Godfrey of Bouillon

This book offers a new appraisal of the ancestry and career of Godfrey of Bouillon (*c.*1060–1100), a leading participant in the First Crusade (1096–1099) and the first ruler of Latin Jerusalem (1099–1100), the polity established by the crusaders after they captured the Holy City. While previous studies of Godfrey's life have tended to focus on his career from the point at which he joined the crusade, this book adopts a more holistic approach, situating his involvement in the expedition in the light of the careers of his ancestors and his own activities in Lotharingia, the westernmost part of the kingdom of Germany. The findings of this enquiry shed new light on the repercussions of a range of critical developments in Latin Christendom in the eleventh and early twelfth centuries, including the impact of the 'Investiture Conflict' in Lotharingia, the response to the call for the First Crusade in Germany, Godfrey's influence upon the course of the crusade, his role in its leadership, and his activities during the initial phases of Latin settlement in the Holy Land in its aftermath.

Simon John is Lecturer in Medieval History at Swansea University. He previously taught at the University of Oxford, and held a Junior Research Fellowship at the Institute of Historical Research. Much of his work to date has focussed upon the crusades and their socio-cultural impact in Latin Christendom. He has published articles in the *English Historical Review*, the *Journal of Medieval History*, and the *Journal of Ecclesiastical History*, and is the co-editor (with Nicholas Morton) of *Crusading and Warfare in the Middle Ages: Realities and Representations. Essays in Honour of John France* (2014).

Rulers of the Latin East
Series editors
Nicholas Morton
Nottingham Trent University, UK
Jonathan Phillips
Royal Holloway University of London, UK

Academics concerned with the history of the Crusades and the Latin East will be familiar with the various survey histories that have been produced for this fascinating topic. Many historians have published wide-ranging texts that either seek to make sense of the strange phenomenon that was the Crusades or shed light upon the Christian territories of the Latin East. Such panoramic works have helped to generate enormous interest in this subject, but they can only take their readers so far. Works addressing the lives of individual rulers – whether kings, queens, counts, princes or patriarchs – are less common and yet are needed if we are to achieve a more detailed understanding of this period.

This series seeks to address this need by stimulating a collection of political biographies of the men and women who ruled the Latin East between 1098 and 1291 and the kingdom of Cyprus up to 1571. These focus in detail upon the evolving political and diplomatic events of this period, whilst shedding light upon more thematic issues such as: gender and marriage, intellectual life, kingship and governance, military history and inter-faith relations.

Godfrey of Bouillon

Duke of Lower Lotharingia, Ruler of Latin Jerusalem, *c.*1060–1100

Simon John

Routledge
Taylor & Francis Group

LONDON AND NEW YORK

First published 2018 by Routledge

2 Park Square, Milton Park, Abingdon, Oxfordshire OX14 4RN
52 Vanderbilt Avenue, New York, NY 10017

Routledge is an imprint of the Taylor & Francis Group, an informa business

First issued in paperback 2019

British Library Cataloguing-in-Publication Data
A catalogue record for this book is available from the British Library

Library of Congress Cataloguing-in-Publication Data
Names: John, Simon (Simon A.), author.
Title: Godfrey of Bouillon : Duke of Lower Lotharingia, ruler of
    Latin Jerusalem, c. 1060–1100 / Simon John.
Description: Milton Park, Abingdon, Oxon ; New York, NY :
    Routledge, 2018. | Includes bibliographical references and index.
Identifiers: LCCN 2017027850 | ISBN 9781472458964 (hardback :
    alkaline paper) | ISBN 9781315585345 (ebook)
Subjects: LCSH: Godfrey, of Bouillon, approximately 1060–1100. |
    Godfrey, of Bouillon, approximately 1060–1100—Family. | Crusades—
    First, 1096–1099—Biography. | Jerusalem—History—Latin Kingdom,
    1099–1244—Biography. | Knights and knighthood—France—
    Biography. | Lorraine (France)—Kings and rulers—Biography.
Classification: LCC D183.3 .J64 2018 | DDC 956/.014 [B]—dc23
LC record available at https://lccn.loc.gov/2017027850

ISBN: 978-1-4724-5896-4 (hbk)
ISBN: 978-0-367-28029-1 (pbk)

Typeset in NewBaskerville
by Apex CoVantage, LLC

Contents

Illustrations

Maps

Figures

Abbreviations

c.p. = continuous pagination

AA	Albert of Aachen, *Historia Ierosolimitana: History of the Journey to Jerusalem*, ed. and tr. Susan B. Edgington (Oxford, 2007).
AAM	*Annales Altahenses Maiores, MGH SS, rer. Germ.*, vol. 4.
Anna	Anna Komnene, *The Alexiad*, tr. E. R. A. Sewter, rev. Peter Frankopan (London, 2009).
ANS	*Anglo-Norman Studies*
Anselm, *Opera*	*Sancti Anselmi Cantuariensis Archiepiscopi, Opera Omnia*, ed. F. S. Schmitt, 6 vols (Edinburgh, 1946–1963), with translations of the letters in *The Letters of Saint Anselm of Canterbury*, tr. Walter Frölich, 3 vols (Kalamazoo, 1990).
Bartolf	'Bartolf of Nangis', *Gesta Francorum Iherusalem Expugnantium, RHC Occ.*, vol. 3, pp. 487–543.
BB	Baldric of Bourgueil, *Historia Ierosolimitana*, ed. Steven Biddlecombe (Woodbridge, 2014).
Benzo	Benzo of Alba, *Ad Heinricum IV, imperatorem libri VII, MGH SS rer. Germ.*, vol. 65.
Bernold	Bernold of St Blasien, *Chronicle*, in *Bertholds und Bernolds Chroniken*, ed. I. S. Robinson (Darmstadt, 2002), pp. 383–540, tr. in *Eleventh-Century Germany: The Swabian Chronicles*, tr. I. S. Robinson (Manchester, 2008), pp. 245–337.
Berthold I	Berthold of Reichenau, *Chronicle* [First Version], in *Bertholds und Bernolds Chroniken*, ed. I. S. Robinson (Darmstadt, 2002), pp. 161–203, tr. in *Eleventh-Century Germany: The Swabian Chronicles*, tr. I. S. Robinson (Manchester, 2008), pp. 99–107.

Berthold II	Berthold of Reichenau, *Chronicle* [Second Version], in *Bertholds und Bernolds Chroniken*, ed. I. S. Robinson (Darmstadt, 2002), pp. 204–381, tr. in *Eleventh-Century Germany: The Swabian Chronicles*, tr. I. S. Robinson (Manchester, 2008), pp. 108–244.
Bonizo	Bonizo of Sutri, *Liber ad amicum, MGH Libelli*, vol. 1, pp. 568–620, tr. in *The Papal Reform of the Eleventh Century: Lives of Pope Leo IX and Pope Gregory VII*, tr. I. S. Robinson (Manchester, 2004), pp. 158–261.
Bruno	*Brunonis Saxonicum Bellum, Q H IV*, pp. 191–405.
Cantatorium	*La Chronique de Saint Hubert dite Cantatorium*, ed. Karl Hanquet (Brussels, 1906).
Carmen	*Carmen de Bello Saxonico, Q H IV*, pp. 143–89.
Cartulaire Gorze	*Cartulaire de l'abbaye de Gorze*, ed. Armand d'Herbomez (Paris, 1898).
CCSSJ	*Le Cartulaire du Chapitre du Saint-Sépulcre de Jérusalem*, ed. Geneviève Bresc-Bautier (Paris, 1984).
ChAnt	*La Chanson d'Antioche*, ed. Suzanne Duparc-Quioc, 2 vols (Paris, 1977–1978), tr. in *The Chanson d'Antioche: An Old French Account of the First Crusade*, tr. Susan B. Edgington and Carol Sweetenham (Farnham, 2011).
Chartes Saint-Hubert	*Chartes de l'abbaye de Saint-Hubert en Ardenne*, ed. Godefroid Kurth, 2 vols (Brussels, 1903).
ChJér	*The Chanson des Chétifs and Chanson de Jérusalem: Completing the Central Trilogy of the Old French Crusade Cycle*, tr. Carol Sweetenham (Farnham, 2016).
CMC	Leo Marsicanus, *Chronica monasterii Casinensis, MGH SS*, vol. 34.
CPC	Heinrich Hagenmeyer, *Chronologie de la Premiére Croisade, 1094–1100* (Paris, 1902).
CW	*Chronicon Wirziburgense, MGH SS*, vol. 6, pp. 17–31.
DK	*Epistulae et Chartae ad Historiam Primi Belli Sacri Spectantes Quae Supersunt Aevo Aequales ac Genuinae: Die Kreuzzugsbriefe aus des Jahren 1088–1100*, ed. Heinrich Hagenmeyer (Innsbruck, 1901).
DULKJ	*Die Urkunden der lateinischen Könige von Jerusalem*, ed. Hans E. Mayer, 4 vols, c.p. (Hannover, 2010).
EC1	Marcus Bull and Norman Housley (eds), *The Experience of Crusading, Volume 1: Western Approaches* (Cambridge, 2003).

EC2	Peter Edbury and Jonathan Phillips (eds), *The Experience of Crusading, Volume 2: Defining the Crusader Kingdom* (Cambridge, 2003).
EHR	*English Historical Review*
Ep. H IV	*Die Briefe Heinrichs IV., Q H IV*, pp. 5–20, 51–141, 469–83.
FC	Fulcher of Chartres, *Historia Hierosolymitana*, ed. Heinrich Hagenmeyer (Heidelberg, 1913), tr. in Fulcher of Chartres, *A History of the Expedition to Jerusalem, 1095–1127*, tr. Frances R. Ryan (Knoxville, 1969).
FCOI	Jonathan Phillips (ed.), *The First Crusade: Origins and Impact* (Manchester, 1997).
FCTJ	Alan V. Murray (ed.), *From Clermont to Jerusalem: The Crusades and Crusader Societies, 1095–1500* (Turnhout, 1998).
Frutolf	*Frutolfi et Ekkehardi Chronica necnon Anonymi Chronica Imperatorum*, ed. Franz-Josef Schmale and Irene Schmale-Ott (Darmstadt, 1972), pp. 47–121, tr. in *Chronicles of the Investiture Contest: Frutolf of Michelsberg and his Continuators*, tr. T. J. H. McCarthy (Manchester, 2014), pp. 84–137.
Frutolf 1106	*Frutolfi et Ekkehardi Chronica necnon Anonymi Chronica Imperatorum*, ed. Franz-Josef Schmale and Irene Schmale-Ott (Darmstadt, 1972), pp. 123–205, tr. in *Chronicles of the Investiture Contest: Frutolf of Michelsberg and his Continuators*, tr. T. J. H. McCarthy (Manchester, 2014), pp. 138–86.
GF	*Gesta Francorum et aliorum Iherosolimitanorum*, ed. and tr. Rosalind Hill (Oxford, 1962).
Gilo	Gilo of Paris and a second anonymous author, *The Historia vie Hierosolimitane*, ed. and tr. C. W. Grocock and Elizabeth Siberry (Oxford, 1997).
GN	Guibert of Nogent, *Dei Gesta per Francos*, ed. R. B. C. Huygens (Turnhout, 1996), tr. in Guibert of Nogent, *The Deeds of God through the Franks*, tr. Robert Levine (Woodbridge, 1997).
Gregory VII, *Register*	*Das Register Gregors VII.*, ed. Erich Caspar, *MGH Ep. sel.*, 2 vols (Berlin, 1920–1923), tr. in *The Register of Pope Gregory VII 1073–1085: An English Translation*, tr. H. E. J. Cowdrey (Oxford, 2002).
Herman	Herman of Reichenau, *Chronicle, MGH SS*, vol. 5, pp. 67–133, tr. in *Eleventh-Century Germany: The Swabian Chronicles*, tr. I. S. Robinson (Manchester, 2008), pp. 58–98.

JG	Susan B. Edgington and Luis García-Guijarro (eds), *Jerusalem the Golden: The Origins and Impact of the First Crusade* (Turnhout, 2014).
JL	*Regesta Pontificum Romanorum ab condita ecclesia ad annum post Christum natum MCXCVII*, ed. Philippe Jaffé, S. Loewenfeld, et al., 2 vols, 2nd edn (Leipzig, 1885–1888).
JMH	*Journal of Medieval History*
Lampert	Lampert of Hersfeld, *Annales*, ed. Oswald Holder-Egger, rev. by Adolf Schmidt and Wolfgang D. Fritz (Darmstadt, 1962), tr. in *The Annals of Lampert of Hersfeld*, tr. I. S. Robinson (Manchester, 2015).
LE	*Letters from the East: Crusaders, Pilgrims and Settlers in the 12th–13th Centuries*, tr. Malcolm Barber and Keith Bate (Farnham, 2010).
MGH	*Monumenta Germaniae Historica.*
Const.	*Constitutiones et acta publica imperatorum et regum.*
DD	*Diplomata Regum et Imperatorum Germaniae.*
DD H III	*Diplomata Heinrici III.*
DD H IV	*Diplomata Heinrici IV.*
Epistolae: Briefe	*Epistolae: Die Briefe der deutschen Kaiserzeit.*
Ep. sel.	*Epistulae selectae.*
Libelli	*Libelli de lite imperatorum et pontificum.*
SS	*Scriptores* (In Folio).
SS rer. Germ.	*Scriptores rerum Germanicarum in usum scholarum separatim editi.*
SS rer. Germ. N.S.	*Scriptores rerum Germanicarum, Nova series.*
Mommsen	*Imperial Lives and Letters of the Eleventh Century*, tr. Theodor M. Mommsen and Karl F. Morrison (New York, 1962).
MvK	Gerold Meyer von Knonau, *Jahrbücher des Deutschen Reiches unter Heinrich IV. und Heinrich V.*, 7 vols (Leipzig, 1890–1909).
NCMH	*The New Cambridge Medieval History*, 8 vols (Cambridge, 1995–2005).
ODEH	*Opera diplomatica et historica*, ed. Aubert Miraeus and Jean-François Foppens, 4 vols (Brussels, 1723–1748).
OFCC	*The Old French Crusade Cycle*, ed. Emmanuel J. Mickel and Jan A. Nelson, 10 vols in 11 (Tucsaloosa, 1977–2003).
1	*La Naissance du Chevalier au Cygne*, ed. Emmanuel J. Mickel and Jan A. Nelson.
2	*Le Chevalier au Cygne and La Fin d'Elias*, ed. Jan A. Nelson.

3	*Les Enfances Godefroi and Le Retour de Cornumarant*, ed. Emmanuel J. Mickel.
4	*La Chanson d'Antioche*, ed. Jan A. Nelson.
5	*Les Chétifs*, ed. Geoffrey M. Myers.
6	*La Chanson de Jérusalem*, ed. Nigel R. Thorp.
7.i	*The Jérusalem Continuations, Part I: La Chrétienté Corbaran*, ed. Peter R. Grillo.
7.ii	*The Jérusalem Continuations, Part II: La Prise d'Acre, La Mort Godefroi, and La Chanson des Rois Baudoin*, ed. Peter R. Grillo.
8	*The Jérusalem Continuations: The London–Turin Version*, ed. Peter R. Grillo.
9	*La Geste du Chevalier au Cygne*, ed. Edmond A. Emplaincourt.
10	*Godefroi de Buillon*, ed. Jan B. Roberts.
OV	Orderic Vitalis, *The Ecclesiastical History of Orderic Vitalis*, ed. and tr. Marjorie Chibnall, 6 vols (Oxford, 1969–1980).
Overmann	Alfred Overmann, *Gräfin Mathilde von Tuscien. Ihre Besitzungen* (Innsbruck, 1895).
Overmann, *Reg. Mat.*	Matilda of Tuscany, *Register*, in Overmann, pp. 123–90.
PL	*Patrologia Latina*, ed. Jacques-Paul Migne, 217 vols.
PSHIGL	*Publications de la section historique de l'institut grand ducal de France*
PT	Peter Tudebode, *Historia de Hierosolymitano itinere*, ed. John H. Hill and Laurita L. Hill (Paris, 1977), tr. in Peter Tudebode, *Historia de Hierosolymitano itinere*, tr. John H. Hill and Laurita L. Hill (Philadelphia, 1974).
Q H IV	*Quellen zur Geschichte Kaiser Heinrichs IV.*, ed. Franz-Josef Schmale and Irene Schmale-Ott (Darmstadt, 1968).
RA	Raymond of Aguilers, *Liber*, ed. John H. Hill and Laurita L. Hill (Paris, 1969), tr. in Raymond of Aguilers, *Historia Francorum qui ceperunt Iherusalem*, tr. John H. Hill and Laurita L. Hill (Philadelphia, 1968).
RBPH	*Revue belge de philologie et d'histoire*
RC	Ralph of Caen, *Tancredus*, ed. Edoardo D'Angelo (Turnhout, 2011), tr. in Ralph of Caen, *Gesta Tancredi*, tr. Bernard S. Bachrach and David S. Bachrach (Aldershot, 2005).
RHC	*Recueil des Historiens des Croisades.*
Arm.	*Documents Arméniens*, 2 vols.
Occ.	*Historiens Occidentaux*, 5 vols.

RHGF	*Recueil des Historiens des Gaules et de la France*, ed. Martin Bouqet, et al., 24 vols.
RM	Robert the Monk, *Historia Iherosolimitana*, ed. Damien Kempf and Marcus Bull (Woodbridge, 2013), tr. in *Robert the Monk's History of the First Crusade: Historia Iherosolimitana* tr. Carol Sweetenham (Aldershot, 2005).
RRR	Revised Regesta Regni Hierosolymitani Database [http://crusades-regesta.com/].
SCH	*Studies in Church History*
Sigebert	Sigebert of Gembloux, *Chronicon, MGH SS*, vol. 6, pp. 300–74.
Table chronologique	*Table chronologique des chartes et diplômes imprimés concernant l'histoire de la Belgique*, ed. Alphonse Wauters, et al., 12 vols (Brussels, 1866–1919).
WEC	Marcus Bull and Damien Kempf (eds), *Writing the Early Crusades: Text, Transmission and Memory* (Woodbridge, 2014).
WM	William of Malmesbury, *Gesta Regum Anglorum*, ed. and tr. R. A. B. Mynors, completed by Rodney M. Thomson and Michael Winterbottom, 2 vols (Oxford, 1998–1999).
WT	William of Tyre, *Chronique*, ed. R. B. C. Huygens, 2 vols, c.p. (Turnhout, 1986), tr. in William of Tyre, *A History of Deeds Done Beyond the Sea*, tr. Ernest A. Babcock and August C. Krey, 2 vols (New York, 1943).

Acknowledgements

I began my doctoral research, upon which this book is based, in 2008. Since that time, I have been the fortunate recipient of a great deal of support and assistance. It is my sincere pleasure to acknowledge that help here. In 2008 I was awarded a Swansea University Research Scholarship, without which I would have been unable to embark on doctoral research. I also benefitted from the award in 2011 of a Scouloudi Junior Research Fellowship by the Institute of Historical Research, for which I would like to thank the Scouloudi Foundation and Miles Taylor, the director of the IHR at that time. Swansea University's College of Arts and Humanities, the History Faculty at Oxford University, and the Royal Historical Society generously provided funding which enabled me to visit libraries or attend conferences. Over the years numerous friends and colleagues have variously read work in draft and offered instructive comments, granted me access to specialist materials or work in advance of its publication, acted as a sounding board for ideas, and generally supported me and my work. These include Johanna Dale, Peter Edbury, Susan Edgington, Leonie Exarchos, M. Cecilia Gaposchkin, Richard Haines, Tom Horler-Underwood, John Law, Jill Lewis, Simon Parsons, Charlie Rozier, Jay Rubenstein, Iris Shagrir, Tom Smith, Matthew Stevens, Carol Sweetenham, Mark Whelan, and Deborah Youngs. Between 2013 and 2016 I taught in Oxford, during which time I was fortunate to work alongside the Balliol history fellows (Lesley Abrams, Martin Conway, John-Paul Ghobrial, and Simon Skinner), and with supportive History Faculty colleagues including Catherine Holmes and Matthew Kempshall. My time in Oxford was greatly enriched by the friendship of Antonia Fitzpatrick, Ingrid Rembold, Alex Paulin-Booth, and Robin Whelan. As a doctoral student at Swansea, I was privileged to work under the supervision of John France and Daniel Power. I owe them both a considerable debt of gratitude. Their advice, encouragement and support were instrumental during my doctoral studies, and have remained so since. I returned to Swansea to take up a lectureship in the autumn of 2016, and I have put the final touches to the book since then. I have taken great pleasure in finishing this project in the same place in which I began it. I would also like to thank all the staff at

Routledge who have assisted me, and Nicholas Morton and Jonathan Phillips, the editors of the *Rulers of the Latin East* series, for their help in guiding my efforts to transform my doctoral thesis into the book that you hold. That thesis was devoted to Godfrey of Bouillon's life and posthumous reputation. The former is the main focus of this book; I intend in the future to return to the latter. Finally, I would like to extend my deepest thanks to my family, and above all my parents, who have always supported me in every way imaginable. I dedicate this book to them, and I offer it with my love and everlasting gratitude.

SAJ
Swansea
May 2017

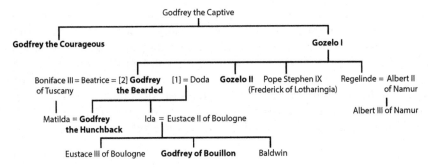

Figure 0.1 Genealogy of the house of Ardennes-Bouillon (simplified)

Dukes of Lower Lotharingia, 1012–1100
Godfrey the Courageous (1012–1023)
Gozelo I (1023–1044)
Gozelo II (1044–1045 or 1046)
Frederick of Luxemburg (1046–1065)
Godfrey the Bearded (1065–1069)
Godfrey the Hunchback (1069–1076)
Conrad, son of Henry IV (1076–1087)
Godfrey of Bouillon (1087–1100)

Dukes of Upper Lotharingia, 1033–1115
Thierry I (978–1026 or 1027)
Frederick II (1019–1026 or 1027, as co-duke with Thierry I)
Frederick III (1027–1033)
Gozelo I (1033–1044)
Godfrey the Bearded (1044–1046)
Adalbert (1047–1048)
Gerard (1048–1070)
Thierry II (1070–1115)

Figure 0.2 The dukes of Lotharingia in the eleventh century

Introduction

Standing high over the cobbles and tramlines of the Place Royale in Brussels is a gigantic bronze statue. It represents a warrior, who sits astride a muscle-bound steed captured in mid-gallop. The warrior holds aloft a war banner in his right hand, and a shield in his left. He wears at his belt a sheathed sword, and atop his head a crown. The warrior is depicted gazing ahead, downhill toward the ornate guild-houses and churches of central Brussels. The identity of the warrior is revealed in the following inscription on the front of the statue's pedestal:

GODEFROID DE BOUILLON
PREMIER ROI DE JERUSALEM
NE A BAISY EN BRABANT
MORT EN PALESTINE LE 17 JUILLET 1100
DECRETE LE 2 NOVEMBRE 1843
INAGURE LE 24 AOUT 1848
SOUS LE REGNE DE LEOPOLD I[1]

The warrior whose statue dominates the Place Royale, then, is Godfrey of Bouillon. By any estimation, Godfrey was a significant historical figure. He was born around 1060, and was the second son of the count of Boulogne, an important figure in northern France and the surrounding regions. Through his maternal ancestry, Godfrey was a member of a prominent dynasty in Lotharingia, the westernmost region of the Western Empire. During his career, he attained the office of duke of Lower Lotharingia, in which capacity he was active in regional politics. In 1096, he set out at the head of a large army on the First Crusade, and, after its forces captured Jerusalem in July 1099, he was selected as the ruler of the incipient Latin polity centred upon the Holy City. Godfrey ruled in Jerusalem for a year, before dying after a brief illness on 18 July 1100.

Godfrey came to enjoy rich fame after his death. In the Middle Ages, he was enshrined as the hero of the First Crusade, and his name became shorthand for the entire crusading 'movement'. He also came to be regarded as an icon of chivalry, and was often held up as an epitome of aristocratic

Figure 0.3 Equestrian statue of Godfrey of Bouillon in the Place Royale, Brussels
(designed by Eugène Simonis, inaugurated 1848)

Photo: Author

values and martial virtues. His reputation continued to develop in the early modern and modern periods.[2] Crucially, however, the various portrayals of Godfrey produced between his death and the present day are generally more revealing of the social, cultural, and political contexts in which those portrayals were created than they are of Godfrey's own career and epoch. The afore-mentioned statue of Godfrey in Brussels, for example, sheds more light on the preoccupations of mid–nineteenth-century Belgium than it does on the life of the historical figure whom the statue purports to depict. The 'historical' Godfrey and the later traditions which surround him are enmeshed so tightly that it is not a straightforward task to unravel them. Even the most rigorous and influential modern historians have some-times discussed Godfrey's life in the light of his later status as a hero of the First Crusade and paragon of chivalry. As a result, many aspects of Godfrey's life have been misconstrued in the past few generations of scholarship.

There is a vast corpus of modern scholarship on the crusades, a not insig-nificant proportion of which is relevant to Godfrey's family and career.[3] Existing biographical studies of Godfrey are, however, far from satisfactory. A few examples will serve to illustrate this. Andressohn's 1947 biography is still generally cited by modern Anglophone scholars as standard.[4] Yet in the seventy years since its publication, scholarship has advanced considerably. Moreover, Andressohn was chiefly interested in Godfrey's exploits on the First Crusade, and so paid rather less attention to his career in Lotharingia. The present book challenges some of Andressohn's findings, particularly those regarding Godfrey's career in the West. Aubé's 1985 biography offers a more comprehensive treatment of Godfrey's life.[5] However, Aubé's study is undermined as a work of scholarship by the lack of a critical apparatus. His analysis features long quotations from primary sources and incorpo-rates arguments formulated by other modern authorities, none of which have full citations. As a result, the uninitiated reader often must guess the origin of Aubé's information from the works listed in his bibliography. Dorchy and Mayer have both carried out useful studies of Godfrey's career before the First Crusade.[6] Focussing on one discrete period of Godfrey's life afforded these scholars the scope to apply sustained critical scrutiny on the pertinent sources to profitable effect. However, this approach also negated the possibility of drawing connections between the different phases of God-frey's life and to the careers of his ancestors. The rich vein of modern writ-ing on the First Crusade will help shed light on Godfrey's preparations for and participation in the expedition. This includes the narrative histories of the expedition by scholars including France, Asbridge, and Rubenstein, and the influential work of Riley-Smith, Bull, and others on its ideological and devotional context.[7] While modern historians of the First Crusade have shed light on Godfrey's involvement in the expedition, however, they have generally relied on the work of other scholars – above all Andressohn – for their assessments of his life in the West, with the result that they have come to problematic conclusions.

The present book draws from scholarship which details Godfrey's ancestry and career in the West. As regards Godfrey's dynastic origin, Parisse has produced a comprehensive genealogy of Godfrey's maternal ancestry (the house of Ardennes-Bouillon), while his paternal lineage, the history of the counts of Boulogne, has been thoroughly investigated by Tanner.[8] Murray has produced a detailed and insightful prosopographical survey of Godfrey's ancestors, family, and companions on the crusade. His work will be invaluable in what follows.[9] The present book also incorporates work on politics and authority in the kingdom of Germany and the Western Empire in the eleventh century, including Cowdrey's biography of Pope Gregory VII, Robinson's biography of Henry IV of Germany, Weinfurter's study of the Salian dynasty, and the range of modern scholarship on the 'Investiture Conflict'.[10]

As a biography of a medieval figure, the present book keys into a recent wave in biographical writing by scholars of the Middle Ages. This trend is perhaps epitomised by the appearance in 2016 of a new biography of William the Conqueror by Bates.[11] Bates' study, an instalment of the *Yale English Monarchs* series, supersedes the earlier biography in that series by Douglas, as well as Bates' own previously published popular biography of the same figure.[12] The *Rulers of the Latin East* series, in which the present book appears, is intended to enhance biographical scholarship on figures who participated in crusading expeditions and those who occupied prominent positions in the Latin East.

The approaches deployed in other modern biographies of medieval figures will provide methodological models for this book. Much has been written on the exigencies of biography.[13] As those discussions have shown, this is rarely a straightforward endeavour. A scarcity of relevant source material often hampers such ventures. Moreover, while the actions of a particular individual from the Middle Ages can sometimes be established, the thoughts, motivations, and feelings upon which those actions were contingent are often very difficult to fathom. The contemporary material which describes Godfrey's life – and especially his involvement in the First Crusade – is such that it will be possible at points to discuss his thinking and worldview in relation to certain key events and issues. However, for the most part it is not the overarching aim of this book to recover the 'inner' Godfrey of Bouillon. Rather, it is conceived as a cultural biography, that is, a study which uses Godfrey as a prism for interrogating the dynamics which shaped the course of his life, the events in which he participated, and the cultures to which he belonged. To emulate Gillingham's approach to the composition of his seminal biography of Richard I, this book is 'less a question of what I think he was "really" like, but rather of the many ways in which contemporaries portrayed him'.[14] A key aim of the book, then, will be to establish how the perceptions that Godfrey's contemporaries had of him can illuminate, *inter alia*, the nature of Lotharingian politics in the age of the 'Investiture Conflict', the recruitment drive for the First Crusade in the kingdom of Germany, the subsequent course of the expedition, and the early phases of Latin settlement in the Holy Land. This book follows a number of recent biographies of individuals who occupied prominent offices in the West before – and in some cases after – participating in crusading expeditions. Gillingham's afore-mentioned study of Richard I constitutes a particularly instructive example, as a key argument of his book is that Richard's formative experiences in the West shaped how he acted whilst on the Third Crusade. Other recent scholarship in this vein includes Freed's work on Frederick Barbarossa, Evergates' study of Henry the Liberal, count of Champagne, and Perry's appraisal of John of Brienne.[15]

This book explores Godfrey's dynastic origins and his career in the West, before turning to his experiences on the First Crusade and in Jerusalem in the expedition's aftermath. It suggests that Godfrey's involvement in the crusade can perhaps best be understood in the light of his experiences in Lotharingia and the familial traditions which helped shape his worldview. In short, Godfrey the duke of Lower Lotharingia is just as important to this book as Godfrey the ruler of Latin Jerusalem.

The first chapter surveys the nature of power in the kingdom of Germany and the Western Empire in the eleventh century, before examining the place of Godfrey of Bouillon's maternal ancestors in Lotharingian and imperial politics. Particular attention is paid to the careers of Godfrey the Bearded (his grandfather) and Godfrey the Hunchback (his uncle), both of whom preceded him as duke of Lower Lotharingia. The chapter pinpoints evidence which suggests that from the mid-1050s until the early 1070s, Godfrey's maternal ancestors had close dealings with the reform papacy. The chapter also explores how Godfrey's predecessors interacted with ecclesiastical authorities in Lotharingia, above all, the bishop of Liège and the monastery of St Hubert. Finally, the chapter examines the lives of Godfrey's parents, Eustace II and Ida of Boulogne, in order to establish the circumstances in which Godfrey and his brothers Eustace (III) and Baldwin were born.

The second chapter investigates Godfrey's career between his birth in about 1060 and the coming of the First Crusade in 1095. It assesses the fragmentary evidence for his earliest years before his emergence in Lotharingian politics in 1076, and then charts his struggles to attain the office of duke of Lower Lotharingia, and his appointment to it in 1087. It is suggested that Godfrey was not firmly aligned with Henry IV of Germany in this period, and that he did not participate in Henry's grand military campaigns in Saxony and Italy in the 1070s and 1080s. It is also contended that, like his uncle and grandfather before him, Godfrey maintained links with the bishop of Liège (who in about 1082 instituted the Peace of God in his diocese at an assembly in which Godfrey participated) and the monks of St Hubert (from whom Godfrey received instruction about sin and penitence).

The third chapter considers how Urban II's appeal for the First Crusade might have reached Godfrey, and discusses his response to that appeal. It suggests that in 1095–1096 Godfrey had access to a number of channels of communication, both ecclesiastical and aristocratic, and that any one of them could have been the conduit along which the official papal message concerning the crusade reached him. It also identifies the dynastic ties which bound Godfrey to the aristocracy of northern France, emphasising the permeable nature of the frontier between the region and Lotharingia. This chapter makes the case that Godfrey's positive response to Urban's appeal for the First Crusade might be best understood in the light of his maternal ancestors' efforts to support the reform papacy, his own participation in the episcopal Peace assembly in Liège, and the influence of the monks of St Hubert on his devotional thoughtworld. The third chapter also examines how Godfrey prepared in 1095–1096 for the First Crusade, and discusses the composition of the army at whose head he departed Lotharingia in August 1096.

The fourth chapter, the longest of the book, is devoted to Godfrey's career on the First Crusade. It charts his exploits from his departure on the expedition through to the capture of Jerusalem by the crusader armies on 15 July 1099. It examines Godfrey's influence on the crusade relative to that of the other leading participants, suggesting that while Godfrey proved himself to be a brave and effective warrior in his own right, he was one of a number of prominent figures who shaped the course of the First Crusade. The chapter suggests that up until the final few months of the expedition, Godfrey remained largely in the shadow of Bohemond, a redoubtable general who possessed a wealth of military experience, and who was the single most dominant participant in the crusade, and Raymond of Toulouse, who was the richest and most distinguished of the leaders. The argument is drawn that it was only in the early months of 1099, at the very end of the expedition, that Godfrey came to the fore and began to surpass the other leaders in influence and authority.

The fifth chapter explores Godfrey's tenure as ruler of Latin Jerusalem. It begins by considering the circumstances of his appointment as ruler of Jerusalem in July 1099. It asserts that he did not take the title of king, and then examines a range of possible explanations for why he did not do so. The chapter then charts his year-long tenure as ruler of the Holy City and traces his efforts to establish the institutions of government in the new Latin polity. The chapter concludes by examining the circumstances of his death on 18 July 1100, and the developments which culminated in him being succeeded by his younger brother, Baldwin, who was inaugurated king of Jerusalem in Bethlehem on Christmas Day 1100.

There follows at the end of the book an epilogue which examines how perceptions of Godfrey developed over the twelfth and thirteenth centuries. It is contended that depictions of Godfrey in that period were shaped by an interconnected series of historical, socio-cultural, political, and literary impulses, the most important of which was the course of crusading history between 1100 and 1300. The fortunes of crusading expeditions and the condition of the Latin states established by the First Crusaders in the Holy Land had a principal influence upon how he was regarded during this time. The epilogue casts the development of Godfrey's reputation as one reflex of the wider process through which the momentous events of the First Crusade were assimilated into the cultural consciousness of Latin Christendom.[16] The success of the First Crusade captured the imagination of the Latin Christian world, and this helped to stimulate interest in Godfrey and his career.

The five core chapters of the book rest on sources which date to the eleventh century or within five or so years after Godfrey's death in 1100. The majority of this evidence consists of texts which this book will, for convenience's sake, refer to as chronicles and charters.[17] Charters yield important information on the careers of Godfrey and his ancestors. Members of the family issued their own charters, and they are also named in documents issued by other parties.[18] The diplomas issued by the kings of Germany/emperors are of particular use, for they contain witness lists which illuminate the crown's political connections at a given moment. The most informative texts for Godfrey's ancestry and early life, however, are chronicles, above all, those which originated in Lotharingia. The most important of these is the chronicle known as the *Cantatorium*, which was written in stages at the monastery of St Hubert down to 1106.[19] The events described in the latter part of the *Cantatorium* took place at the time of the great dispute between Gregory VII and Henry IV. In describing those events, the St Hubert chronicler sided firmly with the papacy. St Hubert was situated close to Bouillon in the diocese of Liège, and its monks had close dealings with members of Godfrey's family. This text therefore contains a wealth of information about their careers. Godfrey and his predecessors acted as advocates for the abbey, and this undoubtedly had a bearing on how they were portrayed in the *Cantatorium*. It should be noted that it was not the principal purpose of this text to record information about members of the house of Ardennes-Bouillon. Its chief aim was to provide a written record of the various lands and properties that St Hubert acquired during the eleventh and early twelfth centuries, and information about Godfrey and his forebears was included only when doing so assisted that function. Other useful sources from Lotharingia include Anselm of Liège's mid–eleventh-century account of ecclesiastical affairs in the diocese, a set of annals compiled at the monastery of St James in Liège, and the account of Sigebert of Gembloux which terminates in 1111, but which was written in stages down to that point, and contains very little about the period after 1099.[20]

The book also draws from eleventh-century sources which originated further afield in the kingdom of Germany. Among these is the set of annals written at the Bavarian abbey of Niederaltaich (the *Annales Altahenses Maiores* or *Annals of Niederaltaich*), a text which details events in the kingdom in the earlier part of the eleventh century.[21] Lampert of Hersfeld's monumental account of events in the Empire in the late eleventh century offers a range of important insights on the exploit of Godfrey's ancestors and relatives.[22] Lampert focussed his account on the struggles between the Salian kings of Germany (of whom he was a fierce critic), and those who rebelled against them, especially the Saxons (for whom he expressed support). Like Lampert, Bruno of Merseburg wrote an important account of the German crown's wars in Saxony.[23] This book also draws from the work of Berthold of Reichenau and Bernold of St Blasien, who wrote in the duchy of Swabia. Both these authors were staunch supporters of Gregory VII.[24] Also of use is the chronicle of Frutolf of Michelsberg.[25] Of particular use is the work of an author who wrote a continuation of Frutolf's account in about 1106. This continuation is a valuable source, providing a German perspective on the First Crusade and the early phases of Latin settlement in the Holy Land.[26] To these will be added sources from Italy which shed light on the conflict between Henry IV and Gregory VII. The pope's own register is a particularly valuable repository of evidence.[27] Also of use are the writings of Gregory's partisan Bonizo of Sutri, the pro-Henry Benzo of Alba, and the account written at the abbey of Monte Cassino by Leo Marsicanus and his continuator.[28]

Godfrey's career on the First Crusade is served by a wide array of evidence. Anna Komnene's account of her father Alexios Komnenos' reign as emperor of Byzantium provides important information.[29] Though Anna wrote later in the twelfth century, her work stands outside Latin Christian historiographical traditions, and so will be used here to illuminate the Byzantine perspective on the expedition. The present book rests above all on the wide range of Latin sources for the First Crusade. The letters written by the leaders of the crusade during the course of the expedition are particularly revealing, for they shed important light on their ideas at particular junctures while the expedition was in progress.[30] This book makes considerable use of the various Latin chronicles of the crusade.[31] The most influential of these is the *Gesta Francorum,* which was probably written soon after the First Crusade ended in August 1099 by an individual who had been associated with Bohemond and his contingent of Normans from southern Italy.[32] Although historians have sometimes regarded the *Gesta Francorum* as a narrative record of events witnessed by the author, studies have shown that it is more sophisticated than it might at first seem. It has been argued, for example, that the author of this account artificially skewed its narrative towards Bohemond, and that he deployed a number of techniques to denigrate Alexios and the Byzantines, from whom Bohemond had become estranged by the end of the crusade.[33]

In the first years of the twelfth century three veterans of the First Crusade used the *Gesta Francorum* as a basis for their own chronicles of the expedition. As a result, there emerged an influential tradition of historical writing on the crusade centred upon this text. The Poiteven priest Peter Tudebode copied the *Gesta Francorum* almost verbatim, but altered certain passages and added a few snippets of information based on his own experiences.[34]

Probably before about 1102, Raymond of Aguilers used the *Gesta Francorum* to write a substantially new account of the First Crusade.[35] He had been a canon of the cathedral church of St Mary in Le Puy, and became a chaplain of Raymond of Toulouse during the course of the crusade. This author provides a great deal of original information, particularly on relations between Raymond of Toulouse and the other leading figures of the crusade.

Fulcher of Chartres was another author who used the *Gesta Francorum* early in the twelfth century to write his own account of the First Crusade.[36] Fulcher set out on the expedition in the company of Robert of Normandy and Stephen of Blois, but during the course of it he joined the contingent of Baldwin (Godfrey's younger brother) and became his chaplain. Fulcher remained in the Holy Land after the end of the crusade, and it was while he was resident in the Latin East that he began to write. He finished the first version of his account of the crusade in 1106, and it soon began to circulate in that form. This first version was used by an author who probably worked soon after in the West to compose a separate account of this expedition. This account, the *Gesta Francorum Iherusalem Expugnantium*, was attributed in the seventeenth century to an otherwise unknown author named Bartolf of Nangis. Though there is no evidence for that attribution, it will be convenient to refer to this source as the 'Bartolf' text as a shorthand.[37] Significantly, Fulcher later extended his account to cover the history of the Latin East down to 1127. He added to his account of the First Crusade (book I) treatments of the reigns of Baldwin I (book II) and Baldwin II (book III). The extant versions of Fulcher's account of the First Crusade likely reflect his later reworking, meaning his work poses difficulties to the diachronic approach being adopted in this book. It is important, then, to consider how Fulcher originally treated the First Crusade by cross-referencing his work with the 'Bartolf' text as far as possible.

By far the most crucial source for charting Godfrey's activities on the First Crusade and thereafter in Jerusalem is the voluminous account written by Albert of Aachen.[38] Working in Lower Lotharingia – not far from Godfrey's chief holdings – Albert wrote about the crusade from an imperial perspective. Significantly, then, Albert's account stands entirely apart from the tradition of near-contemporary historiography on the First Crusade centred upon the *Gesta Francorum*. A reading of his account shows that he treated many aspects of the expedition in a way that differs to the viewpoint advanced in the sources of the *Gesta Francorum* tradition.[39] Moreover, Albert's account is considerably longer and more detailed than any sources of that tradition. It consists of twelve books, the first six of which cover the First Crusade. Edgington has argued that Albert completed these books soon after the events they describe.[40] To these books he added a further six (books 7 to 12) which cover the history of the Latin East down to 1119. Albert did not participate in the First Crusade or go to the Holy Land, and he seems to have drawn his information from oral reports provided by crusaders who had returned to Lotharingia. He was able to accumulate a wealth of unique material on Godfrey's exploits on the expedition and in Jerusalem.

The *Gesta Francorum* and the writings of Peter Tudebode and Raymond of Aguilers all cease immediately after the closing act of the First Crusade (the battle of Ascalon in August 1099). It is thus a smaller corpus of sources that detail Godfrey's tenure as ruler of Jerusalem. In terms of the chronicle accounts, relevant information is contained in the 'Bartolf' text, in the account of Fulcher of Chartres, and, most fully, the work of Albert of Aachen. Also of use for Godfrey's tenure are a few contemporary and near-contemporary letters concerning events in the Holy Land, and a number of charters which describe actions undertaken by or involving Godfrey.[41]

Notes

1 'Godfrey of Bouillon, first king of Jerusalem, born in Baisy in Brabant, died in Palestine on 17 July 1100. [Statue] commissioned on 2 November 1843, inaugurated on 24 August 1848, during the reign of Leopold I'. An equivalent inscription in Flemish features on the back of the pedestal. As this book will show, Godfrey of Bouillon was not king of Jerusalem, he died on 18 July 1100 (not 17 July), and was likely born in Boulogne rather than Baisy. On the statue, see: *Rapports de MM. De Ram, Gachard et de Reiffenberg faits à la séance de la classe des lettres du 5 février 1849 concernant la status de Godefried de Bouillon* (s.l.,1849). On nineteenth-century Belgian attitudes towards the Middle Ages, see: Jo Tollebeek, 'An Era of Grandeur: The Middle Ages in Belgian National Historiography, 1830–1914', in R. J. W. Evans and Guy P. Marchal (eds), *The Uses of the Middle Ages in Modern European States: History, Nationhood and the Search for Origins* (Basingstoke, 2011), pp. 113–35.
2 On the development of Godfrey's reputation see, among others: Marcel Lobet, *Godefroid de Bouillon: Essai de Biographie Antilégendaire* (Brussels, 1943); Gerhart Waeger, *Gottfried von Bouillon in der Historiographie* (Zurich, 1969); Georges Despy, 'Godefroid de Bouillon, myths et réalitiés', *Academie royale de belgique, bulletin de la classe des lettres et des sciences morales et politiques*, 71 (1985), 249–75; David A. Trotter, 'L'ascendance mythique de Godefroy de Bouillon et le Cycle de la Croisade', in Laurence Harf-Lancner (ed.), *Métamorphose et bestiaire fantastique au moyen âge* (Paris, 1985), pp. 107–35; Friedrich Wolfzettel, 'Gottfried von Bouillon. Führer des ersten Kreuzzugs und König von Jerusalem', in Inge Milfull and Michael Neumann (eds), *Mythen Europas. Schlüsselfiguren der Imagination. Mittelalter* (Regensburg, 2004), pp. 126–42.
3 For surveys of crusade scholarship, see: Christopher Tyerman, *The Debate on the Crusades, 1099–2010* (Manchester, 2011), and Giles Constable, 'The Historiography of the Crusades', in Angeliki E. Laiou and Roy P. Mottahedeh (eds), *The Crusades From the Perspective of Byzantium and the Muslim World* (Washington, 2001), pp. 1–22. Modern historiography has drawn attention to the fact that distinct terminology for what modern historians describe as crusades only took shape in the thirteenth century, and the word 'crusade' only entered popular usage in the modern age. It is not the aim of this book to interrogate these terms, however, and so they are used freely in what follows. On this, see: Michael Markowski, 'Crucesignatus: Its Origins and Early Usage', *JMH*, 10 (1984), 157–65; Christopher Tyerman, 'Were There Any Crusades in the Twelfth Century?', *EHR*, 110 (1995), 553–77 (reprinted in his *The Invention of the Crusades* [Basingstoke, 1998], pp. 8–29); Walker R. Cosgrove, 'Crucesignatus: A Refinement

or Merely One More Term Among Many?', in Thomas F. Madden, James L. Naus, and Vincent Ryan (eds), *The Crusades: Medieval Worlds in Conflict* (Farnham, 2010), pp. 95–107. Similarly, this book will render the Latin word 'miles' (pl. 'milites') as 'knight', even though historians have suggested that this may be anachronistic for the eleventh and early twelfth centuries. See: Dominique Barthélemy, *The Serf, the Knight, and the Historian*, tr. Graham R. Edwards (Ithaca, 2009), pp. 137–53.

4 John C. Andressohn, *The Ancestry and Life of Godfrey of Bouillon* (Bloomington, 1947).

5 Pierre Aubé, *Godefroy de Bouillon* (Paris, 1985).

6 Henri Dorchy, 'Godefroid de Bouillon, duc de Basse-Lotharingie', *RBPH*, 26 (1948), 961–99; Hans E. Mayer, 'Baudouin Ier et Godefroy de Bouillon avant la Première Croisade', in Hans E. Mayer, *Mélanges sur l'histoire du Royaume Latin de Jérusalem* (Paris, 1984), pp. 10–48.

7 John France, *Victory in the East: A Military History of the First Crusade* (Cambridge, 1994); Thomas Asbridge, *The First Crusade: A New History* (London, 2004); Jay Rubenstein, *Armies of Heaven: The First Crusade and the Quest for the Apocalypse* (New York, 2011); Jonathan Riley-Smith, *The First Crusade and the Idea of Crusading* (London, 1986); Idem, *The First Crusaders, 1095–1131* (Cambridge, 1997); Marcus Bull, *Knightly Piety and the Lay Response to the First Crusade: The Limousin and Gascony, c.970–c.1130* (Oxford, 1993).

8 Michel Parisse, 'Généalogie de la Maison d'Ardenne', *PSHIGL*, 95 (1981), 9–41; Heather J. Tanner, *Families, Friends and Allies: Boulogne and Politics in Northern France and England, c.879–1160* (Leiden, 2004).

9 Alan V. Murray, *The Crusader Kingdom of Jerusalem: A Dynastic History, 1099–1125* (Oxford, 2000); Idem, 'The Army of Godfrey of Bouillon, 1096–1099: Structure and Dynamics of a Contingent on the First Crusade', *RBPH*, 70 (1992), 301–29.

10 H. E. J. Cowdrey, *Pope Gregory VII, 1073–1085* (Oxford, 1998); I. S. Robinson, *Henry IV of Germany, 1056–1106* (Cambridge, 1999); Stefan Weinfurter, *The Salian Century: Main Currents in an Age of Transition*, tr. Barbara M. Bowlus (Philadelphia, 1999); Uta-Renate Blumenthal, *The Investiture Controversy: Church and Monarchy From the Ninth to the Twelfth Century* (Philadelphia, 1988).

11 David Bates, *William the Conqueror* (New Haven, 2016).

12 David C. Douglas, *William the Conqueror: The Norman Impact on England*, new edn (New Haven, 1999); David Bates, *William the Conqueror*, new edn (Stroud, 2004).

13 For general comments, see: Michael Prestwich, 'Medieval Biography', *Journal of Interdisciplinary History*, 40 (2010), 325–46, and the essays collected in David Bates, Julia Crick, and Sarah Hamilton (eds), *Writing Medieval Biography, 750–1250: Essays in Honour of Professor Frank Barlow* (Woodbridge, 2006).

14 John Gillingham, *Richard I* (New Haven, 1999), p. ix.

15 John B. Freed, *Frederick Barbarossa: The Prince and the Myth* (New Haven, 2016); Theodore Evergates, *Henry the Liberal: Count of Champagne, 1127–1181* (Philadelphia, 2016); Guy Perry, *John of Brienne: King of Jerusalem, Emperor of Constantinople, c.1175–1237* (Cambridge, 2013).

16 For an overview, see: James M. Powell, 'Myth, Legend, Propaganda, History: The First Crusade, 1140–ca.1300', in Michel Balard (ed.), *Autour de la Première Croisade* (Paris, 1996), pp. 127–41. On the circulation of information concerning the First Crusade, see: Carol Sweetenham, 'What Really Happened to Eurvin De Créel's Donkey? Anecdotes in Sources for the First Crusade', in *WEC*, pp. 75–88, and Simon John, 'Historical Truth and the Miraculous Past: The Use of Oral Evidence in Twelfth-Century Historical Writing on the First Crusade', *EHR*, 130 (2015), 263–301. A methodological model for the present study is Benjamin Z.

Kedar, 'The Jerusalem Massacre of July 1099 in the Western Historiography of the Crusades', *Crusades*, 3 (2004), 15–75, which examines accounts of the First Crusaders' capture of Jerusalem in 1099 in chronological sequence, demonstrating how perceptions of that event transformed over time.

17 For introductory comments on chronicles, see: Elisabeth van Houts, *Local and Regional Chronicles* (Turnhout, 1995), esp. pp. 13–16, and David Dumville, 'What is a Chronicle?', in Erik Kooper (ed.), *The Medieval Chronicle II* (Amsterdam, 2002), pp. 1–27. On charters, see: Olivier Guyotjeannin, Jacques Pycke and Benoît-Michel Tock, *Diplomatique Médiévale*, 3rd edn (Turnhout, 2006).

18 On the charters issued by Godfrey and his ancestors in their capacity as dukes of Lower Lotharingia, see: Georges Despy, 'Les actes des ducs de Basse-Lotharingie du XIᵉ siècle', *PSHIGL*, 95 (1981), 65–132.

19 *Cantatorium*; Karl Hanquet, *Étude critique sur la chronique de St Hubert dite Cantatorium* (Brussels, 1900).

20 Anselm of Liège, *Gesta Episcoporum Tungrensium, Trajectensium, et Leodiensium*, *MGH SS*, vol. 7, pp. 161–234; *Annales S. Iacobi Leodiensis*, *MGH SS*, vol. 16, pp. 635–45; Sigebert.

21 *AAM*.

22 Lampert. On Lampert's account, see Robinson's introduction to his translation.

23 Bruno; David S. Bachrach and Bernard S. Bachrach, 'Bruno of Merseburg and His Historical Method, c. 1085', *JMH*, 40 (2014), 381–98.

24 Berthold I; Berthold II; Bernold.

25 Frutolf.

26 Frutolf 1106. This account has long been attributed to Ekkehard of Aura, but McCarthy in his recent translation of these texts convincingly refutes that attribution.

27 Gregory VII, *Register*.

28 Bonizo; Benzo; *CMC*.

29 Anna. On Anna's writings, see: Penelope Buckley, *The Alexiad of Anna Komnene: Artistic Strategy in the Making of a Myth* (Cambridge, 2014), and on her treatment of the First Crusade, see: John France, 'Anna Comnena, the Alexiad and the First Crusade', *Reading Medieval Studies*, 10 (1983), 20–32.

30 Several of these letters are edited in *DK* and translated in *LE*.

31 On these texts, see: Rudolf Hiestand, 'Il cronista medievale e il suo pubblico: alcune osservazioni in margine alla storiografia della crociate', *Annali della Facoltà di lettere e filosofia dell'Università di Napoli*, 27 (1984–1985), 207–27; Susan B. Edgington, 'The First Crusade: Reviewing the Evidence', in *FCOI*, pp. 55–77; Jean Flori, *Chroniqueurs et propagandistes: introduction critique aux sources de la première croisade* (Geneva, 2010).

32 *GF*. On its provenance and influence, see, among others: Jay Rubenstein, 'What Is the *Gesta Francorum* and Who Is Peter Tudebode?', *Revue Mabillon*, 16 (2005), 179–204, and John France, 'The Use of the Anonymous *Gesta Francorum* in the Early Twelfth-Century Sources for the First Crusade', in *FCTJ*, pp. 29–42.

33 Relevant studies include Colin Morris, 'The *Gesta Francorum* as Narrative History', *Reading Medieval Studies*, 19 (1993), 55–71, and Kenneth B. Wolf, 'Crusade and Narrative: Bohemond and the *Gesta Francorum*', *JMH*, 17 (1991), 207–16.

34 PT. The most recent examination of Tudebode's use of the *Gesta Francorum* is Marcus Bull, 'The Relationship Between the *Gesta Francorum* and Peter Tudebode's *Historia de Hierosolymitano Itinere*: The Evidence of a Hitherto Unexamined Manuscript (St. Catharine's College, Cambridge, 3)', *Crusades*, 11 (2012), 1–17.

35 RA.

36 FC.

37 Bartolf. On the origin of this text and its relationship to Fulcher's account, see: Susan B. Edgington, '*The Gesta Francorum Iherusalem expugnantium* of "Bartolf of Nangis"', *Crusades*, 13 (2014), 21–35.
38 AA; Susan B. Edgington, 'Albert of Aachen Reappraised', in *FCTJ*, pp. 55–68.
39 Colin Morris, 'The Aims and Spirituality of the First Crusade as Seen Through the Eyes of Albert of Aachen', *Reading Medieval Studies*, 16 (1990), 99–117.
40 AA, pp. xxiv–xxv.
41 *DULKJ*; Hans E. Mayer, *Die Kanzlei der lateinischen Königen von Jerusalem*, 2 vols in 4 (Hannover, 1996). As Mayer's monumental studies show, some of Godfrey's acts are known only from later reissues, while the authenticity of others is debatable. The present book draws only from the documents deemed authentic by Mayer. Also of use is RRR, an online calendar of documents produced in the Latin East, compiled under the direction of Jonathan Riley-Smith.

1   Ancestry and parentage

Lotharingia and its place in the Western Empire

Godfrey of Bouillon's maternal forebears played a prominent role in the Western Empire in the era in which it was ruled over by the Salian dynasty (1027–1125), particularly during the tumultuous reigns of Henry III (1039–1056) and his son, Henry IV (1056–1105/6).[1] In the eleventh century, the Empire encompassed the constituent kingdoms of Germany, Italy, and, from 1034, Burgundy. Although the three kingdoms notionally had a common ruler, they were not united by any common governmental or institutional framework. The king of the Germans was traditionally elected by the German princes, usually within his father's lifetime. However, the king could only be inaugurated as emperor by the pope in Rome. The length of the duration between an individual's inauguration as king of Germany and his inauguration as emperor thus depended on his relationship with the pope. During the reigns of Henry IV and his son Henry V (1105–1125), the Salian monarchy was embroiled in a bitter dispute with the papacy, a struggle often described by modern scholars as the 'Investiture Conflict'.[2] The clash between Henry IV and Pope Gregory VII (1073–1085) had repercussions which reverberated throughout Latin Christendom.[3]

The chief secular offices in the kingdom of Germany in this period were those of duke, count, and margrave. In the eleventh century, the kingdom consisted of six duchies: Swabia, Bavaria, Carinthia, and Saxony, and to the west, the duchies of Upper Lotharingia and Lower Lotharingia (see Map 1.1). In the Salian era, the office of duke (*dux*) was essentially a military position. The king expected the dukes to assemble the military forces of their duchies and lead them on royal campaigns. The dukes were responsible for maintaining peace and for holding regular assemblies of the counts and other nobility of the duchy. A biographer of Henry II (d.1024), the last Ottonian king of Germany, wrote that as duke of Bohemia Henry 'stood higher than all the counts of the [duchy]'.[4] Although it was not essential for a duke to be a native of his duchy or to possess extensive lands within it to hold the office, in practice, the authority of a duke was determined by the extent and wealth of his personal holdings.[5] The Salian

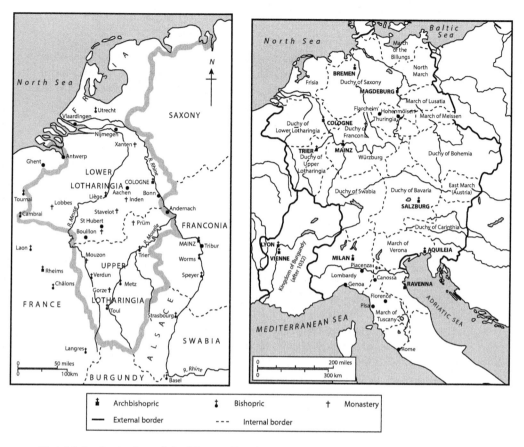

Map 1.1 Lotharingia and the Western Empire

kings regarded dukes as royal officials, whom they could appoint and dismiss at will. According to Weinfurter, over the course of the eleventh century several forces combined steadily to undermine the authority of the dukes. While the Salian kings sometimes considered hereditary principles when appointing a new duke, and would grant the ducal office to the son of the former incumbent if he was politically acceptable, they were often more concerned with aligning ducal offices with the crown.[6] As the biographer of Henry II recognised, the counts of the kingdom of Germany were intended to operate under the authority of the dukes. Over the course of the tenth and eleventh centuries, the nature of comital authority in Germany altered drastically. In the Carolingian age, counts had been public officials appointed by the crown. By the Salian era, however, the title of count essentially denoted an aristocrat who held a monopoly of power in his locality. The counties were not specific areas of land, but, rather, were associated with the exercise of authority over people and places.[7] The office of margrave denoted lordship over a march, that is, authority in an area at the frontier of the kingdom of Germany.[8]

Modern historians have devoted much attention to the nature of the relationship between the Salian monarchy and the Church both in Germany and more widely in the Empire. The Salian kings sought to impose close control over bishoprics throughout the Empire for several reasons. Bishops provided hospitality and financial support to the kings, and facilitated royal itinerations throughout the Empire. The king sought closely to control appointments to high-ranking church offices in the Empire; these often held great wealth, and so selling them to the highest bidder could be lucrative. Perhaps most importantly, bishops often wielded considerable political influence in their dioceses. The kings were thus apt to utilise bishops as agents of central monarchical authority. The tradition of cooperation between the Salian kings and the imperial episcopate has been described in modern historiography as the 'imperial Church system' (*Reichskirchensystem*). The growing dependence of the crown on the episcopate seems to have been one of the factors that served to diminish the power of secular offices in the Empire over the course of the eleventh century.[9] When Henry III intervened in Rome in December 1046 to install Pope Clement II, he seemed even to have incorporated the bishop of Rome into this system.[10] Also important in Germany and the Empire at this time were lay advocates. These were secular lords who were appointed by religious houses to look after their worldly interests.[11]

Godfrey of Bouillon's maternal ancestors were aristocrats in the politically turbulent region of Lotharingia, and Godfrey himself spent most of his adult career there. Some historical context on Lotharingia will therefore be essential for what follows. Lotharingia came into existence in 843 with the Treaty of Verdun, through which the grandsons of Charlemagne, that is, the sons of Louis the Pious (d.840), divided his empire into three kingdoms: West Francia, East Francia, and Middle Francia.[12] The third of these kingdoms was granted to the eldest son, Lothair I. Upon Lothair I's death in 855, his son, Lothair II (d.869) inherited the kingdom, and it subsequently became known as the *regnum Lotharii*: Lotharingia.[13] In 925, the first Ottonian monarch, Henry I, king of the Germans (d.936), brought Lotharingia under his control. He incorporated it into his kingdom as a duchy, although its rulers retained their autonomy. Henry I's son Otto I (d.973) strengthened the crown's hold upon the region. In 959 Otto divided Lotharingia into the duchies of Upper and Lower Lotharingia.[14] He entrusted Upper Lotharingia to Count Frederick of Bar. Frederick was the brother of Bishop Adalberon of Metz (d.962) and Gozelo (d.943), who held Verdun. Gozelo's son, Godfrey 'the Captive' (d.1002), count of Verdun, was the founder of the house of Ardennes-Bouillon, the dynasty of which Godfrey of Bouillon was a member (see Figure 0.1).[15] Crucially, the manner in which the Carolingian Empire fractured in the ninth and tenth centuries created conditions which permitted several inter-connected noble families to assume pre-eminence in Lotharingia.[16] The house of Ardennes-Bouillon was one of the principal beneficiaries of this development.[17]

In the eleventh century, Lotharingia was delineated to the north by Frisia and the North Sea, and to the south by the border with the kingdom of Burgundy. To the west, where Lotharingia bounded the kingdom of France and the county of Flanders, and to the East, where it straddled the other duchies of the kingdom of Germany, its approximate frontiers were marked by the rivers Meuse and Rhine respectively (see Map 1.1).[18] At this time, the count of Flanders was one of the most important vassals of the king of France, but he also owed homage to the emperor for part of the comital territory (so-called imperial Flanders).[19] The duchy of Upper Lotharingia broadly corresponded to the archbishopric of Trier, comprised of the bishoprics of Trier, Verdun, Metz, and Toul. The duchy of Lower Lotharingia roughly correlated with the archbishopric of Cologne, which incorporated the dioceses of Cologne, Utrecht, Liège, and, from 1093, Cambrai. Bouillon and other principal holdings of the house of Ardennes-Bouillon were located in the diocese of Liège, and its members had close dealings with their local bishop throughout the eleventh century.[20] Within the diocese lay several wealthy monasteries, including St Hubert and St Laurent. The diocese also occupied an important place in the 'imperial Church system'. Crucially, Liège lay on the frontier of the king of Germany's authority; while the diocese was nominally subject to the archbishop of Cologne, at times the archbishop of Rheims (who was usually allied to the king of France and the pope) could also exert an influence there.[21] As we shall see, the diocese of Liège proved to be an important battleground in the 'Investiture Conflict'.

It is important to note that the borders of Lotharingia were largely political, rather than ethnic or cultural. While the Lotharingian duchies were components of the Empire in political terms, the region was inhabited by a range of different peoples, including Frisians, Franks, Alemans, and Waloons, who spoke a variety of languages.[22] The inhabitants of the diocese of Liège, where the heartlands of the house of Ardennes-Bouillon lay, spoke a romance tongue rather than German.[23] As a result, the boundary between Lotharingia and the kingdom of France was highly permeable.[24] Aside from the intermingling of languages and culture, other forces served to connect Lotharingia to both east and west. From an economic standpoint, Lotharingia was bisected by the valleys of the Moselle and Meuse rivers, and by east–west land routes.[25] Moreover, the Salian era coincided with an upheaval in the history of communications, and the establishment of new institutional and personal networks which opened up lines of contact that served to shape the history of the Empire and, indeed, of Europe as a whole.[26]

Godfrey's maternal ancestry: the house of Ardennes-Bouillon

As noted above, the house of Ardennes-Bouillon was one of the most powerful families to emerge in Lotharingia amidst the breakup of the Carolingian Empire. The house acquired holdings in both Upper and Lower
Lotharingia, meaning that it retained interests in both ducal offices. Godfrey the Captive, the founder of the house of Ardennes-Bouillon, was count
of Verdun from 963 until his death in 1002. He was also margrave of Antwerp. His son and successor as count of Verdun, Godfrey I 'the Courageous', was the first member of the house of Ardennes-Bouillon to hold
the office of duke; in late 1012, King Henry II of Germany appointed him
duke of Lower Lotharingia, having deemed him to be the best man to
protect the northern border of the duchy. His acquisition of the ducal
office brought considerable prestige and power to the family.[27] When Godfrey I died without a male heir in 1023, he was succeeded as duke by his
brother Gozelo I (Godfrey of Bouillon's great-grandfather). Gozelo I also
succeeded Godfrey the Captive as margrave of Antwerp. As duke of Lower
Lotharingia from 1023, Gozelo I served the crown loyally. This service was
rewarded in 1033, when Conrad II made him duke of Upper Lotharingia.[28] Between 1033 and his death in 1044, then, Gozelo I held both ducal
offices. In the early eleventh century, Gozelo I's daughter Regelinde married Count Albert II of Namur. This was a marriage that would have a significant bearing on the fortunes of the house of Ardennes-Bouillon later
in the century.[29]

During his lifetime Gozelo I associated his eldest son Godfrey (that is,
Godfrey II 'the Bearded') in the rule of the two duchies. Diplomas issued
by King Henry III in 1040–1041 refer to 'Duke Gozelo and Godfrey', indicating that both men were present at the royal court on several occasions.
Moreover, the *Annals of Niederaltaich* twice state that Godfrey the Bearded
ruled over Upper Lotharingia during Gozelo I's lifetime, while Herman
of Reichenau noted that when Gozelo I died, Godfrey the Bearded 'had
long been a duke'.[30] While Lampert of Hersfeld does not explicitly state
that Godfrey shared in his father's power, this chronicler wrote that he was
'extremely experienced in military affairs'.[31] After Gozelo I's death on 19
April 1044, Henry III decided to separate the ducal offices again. He did
not want to allow one man to monopolise power in Lotharingia by holding
both.[32] He thus divided the offices between two of Gozelo's sons, making
Godfrey the Bearded duke of Upper Lotharingia, and appointing Gozelo II
duke of Lower Lotharingia.

The career of Godfrey the Bearded

Godfrey the Bearded's career had a profound impact on the fortunes of
the house of Ardennes-Bouillon, and had repercussions which were felt
throughout the kingdom of Germany and elsewhere in the Empire.[33] The

latter years of Henry III's reign were characterised by enmity between the crown and Godfrey the Bearded, who proved to be the most formidable rebel in the Empire at this time.[34] Godfrey the Bearded was affronted when the king granted his younger brother Lower Lotharingia in 1044. He had fulfilled the duties of duke of Upper Lotharingia during his father's life-time, and fully expected to inherit both ducal offices. Godfrey and the king evidently possessed different conceptions of the hereditability of the ducal office; the king, following the practice of his father, Conrad II, saw it as an office which he could bestow at his discretion, while Godfrey saw it as his rightful inheritance.[35] Godfrey also regarded the division of the Lotharing-ian duchies as a threat to his family's power base.[36] Throughout the latter part of 1044, Godfrey discussed the disposition of the ducal offices with Henry. He promised the king that if he was granted the two duchies, he would remain loyal. The king interpreted this promise as an indication that Godfrey would renounce his loyalty if his request was denied. Henry thus informed Godfrey that if he persisted with his demand, he would oppose him with all the force of the crown.[37] The *Annals of Niederaltaich* record that at an assembly of the princes of the kingdom held towards the end of the year, Godfrey was deprived of all the rights he held from the king, and deposed as duke of Upper Lotharingia.[38] This, Weinfurter suggests, left Godfrey with only the option of rebelling against the king, because he was bound to preserve his family's lands and rights so that he could pass them on to his descendants.[39]

A number of contemporary chroniclers record that Godfrey the Bearded began a rebellion against Henry III in 1044. Sigebert of Gembloux states that after the death of Gozelo I, Godfrey the Bearded inherited the office of duke of Upper Lotharingia, but was denied that of Lower Lotharingia, and so revolted against Henry III.[40] Lampert of Hersfeld noted that Godfrey 'took up arms against the State' because he was denied the ducal office of Lower Lotharingia.[41] Herman of Reichenau castigated Godfrey for his course of action, asserting that he had unlawfully sought to obtain the ducal office that belonged to his brother by right, and when he failed, he 'pre-sumed to rebel against the pious king [Henry]'.[42] The *Annals of Niederalta-ich* state that during his rebellion, Godfrey made contact with Henry I of France, and that the two made common cause against Henry III.[43] The kings of France and Germany were long-standing enemies, and Henry I may have allied with Godfrey in an attempt to increase his authority in Lotharingia.[44]

In late 1044 Godfrey occupied towns and fortified places in Lotharin-gia that were loyal to the crown.[45] Henry's advisers persuaded him at his Christmas court at Speyer to raise an army to combat Godfrey's 'tyranny' and thereby defend his subjects in Lotharingia from the effects of the rebel-lion.[46] At the very end of the year, Henry captured and destroyed one of Godfrey's fortresses.[47] The *Annals of Niederaltaich* record that shortly after Henry's Easter court at Goslar in 1045, he granted to the son of Count Baldwin V of Flanders a march at the frontier, in a region where Godfrey the Bearded was waging war. It is likely that this was the march of Antwerp, which had formerly been held by Godfrey's father, Gozelo I.[48] Godfrey's rebellion did not persist for much longer; in July 1045 he surrendered to Henry III. Herman of Reichenau reports that Godfrey had realised that his rebellion had been defeated, and so came to submit to Henry.[49] He was imprisoned at Giebichenstein near Halle in Saxony, and he remained there for the next ten months.[50] Lampert of Hersfeld wrote that with Godfrey incarcerated, 'for a short time the kingdom remained calm and peaceful'.[51]

In May 1046, Godfrey the Bearded 'made reasonable satisfaction' to the king and so was released from his incarceration in Giebichenstein.[52] Sigebert of Gembloux asserted that Godfrey was released after he sent his son to Henry III as a hostage.[53] Shortly after Godfrey was freed, he came to Henry's Whitsun court at Aachen (18 May 1046), and reportedly prostrated himself on the ground before the king, who 'had compassion on him and restored his ducal office.[54] Godfrey, seemingly becalmed, was thereby restored to royal favour. At some point in 1045 or 1046, probably while Godfrey was languishing in captivity, his brother Gozelo II died.[55] Gozelo left no male heir, and so the office of duke of Lower Lotharingia was lost to the house of Ardennes-Bouillon: Henry III bestowed it upon Frederick of Luxemburg (see Figure 0.2).[56] At the end of 1046, Henry III left Germany and went to Rome to deal with conflicts that had beset the papacy. He sought to prevent the Roman aristocracy interfering in the curia. He also ended a dispute between three men who claimed the office of pope by deposing all three claimants. On Christmas Day, Henry had Bishop Suidger of Bamberg appointed as Clement II (1046–7). On the same day, the new pope crowned Henry III emperor. Henry's intervention also introduced a party of reformers into the papal curia, and instigated a period of close cooperation between the German royal court and the papacy.[57]

Although Godfrey the Bearded recovered the ducal office of Upper Lotharingia in May 1046, he evidently harboured some resentment. Not long after, he embarked on a second rebellion against Henry III. Godfrey may have been motivated by the bestowal of the ducal office of Lower Lotharingia on Frederick of Luxemburg and its consequent loss to the house of Ardennes-Bouillon. Lampert of Hersfeld wrote under the year 1047 that

> when [Godfrey] saw . . . that neither the intercession of the princes nor the act of surrender that he had willingly performed had been of any benefit to him, he was incited by his indignation on this account and by disgust at his own poverty to begin the war afresh.[58]

Sigebert of Gembloux suggested that Godfrey began his new rebellion after the death of the son he had sent to Henry III as a hostage.[59] During his second rebellion, Godfrey made alliances with a number of potentates, including Count Baldwin V of Flanders and Count Thierry IV of Holland. Another of Godfrey's allies at this time was Count Eustace II of Boulogne

(1049–*c.*1087), a vassal of the king of France.[60] As had been the case in 1044–1045, Godfrey's revolt had political ramifications which extended beyond Lotharingia. Henry III, distracted in May and June 1047 by preparations for his planned expedition to Hungary, was slow to perceive the threat that Godfrey posed in Lotharingia. When the emperor finally realised the danger, he abandoned his campaign to Hungary and travelled to Lotharingia. He arrived there by the start of September, and in the period that followed, he fought against Godfrey and his allies.[61]

Godfrey the Bearded's second revolt made a greater impression on contemporary authors than his rebellion on 1044–1045, no doubt because its consequences were more far-ranging. In the course of his second rebellion, he and his allies reputedly caused death and destruction as far as the Rhine.[62] Chroniclers attest that Godfrey destroyed the royal palace in Nijmegen.[63] It is also recorded that in October 1047 he captured the city of Verdun and burned its cathedral.[64] Lampert states that Godfrey later repented of this action. According to this chronicler, he was publicly scourged, personally contributed funds for the rebuilding of the cathedral, and 'very frequently participated personally in the building work, performing the duties of a poor serf'.[65] Another contemporary author suggests that Godfrey and his allies waged a concerted campaign against Bishop Wazo of Liège.[66] In response to Godfrey's renewed hostility, Henry III deposed him from the office of duke of Upper Lotharingia, and conferred the position on Count Adalbert of Châtenois (see Figure 0.2).[67] Godfrey subsequently attacked and killed Adalbert, who had further provoked Godfrey by plundering his lands. In 1048, Henry III appointed Adalbert's brother Gerard duke of Upper Lotharingia, and he held the office until his death in 1070.[68]

Godfrey's second revolt was ended by the intervention of Pope Leo IX (1048/1049–1054).[69] After Leo was consecrated in Rome in February 1049, he travelled to Lotharingia. Herman of Reichenau states that Leo excommunicated Godfrey the Bearded and his ally Count Baldwin of Flanders, and that this sentence prompted Godfrey to seek reconciliation with Henry III at Aachen in July 1049.[70] Godfrey was handed over as a prisoner into the custody of Archbishop Eberhard of Trier.[71] Leo celebrated Christmas in 1050 in Germany with Henry III, and he returned to Italy early in 1051. He was accompanied there by a number of prelates who had joined him in Germany. Among them was Frederick of Lotharingia, archdeacon of the cathedral of St Lambert in Liège, and the younger brother of Godfrey the Bearded.[72]

In mid-1051, Godfrey the Bearded was released from captivity into the care of Archbishop Herman of Cologne, from whom he held a modest fief.[73] This diminished status, coupled with the death of his first wife Doda in about 1053, prompted Godfrey to seek new opportunities beyond Lotharingia. His marriage to Doda had produced a number of children, including a daughter, Ida (born *c.*1040), and a son, also named Godfrey

(Godfrey III 'the Hunchback', born *c*.1045).[74] Soon after Doda's death Godfrey went to Italy, and in late April 1054, he married Beatrice, the widow of Margrave Boniface III of Tuscany (d.1052).[75] He also assumed wardship of Beatrice and Boniface's daughter, Matilda. Beatrice was the daughter of Duke Frederick II of Upper Lotharingia (1019–1026 or 1027), and so was herself Lotharingian. Upon marrying her, Godfrey assumed the office of margrave of Tuscany and gained control of a wide collection of dynastic lands throughout northern Italy. This made him the most powerful secular figure in that region.[76] The marriage of Godfrey and Beatrice also established a new trans-Alpine dynasty, that of Canossa-Lotharingia.

The emperor was gravely alarmed by Godfrey the Bearded's marriage to Beatrice of Tuscany. Herman of Reichenau asserted that Godfrey had gone to Italy in secret and without Henry's permission, and that in doing so, he had 'once more raised up a tyrannical power' against the emperor.[77] Sigebert wrote under the year 1053 that 'Godfrey rebelled again', before noting that he married Beatrice.[78] Lampert of Hersfeld discerned the political ramifications of the union. He noted that after Godfrey married Boniface's widow, 'he claimed for himself his march [of Tuscany] and his other possessions'.[79] The chronicler states that when Henry heard of this development, 'he began to be oppressed by painful anxiety'.[80] With good reason, the emperor regarded the union as a serious threat to his authority. The new dynasty's interests either side of the Alps had the potential to destabilise imperial power in Italy and, perhaps, even to undermine the delicate political balance of the Empire. Henry simply could not afford to stand idly by while Godfrey constructed a new power base in Italy.[81] Between March and November 1055, the emperor conducted an expedition in Italy against Godfrey and Beatrice. When Henry first entered Italy, Godfrey came to protest his innocence in person, reportedly asserting that since he had been deprived of his ancestral lands in Lotharingia, he had simply come to Italy to be supported by his wife's resources.[82] Godfrey failed to mollify the emperor, however. Though Godfrey managed to elude the emperor's clutches and escape from Tuscany to Lotharingia, where he found willing support from allies including Count Baldwin of Flanders, Henry captured Beatrice and Matilda at Florence in June. Henry took them back to Germany with him.[83] The emperor's efforts to undermine the new dynasty did not cease there; at Christmas 1055, he betrothed his infant son Henry (the future Henry IV) to Bertha of Savoy, the daughter of the margravine of Turin. The aim of this union was to undercut the authority of the house of Canossa-Lotharingia in north-west Italy.[84] Although Henry achieved his main aim of checking Godfrey the Bearded's establishment of a power base in Italy, the conflict had serious implications in the longer term. Godfrey's revolts, and Henry's military efforts to counter them, served to undermine the authority of the dukes of Lotharingia. In turn, this destabilised the political balance of the region. With ducal authority in decline, it proved to be more difficult to control the powerful Lotharingian families. The region also became more vulnerable to political interventions from the west, especially from the king of France and the count of Flanders.[85]

In 1056, the emperor pardoned Godfrey and Beatrice. While Berthold of Reichenau states that Godfrey took the initiative and came to submit to the emperor, Bonizo suggests that Henry sensed that he was dying and sought a reconciliation with Godfrey, before beseeching him to promise that he would support the young Henry IV.[86] If Godfrey did submit to Henry III in this way, then he most likely did so when the emperor was at Trier in June.[87] This was one of Henry III's last actions. On 5 October 1056 he died, at the age of only 39. He was succeeded by his six-year-old son, Henry IV. The younger Henry had been inaugurated king of Germany in 1053, though he had yet to be inaugurated emperor by the pope in Rome. Henry III's widow, Agnes of Poitou, acted as regent during the first years of her son's reign. Aware that a minor's accession could precipitate instability, Agnes and her associates in the minority government hastened to restore disaffected lords like Godfrey the Bearded to royal favour. At an assembly of the German nobility in Cologne on 5–6 December, Godfrey the Bearded and his allies were publicly reconciled to the crown. A key participant in the assembly was Pope Victor II (1055–1057), who had come to Germany in order to help ensure that Henry IV succeeded to the throne smoothly. Sigebert of Gembloux wrote that at the assembly, 'through the mediation of Pope Victor, Baldwin [of Flanders] and Godfrey were returned to the king's grace and peace, and all the tumult of war was becalmed'.[88] It is possible that at this juncture Agnes made some kind of promise to Godfrey the Bearded. Both the Lotharingian ducal offices were occupied at that time, but she may have pledged to restore one or other of the duchies to Godfrey should a vacancy arise in the future.[89]

Godfrey the Bearded's reconciliation with the crown in December 1056 set his career off in a new direction. After this point, he was a stalwart supporter of the young Henry IV.[90] One contemporary believed that in this time Godfrey served Henry IV's interests in Italy. The *Cantatorium* relates that Godfrey held the position of prefect of Rome. If this was so, Godfrey was probably appointed to the office at Cologne in December 1056.[91] From 1056 to his death in 1069, Godfrey divided his time between Germany and Italy. While he was in Germany, he administered the lands that he had retained in Lotharingia despite his rebellions, and generally worked to support Henry IV and his government.[92] During these periods, his wife Beatrice administered the family's lands in northern Italy. When Godfrey was in Italy, he played a significant role in regional politics as margrave of Tuscany. Most importantly, in these periods, Godfrey proved to be the most powerful secular ally of the reform papacy in Italy.[93]

The career of Godfrey the Bearded's brother, Frederick of Lotharingia, was instrumental in aligning the family with the reform papacy. As previously noted, Frederick had gone to Rome with Pope Leo IX in 1051. Soon after, Leo made Frederick arch-chancellor of the Church. Frederick played an active role in the papacy's most important diplomatic initiatives at this time. He was, for example, a member of the papal delegation that went to Constantinople in 1054 under the leadership of Cardinal-Bishop Humbert of Silva Candida.[94] Frederick's return to Italy in the following year coincided with Henry III's military campaign against Godfrey the Bearded and Beatrice. While Henry was in Italy at that time, he reportedly ordered Pope Victor II to capture and hand over Frederick as part of his campaign against Godfrey. Frederick thus fled to the abbey of Monte Cassino.[95] Lampert wrote that Frederick served there 'as a warrior of Christ under a holy vow'.[96] Frederick remained at Monte Cassino after Godfrey the Bearded reconciled with the crown in 1056, and in May the following year he was appointed as its abbot. Three days after the death of Pope Victor II on 28 July, Frederick was chosen to be the next pope. Upon his election on 2 August, he took the name Stephen IX.[97] There can be little doubt that the members of the curia hoped that by choosing Frederick they would ensure political and military support from Godfrey the Bearded. At that time, the curia knew that the minority government of Henry IV was too weak to support the papacy as Henry III had between 1046 and 1056.[98] It was to Godfrey that they instead turned. During his pontificate, Stephen sought to enlist his brother's assistance against the Normans of southern Italy.[99] Though Stephen died on 29 March 1058, less than a year after his appointment as pope, Godfrey the Bearded continued to support the papacy in the years that followed. In the aftermath of his brother's death, various members of the curia established themselves at Florence, which lay in Godfrey's territory in northern Italy.[100]

After Stephen's death, a papal schism ensued. The curia split into opposing factions: one group elected Bishop John II of Velletri as Benedict X, while another, comprised of reformers who had realised that no support was forthcoming from the German royal court, elected Bishop Gerard of Florence as Nicholas II. Nicholas was from Godfrey's ambit in the north, and was chosen with the aim of encouraging Godfrey to continue providing support as he had during his brother's pontificate. At a synod at Sutri in December 1058, Nicholas declared Benedict deposed. Bonizo claims that 'the magnificent Duke Godfrey' was present at Sutri.[101] After the synod concluded, Henry IV deemed Nicholas II to be the legitimate pope. This prompted Godfrey to march from northern Italy to Rome to install Nicholas there, and expel his rival, Benedict X. Lampert of Hersfeld explicitly states that Nicholas was set up in Rome 'by the agency of Margrave Godfrey'.[102] Nicholas was enthroned and consecrated in Rome on 24 January 1059, soon after which Godfrey withdrew from the city and returned to northern Italy.[103]

Nicholas II's death in July 1061 precipitated another schism, a development which was exacerbated by a rift which had emerged between the reform party of the papal curial and the German royal court. Henry IV's government – acting in concert with the Romans – set up Bishop Cadalus of Parma as Honorius II, while the reform party elected Bishop Anselm of Lucca, who took the name Alexander II. Once again, the reformers settled on a candidate who was associated with Godfrey the Bearded.[104] Armed confrontations between the opposing factions ensued. Honorius attacked Rome in 1062, and in May Godfrey led an army there in order to confront him. Godfrey assumed the role of mediator, and persuaded the rival popes to return to their bishoprics and await judgement on the situation by the German royal court.[105] Honorius thus returned to Parma, while Alexander departed for Lucca. Honorius attacked Rome, but Godfrey intervened to ward him off.[106] Henry IV and his advisers decided in favour of Alexander, and it was Godfrey who acted to enforce the decision. Repeating his earlier efforts to install Nicholas II in 1059, Godfrey marched on Rome in January 1063 to ensure that Alexander II was appointed pope. By 23 March Alexander was resident in the Lateran.[107] Later that year, Godfrey came to the rescue of a Norman contingent which was fighting for Alexander against Honorius in Rome.[108] The council of Mantua in 1064 confirmed Alexander as the rightful pope, though Honorius II continued to regard himself as the rightful pope until his death in 1072.

On Easter Tuesday (29 March) 1065 the young Henry IV entered his majority. Godfrey the Bearded reportedly played a principal role in the ceremony held on that day at Worms to mark the king's passage from boyhood to adolescence. Berthold of Reichenau asserts that at Worms, Henry 'was girded with the sword in the ninth year of his reign but in the fourteenth year of his life and Duke Godfrey was chosen as his shieldbearer [*scutarius*]'.[109] Robinson interpreted the role of shieldbearer as 'an honorific office conferred on the foremost vassal of the crown'.[110] Godfrey's participation in the ceremony symbolised his allegiance to the German royal court. This accounts for what transpired after Frederick of Luxemburg, the duke of Lower Lotharingia, died later that year. When the royal court was at Goslar around October, Henry appointed Godfrey as Frederick's successor as duke. One author noted that 'Godfrey travelled to the court at Goslar, and there he took on the ducal office . . . and was then made master of the armies of Lotharingia'.[111] The speed with which Godfrey was appointed to the ducal office strongly indicates that he had struck some kind of mutually beneficial deal with the crown before Frederick's death.

After Godfrey the Bearded was appointed duke of Lower Lotharingia, he may have retained the office of margrave of Tuscany. In the ensuing period, he issued charters in which he described himself as 'duke and margrave'.[112] While the latter title could refer to the office of margrave of Tuscany, it could also refer to that of margrave of Antwerp, which his predecessors had held. Despite obtaining the ducal office in 1065, however, Godfrey did not cease supporting the reform papacy. In mid-1067, he was back in Italy, leading troops against an army of Normans that had invaded the region around Rome. Bonizo asserts that 'the magnificent Duke Godfrey' came to 'the aid of St Peter' by expelling the Normans.[113] Bonizo also states that

Godfrey's step-daughter, Matilda, was present during the campaign, claiming that during the encounter she too served St Peter, 'the blessed prince of the apostles'.[114] Godfrey's 1067 campaign had implications for his relations with Henry IV. On one hand, the *Annals of Niederaltaich* claim that Godfrey acted in the king's interests by conducting this campaign.[115] The chronicler Amatus, in contrast, asserts that Henry IV had assembled his army at Augsburg in the expectation of Godfrey joining him there, only to discover that Godfrey had embarked on his own campaign in Italy.[116] Cowdrey found the latter interpretation more convincing, concluding that in 1067 Godfrey commenced his campaign in order to maintain a grip on Italian politics. Had Henry gone to Italy at that time, his presence would have bolstered royal authority south of the Alps. Crucially, Henry's decision to abandon his planned expedition to Italy also meant deferring his inauguration as emperor by the pope in Rome.[117]

After the campaign against the Normans in mid-1067, Godfrey the Bearded remained in Italy until 1069. It seems that in 1068 Godfrey attracted the ire of the reform papacy for communicating with the antipope Honorius II (Bishop Cadalus of Parma). Peter Damian heard rumours that Godfrey had been in contact with Honorius, and so wrote to Godfrey in this year to reproach him.[118] It is related in the *Cantatorium* that Alexander II imposed on Godfrey the penance of living apart from his wife Beatrice until he had founded a monastery.[119] Though the *Cantatorium* does not state what Godfrey had done to earn Alexander's displeasure, the rumours surrounding Godfrey's link to Honorius represent the likeliest explanation. As Robinson suggests, Godfrey's reputed contact with Honorius should be interpreted in the wider context of the German royal court's diplomatic initiatives in Italy in 1068.[120] In that year, Henry IV sent a legation into Italy, perhaps to pave the way for his inauguration as emperor. Henry's legates reportedly met Honorius as well as the bishop of Ravenna, even though both had been excommunicated by Alexander II.[121]

In 1069, Godfrey's health began to fail. Benzo of Alba states that when Godfrey began to feel ill, he decided to leave Italy and return to Lotharingia in the hope that the change of air might benefit him.[122] The *Cantatorium* corroborates this version of events.[123] The same source also provides a detailed report of the events which transpired after Godfrey arrived in Bouillon at the very end of the year. Godfrey reportedly requested that Abbot Thierry of St Hubert (1056–1068) come and visit him.[124] Though Thierry was initially unwilling to leave his monastery, he eventually assented. It is reported that, Godfrey, in the presence of his son, Godfrey the Hunchback, tearfully relinquished his sword into the hands of Abbot Thierry, declaiming that the act signified his renunciation of his life as a man of war.[125] The ailing Godfrey was then carried from the castle of Bouillon across the river Semois to the priory of St Peter, trailed by a number of companions, including his son and his 'best men'.[126] Godfrey placed on the priory's altar an ivory reliquary casket that had belonged to Boniface of Tuscany. At this point he reportedly referred to the penance imposed upon him by Alexander II, and beseeched Thierry to carry out the task with which he had been charged by taking the priory under the control of St Hubert. Thierry responded that he could not do so, because it seemed to him that Godfrey's son was unwilling to give his support. The author of the *Cantatorium* then recounted how the elder Godfrey persuaded his son to take an oath to support the donation of the priory to St Hubert. The author states that this convinced Thierry that Godfrey the Hunchback would support the disposition of the priory, and he therefore agreed to send monks from St Hubert there.[127] Then, Godfrey the Bearded, sensing that his death was approaching, asked to be taken to Verdun, where he had long planned to be buried, to make final restitution for attacking the city during his rebellion against Henry III. On 24 December, about a month after arriving at Verdun, he died.[128] According to the St Hubert chronicler, then, Abbot Thierry played a crucial role in preparing Godfrey the Bearded for his death. As the following pages will show, the link between the house of Ardennes-Bouillon and St Hubert would remain strong under his successors. Lampert of Hersfeld briefly reported Godfrey's death at the very end of 1069, before stating he was widely known and admired for his deeds.[129] Berthold of Reichenau described Godfrey's death, and then accorded him high praise, noting that he had rectified any misdeeds through penance, and had thereby earned himself a place in heaven.[130] The author of the *Cantatorium* at one point listed Godfrey's achievements, recounting that he had been

> patrician of the city of Rome, prefect of Ancona, margrave of Pisa, lord of all the lands around Tuscany and Italy, the unconquered count of Verdun and duke of Lotharingia, and for many years the most redoubtable enemy of Emperor Henry.[131]

Godfrey the Bearded's career marked a crucial phase in the history of the house of Ardennes-Bouillon. The importance of his association to the reform papacy cannot be understated. In the years between his return to Italy in 1057 and his death, contemporaries regarded him as a stalwart supporter of the papacy. Between 1057 and 1063, three men were appointed pope (excluding figures now classed as antipopes). The first, Stephen IX, was Godfrey's brother, and the other two, Nicholas II (bishop of Florence) and Alexander II (bishop of Lucca), were from his political ambit in Tuscany. All three were chosen to secure Godfrey's support for the papacy.[132] Moreover, Godfrey personally installed Nicholas and Alexander in Rome, and fought to expel the antipopes Benedict X and Honorius II. As a result of his exploits, Godfrey was well-regarded by the reformers and their associates. Bonizo of Sutri described Godfrey as 'a magnificent man, most active in military affairs'.[133] The chronicler Berthold of Reichenau wrote a long encomium of Godfrey.[134] By contrast, some of the reform papacy's enemies were hostile to Godfrey. Benzo of Alba, a partisan of the antipope Honorius

II and Henry IV, and a vehement opponent of Gregory VII, was scathingly critical of him, describing him as 'Godfrey who was called duke'.[135] At points in his account, Benzo also employed the caustic terms *Cornefredus* ('Prick-frey') and *Grugnefredus* ('Shitfrey') to refer to Godfrey.[136] In this author's eyes, Godfrey had unscrupulously meddled in the German royal court and in Italian affairs to his own benefit.[137] Benzo's obloquy serves to further underscore just how closely Godfrey was associated with the reform papacy in the eyes of contemporaries.

The career of Godfrey the Hunchback

Godfrey the Bearded's successor was Godfrey the Hunchback, his son from his first marriage.[138] The younger man encountered no problems in succeeding his father to the family's lands or to the office of duke of Lower Lotharingia.[139] As noted above, Godfrey the Hunchback had been born around 1045. He would thus have been around 25 at the time of his father's death. As his cognomen indicates, his physical condition was apparent to contemporaries. Several observers commented that Godfrey's affliction meant that his form was small and unimposing. Lampert wrote that Godfrey was 'small in stature, misshapen, with a hunchback'.[140] Elsewhere the same author stated that Godfrey 'appeared contemptible because of the smallness of his stature and his hunchback'.[141] In a charter of St Hubert, probably drawn up in the year after Godfrey the Bearded's death, Godfrey the Hunchback is listed among the witnesses as 'Duke Godfrey the little'.[142] Nevertheless, other of his qualities struck contemporaries. Lampert of Hersfeld noted that he was 'a young man of outstanding abilities but a hunchback'.[143] In the *Carmen de Bello Saxonico*, it is related that 'the famous Duke Godfrey [the Hunchback] . . . had the heart of his father, but was not his equal in body'.[144] Sigebert of Gembloux stated that although Godfrey the Hunchback was 'small of body, he had an excellent mind'.[145] In this era, noble children with severe disabilities were often sent as oblates to monasteries. In a letter written in about 1080, a monastic author stated that abbots needed to beware of noble families who sent child oblates who were 'lame or infirm, partly deaf or blind, hunchbacked or leprous, or anything else that makes him at all less acceptable to the secular world'.[146] The author warned that oblations such as these were granted not for God's sake, but so that their families did not have to care for them. Crucially, Godfrey the Hunchback's affliction did not inhibit him, and despite it he proved himself to be a formidable warrior and an effective duke.

One of the first issues that confronted Godfrey the Hunchback after his succession was the insistent claim by Abbot Thierry of St Hubert over the bequests made by Godfrey the Bearded just before his death.[147] The author of the *Cantatorium* states that 'young Godfrey' (*junior Gotefridus*) ignored the counsel and help of the abbot, refused to fulfil his father's bequests, and even attempted to intimidate Thierry and the other monks of St Hubert. Godfrey reportedly believed that a new monastic foundation at the priory in Bouillon was less advantageous to him than maintaining the interests of the soldiery of his duchy. After he was reproached by several of the senior men of the castle of Bouillon, Godfrey, moved by shame, admitted that lands bequeathed to St Hubert by his father were being held by his stipendiary warriors (*milites stipendarias*), and that he was neither able nor willing to attempt to recover them. Godfrey entreated the abbot to accept an alternative deal which incorporated rights other than those granted by Godfrey the Bearded. The St Hubert chronicler states that Thierry accepted this offer in the hope that the young man might later atone for his actions. Godfrey then opened a treasure chest bequeathed by his father and removed items worth 700 marks of silver for himself, before giving the rest to the abbot. After this he transferred to St Hubert the rights to Bellevaux, the proceeds of which were assigned to the monks who read the divine office at the priory of St Peter at Bouillon.

Soon after his succession to the ducal office, Godfrey was embroiled in a political crisis which unfolded in the county of Flanders following the death of Count Baldwin VI in July 1070. On his deathbed, Baldwin bequeathed the county to his eldest son, Arnulf III, who was still a minor. Baldwin's widow, Richilde of Mons and Hainaut, was to act as regent for her son until he came of age. The succession was immediately challenged by Baldwin VI's younger brother, Robert 'the Frisian', who sought the county for himself. Richilde secured aid from King Philip I of France, who brought an army to Flanders to challenge Robert. Count Eustace II of Boulogne also supported Arnulf at that time.[148] Arnulf and his allies fought Robert's forces near Cassel on 22 February 1071. Arnulf was killed in the battle, and Robert subsequently captured Flanders. He remained count until his death in 1093.[149] A few months later, Richilde and her younger son, Baldwin, came to the German royal court at Liège to seek Henry IV's assistance against Robert the Frisian. A deal was reached whereby the young Baldwin gave the county of Hainaut to Bishop Theodwin of Liège (1048–1075), who gave it to Godfrey the Hunchback, who in turn passed it as a benefice back to Baldwin.[150] Henry IV then ordered Theodwin, Godfrey, and other Lotharingian princes to go to Flanders and expel Robert the Frisian by force of arms.[151] However, when they discovered that Robert had come to an accommodation with King Philip and had been formally invested as count of Flanders, they abandoned their expedition and returned to Lotharingia.[152] The author of the *Cantatorium* reports that at one juncture some time after this episode, Abbot Thierry of St Hubert bought from Richilde of Mons the rights to Chévigny, which he had long coveted. With Godfrey the Hunchback's approval, Thierry paid for these rights with 500 bezants of gold from Godfrey the Bearded's bequest.[153]

A pivotal moment in Godfrey the Hunchback's life was his marriage to his step-sister, Matilda of Tuscany.[154] The two were at least betrothed before Godfrey the Bearded's death.[155] If they were not wed at that point, they must have married shortly after.[156] Their union was intended to preserve the house of Canossa-Lotharingia. A contemporary charter indicates that in 1071 Godfrey and Matilda had a daughter, but that the child lived for only a few months.[157] Around autumn 1071, the marriage of Godfrey the Hunchback and Matilda broke down. Matilda departed Lotharingia and returned to Italy.[158] Lampert of Hersfeld reports that the two became estranged because Matilda wished to live in Italy rather than in Lotharingia, while Godfrey was too occupied with the responsibilities of the ducal office to leave Germany.[159] The author of the *Cantatorium* states that Matilda left Godfrey and returned to Italy, and spurned all his efforts to persuade her to return.[160]

In late 1072, Godfrey travelled to Italy in the hope of securing a reconciliation with Matilda.[161] He must have made the journey before the end of the year, as he was in Italy in mid-January. While there, he apparently exercised the office of margrave of Tuscany, in conjunction with Beatrice, his mother-in-law. The two held court at Pisa on 17 January, at Arezzo in April, and at Marengo on 18 August.[162] An account of Godfrey's interaction with Matilda at this time is provided in the *Cantatorium.* The author of this text states that before Godfrey departed Lotharingia, he threatened the abbot of St Hubert with violence to compel him to hand over the ivory casket that had formerly belonged to Matilda's father, Boniface of Tuscany, and which had been given to St Hubert by Godfrey the Bearded shortly before his death.[163] The author states that Matilda had asked Godfrey to come to Italy and to bring her the casket, and that, moved by hope of a reconciliation with his wife, he assented. However, Matilda had given Godfrey false hope, for even after he returned the casket, 'he was unable to attain marital grace'.[164] The peace offering failed. Spurned by his wife, Godfrey returned to Lotharingia. His time in Italy in 1073 coincided with the death of Pope Alexander II on 21 April, and the election on the following day of Archdeacon Hildebrand as Gregory VII.[165] Godfrey wrote to congratulate Gregory, and while his letter is lost, Gregory's reply to that missive is preserved in his papal register.[166] After Godfrey's marriage to Matilda broke down, then, he retained interests in Italian politics and the papacy.

The author of the *Cantatorium* appended to his account of Godfrey the Hunchback's visit to Italy a description of an episode which was provoked by his seizure of the ivory casket bequeathed by his father.[167] The author states that after Godfrey appropriated this item, Abbot Thierry of St Hubert and Bishop Herman of Metz went to Italy, in order to confer with Gregory VII. Although the abbot reportedly sought Gregory's absolution from the obligation to fulfil Godfrey the Bearded's deathbed's wishes, the pope ordered Archbishop Anno of Cologne and Bishop Theodwin of Liège to compel Godfrey to uphold his father's bequest. The chronicler also reports that while the two prelates were in Italy, they met Matilda of Tuscany, who had arranged their meeting with Gregory by warmly recommending them to the pope. Matilda presented Abbot Thierry with a white chasuble that had belonged to Leo IX, and a subdeacon's robe which had belonged to Stephen IX, the brother of Godfrey the Bearded. According to the St Hubert chronicler, these developments had repercussions for Godfrey the Hunchback. Though Anno of Cologne and Theodwin of Liège were unable to persuade Godfrey to atone, the situation changed when Herman of Metz paid a visit to Bouillon at the very end of 1074, during a bitterly cold winter.[168] When Herman awoke in Godfrey's chamber one morning, he heard bells pealing, and asked Godfrey about the sound. When Godfrey replied that it signified that the monks placed at his father's wishes in the priory of St Peter in Bouillon were rising to sing Matins, the bishop groaned and commented on how unfortunate he and Godfrey were, that they were resting in the warm while the monks braved the cold outside to perform the divine office. The bishop then addressed Godfrey: 'You, however, are the most unfortunate, because you possess neither the fear of God nor love for your father, whose charity you have cheated, and which you still withhold from such devoted monks!'[169] Godfrey burst into tears at this rebuke, and then thanked the bishop for his intervention. After this, he promised to fulfil his father's bequest. The next day, he called Abbot Thierry of St Hubert to him, and, on his knee, with the bishop and the members of his court looking on, admitted that he had erred and sinned in the eyes of God and his father, but affirmed that he would make amends.[170] Thierry reminded Godfrey of his father's promises, and stated that he would be held to them. Godfrey immediately handed over the requisite funds and certain properties to St Hubert.[171] Just as he had given consolation to the dying Godfrey the Bearded in 1069, Abbot Thierry intervened in 1074 to instruct Godfrey the Hunchback on sinfulness and atonement.

The latter part of Godfrey the Hunchback's career as duke was chiefly shaped by his association with Henry IV. From the time that Henry entered his majority in 1065 he had faced rebellions against his rule in Saxony. Essentially, the Saxon nobility had become aggrieved at what they perceived to be efforts to bolster royal authority in the duchy.[172] A particularly damaging rebellion took place between 1073 and 1075. In that period, Godfrey the Hunchback participated in Henry's military campaigns in Saxony. As noted above, until the late summer of 1073, Godfrey was in Italy attempting to secure a reconciliation with Matilda of Tuscany. By October, he was back in Germany, and present among the royal forces assembled in Saxony. Henry had instructed the princes of his kingdom to gather at Gerstungun on 20 October to confer with the Saxon rebels.[173] Lampert of Hersfeld reports that Henry sent seven representatives to confer with the Saxons, consisting of four ecclesiastical figures and three lay princes. The four prelates were the archbishops of Mainz and Cologne and the bishops of Metz and Bamberg. The three secular representatives were Rudolf of Rheinfelden, duke of Swabia; Berthold of Zähringen, duke of Carinthia; and Godfrey, duke of Lower Lotharingia. Lampert reports that the Saxons convinced the king's seven representatives of the validity of their grievances against him.[174] Lampert also states that Godfrey was one of the princes at the royal court in January 1074 who informed the king that they were unwilling to participate further in military action against the Saxons.[175] (In contrast, Bruno of Merseburg asserted that 'Duke Godfrey was the greatest enemy of the Saxons'.[176]) Godfrey seems also to have conducted a campaign to Frisia at some point in 1074. A brief account written at Iburg in Saxony states that in this year Godfrey went to Frisia accompanied by Bishop William of Utrecht.[177]

Godfrey was again present when the royal army assembled at Breitungun on 8 June 1075. The army fought a battle against the Saxon forces the following day at Homburg on the river Unstrut.[178] Lampert of Hersfeld, Berthold of Reichenau, and the author of the *Carmen de Bello Saxonico* all note that Godfrey and his force of Lotharingians fought in this battle as part of the royal army.[179] Bonizo of Sutri noted that 'the celebrated Duke Godfrey, husband of the most noble Matilda' fought in the battle.[180] Henry IV had evidently come to regard Godfrey as one of his most trusted allies. Hence, after Bishop Theodwin of Liège died on 23 June – soon after the battle of Homburg – the king asked Godfrey to recommend a candidate to fill it. As noted above, Liège was a vitally important diocese, and Henry IV wished to ensure that a loyal supporter was appointed to it. Godfrey nominated his kinsman, Archdeacon Henry of Verdun. Lampert of Hersfeld states that through 'the intervention of Duke [Godfrey] and because of the latter's outstanding service in the war, the king immediately appointed Henry, a certain canon of Verdun, who was a close relative of the duke, as [Theodwin's] successor'.[181] According to Lampert, 'the duke was placed under a great obligation to the king by this favour and he promised his fullest support in the forthcoming expedition'.[182] The author of the *Cantatorium* claims that the nomination of Henry of Verdun provoked some disquiet within the diocese of Liège, and that Godfrey had to persuade the clergy to accept his chosen candidate. After mollifying the clergy, Godfrey accompanied his kinsman Henry to Cologne for his consecration as bishop by the archbishop.[183] Bishop Henry of Liège would be a key ally of both king and duke in the years that followed.[184]

The royal army assembled at Gerstungun on 22 October 1075 for another campaign in Saxony.[185] Though Godfrey the Hunchback and Duke Thierry of Upper Lotharingia were present, the dukes of Swabia, Bavaria, and Carinthia were conspicuously absent. Lampert and Bruno of Merseburg both state that these dukes had come to regret their involvement in earlier royal campaigns against the Saxons.[186] Lampert asserts that the forces brought by Godfrey far surpassed the rest of royal army in quality.[187] After a few days, the king decided to send five representatives to confer with the rebels. Four of these were ecclesiastics, namely, the archbishops of Mainz and Salzburg, and the bishops of Augsburg and Würzburg. The fifth, the only secular representative, was Godfrey the Hunchback. Lampert of Hersfeld states that:

> [Godfrey] exercised the greatest authority in the expedition: he was the supreme power and the point around which all things turned. For although he was small in stature, misshapen, with a hunchback, he nevertheless towered above the rest of the princes because of the splendour of his wealth and the number and excellence of his knights but also because of his mature wisdom and perfect eloquence.[188]

According to this author, the Saxons were relieved when they discovered the identity of the king's five legates, for they trusted those men more than any other members of the royal army. The chronicler states that Godfrey 'and those who were with him showed the greatest energy in these negotiations', and eventually succeeded in persuading the Saxons to come to terms without resorting to battle.[189]

The foregoing has demonstrated that Godfrey the Hunchback was closely associated with King Henry IV in the period 1073–1075. But it is crucial to note that during that same period, Godfrey retained contact with the reform papacy. Although relations between Henry IV and the papacy deteriorated as a result of the royal interventions in Saxony, Godfrey's allegiance to the king did not lead Gregory VII automatically to regard him as an adversary. Before his appointment as pope in 1073, Gregory had been a member of the curia for many years, at least from the time of Stephen IX (1057–1058), Godfrey's uncle. Gregory also knew that Godfrey's father, Godfrey the Bearded, had loyally served Nicholas II and Alexander II, and that he had fought against the antipopes who had challenged them.[190] During the first years of his pontificate, then, Gregory VII hoped that Godfrey the Hunchback would follow in the footsteps of his father and work to support the papacy.

As noted above, Godfrey was in Italy when Gregory was appointed pope in 1073. In the letter that Godfrey sent to Gregory immediately after his elevation, he evidently expressed joy at Gregory's appointment. In his reply of 6 May, Gregory asserted that he welcomed Godfrey's response to his elevation.[191] Gregory then stated that he did not doubt that Godfrey's joy sprang 'from a fount of sincere affection and from a faithful mind'.[192] The pope also affirmed his belief that Godfrey was a supporter of the papacy:

> we recognise that, by God's gift, the power of faith and constancy is implanted in you, and because we have all the confidence in you that is proper in a most beloved son of St Peter, we desire that your mind should in no way be in doubt about our own correspondingly most constant love and most ready goodwill towards your public dignities.[193]

Gregory's characterisation of Godfrey as a 'most beloved son of St Peter' (*karissimo sancti Petri filio*) is particularly striking. The latter part of Gregory's letter of 6 May suggests that Godfrey had asked the pope about his policy toward Henry IV. Gregory responded to the question cautiously, indicating that if the king listened to his advice he would support him completely, but that if the king did not, he would oppose him. The fact that Gregory outlined his attitudes to Henry's kingship to Godfrey led Cowdrey to suggest that the pope probably had Godfrey in mind to act as a mediator with the king.[194] Godfrey and the pope were not confined to epistolary contact; Godfrey may have been present at Gregory's episcopal ordination in Rome on 30 June 1073.[195] Certainly, the two met in person at some point during Godfrey's time in Italy. In a letter sent to Godfrey in 1074, the pope referred to a matter that the two had talked about 'when we were present together'.[196]

Gregory apparently hoped to engineer a reconciliation between Godfrey and Matilda of Tuscany. The pope would have known from the moment that the marriage broke down that the consequences for the reform papacy would be profound.[197] As already indicated, Godfrey the Bearded and his wife Beatrice had been the principal secular supporters of the papacy in the late 1050s and much of the 1060s. After the failure of her marriage to Godfrey the Hunchback, Matilda, along with her mother Beatrice, contemplated leaving the secular world to enter a convent. In a personally dictated letter written on 16 February 1074, Gregory reminded Matilda that he had earlier advised her against taking that course of action. He encouraged her to devote herself to the Virgin Mary whilst remaining in the world.[198] On 4 March, Gregory wrote to both Matilda and Beatrice, and reiterated this advice.[199]

In 1074, the pope envisaged that there would be a reconciliation between Godfrey and Matilda. He hoped that both would participate in a military expedition that he had been planning for the defence of St Peter.[200] Gregory outlined his plan for the expedition in a letter of 2 February to Count William of Upper Burgundy.[201] He stated that the participating forces would assemble in Italy, and after ensuring the papacy was protected from the Normans, cross to Constantinople and aid the Byzantines, who were suffering at the hands of the Turks. Gregory intended to take part in this expedition personally. He instructed Count William that if he planned to join the expedition, he should send a messenger to Rome to signal his intention. The messenger was to come 'by way of Count Beatrice, who with her daughter [Matilda] and son-in-law [Godfrey the Hunchback] has it in train to contend in this business'.[202] This claim is highly significant, for it reveals that in early 1074 Gregory believed that Godfrey was making preparations to render military assistance to the papacy. He must have hoped that Godfrey and Matilda would be able to come to an accommodation so that both could participate. Nevertheless, Gregory was mistaken in his assertion that Godfrey was preparing to assist the papacy at this time. Godfrey may never have had any intention of doing so. Even if he had, he would most likely have been forestalled by his duty to participate in Henry IV's campaigns in Saxony. On 7 April, Gregory wrote to Godfrey to chastise him for failing to follow through on his commitment.[203] The pope stated that when the two had met in person the previous year, Godfrey had promised to participate in the venture, and that he had broken that promise: 'Where is the help that you guaranteed? Where are the knights that you promised us you would lead for the honour and support of St Peter?'[204] Gregory informed Godfrey that because he had reneged on his commitment to him, the pope no longer retained any responsibilities toward him other than those he held to him as a Christian. Nevertheless, Gregory shrewdly left the door open for Godfrey the Hunchback to recover papal favour in the future, asserting to him that

> should you be willing fixedly to stand fast in the thing that you have promised, namely, to adhere to St Peter from the heart, we shall hold you as a most dear son and you will hold us, unworthy though we are, nevertheless as a kind father.[205]

Although Gregory felt deeply aggrieved by Godfrey's failure to support the planned expedition, he did not rule out the possibility of restoring a constructive and friendly relationship with him. When Beatrice and Matilda wrote to Gregory in the autumn of 1075, and asked him about how they should deal with Godfrey, the pope was studiously non-committal in his reply. He noted that Godfrey had broken his promises to Beatrice and Matilda as well as himself, before discussing the prospect of a reconciliation:

> Certainly, if you shall be able to conclude with him any compact that does not conflict with the ordinance of the holy fathers, that seems to us good and praiseworthy . . . Thus, if he shall love you, we shall love him; if, however, by fault of his own he shall begin to engage in hatred, we shall, with God's good will, resist him by loving you in all ways that we shall be able as most dear daughters.[206]

Gregory, then, did not rule out the possibility of securing support from Godfrey in the future. For this reason, he entertained the prospect of Matilda establishing some kind of accommodation with Godfrey which would permit that to happen.

Inevitably, though, Godfrey's continued support of Henry IV influenced Gregory's view of Godfrey. Developments in late 1075 led to the breakdown of relations between Henry and Gregory. The flashpoint was a disagreement over the vacancy in the office of archbishop of Milan.[207] Henry ordered that Tedald, a royal clerk, be appointed to the post. He also had supporters installed in the bishoprics of Fermo and Spoleto, and appears to have been in contact with the Normans of southern Italy, the papacy's long-standing foes. Advice from Godfrey may have shaped Henry IV's Italian policy at this time.[208] Gregory took a dim view of Henry's activities. On 8 December 1075, the pope issued a lengthy letter in which he fiercely upbraided the king.[209] In response, Henry IV instructed the episcopate of the kingdom of Germany to gather at a synod at Worms on 24 January 1076.[210] The attendees there included two archbishops and twenty-four bishops (one of whom was Bishop Henry of Liège).[211] Godfrey the Hunchback, duke of Lower Lotharingia, is the most prominent secular figure attested as present. Only a few other lay princes were there.[212] Those present at the synod swore allegiance to Henry, before condemning Gregory and proclaiming that he should be deposed as pope. The king wrote to Gregory shortly after to inform him of the sentence that had been passed at Worms.[213] The bishops sent a letter to the pope to the same effect, and levelled the additional – and highly inflammatory – accusation that the pope had enjoyed intimate relations with Matilda of Tuscany.[214] At the Lenten synod, which opened in the Lateran on 14 February, the pope responded to the developments at Worms.[215] About a week later, Gregory pronounced his sentence against Henry IV. The pope excommunicated the king, declared that he was suspended from the kingship, and released all Christians from any oath that they had taken to him. Gregory also punished the prelates who had been present at Worms. He excommunicated and suspended the archbishop of Mainz, and gave the remaining prelates until 1 August to make satisfaction, either in person in Rome or by messengers, or face removal from office.[216] Gregory's tactic had the desired aim. At an assembly of the royal court at Tribur in October of that year, the bishops of Germany informed the papal legate that they 'wished henceforth to stand in the party of St Peter'.[217]

Godfrey the Hunchback had spent Christmas 1075 in Flanders, celebrating the feast in great style at Utrecht.[218] His commitments to Henry IV's military campaigns had not stymied his activities in the region; it was from Flanders that he travelled to the synod of Worms. A range of contemporary accounts indicate that he played a prominent role at the synod. Bernold of St Blasien described Godfrey as 'a participant in, or rather the ringleader of the . . . conspiracy [at Worms]'.[219] Similarly, Berthold of Reichenau asserted that Godfrey participated in the 'conspiracy' at Worms, and that he was its 'great supporter and instigator'.[220] It is possible that Godfrey instigated the charge against Gregory of improper behaviour with Matilda for motives that were personal rather than political.[221] Berthold noted that after the participants in the synod decided that Gregory should be replaced by a pope who was loyal to Henry, Godfrey 'boldly promised the king that he would conduct to the Roman see the pope who was to be appointed there'.[222] It is possible that Godfrey envisaged replicating the actions of his father, who had repelled two antipopes from Rome in the course of installing two legitimate pontiffs (Nicholas II and Alexander II). Berthold asserts that Godfrey was excommunicated as a result of his actions at Worms, but there is no indication in Gregory's own letters that this was the case.[223]

In late February 1076, Godfrey was back in Flanders. He had travelled there to provide military assistance to his ally William of Utrecht. It was there that he met his end.[224] Lampert of Hersfeld states that while Godfrey was 'on the frontier of Lotharingia and Flanders in the city called Antwerp, he was murdered'.[225] This author reports that one night, after Godfrey had gone to answer a call of nature when all was quiet, an assailant stabbed him through the buttocks.[226] Berthold of Reichenau recounted a similar story, noting that Godfrey 'was wounded from below by a certain knight while he was sitting in a privy, relieving nature', and that this led to his unhappy death.[227] Likewise, Bernold of St Blasien states that Godfrey 'was wounded in the posterior in a shameful manner by a certain cook, while he was at stool and he died before the middle of Lent'.[228] The *Cantatorium* asserts that Godfrey had gone to Frisia, to the castle at Vlaardingen, where assailants fatally stabbed him through the posterior.[229] Given the connection between St Hubert and the house of Ardennes-Bouillon, this author was arguably best placed to know the precise location of the incident. Lampert and the author of the *Cantatorium* attributed the attack on Godfrey to Robert the Frisian.[230] It may well be the case that Robert was responsible, and that the attack on Godfrey was the product of regional politics.[231] A Milanese author claims that Matilda of Tuscany arranged the assassination of her husband so that she could gain control of her family's lands.[232] However, this is a rather unconvincing claim, as Matilda's activities in this period were confined to Italy. Godfrey did not lack enemies closer to home.[233] Both Robinson and Hay connect the attack on Godfrey to his participation in the synod of Worms, and suggest that his resolute support for Henry IV had made him some powerful enemies.[234] Godfrey lived for a few days after the attack. His associates transported him to Utrecht, and he died there on 26 February. He was probably not much older than thirty. While he still lived, he asked to be buried in Verdun alongside his father. The author of the *Cantatorium* states that on the way to Verdun, his body was taken to Liège, where it was received by Bishop Henry, the clergy, and the people of the city, who observed a solemn ceremony in Godfrey's honour. Henry accompanied Godfrey's body part of the way to Verdun, but severe grief prevented him from proceeding further, and so he asked Abbot Thierry of St Hubert to do so in his place.[235]

Godfrey the Hunchback's career inevitably has to be judged in comparison to that of his father. While Godfrey the Bearded's exploits cast a shadow over the activities of his son, contemporary evidence indicates that Godfrey the Hunchback exerted considerable influence as duke of Lower Lotharingia. An annalist in Liège described him as 'the pride of Gaul' (*decus Galliae*).[236] The author of the *Cantatorium* states that when Godfrey was killed, all of Lotharingia lamented, because the justice and peace that he had worked to restore died with him.[237] His activities also extended to Flanders and Italy, though the failure of his marriage to Matilda of Tuscany scuppered his chances of maintaining long-term interests south of the Alps.

Like Godfrey the Bearded before him, as duke of Lower Lotharingia, Godfrey the Hunchback exerted his authority at the highest level of politics in the kingdom of Germany. He was a stalwart supporter of Henry IV in an era in which the king faced mounting opposition from the Saxon nobility and the papacy. Godfrey conducted his own interactions with the papacy. Gregory VII's letters of 1073 and early 1074 indicate that at that time the pope regarded Godfrey as a faithful servant and supporter of the papacy. Godfrey's failure to participate in Gregory's planned expedition of 1074 harmed relations between the two, and Godfrey's prominent role at the synod of Worms hardly endeared him to the pope. But Godfrey did not irrevocably lose the pope's good graces.[238] The sentences of punishment that Gregory levied against those who had been at the synod contain no mention of Godfrey. A few months after Godfrey the Hunchback's death, Bishop Herman of Metz wrote to Gregory to seek clarification about the punishments meted out to the associates of Henry IV. (Herman had been present at Worms, but had later repented of his actions.) The bishop appears to have asked specifically about the late Godfrey's fate. This was the same prelate, after all, who had visited Godfrey at the end of 1074 and compelled him to uphold Godfrey the Bearded's bequests to St Hubert.[239] In his reply, dated 15 August 1076, Gregory outlined his thoughts on Godfrey:

> But of Godfrey [Matilda of Tuscany's] late husband, you may know for a certainty that I, although a sinner, frequently make memorial before God; for neither his enmity nor any vain consideration hold me back and, moved by your own brotherly love and Matilda's pleading, I long for his salvation.[240]

Although their relationship had soured, then, Gregory affirmed that he prayed for Godfrey's soul. Elsewhere in his missive to Herman of Metz, Gregory stated that he had received letters from repentant 'brother bishops and dukes', and affirmed that he had authorised their absolution from excommunication.[241] It is possible, then, that if Godfrey not been killed a month after the synod of Worms, he might also have reconciled with Gregory and regained papal favour. Taking Gregory at his word, the pope regarded Godfrey as a servant of the papacy who had lost his way.

Godfrey's parents: Count Eustace II and Ida of Boulogne

In 1057, Ida (the sister of Godfrey the Hunchback and daughter of Godfrey the Bearded) married Count Eustace II of Boulogne. Ida and Eustace were the parents of Godfrey of Bouillon. Eustace was a prominent figure in the politics of northern France.[242] The county of Boulogne had its origins in the early tenth century. Count Baldwin II of Flanders acquired the strategically important territory around Boulogne in 879. Upon his death in 918, he gave Flanders to his son Arnulf I (d.965), and Boulogne to a younger son, Adelolf (d.933). Adelolf's successors steadily consolidated the county of Boulogne over the tenth and early eleventh centuries.[243] In the eleventh century, the counts of Flanders and the kings of France both attempted to extend their authority in Boulogne.[244] This situation prompted the counts of Boulogne to seek alliances with potentates from nearby regions, including Lotharingia. As a result, the counts were often drawn into the vortex of Lotharingian politics.

Eustace II became count of Boulogne upon the death of his father, Eustace I, in late 1046.[245] By this time, the county of Boulogne incorporated, in addition to Boulogne itself, towns including Guînes and Thérouanne. Eustace II's first wife, whom he married in 1036, was Goda, daughter of King Æthelred II of England (978–1013, 1014–1016), and sister of Edward the Confessor (1042–1066).[246] This marriage provided Eustace with important ties to England, and sealed an alliance with the English crown against the burgeoning power of the count of Flanders. Eustace retained his interests in England after Goda's death in about 1048. It is possible that Eustace and Goda had a child, which would have yielded to the family an interest in the succession to the crown of England.[247] As noted above, Eustace II was one of Godfrey the Bearded's allies in his rebellion against Henry III of Germany of 1047–1049. In September 1051, Eustace visited Edward the Confessor's court. A laconic passage in the 'E' version of the Anglo-Saxon Chronicle states that Eustace 'went to the king and told him what he wished, and then went homewards'.[248] Barlow argues that while this may simply have been a quotidian meeting between political allies, it is more likely Eustace sought to promote the interests of his family in the royal succession.[249] During this visit to England, Eustace and his men were reportedly involved in a confrontation at Dover, which led Eustace to seek help from the king. King Edward apparently instructed Earl Godwin of Wessex to punish those responsible. Godwin failed to do so, and this precipitated a rift with the king. As a result, Godwin and his sons were exiled from England, and their lands were confiscated.[250] As indicated above, Eustace married Ida of Boulogne in 1057.[251]

After Edward the Confessor's death on 5 January 1066, Count Eustace became involved in the struggle for the succession. Eustace agreed to participate in Duke William of Normandy's campaign to secure the English throne. William and Eustace had previously been enemies, and the former evidently did not fully trust the latter; the chronicler William of Poitiers states that before the campaign commenced in the autumn of 1066, Eustace was obliged to send his son as a hostage to Duke William in Normandy.[252] Eustace's participation in William's campaign in England brought considerable attention and prestige to his family.[253] There can be little doubt that Eustace participated in the hope of gaining land and wealth.[254] He may have envisaged capitalising upon the links to England that he had established through his first marriage to Goda. In essence, he took a calculated risk with the aim of securing profit.

Eustace evidently acquitted himself well during the battle of Hastings on 14 October. The author of the *Carmen de Hastingae Proelio* recorded that when Duke William became isolated at one point during the battle, Eustace courageously sped on horseback to his rescue:

> Then Count Eustace, scion of a noble dynasty, accompanied by a large escort of soldiers, hastened to be the first to give him aid. He dismounted so that the duke could get away in the saddle. And then one of Eustace's household knights did for his lord what the count had done for his. After these auspicious events the count and duke return together to fight where the weapons gleamed the most.[255]

This author credited William and Eustace with inflicting the greatest number of casualties among the English forces. He then claimed that William and Eustace, accompanied by two other men, killed King Harold during the battle.[256] Eustace seems also to have been immortalised in the Bayeux Tapestry. One of the Tapestry's last scenes portrays a mounted warrior named *Eustatius* holding aloft the papal banner and riding ahead of William and his troops in the midst of the battle of Hastings.[257] Historians generally concur that this figure is Eustace II. One modern author has even suggested that Eustace's prominence in the Tapestry indicates that he was its patron, rather than Bishop Odo of Bayeux, as is traditionally thought.[258] Other contemporary authors, however, were less positive about Eustace's role in the campaign. William of Poitiers claims that at one point during the battle of Hastings, Eustace and fifty knights began to flee, only for Duke William to order them to stand fast. Eustace reportedly attempted to sound the retreat, fearing that if he pressed forward he would soon be killed. The chronicler states that as Eustace uttered these words, he was struck from behind by a blow that landed between his shoulders: 'its violence was immediately shown by blood streaming from his nose and mouth; and, half dead, he escaped with the help of his companions'.[259] The chronicler William of Jumièges made no mention at all of Eustace in his account of the campaign.[260]

William of Poitiers's depiction of Eustace was no doubt influenced by the events that transpired after the battle of Hastings. At some point, Eustace became estranged from Duke William, the new king of England. No source specifies that Eustace was present at William's coronation on Christmas Day 1066, so it is likely that the rift emerged before that point.[261] Eustace had most probably become disaffected by how William had divided the conquered lands. He may have been frustrated at not receiving the lands that had formerly belonged to Goda.[262] More likely, he had been aggrieved by the fact that, while he had been granted lands, he had not received any significant holdings in Kent, which lay directly across the channel from the county of Boulogne. Before the conquest Eustace probably envisaged securing lands there in order to enjoy the commercial and strategic advantages that the resultant tightly-knit cross-channel axis would bring.[263] In early 1067 Eustace was back in Boulogne, but he returned to England later in the year and attacked the Norman castle at Dover. William of Poitiers reports that the native men of Kent knew of Eustace's prowess as a warrior, and so convinced him to participate in their assault upon Dover. The chronicler lucidly explained what attracted Eustace to the plan: 'If indeed he had been able to gain possession of that strong site with its seaport his power would have been extended more widely and that of the Normans correspondingly diminished'.[264] Eustace and his men surreptitiously sailed across the channel from Boulogne, but the garrison at Dover were alert and quickly defeated them.[265] King William subsequently condemned Eustace, and confiscated the lands he had been granted after Hastings. As a result, Eustace's activities were confined to the continent for the next few years.[266]

Eustace – along with his brother-in-law Godfrey the Hunchback – was involved in the succession crisis in Flanders after the death of Count Baldwin VI in 1070. Eustace supported Arnulf III against Robert the Frisian, and fought in the battle of Cassel in February 1071. Siding against Robert probably helped Eustace to regain the favour of King William, and the two were reconciled in the mid-1070s.[267] At the end of his account, William of Poitiers noted that at the time he was writing (probably around 1077), King William and Eustace were once again allies. This author wrote that although Eustace had fully deserved the punishments he had suffered after the failed attack on Dover, 'we feel that this man, illustrious in many ways and a distinguished count, ought to be spared because he is now reconciled and honoured among those closest to the king'.[268] Eustace was subsequently rewarded with extensive lands in England. These lands were assessed in King William's survey of 1086 and recorded in Domesday Book. Domesday shows that in 1086 Eustace held lands in twelve counties, though most of these were in Essex.[269] These lands – known as the Honour of Boulogne – produced a combined annual income of about £770, a sum which made the count of Boulogne one of the wealthiest secular landowners in post-conquest England.[270]

Eustace II and Ida had three sons. The first, Eustace, was born in about 1058. When Eustace II died around 1087, this eldest son succeeded him as count of Boulogne, and inherited the family's lands in England.[271] Like his father, Eustace III was heavily involved in politics in England. In 1088, he participated in a rebellion against King William Rufus (1087–1100) in favour of the king's brother, Robert Curthose, duke of Normandy. When the rebellion was defeated, William deprived Eustace of the Honour of Boulogne.[272] Godfrey, the second son, was born in about 1060. The third, Baldwin, was born about two years later.[273] Eustace II also fathered an illegitimate son named Geoffrey.[274] At some point in the mid-1080s, a monk of the abbey of St Amand wrote a genealogy of the comital line.[275] This genealogy traces the lineage of the house from King Priam of Troy, and charts its descent through the Merovingians and the Carolingians, and ends with the birth of the sons of Eustace II. Tanner has argued that the links between the comital house and St Amand were not particularly close, meaning that the genealogy probably sheds light on wider contemporary perceptions of the dynasty.[276]

Eustace II's wife, Ida, had a considerable influence upon the fortunes of the comital house.[277] The author of the St Amand genealogy claimed that Eustace specifically chose to marry Ida for her 'noble birth and character'.[278] Over the course of her lifetime, Ida was responsible for reforming one abbey in the county of Boulogne (St Wulmer at Samer), and for founding three others (St Wulmer at Boulogne, Le Wast, and Capelle).[279] Ida also maintained contacts with a number of prominent ecclesiastical figures. At some point between 1082 and 1096, she wrote to Osmund, bishop of the Spanish diocese of Astorga, in relation to several Marian relics in his possession.[280] She also maintained contact with Hugh, abbot of Cluny, the most influential monastic order of the age. Hugh and his order had close links with the reform papacy throughout the last quarter of the eleventh century.[281] At Ida's request, at some point around 1096, Hugh sent monks from Cluny to Ida's foundation of Le Wast.[282] Most significant was Ida's relationship with Anselm, abbot of Bec (1078–1093) and archbishop of Canterbury (1093–1109). Crucially, Anselm was a close associate of the reform papacy. Six of Anselm's letters to Ida survive. Their correspondence began at the start of his time at Bec, and continued during his career as abbot and then archbishop.[283] They also met in person on several occasions.[284] In one of his letters, written shortly after his appointment as archbishop, Anselm addressed Ida as his beloved sister and sweetest daughter in God, and reminded her that she had earlier entrusted her soul to him. He also noted that he knew that she always held him in her heart.[285] Crucially, Anselm's exchanges with Ida indicate that he had a concern not just for her but for the house of Boulogne as a whole. In one of his letters, written sometime before 1093, Anselm asked Ida to greet her husband and their children on his behalf.[286] In another letter, Anselm informed Ida that he had spoken with her son – he does not specify which – and stated that he had asked that son about her.[287] Vaughn dates this letter to the years 1093–1097, during which period Anselm could conceivably have talked with any of Ida's three sons.[288] In 1102, after the youngest of Ida's sons, Baldwin, had been appointed king of Jerusalem, Anselm wrote to him in familiar terms. He referred to the close relationship he had maintained with the comital family, stating that he was 'mindful of the great love and generosity shown to me by your father and mother and their children'.[289] On the basis of this evidence, Vaughn has posited that Ida's sons benefitted from Anselm's advice and teaching during their formative years.[290] Ida's epistolary activities, then, connected her family to prominent ecclesiastical figures, at least one of whom maintained links to the papacy.

Notes

1 On the Salian dynasty, see: Weinfurter, *Salian Century*. On Henry IV, see: Robinson, *Henry IV*.
2 For an overview, see: Blumenthal, *The Investiture Controversy*. The repercussions in Lower Lotharingia are considered in Alfred Cauchie, *La Querelle des investitures dans les dioceses de Liège et de Cambrai*, 2 vols (Louvain, 1890–1891).
3 On Gregory and his pontificate, see: Cowdrey, *Gregory VII*.
4 'ducatus sui ultra omnes comites regni huius ditaverat'. *Vita Heinrici II. Imperatoris, auctore Adalboldo, MGH SS*, vol. 4, pp. 679–95, at p. 686.
5 On the nature of the ducal office in the Empire in the Salian era, see: Robinson, *Henry IV*, pp. 2–3; Benjamin Arnold, *Princes and Territories in Medieval Germany* (Cambridge, 1991), pp. 88–92. On the Lotharingian dukes, see: Georges Despy, 'La fonction ducale en Lotharingie, puis en Basse-Lotharingie de 900 à 1100', *Revue du Nord*, 48 (1966), 107–9; Arlette Laret-Kayser, 'La function et les pouvoirs ducaux en Basse-Lotharingie au XIe siècle', *PSHIGL*, 95 (1981), 133–52; Matthias Werner, 'Der Herzog von Lothringen in salischer Zeit', in Stefan Weinfurter (ed.), *Die Salier und das Reich*, 3 vols (Sigmaringen, 1991), vol. 1, pp. 367–473.
6 Weinfurter, *Salian Century*, pp. xiii, 52–3.
7 Arnold, *Princes and Territories*, pp. 112–20.
8 Arnold, *Princes and Territories*, p. 122.
9 Robinson, *Henry IV*, pp. 6–7; Weinfurter, *Salian Century*, pp. 56–8, 102–3; Timothy Reuter, 'The "Imperial Church System" of the Ottonian and Salian Rulers: A Reconsideration', *Journal of Ecclesiastical History*, 33 (1982), 347–74.
10 Weinfurter, *Salian Century*, pp. 93–6.
11 On ecclesiastical advocacy in the Empire at this time, see: Weinfurter, *Salian Century*, pp. 70–1. On the practice in Lotharingia, see the essays collected in 'L'avouerie en Lotharingie', *PSHISGL*, 98 (1984). See also: Charles West, 'Monks, Aristocrats and Justice: Twelfth-Century Monastic Advocacy in a European Perspective', *Speculum*, 92 (2017), 372–404, which considers a wider geographic area.
12 On the breakup of the Carolingian Empire and the formation of Lotharingia, see: Charles West, *Reframing the Feudal Revolution: Political and Social Transformation Between Marne and Moselle, c.800–c.1100* (Cambridge, 2014); Hans-Walter Herrmann and Reinhard Schneider (eds), *Lotharingia: Eine europäische Kernlandschaft um das Jahr 1000* (Saarbrücken, 1995); Michel Parisse, 'Lotharingia', in *NCMH*, vol. 3, pp. 310–27.
13 Parisse, 'Lotharingia', p. 312, notes that by the end of the tenth century, the region was widely known as Lotharingia.
14 Though see West, *Reframing*, pp. 129–32, which notes that it is important not to overstate the political coherence of Lotharingia as a result of these developments.
15 As Parisse has written, Godfrey the Captive was 'one of those Godfreys whose name was to dominate Lotharingian history up to the time of Godfrey of Bouillon'. Parisse, 'Lotharingia', p. 318. He was Godfrey of Bouillon's great-great-grandfather. As regards the nomenclature 'Ardennes-Bouillon', the present book follows Murray, *Crusader Kingdom*, pp. 4–5.
16 See in general: Michel Parisse, *La Noblesse Lorraine, XIe – XIIIe siècles*, 2 vols (Paris, 1976).
17 West, *Reframing*, p. 123.
18 Parisse, 'Lotharingia', p. 310.
19 For an overview, see: David Nicholas, *Medieval Flanders* (London, 1992). On 'imperial Flanders', see: François-Louis Ganshof, 'Les origines de la Flandre

impériale: contribution à l'histoire de l'ancien Brabant', *Annales de la Société royale d'archéologie de Bruxelles*, 46 (1942–1943), 99–173.

20 On the diocese of Liège in this era, see: Steven Vanderputten, Tjamke Snijders, and Jay Diehl (eds), *Medieval Liège at the Crossroads of Europe: Monastic Society and Culture, 1000–1300* (Brepols, 2016); Julien Maquet, *'Faire Justice' dans le diocèse de Liège au Moyen Âge (VIIIe–XIIe siècles): Essai de droit judiciaire reconstitute* (Geneva, 2008); and Jean-Louis Kupper, *Liège et l'Église impériale (XIe–XIIe siècle)* (Paris, 1981). On the interactions of its bishops with the house of Ardennes-Bouillon, see: Jean-Louis Kupper, 'La maison d'Ardenne-Verdun et l'eglise de Liège: Remarques sur les origines d'une principauté épiscopale', *PSHIGL*, 95 (1981), 201–15.

21 On the archbishopric of Rheims at this time, see: John S. Ott, *Bishops, Authority and Community in Northwestern Europe, c.1050–1150* (Cambridge, 2015).

22 Parisse, 'Lotharingia', p. 312.

23 Parisse, 'Lotharingia', p. 312. Historians in modern France and Germany have generally focussed on the areas either side of the Meuse. That to the west is seen as an historical part of France, and that to the east part of Germany. On this, see: West, *Reframing*, pp. 232–5.

24 Michel Bur, 'La Frontière entre la Champagne et la Lorraine du milieu du Xe à la fin du XIIe siècle', *Francia*, 4 (1976), 237–54.

25 Parisse, 'Lotharingia', p. 324. On the economic dimensions of the region, see: Bas van Bavel, *Manors and Markets: Economy and Society in the Low Countries* (Oxford, 2010), esp. pp. 24–8, on the Ardennes.

26 Thomas Wetzstein, 'Europäische Vernetzungen: Straßen, Logistik und Mobilität in der späten Salierzeit', in Bernd Schneidmüller and Stefan Weinfurter (eds), *Salisches Kaisertum und neues Europa: Die Zeit Heinrichs IV. und Heinrichs V.* (Darmstadt, 2007), pp. 341–70.

27 Laret-Kayser, 'La function', pp. 134–6.

28 Sigebert, p. 357.

29 See below, pp. 59–66.

30 *MGH DD H III*, nos. 52 (Stavelot, 5 June 1040), 74 (Maastricht, 15 February 1041), and 80 (Aachen, 3 June 1041); *AAM*, pp. 34, 41; 'iam dudum dux'. Herman, p. 124, tr. p. 75.

31 'in re militari admodum exercitatus'. Lampert, p. 44, tr. p. 54.

32 On Henry III's policy toward Lotharingia in 1044, see: Weinfurter, *Salian Century*, pp. 104–8; West, *Reframing*, pp. 126–7; Andressohn, *Godfrey*, p. 9; Egon Boshof, 'Lothringen, Frankreich und das Reich in der Regierungszeit Heinrichs III.', *Rheinische Vierteljahrsblätter*, 42 (1978), 63–127, at pp. 65–70. Herman wrote that Gozelo I suggested that the duchies be divided in 1044: Herman, p. 124, tr. p. 75.

33 Eugene Dupréel, *Histoire Critique de Godefroid le Barbu, Duc de Lotharingie, Marquis de Toscane* (Brussels, 1904).

34 Robinson, *Henry IV*, p. 20. Cowdrey, *Gregory VII*, p. 82, describes Godfrey as 'a figure of especially disturbing augury'.

35 *AAM*, p. 34, speaks of a struggle (*contentio*) between Godfrey the Bearded and Gozelo II over their father's property after his death, and says that the former did not consent to the latter being made duke of Lower Lotharingia.

36 Weinfurter, *Salian Century*, pp. 104–6.

37 *AAM*, pp. 37–8; Dupréel, *Godefroid le Barbu*, pp. 23–4.

38 *AAM*, p. 38. Dupréel, *Godefroid le Barbu*, pp. 25–6, places this assembly at Aachen in late September: *MGH DD H III*, no. 128 (Aachen, 25 September 1044).

39 Weinfurter, *Salian Century*, pp. 107–8. A parallel development from the reign of Henry III's son may illuminate how Godfrey the Bearded felt in 1044. When in

1071 King Henry IV told Magnus Billung, the son of Duke Otto of Saxony, and would-be heir as duke, that he had to renounce the ducal office and his inheritance if he wanted to be set free from captivity, Magnus reportedly declared that he would rather remain in prison and suffer torture than relinquish what was rightfully his. Lampert, p. 178, tr. pp. 174–5.

40 'Gothelo dux obiit, cuius filius Godefridus, dum ei ducatus Mosellanorum denegatur, altero ducatu repudiato, contra imperatorem rebellat'. Sigebert, p. 358.

41 'arma contra rem publicam corripuit'. Lampert, p. 44, tr. p. 54.

42 'rebellare pio regi praesumit'. Herman, p. 124, tr. p. 79. Cf. *CW*, p. 30, and Frutolf, p. 64, tr. p. 98.

43 *AAM*, p. 38.

44 On the suggestion of collusion between Godfrey and Henry I of France in 1044–1045, see Dupréel, *Godefroid le Barbu*, pp. 24–5.

45 *AAM*, pp. 38–41.

46 *AAM*, pp. 38–9.

47 Herman, p. 125, tr. p. 77.

48 *AAM*, p. 39; Dupréel, *Godefroid le Barbu*, p. 30. The march of Antwerp was restored to Henry III in about 1050.

49 Herman, p. 125, tr. p. 78. Godfrey's submission is also mentioned in Sigebert, p. 358, and Anselm of Liège, *Gesta Episcoporum*, p. 223. The king's diplomas detail his movements in Lotharingia throughout July 1045: *MGH DD H III*, nos. 138–40 (Cologne, 10–12 July), no. 141 (Aachen, 15 July), and no. 142 (Maastricht, 22 July). Godfrey must have submitted at one of these locations.

50 Frutolf, p. 64, tr. pp. 98–9; Lampert, p. 46, tr. p. 55; Herman, p. 125, tr. p. 78; *CW*, p. 30.

51 'Dux Gotefridus . . . missus est custodiendus, sicque regnum brevi tempore quietum et pacatum mansit'. Lampert, p. 46, tr. p. 55.

52 'Gothefridus . . . in castello Gibichenstein usque ad dignam satisfactionem sub custodia mancipatur'. *CW*, p. 30; Frutolf, p. 64, tr. p. 98. Robinson, *Henry IV*, pp. 25–6, notes that Henry III usually pardoned defeated princes and received them back into favour, rather than alienate them and their allies and thereby risk a feud.

53 'Godefridus hortatu quorundam Dei fidelium ad recuperandam imperatoris gratiam adductus, ab imperatore capitur et custodiae mancipatur; sed filium suum obsidem dans, relaxatur'. Sigebert, p. 358.

54 'ducatum suum misertus reddidit'. Herman, p. 126, tr. pp. 78–9. The *Annals of Niederaltaich* concur that Godfrey was restored to the office of duke of Upper Lotharingia at this point: *AAM*, p. 41. On the date of Godfrey's release from prison, see: Dupréel, *Godefroid le Barbu*, p. 31.

55 The chronology of Godfrey's release from prison and the death of his brother Gozelo II is unclear. Dupréel, *Godefroid le Barbu*, pp. 32–3, suggests on the basis of evidence contained in charters that Gozelo II died early in 1046, at some point before Easter (3 March).

56 On Frederick's appointment as duke, see: Herman, p. 126, tr. p. 79; Sigebert, p. 359; *AAM*, p. 41. Frederick held the office until his death in 1065.

57 On Henry III's dealings with the papacy, and the events of 1046–1047 in Rome, see: Robinson, *Henry IV*, p. 20; Weinfurter, *Salian Century*, pp. 89–93; Blumenthal, *Investiture Controversy*, pp. 49–58.

58 Lampert, p. 46, tr. p. 55. Cf. *AAM*, p. 44.

59 'Quo [filio] defuncto in obsidatu, ad rebellandum grassatur'. Sigebert, p. 358.

60 Herman, p. 127, tr. pp. 82–3; Lampert, pp. 46–8, tr. pp. 56–7; *AAM*, p. 44; *CW*, p. 31; Frutolf, pp. 66–7, tr. p. 99; Tanner, *Families*, p. 86.

61 Dupréel, *Godefroid le Barbu*, pp. 40–1.

62 Lampert, p. 44, tr. p. 54. Though Lampert made this claim in relation to Godfrey the Bearded's first rebellion of 1044–1045, Dupréel, *Godefroid le Barbu*, p. 43, n. 4, argues convincingly that it relates to Godfrey's second rebellion of 1047–1049.

63 Lampert, p. 46, tr. p. 56; *AAM*, p. 44; Sigebert, p. 358.

64 Lampert, p. 46, tr. p. 56; Herman, p. 127, tr. p. 83; Sigebert, p. 358; Dupréel, *Godefroid le Barbu*, pp. 43–4.

65 'in opere cementario per seipsum plerumque vilis mancipii ministerio functus deserviret'. Lampert, p. 46, tr. p. 55–6.

66 Anselm of Liège, *Gesta Episcoporum*, pp. 221–2; Dupréel, *Godefroid le Barbu*, pp. 49–51.

67 Herman, p. 127, tr. p. 83.

68 Herman, p. 128, tr. p. 85.

69 Bishop Bruno of Toul was elected as Leo IX in December 1048 and consecrated in February 1049.

70 Herman, p. 129, tr. p. 86. *AAM*, p. 45, and Lampert, p. 48, tr. p. 58, also refer to Leo's intervention. See also: Weinfurter, *Salian Century*, p. 106; Dupréel, *Godefroid le Barbu*, pp. 54–5.

71 *AAM*, p. 45.

72 Lampert, p. 50, tr. pp. 58–9, explicitly mentions Leo's return to Rome with Frederick, though mistakenly claims that Godfrey the Bearded went with them. As will be seen below, Frederick of Lotharingia became pope in 1057, taking the name Stephen. He is generally known as Stephen IX, though sometimes he is described as Stephen X. On his career in Lotharingia, see: Georges Despy, 'La carrière lotharingienne du pape Étienne IX', *RBPH*, 31 (1953), 955–72. On his pontificate, see: Ulysee Robert, *Un pape belge: histoire du Pape Étienne X* (Brussels, 1892).

73 *AAM*, p. 47; Dupréel, *Godefroid le Barbu*, p. 59.

74 Lampert, p. 122, tr. p. 126, describes Godfrey the Hunchback as 'a young man' (*adolescens*) at the time of his father's death in 1069. On the births of Godfrey the Bearded's children, see: Aubé, *Godefroy*, p. 25.

75 Some contemporaries deemed Henry III responsible for the killing of Boniface of Tuscany in 1052. On Godfrey's marriage to Beatrice in 1054, see: Henri Glaesener, 'Un mariage fertile en conséquences (Godefroid le Barbu et Béatrice de Toscane)', *Revue d'histoire ecclésiastique*, 42 (1947), 379–416.

76 For a survey of the lands held by the house of Canossa at this time, see Overmann, pp. 4–37. It is also of note that Beatrice held dynastic lands in Lotharingia. On the extent of Godfrey's power in Italy, see the comments in Robinson, *Henry IV*, pp. 32–3. See also: Georges Despy, 'Notes sur les actes de Godefroid le Barbu, comme marquis de Toscane (1054–1069)', in *Mélanges offerts par ses confrères étrangers à Charles Braibant* (Brussels, 1959), pp. 65–81.

77 Herman, p. 133, tr. p. 98. See also: Lampert, p. 56, tr. pp. 64–5; *AAM*, p. 50; Bonizo, p. 590, tr. p. 194.

78 Sigebert, p. 359.

79 'accipiens marcham et caeteras sius possessiones'. Lampert, p. 52, tr. p. 61.

80 'Quo comperto imperator Heinricus gravi scrupulo perurgeri cepit'. Lampert, p. 52, tr. p. 61.

81 Rumours emerged at this time that Godfrey hoped to seize the kingdom of Italy for himself. See: Lampert, p. 56, tr. pp. 64–5. On the wider threats posed to Henry III by the marriage of Godfrey the Bearded and Beatrice, see: Weinfurter, *Salian Century*, pp. 106–7; Robinson, *Henry IV*, p. 24; David Hay, *The Military Leadership of Matilda of Canossa, 1046–1115* (Manchester, 2008), pp. 33–4.

82 Lampert, pp. 54–6, tr. p. 64.

83 On Henry III's campaign against Godfrey the Bearded and Beatrice, see: Lampert, p. 56, tr. pp. 64–5; *AAM*, pp. 50–1; Berthold II, p. 44, tr. pp. 112–13; Bonizo, p. 590, tr. pp. 194–5; *CW*, p. 31; Frutolf, p. 70, tr. p. 102; Sigebert, p. 359. For comment, see: Robinson, *Henry IV*, pp. 24–5.

84 Bonizo, p. 590, tr. p. 194; Robinson, *Henry IV*, p. 25; Cowdrey, *Gregory VII*, p. 82.

85 On the implications of Henry's treatment of Godfrey the Bearded for Lotharingian politics, see Weinfurter, *Salian Century*, pp. 106–7, Robinson, *Henry IV*, p. 24, and Hay, *Military Leadership*, p. 34.

86 Berthold II, p. 44, tr. p. 113; Bonizo, p. 590, tr. p. 194. These differing perspectives are reflected in modern accounts. Robinson, *Henry IV*, pp. 35–6, suggests that Godfrey the Bearded once again feared that his rebellion was doomed to fail, and so sought a reconciliation with the emperor, while Weinfurter, *Salian Century*, pp. 106–7, and Hay, *Military Leadership*, p. 34, assert that it was the emperor who instigated the reconciliation with Godfrey.

87 *MGH DD H III*, no. 372 (Trier, 31 May–30 June 1056); *CW*, p. 31; Frutolf, p. 70, tr. p. 103.

88 'Coloniae generali convenu habito, Balduinus et Godefridus mediante Victore papa ad gratiam regis et pacem reducuntur, et omnes bellorum motus sedantur'. Sigebert, p. 360. On the reconciliation, see: Robinson, *Henry IV*, p. 31; Weinfurter, *Salian Century*, p. 112.

89 Robinson, *Henry IV*, p. 32; Aubé, *Godefroy*, p. 24; Weinfurter, *Salian Century*, p. 107.

90 Robinson, *Henry IV*, p. 32.

91 *Cantatorium*, p. 58; Dupréel, *Godefroid le Barbu*, pp. 74–5.

92 Dupréel, *Godefroid le Barbu*, pp. 73–106, argues that in the period between Henry IV's accession in 1056 and his coming of age in 1065, Godfrey was closely associated with the minority government, particularly after the coup of Kaiserwerth in April 1062, when a court faction led by Archbishop Anno of Cologne kidnapped the young king and assumed control of the government.

93 In this respect, Godfrey followed in the footsteps of his predecessor as margrave of Tuscany, Boniface, who had also been a close political ally of the papacy. In 1047, Boniface had escorted Damasus II to Rome.

94 Bonizo, p. 589, tr. p. 192; *CMC*, p. 687. While the representatives were at the Byzantine capital, Humbert of Silva Candida and the patriarch of Constantinople, Michael Keroularios, excommunicated one another. This development is often seen as the starting point of the schism between the Latin and Byzantine Orthodox Churches.

95 *CMC*, p. 687.

96 'ibi deinceps Christo sub sanctae professionis titulo militaturus'. Lampert, p. 54, tr. pp. 62–3.

97 *CMC*, pp. 692–3; Bonizo, p. 190, tr. p. 196; Berthold I, p. 24, tr. p. 102; Berthold II, p. 46, tr. p. 114.

98 Robinson, *Henry IV*, pp. 32–3, 36–7.

99 *CMC*, p. 694. One chronicler reports that Stephen ransacked the treasury of St Benedict in order to provide the funds needed to persuade Godfrey to attack the Normans: *Storia de'Normanni di Amato di Montecassino volgarizzata in antico francese*, ed. Vincenzo de Bartholomaeis (Rome, 1935), pp. 166–7, tr. in Amatus of Montecassino, *The History of the Normans*, tr. Prescott N. Dunbar, 'rev. by Graham A. Loud (Woodbridge, 2004), p. 104.

100 Blumenthal, *Investiture Controversy*, p. 84.

101 'magnificus dux Gotefridus'. Bonizo, p. 593, tr. p. 202.

102 'per Gotefridum marchionem'. Lampert, p. 66, tr. p. 74.

103 Bonizo, p. 593, tr. p. 202; Berthold I, p. 24, tr. p. 102; Berthold II, p. 48, tr. pp. 114–15. Nicholas II referred to Godfrey the Bearded's loyal service in a letter to Archbishop Gervase of Rheims in 1059: *RHGF*, vol. 11, pp. 492–3. For comment see: Cowdrey, *Gregory VII*, p. 37; Dupréel, *Godefroid le Barbu*, pp. 82–6.

104 As Cowdrey, *Gregory VII*, p. 49, notes, 'for the third successive time, thought turned to a candidate for the papacy who was associated with the politically powerful Duke Godfrey of [Lotharingia], together with his wife, Countess Beatrice of Tuscany'. On Godfrey's role in the schism which ensued, see: Dupréel, *Godefroid le Barbu*, pp. 92–103.

105 *AAM*, pp. 60–1; Bonizo, p. 595, tr. p. 207; Benzo, pp. 228–9; Cowdrey, *Gregory VII*, p. 50.

106 *AAM*, pp. 60–1; Bonizo, p. 595, tr. p. 207.

107 Cowdrey, *Gregory VII*, p. 50; The German court decided to support Alexander II at the council of Augsburg (28 October 1062).

108 Benzo, pp. 242–54; Cowdrey, *Gregory VII*, p. 51.

109 'Et ibidem accincus est gladio, anno regni sui IX., aetatis autem suae XIIII. et dux Gotifridus scutarius eius eligebatur'. Berthold I, p. 30, tr. p. 105; Berthold II, p. 54, tr. p. 118. The ceremony is also mentioned in Lampert, p. 94, tr. p. 98. See the discussion in Robinson, *Henry IV*, pp. 51–2. Weinfurter, *Salian Century*, p. 131, describes the ritual as a knighting ceremony.

110 Robinson, *Henry IV*, p. 51. Dupréel, *Godefroid le Barbu*, pp. 97–8, 106–7, posits that Godfrey was chosen to fulfil this role at the ceremony because he had been responsible for giving the young Henry IV his military training.

111 Sigebert, p. 358; 'Godefrido ad curiam Goslar abbas proficiscitur, ubi ille ducamen . . . adeptus, magister militiae Lotharingiae denuo sublimatur'. *Triumphus Sancti Remacli*, *MGH SS*, vol. 11, pp. 433–61, at p. 443. For the court's stay at Goslar: *MGH DD H IV*, nos. 172 (16 October) and 173 (19 October).

112 'dux et marchio'. See, for example, the charter issued at Bouillon in 1069: *Cartulaire Gorze*, pp. 240–2 (no. 188); Despy, 'Les actes', pp. 68–9.

113 'Ildebrandus, continuo magnificum ducem Gotefridum in auxilium sancti Petri evocat'. Bonizo, p. 599, tr. p. 215. Bonizo credited Archdeacon Hildebrand (the future Gregory VII) with summoning Godfrey in this instance, a claim that Cowdrey, *Gregory VII*, p. 61, n. 134, describes as 'improbable'. Bonizo also noted that it was by luck that Godfrey was in Italy at this time, suggesting that this author knew that Godfrey spent some of his time north of the Alps. The episode is considered in Dupréel, *Godefroid le Barbu*, pp. 115–23.

114 'beato apostolorum principi'. Bonizo, p. 599, tr. p. 216.

115 *AAM*, pp. 72–3.

116 *Amato di Montecassino*, p. 271, tr. p. 153.

117 Cowdrey, *Gregory VII*, pp. 83, 130; Robinson, *Henry IV*, p. 108. Dupréel, *Godefroid le Barbu*, p. 123, in contrast, suggests that Godfrey acted as Henry IV's representative in Italy at this time.

118 Peter Damian, *Die Briefe des Petrus Damiani*, *MGH Epistolae: Briefe*, vol. 4, pp. 67–71 (no. 154).

119 *Cantatorium*, p. 59.

120 Robinson, *Henry IV*, pp. 108–9. Cf. Dupréel, *Godefroid le Barbu*, pp. 126–7.

121 *AAM*, p. 74.

122 Benzo, pp. 298–300.

123 *Cantatorium*, p. 58.

124 On his abbacy, see: Brigitte Meijns, 'Obedience to the Bishop, Apostolic Protection and Appeal to Rome. The Changing Representation of Abbot Theodoric I of St-Hubert (1055–1086) Against the Backdrop of the Investiture Conflict in the Diocese of Liège', *RBPH*, 91 (2013), 1–28.

125 *Cantatorium*, p. 58.

126 'optimatibus suis'. *Cantatorium*, p. 59.

127 *Cantatorium*, pp. 59–62. On the priory, see: Wolfgang Peters, 'Zur Gründung und frühen Geschichte des Benediktinerpriorates St. Peter in Bouillon', *Revue Bénédictine*, 109 (1999), 341–58.

128 *Cantatorium*, pp. 62–3. On the date of his death, see: Dupréel, *Godefroid le Barbu*, p. 132.

129 Lampert, p. 122, tr. p. 126.

130 Berthold II, p. 64, tr. pp. 123–4.

131 'Romane urbis patricii et prefecti Anchonitani et Pisani marchonis et tocius interjacentis Tuscie et Italie dominatoris, invicti quoque Virdunensium comitis et Lotharingie ducis, Henrici etiam imperatoris per tot annos acerrimi impugnatoris'. *Cantatorium*, pp. 58–9.

132 Cowdrey, *Gregory VII*, p. 53.

133 'Gotefridus dux, vir magnificus et in bellicis rebus strennuissimus'. Bonizo, p. 590, tr. p. 194.

134 Berthold II, p. 64, tr. pp. 123–4. Cowdrey, *Gregory VII*, p. 82, is surely right that Godfrey acted out of self-interest when he aided the papacy. This was not, however, how many contemporaries saw it.

135 'Gotefredus dictus dux'. Benzo, p. 594.

136 Benzo, p. 242. and 300. The translations of these colourful terms are borrowed from Christopher Tyerman, *God's War: A New History of the Crusades* (London, 2006), p. 48.

137 On Benzo's perspective on Godfrey and the reform papacy, see Cowdrey, *Gregory VII*, p. 51.

138 On the succession of Godfrey the Hunchback: *AAM*, p. 78; Lampert, p. 122, tr. p. 126; Sigebert, p. 362. On his career, see: Friedrich Dieckmann, *Gottfried III der Bucklige, herzog von Niederlothringen und gemahl Mathildens von Canossa* (Erlangen, 1885).

139 Indeed, the *Annals of Niederaltaich* state explicitly that at Godfrey the Bearded's death, his son succeeded to his inheritance and his 'principate' ('in hereditate et principatu successit'). *AAM*, p. 78.

140 'ducem Gozelonem . . . licet statura pusillus et gibbo deformis esset'. Lampert, p. 316, tr. p. 283.

141 '[Godfrey] licet staturae pusillitate atque gibbo despicabilis videretur'. Lampert, p. 348, tr. p. 308.

142 'Godefridi ducis parvi'. *Chartes Saint-Hubert*, vol. 1, pp. 34–5 (no. 30).

143 'Gozelo . . . prestantis quidem animi adolescens, sed gibbosus'. Lampert, p. 122, tr. p. 126.

144 'insignis dux . . . Gotefridus, Corda gerens patris, quamvis sit corpore dispar'. *Carmen*, p. 176.

145 Sigebert, p. 362.

146 'claudus erit aut mancus, surdaster aut caecus, gibbosus aut leprosus, vel aliud quid hujusmodi quod eum aliquo modo saeculo facit minut acceptum'. Udalric of Zell, *Consuetudines Cluniacenses*, PL, vol. 149, cols 635–778, at col. 635.

147 *Cantatorium*, pp. 64–5.

148 Eljas Oksanen, *Flanders and the Anglo-Norman World, 1066–1216* (Cambridge, 2012), pp. 16–17.

149 See: Charles Verlinden, *Robert Ier le Frison, comte de Flandre. Étude d'histoire politique* (Antwerp, 1935), esp. pp. 40–72, which cover the capture of Flanders.

150 Lampert, p. 142, tr. p. 142. The transaction is recorded in *MGH DD H IV*, no. 242 (Liège, 11 May 1071).

151 Lampert, p. 142, tr. p. 142. On Godfrey the Hunchback's involvement in Flanders at this time, see: Dieckmann, *Gottfried III der Bucklige*, pp. 21–41; Aubé, *Godefroy*, pp. 40–2; Andressohn, *Godfrey*, p. 14.

152 Lampert, p. 142, tr. p. 142. Verlinden, *Robert Ier*, p. 80, notes that Robert and King Philip reached their accommodation in late March or early April 1071.

153 *Cantatorium*, pp. 68–9.
154 Paolo Golinelli, *Matilde e i Canossa* (Milan, 2004), pp. 169–84; Overmann, pp. 241–4; Dieckmann, *Gottfried III der Bucklige*, pp. 14–21.
155 *Cantatorium*, p. 61. Overmann, *Reg. Mat.*, p. 124, item h, dates the betrothal to around 1057. Most modern commentators have written that the betrothal was long-standing at the death of Godfrey the Bearded. See, for example, Dieckmann, *Gottfried III der Bucklige*, pp. 14–21, Andressohn, *Godfrey*, p. 14, and Hay, *Military Leadership*, p. 43.
156 Overmann, *Reg. Mat.*, p. 125, item d; Hay, *Military Leadership*, p. 43, and n. 79; Golinelli, *Matilde e i Canossa*, p. 171; Cowdrey, *Gregory VII*, pp. 296–7.
157 A charter issued by Beatrice on 29 August 1071 at Frassinoro records a donation she made for the souls of her daughter and her granddaughter, who was also called Beatrice ('pro incolomitate et anima Matilde dilecte filie mee ... et pro mercede anime Beatricis quondam aneptis mee'). *Codice Diplomatico Polironiano (961–1125)*, ed. Rosella Rinaldi, Carla Villani and Paolo Golinelli (Bologna, 1993), pp. 136–9 (no. 30). The document is discussed in Golinelli, *Matilde e i Canossa*, p. 172. Golinelli describes the daughter of Godfrey the Hunchback and Matilda of Tuscany as 'Beatrice of Lotharingia'.
158 Aubé, *Godefroy*, p. 40; Hay, *Military Leadership*, pp. 43–4. Cowdrey, *Gregory VII*, p. 97, asserts that the marriage 'failed from the start'.
159 Lampert, pp. 398–400, tr. p. 349.
160 *Cantatorium*, pp. 69–70.
161 On Godfrey the Hunchback's time in Italy, see: Dieckmann, *Gottfried III der Bucklige*, pp. 41–5; Andressohn, *Godfrey*, p. 15, Aubé, *Godefroy*, pp. 43–5, Hay, *Military Leadership*, p. 43, and n. 82.
162 Overmann, *Reg. Mat.*, pp. 127–9, items 9, 13, and 15.
163 *Cantatorium*, p. 69.
164 'Sed nec sic quidem apud eam maritalem gratiam obtinuit, spretusque ab ea et inactus ab Italia Lotharingiam rediit'. *Cantatorium*, p. 70.
165 Cowdrey, *Gregory VII*, pp. 71–4.
166 Gregory VII, *Register*, pp. 13–15 (no. 1.9), tr. pp. 9–10.
167 *Cantatorium*, pp. 70–6.
168 *Cantatorium*, p. 84.
169 'Tu quoque infelicior infelicissimis, quem necdum emolliunt vel timor Dei vel amor patris tui, qui elemosinam ejus defraudaveris, et fratribus tam devotis adhuc eam detraxeris!' *Cantatorium*, pp. 84–5.
170 'se errasse, se peccasse in Deum et patrem suum est confessus, erroremque suum amodo se correcturum professus'. *Cantatorium*, p. 85.
171 *Cantatorium*, pp. 85–6.
172 Robinson, *Henry IV*, pp. 63–104, surveys Henry's dealings with the Saxons between 1065 and 1075.
173 Robinson, *Henry IV*, pp. 91–2; Aubé, *Godefroy*, p. 45.
174 Lampert, p. 202, tr. p. 195.
175 Lampert, p. 218, tr. p. 209.
176 'Godefrodus dux ... fuit maximus hostis Saxoniae'. Bruno, p. 318.
177 *Annales Yburgenses*, MGH SS, vol. 16, pp. 434–8, at p. 436; Verlinden, *Robert Ier*, p. 96.
178 On the battle, see: Robinson, *Henry IV*, pp. 100–1.
179 Lampert, p. 292, tr. p. 264; Berthold II, p. 86, tr. p. 136; *Carmen*, p. 176.
180 'preclarum ducem Gotefridum, nobilissime Matilde coniugem'. Bonizo, p. 606, tr. p. 233. Bonizo gives no hint that the marriage broke down.
181 'rex per interventum Gozelonis ducis propter eius excellens in milicia meritum successorem constituit Heinricum quendam Vertunensem canonicum, ipsi duci consanguinitate proximum'. Lampert, p. 300, tr. p. 270. Lampert

does not indicate precisely how Godfrey the Hunchback and Henry of Verdun were related.

182 'Quo ille beneficio regi devinctus operam suam futurae expeditioni quam maximam pollicebatur'. Lampert, p. 300, tr. p. 270.

183 *Cantatorium*, pp. 86–8.

184 Kupper, 'La maison d'Ardenne-Verdun et l'eglise de Liège', p. 212; Cauchie, *Querelle*, vol. 1, p. 30; Andressohn, *Godfrey*, p. 16.

185 Robinson, *Henry IV*, p. 102.

186 Lampert, p. 314, tr. pp. 281; Bruno, pp. 266–8.

187 Lampert, p. 314, tr. p. 281.

188 'ducem Gozelonem, cuius potissimum in ea expeditione auctoritas valebat, et in eo omnium quae agenda erant summa et cardo vertebatur, pro eo quod, licet statura pusillus et gibbo deformis esset, tamen opum gloria et militum lectissimorum copia, tum sapientiae et eloquii maturitate caeteris principibus quam plurimum eminebat'. Lampert, p. 316, tr. pp. 282–3. The chronicler repeated this passage almost verbatim later in his account when describing Godfrey's death.

189 'Gozelo dux et qui cum eo erant satis imprigos se exhibuerunt negocio'. Lampert, p. 320, tr. p. 285.

190 On Gregory's early experiences at the curia: Cowdrey, *Gregory VII*, pp. 35–9, 43–53.

191 'Grata nobis est lętitia tua, quam in litteris tuis de promotione nostra te habere cognovimus'. Gregory VII, *Register*, pp. 13–15 (no. 1.9), tr. pp. 9–10.

192 'ex fonte sincere dilectionis et fideli mente derivatam esse non dubitamus'. Gregory VII, *Register*, pp. 13–15 (no. 1.9), tr. pp. 9–10.

193 'Cęterum, quia fidei et constantię virtutem donante Deo in te sitam esse cognovimus, omnem, quam oportet in karissimo sancti Petri filio, in te fiduciam habentes, animum tuum de nostra itidem constantissima dilectione et erga honores tuos promptissima voluntate nequaquam dubitare volumus'. Gregory VII, *Register*, pp. 13–15 (no. 1.9), tr. pp. 9–10.

194 Cowdrey, *Gregory VII*, p. 96.

195 Cowdrey, *Gregory VII*, p. 93.

196 'nihil aliud mandamus, quam quod presentes simul diximus'. Gregory VII, *Register*, pp. 103–4 (no. 1.72), tr. pp. 75–6.

197 Hay, *Military Leadership*, p. 44.

198 Gregory VII, *Register*, pp. 71–3 (no. 1.47), tr. pp. 51–3.

199 Gregory VII, *Register*, pp. 76–7 (no. 1.50), tr. pp. 55–6.

200 On Gregory's proposed expedition, see: H. E. J. Cowdrey, 'Pope Gregory VII's "crusading" plans of 1074', in Benjamin Z. Kedar, Hans E. Mayer and R. C. Smail (eds), *Outremer: Studies in the History of the Crusading Kingdom of Jerusalem Presented to Joshua Prawer* (Jerusalem, 1982), pp. 27–40.

201 Gregory VII, *Register*, pp. 69–71 (no. 1.46), tr. pp. 50–1.

202 'et idem vester nuntius veniat per comitissam Beatricem, quę cum filia et genero in hoc negotio laborare procurat'. Gregory VII, *Register*, pp. 69–71 (no. 1.46), tr. pp. 50–1.

203 Gregory VII, *Register*, pp. 103–4 (no. 1.72), tr. pp. 75–6.

204 'Ubi est auxilium, quod pollicebaris, ubi milites, quos ad honorem et subsidium sancti Petri te ducturum nobis promisisti?' Gregory VII, *Register*, pp. 103–4 (no. 1.72), tr. pp. 75–6.

205 'Denique, si in his, quę nobis promisisti, videlicet sancto Petro ex corde adhęrere, immobiliter perstare volueris, te sicut karissimum filium habebimus et tu nos, quamquam indignum, dulcem tamen habebis patrem.' Gregory VII, *Register*, pp. 103–4 (no. 1.72), tr. pp. 75–6.

206 'Verum si aliquod foedus, quod a sanctorum patrum sanctione non discrepet, inire cum eo poteris, nobis [bonum] laudandumque videtur . . . Unde, si vos dilexerit, eum diligemus, si vero ex sua culpa odio habere ceperit, sicut karissimas filias modis quibus poterimus vos diligendo ei Deo favente resistemus'. Gregory VII, *Register*, pp. 251–2 (no. 3.5), tr. pp. 179–80. On this letter, see: Cowdrey, *Gregory VII*, p. 130; Robinson, *Henry IV*, p. 138.

207 Cowdrey, *Gregory VII*, pp. 130–1; Robinson, *Henry IV*, pp. 138–40.

208 This is the suggestion of Cowdrey, *Gregory VII*, p. 130.

209 Gregory VII, *Register*, pp. 263–7 (no. 3.10), tr. pp. 187–90; Cowdrey, *Gregory VII*, pp. 131–4.

210 On the synod of Worms, see: Robinson, *Henry IV*, pp. 143–6; Cowdrey, *Gregory VII*, pp. 135–9; Hay, *Military Leadership*, p. 44; Dieckmann, *Gottfried III der Bucklige*, pp. 80–1; Cauchie, *Querelle*, vol. 1, p. 30.

211 All but one of these bishops were from dioceses in the kingdom of Germany. The other was Bishop Bruno of Verona.

212 Henry subsequently exaggerated the scale of the attendance at Worms in a letter to Gregory, describing the synod as a 'general meeting of all the princes of the kingdom' ('generalem conventum omnium regni primatum'). *Ep. H IV*, pp. 62–4 (no. 11), tr. in Mommsen, pp. 146–7 (no. 11).

213 *Ep. H IV*, pp. 62–4 (no. 11), tr. in Mommsen, pp. 146–7 (no. 11a).

214 *MGH Const.*, vol. 1, pp. 106–8 (no. 58), tr. in Mommsen, pp. 147–9 (no. 11b).

215 On the Synod, see: Cowdrey, *Gregory VII*, pp. 140–2.

216 For Gregory's sentences against the participants in the synod of Worms, see: Gregory VII, *Register*, pp. 252–4, 268–71 (nos. 3.6 and 3.10a), tr. pp. 181, 191–3.

217 'in parte sancti Petri stare voluissent'. Berthold II, p. 116, tr. p. 153.

218 *Cantatorium*, p. 90; Andressohn, *Godfrey*, p. 17.

219 'Gotefridus dux . . . particeps immo auctor . . . conspirationis'. Bernold, pp. 300–2, tr. p. 256. On the basis of this testimony, Cowdrey, *Gregory VII*, p. 135, suggests that Godfrey played the key role in ensuring the bishop's obedience to Henry.

220 'dux Gotifridus . . . Wormaciensi conspiratione, non minimus suffragator et incentor'. Berthold II, p. 102, tr. p. 146. Lampert of Hersfeld singled out Bishop William of Utrecht for his actions: Lampert, p. 346, tr. p. 306. Gregory VII himself held Archbishop Siegfried of Mainz chiefly responsible for the developments at Worms: Gregory VII, *Register*, pp. 268–71 (no. 3.10a), tr. pp. 191–3.

221 Cowdrey, *Gregory VII*, p. 137, n. 267, and Hay, *Military Leadership*, p. 63, connect the charges concerning Matilda to Godfrey's presence at Worms.

222 'Gotifridus . . . papam illic constituendum ad sedem Romanam se perducturum iam regi audacter promiserat'. Berthold II, p. 106, tr. p. 148.

223 Berthold II, pp. 102, 106–8, tr. p. 146, 148.

224 On the fatal wounding and death of Godfrey the Hunchback, see: Cowdrey, *Gregory VII*, p. 142; Dieckmann, *Gottfried III der Bucklige*, pp. 81–5; Hay, *Military Leadership*, pp. 65–6; Andressohn, *Godfrey of Bouillon*, p. 18; Overmann, *Reg. Lat.*, p. 137, item 23a; Verlinden, *Robert Ier*, p. 97; Kees Nieuwenhuijsen, 'De moord op Godfried met de Bult', *Terra Nigra*, 70 (2007), 42–55.

225 '[Godfrey] . . . cum esset in confinio Lotheringiae et Flandriae in civitate quae dicitur Antwerpha occisus est'. Lampert, p. 348, tr. p. 308.

226 Lampert, p. 348, tr. p. 308.

227 'a milite quodam ad requisita naturae in secessu sedens de deorsum vulneratus, infeliciter exspiravit'. Berthold II, p. 102, tr. p. 146.

228 'turpiter a quodam coquo per posteriora cum ad necessarium sederet vulneratus, ante medium quadragesimae expiravit'. Bernold, p. 302, tr. p. 256.

229 *Cantatorium*, p. 90. Sigebert of Gembloux just wrote that 'an assassin killed Duke Godfrey in Frisia' ('Sicarius in Fresonia Godefridum ducem perimit'). Sigebert, p. 363. The annalist of St James in Liège simply wrote that he was killed by an assassin: *Annales S. Iacobi Leodiensis*, p. 639.

230 Lampert, p. 348, tr. p. 308, refers to rumours that Robert's 'cunning' (*insidias*) was behind the attack, while it is related in the *Cantatorium*, p. 90, that Godfrey's assailants were 'certain associates' (*quosdam necessarios*) of Robert.

231 Cowdrey, *Gregory VII*, p. 142.

232 Landulf Senior, *Historia Mediolanensis, MGH SS*, vol. 8, pp. 32–100, at pp. 97–8.

233 Hay, *Military Leadership*, pp. 66–7.

234 Robinson, *Henry IV*, pp. 147–8; Hay, *Military Leadership*, p. 66.

235 *Cantatorium*, pp. 90–1; Aubé, *Godefroy*, pp. 57–8.

236 *Annales S. Iacobi Leodiensis*, p. 639.

237 *Cantatorium*, pp. 90–1.

238 Of those who were present at Worms other than Henry IV, Gregory bore the deepest animosity toward the archbishop of Mainz: Gregory VII, *Register*, pp. 268–71 (no. 3.10a), tr. pp. 191–3; Lampert, p. 346, tr. p. 306.

239 See above, p. 31.

240 'Gotifredi autem quondam illius viri indubitanter scias, quod frequenter apud Deum licet peccator, habeam memoriam, quia non me illius inimicitia vel aliqua impedit vanitas, sed motus fraterna dilectione tua et Mathildae deprecatione illius exopto salutem'. Gregory VII, *Register*, pp. 293–7 (no. 4.2), tr. pp. 208–11.

241 'litteris acceptis quorundam fratrum nostrorum presulum et ducum'. Gregory VII, *Register*, pp. 293–7 (no. 4.2), tr. pp. 208–11.

242 Tanner, *Families*, provides an excellent political overview of the comital house between the ninth and twelfth centuries.

243 On the counts of the ninth and tenth centuries, see: Tanner, *Families*, pp. 20–68.

244 Tanner, *Families*, p. 69.

245 For an overview of his career, see: Heather J. Tanner, 'The Expansion of the Power and Influence of the Counts of Boulogne Under Eustace II', *ANS*, 14 (1992), 251–77.

246 Tanner, *Families*, pp. 79, 113, 258.

247 Frank Barlow, *Edward the Confessor*, new edn (New Haven, 1997), pp. 307–8 (Appendix C).

248 *The Anglo-Saxon Chronicle*, tr. Dorothy Whitelock and David C. Douglas (London, 1961), p. 117.

249 Barlow, *Edward the Confessor*, pp. 109–11.

250 *Anglo-Saxon Chronicle*, pp. 117–19 (the testimony of the 'D' and 'E' versions); Barlow, *Edward the Confessor*, pp. 110–16.

251 On the timing of the marriage, see: Mayer, 'Baudouin Ier', pp. 15–16.

252 *The Gesta Guillelmi of William of Poitiers*, ed. and tr. R. H. C. Davis and Marjorie Chibnall (Oxford, 1998), pp. 182–3; Tanner, 'The Expansion', p. 270.

253 Tanner, *Families*, pp. 100–2; Eadem, 'The Expansion', pp. 270–5.

254 Tanner, 'The Expansion', p. 273.

255 'At comes Eustachius, generosis patribus ortus, | Septus bellantum multiplici cuneo, | Ad ducis auxilium festinat primus haberi; | Efficiturque pedes dux ut abiret eques. | Miles erat quidam comitis, nutritus ab illo, | Fecerat ut domino, fecit et illi sibi. | Talibus auspiciis, comes et dux associati | Quo magis arma micant, bella simul repetunt'. *The Carmen de Hastingae Proelio of Guy Bishop of Amiens*, ed. and tr. Frank Barlow (Oxford, 1999), pp. 30–3.

256 *Carmen de Hastingae Proelio*, pp. 32–3.

257   Lucien Musset, *The Bayeux Tapestry*, new edn, tr. Richard Rex (Woodbridge, 2005), pp. 250–1.

258   Andrew Bridgeford, 'Was Count Eustace II of Boulogne the patron of the Bayeux Tapestry?', *JMH*, 25 (1999), 155–85. See also: Shirley A. Brown, 'The Bayeux Tapestry: Why Eustace, Odo and William?', *ANS*, 12 (1990), 7–28.

259   'Haec inter uerba percussus Eustachius inter scapulas ictu sonoro, cuius grauitatem statim sanguis demonstrabat naribus et ore, quasi moribundus euasit ope comitum'. *Gesta Guillelmi*, pp. 138–9.

260   *The Gesta Normannorum Ducum of William of Jumièges, Orderic Vitalis and Robert of Torigni*, ed. and tr. Elisabeth van Houts, 2 vols (Oxford, 1992–5).

261   Tanner, 'The Expansion', p. 272.

262   Tanner, 'The Expansion', p. 273.

263   Tanner, *Families*, p. 102; Eadem, 'The Expansion', pp. 273–4. I am grateful to Stephen Baxter for clarifying my understanding of Eustace's intentions towards Kent in the period after the battle of Hastings.

264   'Equidem fore, si firmissimo loco hoc sit potitus cum portu marino, ut potentia eius latius distendatur, sicque potentiam Normannorum diminutum iri'. *Gesta Guillelmi*, pp. 182–3.

265   *Gesta Guillelmi*, pp. 182–5.

266   Tanner, 'The Expansion', p. 272.

267   Tanner, 'The Expansion', pp. 274–6.

268   'Sed parcendum sentimus personae multifariam illustri, comiti nominato, qui reconciliatus nunc in proximis regis honoratur'. *Gesta Guillelmi*, pp. 184–5.

269   Tanner, *Families*, pp. 335–8 (Appendix 2), with a map at p. xvii. The counties in which Eustace held land were Bedfordshire, Cambridgeshire, Dorset, Essex, Hertfordshire, Huntingdonshire, Kent, Norfolk, Oxfordshire, Somerset, Suffolk, and Surrey.

270   Tanner, 'The Expansion', p. 276; Judith A. Green, *The Aristocracy of Norman England* (Cambridge, 1997), pp. 41–2. See also the entry for Eustace in K. S. B. Keats-Rohan, *Domesday People: A Prosopography of Persons Occurring in English Documents: 1066–1166, Vol. I: Domesday Book* (Woodbridge, 1999), pp. 196–7. At the time of the issue of Magna Carta in 1215, these lands were still known as the Honour of Boulogne. See: J. C. Holt, *Magna Carta*, 3rd edn (Cambridge, 2015), pp. 289–90.

271   The 'E' version of the Anglo-Saxon Chronicle refers to 'Eustace the Young' under the year 1088, so the son had evidently succeeded his father by that point. *Anglo-Saxon Chronicle*, pp. 167. Note, however, that Tanner, *Families*, p. 129, suggests that Eustace III's rule as count began '*c.*1089', while Mayer, 'Baudouin Ier', pp. 16–18, suggests that Eustace II died around 1082 and was succeeded as count by his eldest son at that point.

272   Frank Barlow, *William Rufus*, new edn (New Haven, 2000), pp. 77, 90–1. *Anglo-Saxon Chronicle*, p. 177, records that the lands were restored to Eustace in 1101.

273   On Godfrey's elder brother, Eustace, see Heather J. Tanner, 'In His Brothers' Shadow: The Crusading Career and Reputation of Eustace III of Boulogne', in Khalil I. Semaan (ed.), *The Crusades: Other Experiences, Alternate Perspectives* (Binghamton, 2003), pp. 83–99. On Baldwin, see: Murray, *Crusader Kingdom*, pp. 30–6.

274   Geoffrey fitzEustace married a daughter of Geoffrey de Mandeville, another of the chief post-conquest magnates of England. See Keats-Rohan, *Domesday People*, p. 229, and the genealogical table in Tanner, *Families*, p. 290.

275   *Genealogia Comitum Buloniensium*, *MGH SS*, vol. 9, pp. 299–301. For a critical study of this text, see Léopold Genicot, 'Princes territoriaux et sang Carolingien: La Geneaologia Comitum Buloniensium', in his *Études sur les Principautés Lotharingiennes* (Louvain, 1975), pp. 217–306.

276   Tanner, *Families*, p. 266.

277 On Ida, see: Nicholas Huyghebaert, 'La mère de Godefroid de Bouillon: La comtesse Ide de Boulogne', *PSHIGL*, 95 (1981), 43–63; Renée Nip, 'Godelieve of Gistel and Ida of Boulogne', in Anneke B. Mulder-Bakker (ed.), *Sanctity and Motherhood: Essays on Holy Mothers in the Middle Ages* (London, 1995), pp. 191–223; Jean-Pierre Dickès, *Sainte Ide de Boulogne: mère de Godefroy de Bouillon* (Paris, 2004).

278 'Eustachius vero accepit uxorem filiam Godefridus ducis, Idam nomine, nobilem genere et mobus'. *Genealogia Comitum Buloniensium*, p. 301.

279 Tanner, *Families*, pp. 258, 263; Dickès, *Sainte Ide*, pp. 81–115.

280 Baudouin de Gaffier, 'Sainte Ide de Boulogne et l'Espagne', *Analecta Bollandiana*, 86 (1968), 67–82.

281 H. E. J. Cowdrey, *The Cluniacs and the Gregorian Reform* (Oxford, 1970).

282 Tanner, *Families*, pp. 123–4.

283 For the letters, see: Anselm, *Opera*, vol. 3, pp. 206–7 (no. 82); p. 249 (no. 114); pp. 273–4 (no. 131); vol. 4, pp. 41–2 (no. 167); pp. 154–5 (no. 244); p. 157 (no. 247). For translations, see: Frölich, vol. 1, pp. 216–07 (no. 82); p. 274–5 (no. 114); pp 307 (no. 131); vol. 2, pp. 62–4 (no. 167); pp. 227–8 (no. 244); pp. 230–1 (no. 247).

284 On Anselm's correspondence with Ida, see: Sally N. Vaughn, *St Anselm and the Handmaidens of God: A Study of Anselm's Correspondence With Women* (Turnhout, 2002), pp. 126–59; Eadem, 'Anselm in Italy, 1097–1100', *ANS*, 16 (1994), 245–70.

285 Anselm, *Opera*, vol. 4, pp. 41–2 (no. 167), tr. vol. 2, pp. 62–3.

286 Anselm, *Opera*, vol. 3, p. 249 (no. 114), tr. vol. 1, pp. 274–5.

287 Anselm, *Opera*, vol. 4, pp. 154–5 (no. 244), tr. vol. 2, pp. 227–8.

288 Vaughn, *St Anselm and the Handmaidens of God*, p. 139.

289 'memor magnae dilectionis et beneficiorum, quae in patre et matre vestra et filiis eorum erga me sum expertus'. Anselm, *Opera*, vol. 4, pp. 142–3 (no. 235), tr. vol. 2, pp. 210–12.

290 Vaughan, 'Anselm in Italy', p. 252.

2 Godfrey's career in the West, c.1060–1095

Godfrey's early years and arrival in Lotharingia

No contemporary source records where the three sons of Eustace II and Ida of Boulogne were born. However, Boulogne itself, the most important of the comital house's possessions, is the likeliest location.[1] The genealogy of the counts of Boulogne lists the three sons in the following order: Eustace (born c.1058), named for his father, then Godfrey (born c.1060), and Baldwin (born c.1062).[2] Although the genealogy does not explicitly state which was the eldest, the order in which they are listed in this text must indicate the order in which the three sons were born. The middle son became better known within his own lifetime as Godfrey of Bouillon. While 'Godfrey' was the leading name of the house of Ardennes-Bouillon, it should be noted that it was also the name of several members of the comital house of Boulogne. Indeed, it was the name of one of Eustace II's own brothers.[3] The eldest of the three sons, the future Eustace III, was evidently earmarked from birth to inherit the comital title and all the patrilineal holdings. As a result, the two younger sons may not have anticipated gaining titles and lands of their own during their early years.

Contemporary sources reveal much about the lifestyle and pursuits of a typical aristocratic youth in this era.[4] The course of Godfrey's youth can therefore be surmised. He would most likely have begun military training before the age of ten. Thereafter, he would have spent much time in the study of arms, learning how to ride a horse, and how to use a sword, shield, and lance while mounted.[5] Godfrey's exploits on the First Crusade indicate that during his military training he also learned how to use the crossbow.[6] Most likely at the age of about fifteen, he would have undergone a coming of age ritual which signified that he had passed from boyhood to adolescence, and had thereby acquired the status of a warrior. William of Poitiers wrote that when William of Normandy, future king of England, reached adulthood and took up arms, news reverberated throughout all of France.[7] As noted in the previous chapter, Henry IV of Germany performed a coming of age ceremony at Easter 1065.[8] In the eleventh century, aristocratic youths typically spent time serving as a squire in the retinue of a relative (often an uncle) or an associate of his family. When one noble sent his son to the court of another, it signified a political bond between the two families. Contemporaries accorded the relationship between nephew and uncle with particular significance. This is apparent in texts such as the *Chanson de Roland*, whose eponymous lead character is depicted as the nephew of Charlemagne. As the following pages will suggest, this may well have been Godfrey's experience.

Godfrey emerges in historical record with his entry into Lotharingian politics. He is first mentioned in relation to the death of his uncle Godfrey the Hunchback in February 1076. Lampert of Hersfeld, writing almost contemporaneously, states that at the point of his uncle's death, Godfrey – aged about sixteen – was 'an energetic young man, very eager for military action'.[9] A revealing contrast may be drawn with Lampert's description of another young noble, Ekbert II of Meissen. Lampert reports that when Margrave Ekbert I of Meissen died in January 1068, he was succeeded by Ekbert II, his son, who at that time was a 'little child of a very tender age'.[10] Later in his account, Lampert asserted that in 1073, Ekbert II was still a boy 'under the age of knighthood'.[11] While Lampert explicitly noted that Ekbert II had yet to assume formally the status of a warrior in 1073, this author made no such claim in connection to Godfrey of Bouillon's status at the death of his uncle. Lampert thus seems to have believed that Godfrey had already come of age and held the status of a warrior by the time his uncle died in 1076.

Before Godfrey the Hunchback died, he designated his young nephew as his heir. Berthold of Reichenau asserts by the time Godfrey the Hunchback died, he had already granted the ducal office to his nephew.[12] Similarly, it is related in the *Cantatorium* that while Godfrey the Hunchback was alive, he 'had adopted' (*adoptaverat*) as his heir his nephew, 'young Godfrey' (*Godefrido adolescenti*).[13] Modern scholars have generally concluded on the basis of this evidence that Godfrey the Hunchback nominated his nephew on his deathbed, in the few days he lived after his fatal wounding in Flanders.[14] This possibility cannot be ruled out. In 1076, Godfrey the Hunchback was only about thirty, and he had been able to fulfil all his duties as duke despite his physical affliction. He had married, and though his union with Matilda of Tuscany had failed, it had evidently produced at least one child (a daughter who died in infancy).[15] Up until the attack upon him in Flanders in 1076, then, Godfrey may have thought that he would produce a male heir of his own. It is, however, important to note that the chroniclers do not pinpoint the precise moment at which he adopted his nephew as his heir. In other words, it is possible that the elder Godfrey nominated his heir *before* he was mortally wounded in 1076. The author of the *Cantatorium* employed the pluperfect tense to relate that Godfrey the Hunchback 'had adopted' Godfrey as his heir, a tense which can convey the sense of an action taken some time in the past. One moment in Godfrey the Hunchback's career stands out at a point at which he may have decided to turn to his nephew: Matilda of Tuscany's departure from Lotharingia to

Italy in 1071. It is conceivable that after Matilda's departure, Godfrey began actively looking to other members of his family with the succession in mind.

Even if Godfrey the Hunchback did formally designate his nephew as his heir as he lay on his deathbed and not before, there must have been a pre-existing bond between the two men. It is very difficult to believe that Godfrey the Hunchback would nominate a successor whom he did not already know and trust. It is likely the case that before Godfrey was fatally attacked in February 1076, he had become sufficiently familiar with his nephew to regard the young man as a suitable successor. Contemporary evidence provides several hints that this was exactly what happened in the years before Godfrey the Hunchback's death. The author of the *Cantatorium* implies that Godfrey attended his uncle's burial in Verdun, or at the very least, was in Lotharingia when the funeral took place. According to this account, after his uncle was laid to rest, the younger Godfrey spent a period at St Hubert in the company and protection of his kinsman, Bishop Henry of Liège.[16] The *Cantatorium* records that he needed Bishop Henry's care because with Godfrey the Hunchback's death, he had been 'deprived of his uncle's assistance (*auxilio*)'.[17] One manuscript of the *Cantatorium* replaces *auxilio* with the word *solatio*, which can be rendered as 'support'.[18] The author of this account clearly believed that before Godfrey the Hunchback died he had supported his nephew. It is also of note that the younger man kept in his company individuals who had formerly been associated with his uncle. Not long after Godfrey the Hunchback's death, Godfrey's retinue included a monk of St Hubert named Adalberon. This man, a Swabian, had formerly been at the abbey of Constance, and had been a close associate of Godfrey the Hunchback.[19] In addition, Heriband, the castellan of Bouillon, witnessed charters issued by Godfrey the Hunchback as well as by Godfrey of Bouillon, indicating that he was a member of both of their households.[20] Though this evidence is far from conclusive, Godfrey's associations with figures who had been companions of Godfrey the Hunchback suggests a degree of continuity in the household over the succession.[21] Moreover, Godfrey's parents certainly sent at least one of their sons to the household of an associate. As noted in the previous chapter, shortly before William of Normandy's invasion of England in 1066, Eustace II and Ida sent one of their sons – it is not specified which – as a hostage to William's ducal court at Rouen.[22] It is thus wholly plausible that they sent their second son to join the household of Ida's brother.

The main territories of the house of Ardennes-Bouillon were in the romance-speaking diocese of Liège, meaning that in many situations Godfrey could probably have communicated in the French he would have learned growing up in the county of Boulogne. However, entering Lotharingian politics apparently induced Godfrey to learn German too. Frutolf of Michelsberg's 1106 continuator explicitly states that Godfrey had 'innate skill' in both French and German.[23]

Information on Godfrey's career in Lower Lotharingia after 1076 is provided only in a handful of charters and a number of fleeting references in local chronicles.[24] This evidence is so equivocal that modern scholars have come to opposing conclusions regarding this phase of his life. Andressohn concluded that after 1076 Godfrey's career was firmly aligned with Henry IV, an allegiance typified by his participation in the king's military campaigns in Saxony and Italy.[25] In contrast, other historians have asserted that Godfrey took no part in Henry IV's campaigns, and that his activities were largely confined to the protection of his inheritance in the region around Bouillon.[26] The following pages appraise these fragmentary sources for this period in Godfrey's career, and demonstrate that the latter interpretation has the firmer basis in the evidence.

The succession to the office of duke of Lower Lotharingia in 1076

It has already been noted that Godfrey the Hunchback designated his nephew as his successor. But to what did the younger Godfrey succeed after his uncle's death in February 1076? Before attempting to answer this question, it is crucial to reiterate that the familial holdings of the house of Ardennes-Bouillon were distinct from the office of duke of Lower Lotharingia. While Godfrey the Hunchback may have intended his nephew to succeed to both after his death, Henry IV did not immediately appoint the younger man to the ducal office. Around a month after Godfrey the Hunchback's death, the king came to Utrecht to celebrate Easter, holding a synod there on Holy Saturday and Easter Sunday (26 and 27 March). This, it should be pointed out, was in the immediate aftermath of Gregory VII's February proclamation that Henry was excommunicated and deposed. The purpose of the Easter court at Utrecht was to convey the strength and legitimacy of Henry's kingship. To that end, Henry had Bishop William of Utrecht publicly excommunicate Gregory, and the king himself performed a solemn crown-wearing in the city's cathedral.[27] Henry's most pressing issue at the synod regarding affairs in Germany was to appoint a new duke of Lower Lotharingia to succeed Godfrey the Hunchback. The two closest male relations of the late duke were his nephew Godfrey (the named heir), and Count Albert III of Namur. Albert had a strong claim: as the son of Albert II of Namur and Regelinde (the sister of Godfrey the Bearded) he had a dynastic connection to the house of Ardennes-Bouillon. Moreover, Albert III's wife was Ida, the widow of Frederick of Luxemburg (duke of Lower Lotharingia between 1046 and his death in 1065), and this would have bolstered his claim on the office (see Figure 0.2).

Rather than appointing Godfrey or Albert III as duke, however, the king instead bestowed the office upon his son Conrad, a boy of about two. Henry appointed Godfrey margrave of Antwerp, an office which several of his predecessors had held. The annalist of St James in Liège lucidly described these developments, noting that after Godfrey the Hunchback was killed, 'Godfrey the son of his sister replaced him as margrave. Conrad, the little boy of King Henry, was appointed duke'.[28] Similarly, Lampert of Hersfeld noted that Henry 'celebrated Easter at Utrecht, and there he conferred the duchy of Lotharingia on to his son Conrad, but granted the march that is called Antwerp to Godfrey, the nephew of Duke [Godfrey], and son of Count Eustace'.[29] Berthold of Reichenau wrote that after Godfrey the Hunchback's death, his nephew,

> who bore his name, came into possession of his march, purchasing it from the king for forty pounds of gold, but he was unjustly deprived of his duchy, although his uncle had already granted it to him and he had obtained it from [Henry IV]. The king caused his own son [Conrad], who was barely two years old, to rule over it.[30]

Both Lampert and Berthold were highly critical of Henry IV's decision to overlook Godfrey for the office, portraying the king's policy as an attack on the young man's hereditary rights.[31] These chroniclers seized upon Henry's disposition of the office as a chance to heap obloquy on the king. While some modern commentators have suggested that Henry used Godfrey the Hunchback's death to strengthen royal influence in Lotharingia – as he had apparently earlier sought to do in Saxony – Robinson refutes this, arguing that Henry's intention was simply to maintain order in the region.[32]

Henry's policy towards Lower Lotharingia in 1076 makes sense when viewed in its wider context.[33] With his disputes with the Saxons and the papacy ongoing, Henry was anxious to appoint a reliable ally to the office. Henry knew only too well the cost of appointing the wrong man as duke. During his minority (1056–1065), his mother Agnes, acting as regent, had appointed three powerful princes to ducal offices. One of those princes, Otto of Northeim, selected as duke of Bavaria in 1061, had been one of the ringleaders of the Saxon rebellion against Henry's rule in 1073–1075.[34] In the aftermath of the synod of Worms, and particularly after Gregory VII's sentence against Henry became widely known, much of Henry's support had melted away, leaving him with only a small core of allies.[35] Henry had to ensure that Godfrey the Hunchback's successor would be a man who would protect royal interests in the duchy and, if possible, ensure that military support from Lower Lotharingia was assembled for royal campaigns. From Henry's perspective, not only were the young Godfrey's military talents unproven, but he was also the son of Count Eustace II of Boulogne, one of the most important vassals of the king of France, a longtime adversary. For these reasons, Henry IV could not appoint him duke in 1076.[36] This is not to suggest that Henry doubted Godfrey the Hunchback's judgement when it came to filling important offices; as noted above, in mid-1075, the king appointed Henry of Verdun as bishop of Liège on Godfrey's recommendation.[37] Henry wished simply to align the ducal office more firmly with the crown, and believed that this was best achieved by appointing his infant son Conrad to it. Crucially, Henry's policy in 1076 was in keeping with how the Salian monarchs had dealt with vacancies in the ducal offices in Germany before. In 1053, Henry III deposed the duke of Bavaria, and conferred the office on his eldest son Henry (that is, the future Henry IV), who at that point was two years old. Henry III appointed Bishop Gebhard of Eichstätt, the future Pope Victor II, as regent in the duchy.[38] After Henry III had his son inaugurated king of Germany on 17 July 1054, he transferred the office of duke of Bavaria to his second son, the two-year-old Conrad. Henry IV may have been aware of these precedents when he disposed of the ducal office of Lower Lotharingia in 1076.

Conrad's authority over the duchy was symbolic. In practice, he was an absentee duke, spending most of the period between 1076 and 1085 representing his father's interests in the kingdom of Italy.[39] To safeguard royal interests in Lower Lotharingia, the king installed Albert III of Namur as his representative in the duchy, just as Henry III had charged Gebhard of Eichstätt with a similar role in Bavaria in 1053. A contemporary charter indicates that Albert of Namur held the 'principate' (i.e. the ducal office) as 'vice-duke'.[40] From Henry's perspective, this was a sound appointment: Albert loyally supported the crown in the era that followed.[41] It was probably with the aim of placating Godfrey that Henry appointed him margrave of Antwerp.[42] While that office had been associated with the house of Ardennes-Bouillon from the time of Godfrey the Captive, it was a position that technically subordinated Godfrey to the duke. Moreover, since Godfrey did not hold substantial lands near Antwerp, the title bore him no real authority.[43] Nevertheless, Henry's decision to appoint Godfrey to this office suggests that the king intended to keep the young man in mind for the future. Hence, while contemporary chroniclers painted Henry's disposition of the ducal office as an attack on Godfrey, the policy was more likely a compromise, to which the young man must have agreed in the hope of later rewards.[44] Most crucially, these arrangements did not exclude Godfrey from the ducal succession in the future.

Godfrey's matrilineal inheritance

Upon Godfrey the Hunchback's death, Godfrey of Bouillon inherited the lands and holdings of the house of Ardennes-Bouillon, a relatively limited collection of properties chiefly located around the Middle Meuse (see Map 2.1).[45] Murray has helpfully divided Godfrey's inheritance into four groups. The first and most important of these centred upon Bouillon itself.[46] The castle of Bouillon was Godfrey's principal stronghold. Reputedly founded by Charles Martel, the castle was well-defended by nature, situated as it was on a steep rocky bank, and almost entirely encircled by a tight 'U'-shaped curve of the river Semois (a tributary of the Meuse).[47]

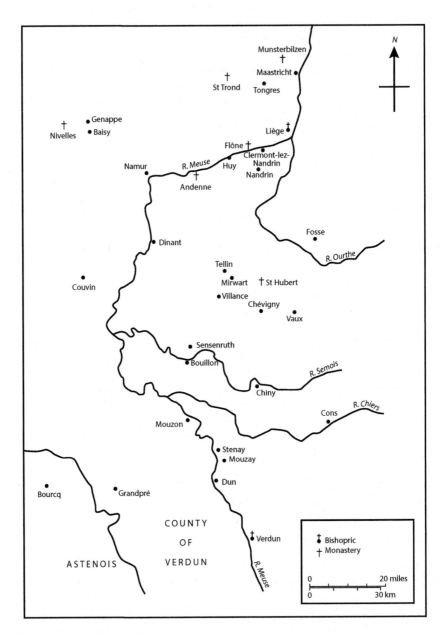

Map 2.1 Bouillon and its environs

Across the Semois from the castle was the priory of St Peter, established as a satellite of St Hubert by Godfrey the Bearded in 1069.[48] Bouillon was the nexus of a wider array of allodial properties and rights in several nearby villages. Adjoining that allodial territory to the south was a fief held from the archbishop of Rheims.[49] Also associated with these holdings around Bouillon were a number of local responsibilities and offices, including the advocacy of St Hubert. As the following pages will show, like his uncle and grandfather before him, Godfrey acted as the lay advocate of St Hubert, in which capacity he maintained close ties with its monks.[50] The second element of Godfrey's inheritance was the office of count of Verdun. Verdun had first been associated with the house of Ardennes-Bouillon when Godfrey the Captive became its count in 963. After Godfrey the Bearded captured Verdun in 1047, it had remained in the family's ambit. However, from the middle of the eleventh century, beginning with the episcopate of Thierry (1047–1089) and continuing through that of Richer (1089–1107), the authority of the bishop of Verdun came to supplant that of its count in the region. Murray interprets this as an outcome of the wider Salian policy of utilising bishoprics in the kingdom of Germany as nodes of royal authority.[51] The third principal component of Godfrey's inheritance consisted of the allods of Stenay and Mouzay. These were located on the Meuse, about thirty miles south of Bouillon, and about the same distance north of Verdun. These had come to the house of Ardennes-Bouillon as part of the dowry granted when Godfrey the Bearded married Beatrice of Tuscany in 1054. As Murray points out, since Godfrey and Beatrice had had no children, these allods were open to the claims of Matilda of Tuscany (the daughter of Beatrice and Margrave Boniface of Tuscany).[52] The fourth component of Godfrey's inheritance comprised two blocs of land to the north of Bouillon. One of these lay in Brabant, and included the allods of Baisy and Genappe, while the other was largely located further to the north, on the west bank of the Meuse near Maastricht. Godfrey's mother, Ida, also appears to have held land in both these northern blocs.[53]

As Murray has suggested, the holdings of the house of Ardennes-Bouillon had become markedly less lucrative over the course of the eleventh century. In that period, the family lost lands and rights in three main ways. Firstly, land had been donated to the Church. Secondly, other territory had been used as dowries in marriage contracts. Thirdly, and most significantly, Godfrey the Bearded's rebellions of 1044–1045 and 1047–1049 had prompted the king to confiscate a number of offices and territories.[54] While these various holdings did not supply Godfrey of Bouillon with substantial revenues after 1076, they did have a strategic value, as they bisected important lines of regional communication and trade. Bouillon itself was particularly important, as it straddled the frontier between the county of Champagne (part of the kingdom of France) and that of Luxemburg (which belonged to the kingdom of Germany).

In the following pages, it will be shown that after Godfrey the Hunchback's death, several claimants asserted their rights to certain parts of Godfrey of Bouillon's inheritance.[55] Bishop Henry of Liège had no qualms in using his influence over Godfrey, his young kinsman, to advance ecclesiastical interests in his diocese. Count Thierry of Veluwe apparently claimed lands north of Bouillon. Albert of Namur, Henry IV's representative in Lower Lotharingia, perhaps asserting his dynastic connection to the house of Ardennes-Bouillon, appears to have demanded Bouillon itself. Matilda of Tuscany, the widow of Godfrey the Hunchback, also asserted a claim. Though Matilda had assumed control of her family's extensive lands in northern Italy after her husband's death, she also sought some of her husband's lands in Lotharingia, namely the allods of Stenay and Mouzay.[56] As Gregory VII's most ardent supporter in Italy, she was able to enlist papal support. Matilda, Albert, and Thierry made common cause against Godfrey, and he would have to counteract their efforts to protect his inheritance.

Godfrey's career in Lotharingia, 1076–1087

While contemporary sources yield only sporadic glimpses into Godfrey's career in Lotharingia in the decade after his uncle's death, the extant evidence strongly suggests that his prime concern in that period was the protection and maintenance of his inheritance. It was previously noted that after the death of Godfrey the Hunchback in February 1076, Godfrey spent some time at St Hubert in the company of his kinsman, Bishop Henry of Liège.[57] The *Cantatorium* records that in that time the bishop often discussed with 'the young Margrave Godfrey' the allod of Tellin, a small village eight miles north-west of St Hubert. Henry apparently claimed that Godfrey's ancestors had violently captured the allod from St Hubert. After receiving advice and encouragement from his 'best men', Godfrey ceded the allod, and voluntarily recognised that it belonged to St Hubert.[58] The allod was formally restored in a ritual performed on Palm Sunday (20 March). After the solemn procession for the feastday, Godfrey, accompanied by his nobles, went with Bishop Henry to the altar dedicated to St Peter in the abbey of St Hubert. Henry, holding his pastoral staff and wearing his episcopal stole, took Godfrey's hand into his own right hand, and formally received the allod. He then pronounced that it was now under God's protection, and declared that anyone who attacked it would be excommunicated. Godfrey 'humbly admitted his and his ancestors' crime', for which the bishop then granted absolution. A document recording the transfer was then drawn up, and Godfrey and his men confirmed it.[59] This episode sheds important light onto Godfrey's early career in Lotharingia. Firstly, it reveals that Godfrey quickly forged a close relationship with Bishop Henry of Liège, and that the latter was content to use his influence over his young kinsman to benefit ecclesiastical interests in the area. Secondly, it suggests that the bishop of Liège and the monks of St Hubert acted in tandem to instruct Godfrey about sin and absolution. As demonstrated in the previous chapter, Godfrey the Hunchback and Godfrey the Bearded had had similar experiences in their interactions with the bishop and St Hubert.

Almost immediately after Godfrey of Bouillon succeeded his uncle, he came into conflict with Albert of Namur. It seems that Albert claimed from Godfrey the castle of Bouillon itself. The *Cantatorium* relates that Albert travelled to meet Godfrey at St Hubert in order to assert his claim in person, recording that at the ensuing meeting 'a very serious conflict over the castle of Bouillon' arose between the two men.[60] Though the text does not record either the nature or the outcome of these discussions, it is clear that Albert departed the meeting feeling unfulfilled. (The *Cantatorium* records that Godfrey was accompanied at the meeting with Albert of Namur at St Hubert by Adalberon, his uncle's former associate. The text relates that shortly after, the bishop of Laon, a suffragan of the archbishop of Rheims, appointed Adalberon abbot of St Vincent of Laon.[61]) As indicated above, Matilda of Tuscany allied her claim to those of Albert of Namur and Bishop Thierry of Verdun. Thierry's aim appears to have been to bolster his influence in the diocese of Verdun at Godfrey's expense. It seems that in the aftermath of Godfrey the Hunchback's death, Thierry granted the county of Verdun to Matilda, who in turn entrusted it to Albert of Namur. This is recorded in a charter dated September 1082. In that document, Thierry states that after Godfrey the Hunchback died, he had recognised Matilda of Tuscany as countess 'according to hereditary law', and that Matilda had then passed the office on to Albert of Namur.[62] Matilda travelled from Italy to Lotharingia at least once between 1076 and 1080, and it is possible that the purpose of that journey was to discuss the matter of Verdun with Thierry and Albert.[63] This triumvirate of Matilda, Thierry, and Albert worked together with the aim of depriving Godfrey of his family's former influence in Verdun.[64]

Matilda also enlisted support for her dispute with Godfrey from her close ally Pope Gregory VII. Though Matilda's communication with Gregory on this matter has not survived, the pope evidently wrote to Archbishop Manasses I of Rheims and instructed him to arbitrate on the dispute. Manasses' involvement may denote that the dispute between Matilda and Godfrey pertained to the fief south of Bouillon that Godfrey's predecessors had held from the archbishopric of Rheims.[65] In a letter of about 1078, Manasses reported to Gregory on the matter, and affirmed to the pope that he was 'prepared to carry out whatever [Matilda] will demand with regard to rejecting [Godfrey] and in accepting Count [Albert]'.[66] He then stated that he had gone to Verdun to discuss the matter with Bishop Thierry. It is possible that Gregory instructed Manasses to find in Matilda's favour rather than neutrally weigh the merits of both sides. In the late 1070s, Manasses had a difficult relationship with the pope. In that era, he intervened in the abbacy of St Remi in Rheims, to Gregory's consternation.[67] Hence, Manasses' underlying aim at this time must have been to regain papal favour, and this may have been why he was content to follow Gregory's instructions and find in Matilda's favour.[68] Manasses' letter of *c.*1078 is a vital source for understanding the challenges which Godfrey faced during his career in Lotharingia after 1076. It reveals that opposition to Godfrey united figures as powerful and diverse as Manasses, Gregory VII, Matilda of Tuscany, Albert of Namur, and Thierry of Verdun.[69] Some of this pressure was released in late 1080 or early 1081, however, after Thierry of Verdun renounced his alliance with Matilda in order to regain favour with Henry IV.[70] The danger confronting Godfrey diminished further in 1081, when Henry accused Matilda of Tuscany of treason and formally deprived her of her lands and property on both sides of the Alps.[71] While these developments may have lessened the threat to Godfrey's inheritance in Lotharingia, however, they did not wholly remove it.

Godfrey's conflict with Count Thierry of Veluwe ignited around 1081–2. Since Thierry held lands near the point where the Semois joined the Meuse, not far from Bouillon, it is likely that two were jostling for influence in the region. According to the *Cantatorium*, around this time Godfrey captured Thierry and had him imprisoned in the castle of Bouillon. The author states that Thierry was intimately familiar with Henry IV, prompting Godfrey to command his men that Thierry be well treated in his captivity. Nevertheless, Thierry died after about six months of confinement. His death no doubt permitted Godfrey to extend his influence in the region around Bouillon.[72] The same text records that Godfrey was once again in conflict with Albert of Namur around 1082, relating that 'after enmity grew between Albert of Namur and Godfrey of Bouillon [*Godefridum Bulloniensem*]', the former 'secretly committed' to repair Mirwart castle, from which he planned to 'wage war on Bouillon'.[73] Mirwart was a stronghold located about halfway between Bouillon and Namur.[74] Bishop Henry of Liège, however, learned of Albert's plan and hastened to thwart it, because, in the words of the chronicler, he 'favoured Godfrey in all ways', and because he feared the fortification of Mirwart might create problems in the diocese.[75] Henry thus purchased Mirwart from its vendor, Richilde of Mons. After some time, he transferred it to St Hubert.[76] While the author of the *Cantatorium* included this episode in his account to record how St Hubert acquired Mirwart rather than to illuminate Godfrey's career, it does indicate that Godfrey continued to have close dealings with Bishop Henry of Liège in the early 1080s.

In about 1082, Godfrey supported Bishop Henry of Liège's efforts to institute of the Peace of God in his diocese. Originating in Aquitaine in the late tenth century, the Peace of God was a movement instigated by ecclesiastical authorities in order to counteract endemic warfare. Under its precepts, prelates banned military activity on certain days of the week and in certain periods of the year. Those who contravened the Peace would suffer both worldly and spiritual punishments. The Peace was instituted in other parts of France during the eleventh century.[77] Henry of Liège – who was, it should be reiterated, Godfrey's kinsman – was the first bishop in Germany to institute the Peace in his diocese, and historians have rightly recognised this as a significant development.[78] The following pages discuss the significance of Godfrey's involvement in the bishop's efforts.[79]

Henry of Liège seems to have instituted the Peace at an assembly held at Easter 1082.[80] While no contemporary record of the decrees of the Liège Peace assembly survives, the mid-thirteenth-century chronicler Giles of Orval had a copy of them, which he used to write about the assembly.[81] The establishment of the Liège peace influenced other prelates in Germany to make similar institutions. On 20 April 1083, Archbishop Sigewin of Cologne instituted the Peace in his archdiocese, the original decrees of which do survive.[82] Crucially, Giles of Orval's account of the Liège Peace decrees bears a striking resemblance to those issued in Cologne in 1083, indicating that the chronicler used reliable evidence from the Liège Peace assembly.[83] In 1085, the Peace was instituted throughout the whole Empire, and the decrees of that institution likewise survive.[84] Robinson has suggested that this 1085 Peace was directly inspired by those instituted earlier in Liège and Cologne.[85] The evidence provided by Giles of Orval indicates that the Liège Peace prohibited warfare from Advent to Epiphany, and from the Sunday of Septuagesima to the octave of Pentecost. The Peace was also to be observed from Friday morning to Monday morning throughout the year, and on two important local feasts in the diocese (the feast of St Lambert on 17 September and the anniversary of the dedication of the cathedral of Liège on 28 October).[86] The Peace also instituted secular and spiritual sanctions against those who contravened its decrees. Any free man who violated it would lose his patrimony, be deprived of his benefice, and expelled from the diocese. Any serf or cleric who did so would lose all they possessed and have their right hand amputated. Although a free man could request twelve supporters to give testimony that would exculpate him, the non-free figures who violated its terms had to resort to the judgment of God or the testimony of seven (unspecified) persons.[87] Violators of the Peace also risked excommunication.[88] The Peace was supported by a range of Lotharingian nobles, including Albert of Namur, Herman II (count palatine of Lotharingia), and Godfrey of Bouillon, in his capacity as margrave of Antwerp.[89] Henry of Liège no doubt instituted the Peace in his diocese in response to instability which troubled the region after Godfrey the Hunchback's death. Moreover, Henry IV's extended absence on campaign in Italy (from March 1081 to August 1084) created unrest throughout the kingdom of Germany.[90] The institution of the Peace of God in Liège in *c.*1082 signified that by this time episcopal authority in Lower Lotharingia had grown, while ducal authority had diminished.[91] Godfrey's participation in the Peace assembly yields important information on this phase of his career. Firstly, it strongly suggests that he was present in Lotharingia at the time it was held. Secondly, it indicates that his activities continued to align with those of Bishop Henry of Liège. Thirdly, it shows that he was in contact with an ecclesiastical authority which sought to intervene in the lives of armsbearers and impose spiritual sanctions on those who contravened its decrees on the waging of warfare.

Contemporary sources yield a few glimpses into Godfrey's activities in the 1080s. Around 1084, he was required to fulfil his responsibilities as advocate of St Hubert.[92] When Richilde of Mons went to visit her fief of Chévigny after returning from Rome, she was attacked by Count Arnulf II of Chiny. Abbot Thierry granted her refuge at St Hubert, where she stayed for a week. The *Cantatorium* states that her time with the monks there made such an impression on her that she decided to sell Chévigny to St Hubert. On a fixed day at the castle of Fosse, the transfer of Chévigny was carried out by means of a formal ritual. Albert of Namur, acting at the behest of Thierry, provided Richilde and her son Baldwin with safe passage to Fosse. Then, in the presence of Bishop Henry and Godfrey, the transaction took place.[93] After the price was agreed, Richilde and Baldwin relinquished the fief into the hands of Bishop Henry, Abbot Thierry, and Godfrey, the advocate of St Hubert.[94] An act confirming the transfer was drawn up in public, in the presence of Henry and Godfrey, and ratified by suitable witnesses. Thierry then returned to St Hubert, and received 'legal investiture' (*vestituram legalem*) of Chévigny from the hand of Godfrey on the altar dedicated to St Peter.[95] While the author of the *Cantatorium* was chiefly interested with detailing how St Hubert acquired this fief, once again, in doing so, he detailed Godfrey's activities.[96]

In the summer of 1085 Henry IV visited Metz. There, he confiscated Stenay and Mouzay from Matilda of Tuscany, and granted them to Bishop Thierry of Verdun.[97] The nineteenth-century scholar Clouet suggested that it was at this juncture – nearly a decade after Godfrey the Hunchback's death – that Godfrey of Bouillon was named count of Verdun.[98] Clouet surmised that the removal of Matilda's influence in Verdun created a vacancy in the comital office which Godfrey filled. A number of historians writing after Clouet have accepted this suggestion.[99] Mayer, in contrast, exercised rather more caution on the subject of Godfrey's influence in Verdun, questioning the authenticity of the Metz diploma, and pointing out that while Godfrey did hold the office of count of Verdun at the point at which he departed on the First Crusade in 1096, no contemporary source is explicit on precisely when he acquired it. While Henry IV's visit to Metz in 1085 is a plausible juncture, then, it is no more than that.[100] The *Cantatorium* recounts that after Abbot Thierry of St Hubert died on 25 August 1086, Godfrey – once again referred to as *Godefridus Bulloniensis* – and other lords, including Albert of Namur and Arnulf of Chiny, participated in the funeral rites. The monks celebrated mass and chanted psalms for two days before the abbot was buried on 27 August.[101] His successor as abbot was Thierry, prior of St Hubert. Thierry II was elected abbot on the day of his predecessor's burial, and consecrated by Bishop Henry of Liège on 1 September.

The military campaigns of Henry IV of Germany

The foregoing pages examined Godfrey's career in Lotharingia in the decade after the death of his uncle. At this point, the focus shifts to consider the nature of Godfrey's relationship with Henry IV in that period. This is a topic which has been subject to radically diverging interpretations among modern scholars. Writing in 1947, Andressohn characterised Godfrey as a stalwart ally of Henry IV.[102] Following him, many modern historians of the crusades have described Godfrey as an avowed supporter of Henry IV, and suggested that he participated in Henry's military campaigns in the 1070s and 1080s.[103] A close inspection of contemporary sources suggests that in fact the relationship between Godfrey and Henry was more limited than Andressohn concluded. Particularly important evidence on this subject can be gleaned from Henry IV's diplomas, which list high-ranking figures who were in attendance on him at a given moment. Also of use is the testimony of contemporary chroniclers who were well-informed on Henry's activities and political associations. A scrutiny of this evidence suggests that Godfrey had very few dealings with Henry IV in the period between 1076 and 1087. When sources do refer to Godfrey and his whereabouts in this period, it is in relation to events in Lotharingia rather than in the context of Henry's military activities. Modern assessments of Godfrey have overlooked the fact that these contemporary sources are almost silent on his relationship with Henry. While arguments from silence are problematic, the crucial point here is that Henry's political aims in the 1070s and 1080s were such that silence of this kind had a particular significance to contemporaries. If Godfrey regularly attended Henry's court in this period, it would have been recorded. Lampert of Hersfeld discussed at one point in his account how Henry and his intimates approached political interactions with the nobility of Germany in the periods of his reign in which he faced serious opposition. According to Lampert, if a prince did not attend the royal court when he was called, the king might begin to suspect him of being a rebel. For this reason, Lampert states, princes came to Henry's court not because they wanted to, but because they did not want to be branded traitors.[104] As opposition to Henry's rule mounted, Henry sought to attract dukes, counts, and high-ranking ecclesiastical figures to gatherings of his court, in order to convey the impression that he still possessed strong support from the political community. In other words, contemporary sources generally record when prominent figures attended Henry's court because it was in his interests to do so.

Gregory VII's excommunication and deposition of Henry IV in early 1076 had a profound bearing on the subsequent course of his reign. At an assembly at Tribur in October 1076, a portion of the German nobility compelled Henry to promise that he would absolve himself of his excommunication within a year, and threatened to elect another king if Henry did not do so.[105] Bonizo of Sutri recorded that Godfrey the Hunchback was not present at the Tribur assembly because he had recently died, but said nothing of the involvement of Godfrey's successor.[106] It is worth noting that in the period after the Tribur assembly, Henry's key adviser was Bishop Thierry of Verdun, who, as noted above, allied with Matilda of Tuscany against Godfrey of Bouillon after 1076.[107] The demands presented to Henry IV at Tribur precipitated his famous meeting with Gregory VII at Canossa in January 1077.[108] Though the king seemingly recovered his position at Canossa, some members of the German nobility continued to call for his deposition. In March 1077, a number of them met in Forchheim and declared that Henry IV was deposed, before electing Duke Rudolf of Swabia as 'king' of Germany. Rudolf was inaugurated in Mainz on 26 March. Rudolf and his supporters, however, had overestimated the scale of their support. After Henry returned to Germany from Canossa, the anti-king and his associates were confined to Saxony.[109]

Though Rudolf of Swabia could not exert any influence outside Saxony, Henry knew that he needed to defeat his rival before his kingship was further undermined. Between 1077 and 1080, Henry fought a number of battles as part of a concerted military campaign against Rudolf and his allies.[110] They fought in August 1077 at Würzburg, in August 1078 at Mellrichstadt, and in January 1080 at Flarcheim. The campaign culminated in a battle fought close to Hohenmölsen near the river Elster on 15 October 1080. Though Henry IV's forces were defeated in the battle, Rudolf was mortally wounded during it. Both Frutolf of Michelsberg and the anonymous author of Henry's *Vita* report that during the fighting Rudolf lost his right hand, that is, the hand with which he had earlier sworn fealty to Henry.[111] Bruno of Merseburg claims that Rudolf suffered two injuries in the battle: one which was disfiguring (the loss of his hand) and another which was mortal (a serious wound which extended from his stomach down to his groin).[112] Rudolf died from his injuries, either on the evening of the battle or the following day.[113] His death denuded the Saxon rebellion against Henry IV of much of its momentum.

No source written before about 1105 states that Godfrey of Bouillon was present among Henry IV's forces in the battle on the Elster.[114] Contemporaries do specify that Lotharingians fought on the royal side. William of Apulia, who wrote in the 1090s, claimed that Lotharingians had taken part in the battle on Henry's side, without identifying any individual from the region.[115] Bruno of Merseburg noted that the Lotharingian Count Henry of Laach was among the royal forces at the battle, and Robinson has asserted that the Lotharingians who took part were under his command.[116] While some sources do place Godfrey at the battle of the Elster, crucially, they were all composed many years after the First Crusade.[117] Modern historians including Breysig, Andressohn, and Aubé nevertheless accepted those non-contemporary sources as evidence for Godfrey's participation.[118] Dorchy, on the other hand, asserted that Godfrey had been fighting to defend his inheritance from Albert of Namur and others since 1076, and had therefore remained in the region of Bouillon in the era in which Henry IV campaigned against Rudolf of Swabia.[119] Given the silence of contemporary sources on Godfrey's involvement, the latter position is the more convincing.

On 7 March 1080 Gregory VII again declared that Henry IV was excommunicated and deposed, and affirmed his support for Rudolf of Swabia.[120] In response, Henry resolved to deal with Gregory once and for all.[121] After he concluded his campaign against Rudolf and the Saxon rebels, Henry departed for Italy, where he arrived in March 1081. He would remain there until his return to Germany in August 1084. While he was in Italy, Henry divided his time between besieging Rome with the aim of unseating Gregory, attacking his enemies in northern Italy (the most important of which was Matilda of Tuscany), and campaigning in the south.[122] Henry's troops first reached Rome in May 1081, but they were unable to make any progress in capturing the city. He thus spent the summer and autumn of that year in northern Italy. By the end of February 1082, he was again camped before Rome, and he stayed there during Lent. The onset of warmer weather prompted him to depart for the north in order to campaign in Tuscany. In November he was once again at Rome, and he remained there in the ensuing months. In June 1083, his forces captured the Leonine city, although the old city remained under Gregory's control. Henry built a fortress on the Palatine Hill, and then departed Rome to spend the late summer and autumn in Tuscany. After Henry left, Rome's summer heat caused death and disease among the soldiers he had placed in the new Palatine fortress. In February and early March 1084, Henry was in the south of Italy, attacking Robert Guiscard, Gregory's ally. He returned to Rome and ceremonially entered the city on 21 March. Three days later, on Palm Sunday, he had Archbishop Wibert of Ravenna enthroned as Clement III. A week later, on Easter Sunday, Clement inaugurated Henry as emperor in St Peter's.[123] Henry remained in Rome until the approach of a Norman army prompted him to depart on 21 May. The new emperor remained in Italy for two months, before he returned to Germany in August 1084.

In contrast to the sources for Henry IV's earlier campaign against Rudolf of Swabia, one near-contemporary author claims that Godfrey took part in Henry's Italian campaign of 1081–1084. Albert of Aachen – whose account of the First Crusade features prominently in the following chapters – claims that Godfrey took part in one of Henry IV's assaults on Rome. According to Albert, in 1098, amidst a particularly arduous phase of the siege of Antioch during the First Crusade, disease spread among the crusaders, reminding Godfrey of the suffering endured by Henry IV's troops at Rome:

> Duke Godfrey left Antioch, fearing that this was the same illness which he remembered had afflicted Rome long ago with a very similar disaster when he was on an expedition with King Henry IV . . . in which five hundred of the strongest soldiers and many nobles had died during the

plague-bearing month of August, and many had been terrified and had left the city along with the emperor himself.[124]

Albert's claim regarding the spread of disease in Rome is broadly compatible with that of Frutolf of Michelsberg, who states that at the height of summer 1083, some of the troops Henry had placed to garrison the fort on the Palatine Hill perished on account of the warm climate.[125] On balance, however, it is difficult to accept Albert's claims as authentic. While Albert provides a wealth of original information concerning Godfrey's exploits on the First Crusade, this passage concerning the siege of Rome represents his only substantial reference to Godfrey's life before his departure on the expedition. Since one of Albert's principal aims in writing his account was to emphasise the German contribution to the First Crusade, the aim of this passage was probably to cast Godfrey as a member of the nobility of the kingdom of Germany. More significantly, Henry IV issued over thirty diplomas during his three-year campaign in Italy. Godfrey does not appear in a single one of these documents, which strongly suggests that he was not present at Henry's court in that period.[126]

In addition to this, evidence provided in the *Cantatorium* – that is, the passage which relates Godfrey's conflicts with Thierry of Veluwe and Albert of Namur – suggests that Godfrey was in Lotharingia around 1081–1082.[127] Moreover, the author of the *Cantatorium* noted at one point that Henry IV attacked Rome and installed Clement III as pope, but made no mention of Godfrey participating in those events. It is reasonable to suppose that if one of the most important secular lords in the diocese of Liège had been present during those momentous events, the St Hubert chronicler would not have neglected to mention it.[128] Also relevant to this question is the evidence which places Godfrey at Bishop Henry of Liège's Peace assembly in the diocese, which probably took place at Easter 1082. The equivocal evidence of Godfrey's presence in Henry's campaign in Italy has precipitated differing interpretations among modern historians.[129] While the possibility should not be ruled out that Godfrey did participate in at least part of the campaign – perhaps in his capacity of margrave of Antwerp – the silence of sources emanating from Henry's circles seems fairly conclusive.

Godfrey's career as duke of Lower Lotharingia, 1087–1095

One school of thought, reflected in the work of Breysig and Dorchy, suggests that Godfrey was so successful in his efforts to protect his inheritance in Lotharingia after 1076 that he effectively acquired the authority associated with office of duke of Lower Lotharingia in the early 1080s. These historians suggest that Godfrey had come to hold the ducal office in practice – if not in title – by about 1082. In support of this argument, they cite a number of charters which they dated to the early to mid-1080s in which Godfrey is styled as duke. Dorchy also highlighted a passage in the *Cantatorium* which refers to Godfrey as duke in relation to an event which took place in 1084.[130] However, in a critical study, Despy conclusively demonstrated that the charters in question are either false or highly suspect, and pointed out that the chronology of the *Cantatorium* is too unreliable for the passage in question to be used as evidence for Godfrey's acquisition of the ducal title by 1084.[131]

Contemporary evidence makes it clear that Godfrey was finally appointed duke of Lower Lotharingia in 1087.[132] Henry IV gathered together much of the nobility of the kingdom of Germany at an assembly at Aachen in May of that year. On that occasion, Godfrey was present at the royal court. He is listed in his capacity as margrave of Antwerp in a diploma issued at the assembly. The document also records the presence at Aachen of Albert of Namur and Henry IV's son Conrad, the duke of Lower Lotharingia, who by now was thirteen years old.[133] This was Conrad's last appearance as duke in a royal diploma. During this visit, Henry had Conrad inaugurated king of Germany in a ceremony held on 30 May in Aachen Cathedral. Conrad's appointment to the kingship created a vacancy in the office of duke of Lower Lotharingia. On the same day, or shortly after it, Henry IV appointed Godfrey to succeed Conrad as duke. The monastic annalist who wrote at St James in Liège described these events in succinct terms: 'The boy Conrad, the son of Emperor Henry, was made king at Aachen, and Margrave Godfrey was made duke'.[134] A number of sources indicate that Godfrey held the title of duke from 1087. A charter recording Bishop Henry of Liège's donation of the allod of Bras to St Hubert refers to Godfrey as 'duke and advocate' of that monastery. Though the document purports to date to 1082, Despy argues that the text of the document was altered in 1087.[135] Bishop Conrad of Utrecht issued a charter on 1 November 1087 to confirm the privileges for the cathedral of St Martin, and the witness list of that document refers to Godfrey as duke.[136] In late 1088, Heldebold, a monk of St Trond, issued a charter whose dating clause relates that at that time Godfrey held the ducal office.[137] The *Cantatorium* refers to Godfrey as duke in relation to an event which took place in 1088.[138] The genealogy of the counts of Boulogne states that Godfrey was 'now duke of Lotharingia', which might be interpreted as a sign that this he had only recently acquired the office when the genealogy was written.[139] Sigebert of Gembloux, however, wrote that Godfrey gained the office of duke in the year 1089. Under that year in his account, he asserted that 'Godfrey, nephew of Godfrey the Hunchback, was at last [*tandem*] given the ducal office of Lotharingia'.[140] The use of the term *tandem* in this passage was a subtle rebuke of Henry IV for overlooking Godfrey for the office in 1076. Several modern scholars, including Meyer von Knonau and Robinson, have accepted Sigebert's claim that Godfrey was appointed duke in 1089.[141] Given the weight of the available evidence, however, there can be little doubt that 1087 is the correct date. Like the author of the *Cantatorium*, Sigebert sometimes confused his chronology.[142]

Godfrey retained his office of margrave of Antwerp after his appointment as duke in 1087, issuing charters in which he was styled 'duke and margrave'.[143] Godfrey also used a seal which attributed both titles to him. A now-lost charter of 1096 which carried the seal of Ida and those of her sons Eustace and Godfrey was seen in the seventeenth century by Van Riedwijck, who produced drawings of all three seals.[144] In 1846 De Ram published a study of Godfrey's seal using Van Riedwijck's drawings.[145] In the 1940s, Martens found another reproduction of the 1096 act and its seals produced by Regaus in the late eighteenth century. Martens compared the Van Riedwijck and Regaus images and concluded that they portray what was an authentic example of Godfrey's seal.[146] De Ram's reproduction of Van Riedwijck's drawing of Godfrey's seal clearly records its form and appearance (see Figure 2.1). Above all, the seal emphasises Godfrey's status as a warrior. The seal is circular, and depicts Godfrey as a mounted warrior, with his horse captured in mid-gallop. Godfrey is portrayed wearing armour and a helmet. In his left hand he holds a round shield, and in his right a long lance bearing at its tip a fluttering banner, which he points ahead. Around the image of the mounted Godfrey is a circular inscription which reads: GODEFRIDUS: GRA[TIA] D[E]I DUX ET MARCHIO ('Godfrey, by the

Figure 2.1 Godfrey of Bouillon's seal (from Pierre de Ram, 'Notice sur un sceau inédit de Godefroi de Bouillon', *Bulletin de l'académie royale des sciences, des lettres et des beaux-arts de Belgique*, 13 (1846), 355–600, annexe, plate 1)

grace of God, Duke and Margrave'). This equestrian image is entirely typical of seals used by aristocrats in the latter half of the eleventh century.[147] Indeed, De Ram's illustrations of the seals appended to the 1096 charter indicate that Godfrey's own brother Eustace adopted a similar image on the seal he used as count of Boulogne. After William of Normandy obtained the throne of England in 1066, he adopted a seal which depicted him on its obverse as duke of Normandy, using an equestrian image which closely resembles that depicted on Godfrey's.[148]

Henry IV spent the spring and summer of 1089 in Lotharingia. He was in Cologne in August for his wedding to his second wife, Eupraxia of Kiev, and her ensuing inauguration as queen.[149] During this visit to Lotharingia, Henry hosted a gathering of the royal court at Metz on 5 April. A diploma issued at that point shows that Godfrey was present at Henry's court in his capacity of duke of Lower Lotharingia.[150] This is Godfrey's last appearance in a royal diploma. Not one document issued after this point records that he attended Henry IV's court, even during gatherings held when the emperor was in Lotharingia. While Godfrey obviously owed his appointment to Henry, the contemporary sources do not convey the sense that the former repaid the latter for the bestowal of the office with concerted political support after 1087. Given the propensity of the other dukes of Germany to participate in rebellions against Henry's rule, the emperor may simply have been content to appoint a duke who, while he was not an active supporter, was not an active opponent either. Since there is no indication that Godfrey was hostile to Henry, he may well have regarded the appointment as a successful one.

While in 1087 Godfrey attained the office that had been so closely associated with his family throughout the eleventh century, very little is recorded about his career as duke.[151] Prominent figures in the region did recognise his authority as duke; for example, in May 1091 Baldwin of Mons, count of Hainaut issued a charter whose dating clause indicates that it was written in the time when Godfrey held the ducal office.[152] But such references to Godfrey are rare, and reveal nothing of Godfrey's own activities. The lack of information on Godfrey in contemporary written record must signal that his career as duke was not an especially auspicious one. When the evidence from this period does detail his actions for the years between 1087 and 1095, he is generally mentioned in a manner which suggest his activities were largely confined to his personal holdings around Bouillon, and to the offices he had held before his appointment as duke, particularly that of advocate of St Hubert.

In 1088, Godfrey was in the company of Abbot Thierry II of St Hubert the castle of Thuin during negotiations with Baldwin of Mons (the son of Richilde of Mons) over the fief of Chévigny, which St Hubert had acquired from the comital house in *c.*1084.[153] In the same year, Godfrey travelled to the abbey of Prüm, which was in Upper Lotharingia, but which lay close to Lower Lotharingia. The purpose of his visit was to secure an agreement for the transfer of the church of Chévigny from Prüm to St Hubert. The discussions were conducted by the abbots and the advocates of the respective houses: Godfrey for St Hubert, and Berthold of Hamm for Prüm.[154] A charter shows that in 1091 Godfrey acted as a witness alongside a number of ecclesiastical and secular figures when Bishop Henry of Liège approved the foundation of a hospice and an oratory dedicated to St Matthew at the abbey of Flône.[155] A letter apparently sent to Godfrey in the early 1090s offers hints about his political connections in that era. The author of the letter identified himself only as 'A.', and the recipient as 'his most dear son G.' (*Dilectissimo filio G.*). In the letter, 'A.' praises 'G.' for his qualities and conduct in military affairs, and compared him favourably to other nobles who sought only to increase their own authority. Morin, who published an edition of this letter in 1922, suggested at that point that the sender was Archbishop Anselm of Canterbury, and its recipient was Godfrey. He noted the long-standing epistolary connection between Anselm and the comital house of Boulogne, and detected similarities between the letter and other missives authored by Anselm.[156] However, in 1930 Morin revised his argument and suggested that the 'A.' who sent the letter was not Anselm, but was instead Adalberon, the former associate of Godfrey the Hunchback. As previously noted, Adalberon had spent time in the younger Godfrey's company before being appointed abbot of St Vincent of Laon.[157] If Godfrey was indeed the 'G.' to whom this letter was addressed, his connections extended beyond Lotharingia and the kingdom of Germany, either to Anselm in England or to Adalberon in the archdiocese of Rheims.

The best-documented episode in Godfrey's career as duke centred upon his involvement in a crisis which reverberated throughout the diocese of Liège in the early 1090s. This episode is described in great detail in the *Cantatorium*. After Henry IV's return from Italy in 1084, he pursued a policy of appointing staunch allies to episcopal offices throughout the Empire. Simultaneously, he attempted to forestall the appointment of candidates favoured by Gregory VII and his successors.[158] After Bishop Henry of Liège died on 31 March 1091, the emperor implemented this policy. When the post became vacant, the emperor was on campaign in Italy, having left Germany in the spring of 1090.[159] Though he was absent from the kingdom, Henry named Otbert, the provost of St Cross in Liège, as his appointee to the episcopal office. Accordingly, Otbert was consecrated by the archbishop of Cologne early in 1092. Like Henry of Liège before him, Otbert proved to be an ardent supporter of Henry IV. His appointment caused disquiet in the diocese, however. The author of the *Cantatorium*, whose abbey suffered greatly at the hands of Otbert, states that Henry of Liège had previously expelled Otbert from the diocese, and that the new bishop had obtained the office not through canonical election but by buying it from Henry IV.[160] Otbert soon began to intervene in ecclesiastical affairs in the diocese with the aim of advancing Henry's interests. The information contained in the

Cantatorium regarding Godfrey's involvement in this episode is crucial for understanding this phase of his career.[161]

The *Cantatorium* states that very soon after Otbert was consecrated bishop, he caused alarm by attempting to depose Abbot Berenger of St Laurent and Abbot Lanzon of St Trond and replace them with 'pseudoabbots' named Wobold (at St Laurent) and Lupon (at St Trond). These two prelates were reportedly convicted criminals whom Henry of Liège had earlier excommunicated, and who had apparently promised to pay Henry IV in return for obtaining these offices.[162] According to the St Hubert chronicler, the very day Otbert returned to Liège after his consecration at Cologne, he demanded that Berenger resign the abbacy in order to allow Wobold to assume it. Berenger refused to do so, however, and instead went to Otbert to complain publicly of the injustice. Berenger quickly spread word of Otbert's disreputable activities among other ecclesiastical houses in the diocese. However, his position at St Laurent became untenable and so he was forced to flee. Abbot Thierry II, 'preferring to offend Otbert rather than God', granted Berenger sanctuary at St Hubert. Both abbots quickly resolved to leave St Hubert to escape Otbert's clutches, and so went to discuss the affair with the archbishop of Rheims, Renaud du Bellay.[163] In the aftermath of Thierry II's flight, Otbert attempted to install Ingobrand, a monk of St Peter's in Lobbes, as the new abbot of St Hubert.[164] In the ensuing period, the monks of St Hubert decided to send some of the abbey's revenues to Thierry II and other exiled associates. The chronicler states that Godfrey, the duke of Lower Lotharingia, and Thierry II, the duke of Upper Lotharingia, instructed their men not to interfere with that arrangement.[165] Ingobrand accordingly complained to Otbert about the loss of some of St Hubert's revenues, and Otbert went in turn to Godfrey, the abbey's advocate, to enquire why they were being diverted. Godfrey replied that the revenues of St Hubert belonged to its monks, and that it was Otbert who had disrupted its financial prosperity by attempting to overthrow Thierry II, the legitimate abbot, and install Ingobrand in his place.[166] Godfrey may also have profited at Otbert's expense around this time. The *Cantatorium* states that a certain man from Bouillon (*quidam Bullonienses*) and some companions hid in a forest near Grupont and attacked a convoy of twelve carts carrying Otbert's provisions, before taking their cargo for themselves.[167] Though the author did not explicitly link this to Godfrey, the fact that the culprit was from Bouillon implies the author thought Godfrey was at least partially culpable.

Malcontent with Otbert's episcopacy came to a head in the first part of 1095. In that period, a dispute arose between Otbert and Count Godfrey of Louvain. The latter had reportedly attacked the city of Liège on several occasions. This prompted Otbert to call together the princes of the diocese to wage a military campaign against the count. On the assigned day, the princes assembled in Liège to deliberate how to proceed. Otbert declared that he had excommunicated Godfrey of Louvain, prompting Godfrey of

Bouillon to intervene in the count's defence. According to the *Cantato-rium*, 'Duke Godfrey, smiling' (*dux Godefridus irridens*), related to Otbert that Godfrey of Louvain had already informed him about the sentence of excommunication, but affirmed to the bishop that the sentence would only stand if Abbot Thierry II of St Hubert confirmed it, or if Otbert absolved Thierry II. Godfrey reputedly stated that if neither eventuality occurred, he would consider Otbert excommunicated from the universal Church. God-frey's words provoked Otbert to fly into a rage, and the bishop declaimed that he would not suffer such a humiliation by the princes, before lambast-ing them for lacking respect for the Holy Virgin, St Lambert, and his own episcopal authority. The princes, led by Godfrey of Bouillon, and including other lords such as Albert of Namur, Cono of Mons, and Arnulf of Chiny, were offended by Otbert's reproach. They responded that, on the contrary, they remained faithful to the Holy Virgin and St Lambert, and that if they had been negligent in their faith, it was because they had failed properly to investigate the causes of the problems wracking the diocese. The nobles unanimously insisted that Thierry II ought to be granted a public audience to answer the charges against him. The exiled abbots sought this so that they could air their grievances against Otbert before the most prominent figures of the diocese. Though Otbert was 'stupefied' (*obstupuit*) by this demand, he reluctantly agreed to set a day to hear the abbot's case. How-ever, when it came to it, Otbert was unwilling to provide Thierry II with safe passage to the hearing. The result of all this was that many in the diocese began to regard Otbert's actions as unjust and dishonourable. At last, the St Hubert chronicler states, Otbert promised to take counsel with Duke Godfrey and reach a conclusion in accordance with his advice.[168]

When Thierry II received word of these developments, he resolved to return to the diocese of Liège. He contacted a number of prelates in the region, including Archdeacon Paul of Metz and Berenger of St Laurent, who was himself in exile at Évernicourt (in the diocese of Laon). Thierry II went to Dudo of Cons, who accompanied him to a meeting with Godfrey in Bouillon. The abbot asked Godfrey about his safe conduct to Liège, and Godfrey responded that he had often discussed the matter with Otbert, but that the bishop had evaded giving a firm answer. Godfrey said that on the next day, he would take Dudo of Cons with him to a colloquium with Otbert at Villance, and report back to the abbot. At Villance, Otbert told Godfrey that he knew Thierry II was supported in the diocese, and how unhappy the people of Liège were that figures from outside the diocese – figures such as Archdeacon Paul of Metz – had become involved in the matter. Otbert affirmed to Godfrey that he was determined to avoid a public hear-ing of Thierry's case. Godfrey and Otbert thus came to an agreement; the bishop doubled the (unspecified) sum of money he had earlier promised to Godfrey, while Godfrey agreed that on the day of Thierry's hearing (29 June – the feast of the Apostles Peter and Paul), he would be away from the diocese with Count Arnulf of Chiny, instead travelling to Rheims, to confer with Archbishop Renaud over Arnulf's earlier attack on the castle of Mouzon.[169] Godfrey's convenient absence from the hearing was intended to work in Otbert's favour. The author of the *Cantatorium* stated that through Otbert and Godfrey's shady deal, 'malignant impiety united with avarice to crush the truth'.[170]

Dudo of Cons realised that the bishop and the duke had conspired against Thierry II, and so he went to the abbot and informed him what had happened at Villance. Thierry was gravely wounded by Godfrey's actions, and wrote to Berenger to inform him that 'their hope had been frustrated by Otbert and the duke'.[171] Berenger was indignant, and at once wrote a letter intended for circulation among the high clergy of the diocese of Liège. He then went to Rheims, whence Godfrey had already travelled. According to the author of the *Cantatorium*, in that place, the abbot subtly rebuked Godfrey for his deal with Otbert. He spoke to Godfrey about the injuries being done to the Church by Otbert, and accused the bishop of forestalling Thierry's hearing. Berenger then praised Godfrey, along with the other princes of the diocese, for attempting to compel Otbert to hold the hearing. At this underserved praise, the chronicler states, Godfrey blushed profusely, for by giving it the abbot had pricked his conscience. Archbishop Renaud then intervened to ask why Godfrey and the other protectors of monasteries in the diocese left them to ruin, when they could easily compel Otbert to follow their will, either by violence or persuasion. The chronicler states that Godfrey was moved by the archbishop's words, and promised that he would begin working to defend the Church and restore the legitimate abbots. 'In this way', the chronicler asserts, 'divine providence brought forth mercy'.[172]

Significantly, Berenger's epistolary activities around this time extended beyond Liège to the highest level of the Church. He was in communication over the Otbert affair with Pope Urban II. One letter on the matter sent between the two has survived. At some point between 1093 and 1095, possibly at the time of the council of Piacenza in March 1095, Urban II wrote a letter of support to Berenger, encouraging him to maintain his commitment to reform and castigating 'the Antichrist's standard-bearer' (*Antichristi signifer*) Otbert for his simoniacal activities.[173]

In July 1095, Otbert resolved to attack the castle of Clermont-lez-Nandrin, which was located midway between Huy and Liège. The garrison of that castle was causing problems by interfering with the navigation of the Meuse between those two towns. Otbert commenced a siege upon the castle – he seems to have initially had his own troops under his command – before calling on Godfrey and the other princes of the diocese to provide assistance.[174] Soon after Godfrey arrived at Clermont-lez-Nandrin, he scolded Otbert, and affirmed that he could not provide counsel or support unless the bishop restored St Hubert and St Laurent to their proper states by expelling the prelates who had bought their abbacies, and restoring Thierry and Berenger, who had been legitimately ordained to those offices. According to the St Hubert chronicler, Godfrey then made an impassioned speech to those assembled in support of the exiled abbots:

> What assistance, fellow warriors [*commilitones*], can we hope for from God, we who, while His churches are perishing, not only do not come to their defence, but do not even put forward any word of objection? Certainly the most benign plan of the Creator has deserved this much of us, having constituted us ministers of His realm, that each of us individually refuse [Otbert] our service, we who were chosen by His general dominion to protect His law in this our time.[175]

While it is unlikely that the chronicler knew the precise words spoken by Godfrey during the siege of Clermont-lez-Nandrin, this passage suggests that he did publicly intervene on behalf of Thierry and Berenger at this juncture. The chronicler states that Godfrey's speech was interrupted by the other princes, who began to voice their assent to the conditions he had imposed upon Otbert. The matter was decided when some prelates present at the siege provided evidence of Otbert's simoniacal dealings. The bishop had no choice but to relent. He agreed to expel Wobold and Ingobrand, and restore Berenger and Thierry to their abbeys.[176] Soon after, Otbert and Berenger were reconciled publicly in a ceremony held in Liège, in the presence of 'Duke Godfrey and the principle inhabitants of the city'.[177] Thierry II, hearing of these developments, returned to St Hubert. After his return to the abbey, peace with Otbert was brokered by Berenger and Henry, archdeacon of Liège.[178] Otbert circulated a letter to the clergy of the diocese, attempting to defend his actions. At one point in that letter he asserted that he had acted on the 'advice of Duke Godfrey and other wise men'.[179] Nevertheless, the return of the two abbots to their houses brought to an end a crisis which had destabilised the diocese of Liège since the death of Bishop Henry.

Godfrey's actions during the crisis in Liège, and above all, his inertia during the early stages of the conflict, have provoked varied assessments by modern historians. Aubé drew the exceedingly unconvincing argument that Godfrey's ultimate motive was the maintenance of peace in the diocese, and it was in the pursuit of that goal that he attempted to remain neutral to avoid undermining Otbert's episcopal authority and thereby further destabilising the diocese.[180] Cauchie believed that during this episode Godfrey acted out of self-interest rather than any particular devotion to either side.[181] The latter interpretation correlates more closely with the account provided in the *Cantatorium*. Otbert's expulsion of St Hubert's canonically elected abbot did not immediately spur Godfrey, the advocate of the abbey, into defending its interests. Godfrey initially turned a blind eye to Otbert's activities, and it was only when he was rebuked by the exiled Abbot Berenger that he finally began to intervene meaningfully in the affair. After that point, Godfrey sided with Abbots Thierry II and Berenger (the latter of whom Urban II regarded as a stalwart supporter of reform) against Otbert, the creature of Henry IV. Crucially, Godfrey's repeated and public criticism of Otbert, coupled with his eventual support for the deposed abbots, confirm that he was no ardent stooge of Henry IV when it came to implementing imperial policy in the diocese of Liège.

The *Cantatorium*'s account of the crisis in the diocese of Liège in the early 1090s represents the only substantial information on Godfrey's activities at that time. There is only fleeting information on the rest of his doings in this period. In a charter drawn up at Bouillon in 1093, Godfrey confirmed that the rights of the church of St Dagobert at Stenay belonged to the abbey of Gorze. The church had earlier been appropriated by Count Arnulf of Chiny, who was forced by Godfrey to compensate Gorze.[182] In 1094 Godfrey issued a confirmation charter for the priory of St Peter at Bouillon. In that document, Godfrey noted that his grandfather Godfrey the Bearded had earlier assigned the priory to St Hubert. Godfrey of Bouillon stated that his confirmation was supported by his mother, Ida, and his brothers, Baldwin and Eustace. What is perhaps most revealing about this charter is that Godfrey describes himself as 'Godfrey, legitimate successor and heir of Duke Godfrey the Bearded, and his son, the most powerful and just Duke Godfrey, my uncle'.[183] Evidently, as late as 1094, about eighteen years after the death of Godfrey the Hunchback in 1076 and about nine years after his own appointment as duke in 1087, Godfrey of Bouillon was anxious to assert his legitimacy through his connection to his uncle and grandfather. In 1095, Godfrey acted as a witness when Count Henry of Louvain issued a document approving the donation of Incourt to Flône.[184] Godfrey seems to have been at Huy on 15 August 1095 in order to mediate a dispute between the monks and nuns of the abbey of Andenne and their advocate, Walter of Dun. Also present at this meeting were Otbert of Liège, Albert of Namur, and a number of other nobles from both Upper and Lower Lotharingia. The inmates of Andenne accused Walter of Dun of making exactions against the abbey's fief at Sassey (located halfway between Bouillon and Verdun). A charter was drawn up to record the resolution of the dispute. Its dating clause states that it was written 'in the time when Godfrey was holding the ducal office of the kingdom of the Lotharingians and administering the march [of Antwerp], and he himself was present'.[185] At the end of 1095, at some point between 24 September and 31 December, Godfrey helped to end a lengthy dispute between the abbeys of Stavelot and St Adalbert of Aachen. Godfrey, acting as the advocate of St Adalbert, and Albert of Namur, holding the same role for Stavelot, had agreed that the matter should be settled by a judicial duel between champions. With Godfrey and Albert present, St Adalbert's warrior defeated that of Stavelot. Abbot Rudolf of Stavelot wrote an account of the episode, in which he referred to Godfrey as 'Duke Godfrey of Bouillon, son of Eustace of Boulogne'.[186] Godfrey's involvement in this small-scale and highly localised activity encapsulates the character of his wider career as duke of Lower Lotharingia. In contrast to his predecessors Godfrey the

Bearded and Godfrey the Hunchback, the career of Godfrey of Bouillon as duke of Lower Lotharingia played out within more narrow horizons.

Notes

1 On this, see: Andressohn, *Godfrey*, p. 27; Aubé, *Godefroy*, p. 31.
2 'genuit ex ea [Ida] tres filios, Eustachium et Godefridum . . . et Balduinum'. *Genealogia Comitum Buloniensium*, p. 301. For the birth dates of the three sons, see: Andressohn, *Godfrey*, p. 27; Aubé, *Godefroy*, pp. 29–30; Mayer, 'Baudouin Ier', pp. 18–20, 22.
3 Eustace II's brother, Godfrey (d.1095), was bishop of Paris from 1061 and chancellor to King Philip I of France. Tanner, *Families*, pp. 97, 103 and 290 (a genealogical table). On the importance of the name to the house of Ardennes-Bouillon, see: Murray, *Crusader Kingdom*, p. 6. Cf. Andressohn, *Godfrey*, p. 28, who concludes that Eustace II and Ida named their second son after Ida's father, Godfrey the Bearded.
4 On what follows, see: Matthew Bennett, 'Military Masculinity in England and Northern France, c.1050–c.1225', in Dawn M. Hadley (ed.), *Masculinity in Medieval Europe* (London, 1999), pp. 71–88, esp. pp. 73–9.
5 On the equipment used by mounted warriors in this era, see: Ian Peirce, 'The Knight, His Arms and Armour in the Eleventh and Twelfth Centuries', in Christopher Harper-Bill and Ruth Harvey (eds), *The Ideals and Practice of Medieval Knighthood* (Woodbridge, 1986), pp. 152–64.
6 On Godfrey's proficiency, see: France, *Victory*, p. 49. On the use of bows in warfare in general at this time, see: Jim Bradbury, *The Medieval Archer* (Woodbridge, 1985), esp. pp. 1–38.
7 *Gesta Guillelmi*, pp. 6–7.
8 See above, p. 25. Some modern historians are content to describe rituals such as these as the act of 'knighting', though others are wary of using that term to refer to ceremonies carried out before about 1100. On this, see: Jean Flori, 'Les origines de l'adoubement chevaleresque: étude des remises d'armes et du vocabulaire qui les exprime dans les sources historiques latines jusqu'au début du XIIIe siècle', *Traditio*, 35 (1979), 209–72; Max Lieberman, 'A New Approach to the Knighting Ritual', *Speculum*, 90 (2015), 391–423.
9 'Gotefrido, consobrino Gozelonis ducis, filio Eustachii comitis, impigro et ad rem militarem acerrimo adolescenti'. Lampert, p. 350, tr. 310. This description may be a topos: the same chronicler uses not dissimilar vocabulary to describe Godfrey the Bearded in 1044 and Godfrey the Hunchback in 1069: Lampert, pp. 44, 122, tr. pp. 54, 126. The suggestion that Godfrey was born around 1060 is extrapolated from Lampert's description of him in 1076. See: Mayer, 'Baudouin Ier', p. 22.
10 'tenerrimae aetatis infantulo'. Lampert, p. 112, tr. p. 115.
11 'puer adhuc infra militares annos'. Lampert, p. 180, tr. p. 176.
12 Berthold II, pp. 103–4, tr. p. 146.
13 'Godefrido adolescenti, quem avunculus adhuc vivens adoptaverat heredem sibi'. *Cantatorium*, p. 100.
14 For example: 'On his death-bed Godfrey [the Hunchback] formally designated as heir his nephew Godfrey'. Murray, *Crusader Kingdom*, p. 8; 'In his last moments [Godfrey the Hunchback] designated his nephew, Godfrey of Bouillon, as his heir'. Andressohn, *Godfrey*, p. 18. Cf. Aubé, *Godefroy*, p. 56; Mayer, 'Baudouin Ier', p. 21.
15 See above, pp. 30–1, and 31, n. 157.

16 'Morabatur tunc junior Godefridus marchio cum illo [Henry] . . . ejusdem episcopi tuebatur patrocinio'. *Cantatorium*, pp. 91–2; Aubé, *Godefroy*, p. 57. Lampert
of Hersfeld had described Henry of Liège as a close relative of Godfrey the
Hunchback: Lampert, p. 300, tr. p. 270.

17 'junior Godefridus . . . avunculi sui destitutus auxilio'. *Cantatorium*, pp. 91–2.

18 *Cantatorium*, p. 92, n. *a*.

19 *Cantatorium*, pp. 99–102. This text reports that Adalberon and Godfrey the
Hunchback had become close friends after the latter returned from Italy, which
must denote his journey there in 1072–1073. See above, pp. 30–1.

20 Murray, *Crusader Kingdom*, pp. 209–10.

21 Aubé, *Godefroy*, pp. 45–7, is less cautious on this point, stating that 'Godefroy . . .
complétait son éducation chevaleresque dans l'entourage ducal, sans doute à
Bouillon'.

22 *Gesta Guillelmi*, pp. 182–3; Tanner, *Families*, pp. 100 and 130.

23 'innatam sibi utriusque linguę peritiam'. Frutolf 1106, p. 158, tr. p. 158.

24 On this phase of Godfrey's career see: Kurt Breysig, 'Gottfried von Bouillon vor
dem Kreuzzüge', *Westdeutsche Zeitschrift für Geschichte und Kunst*, 17 (1898), 169–
201; Herman Vanderlinden, 'La date de la nomination de Godefroid de Bouillon comme duc de Lotharingie (1087)', *Bulletin de la commission royale d'histoire*,
90 (1926), 189–92; Dorchy, 'Godefroid'; Georges Despy, 'La date de l'accession
de Godefroid de Bouillon au duché de Basse-Lotharingie', *RBPH*, 36 (1958),
1275–84; Mayer, 'Baudouin Ier'.

25 Andressohn, *Godfrey*, pp. 28–46.

26 Dorchy, 'Godefroid'; Despy, 'La date de l'accession'; Murray, *Crusader Kingdom*,
pp. 20–6.

27 Robinson, *Henry IV*, pp. 147–9.

28 'Godefridus dux et decus Galliae a sicario perimitur. Godefridus filius sororis
eius marchio subrogatur. Cuonradus puer filius Heinrici regis dux substituitur'.
Annales S. Iacobi Leodiensis, p. 639.

29 'Rex . . . Pascha Traiecti celebravit, ibique ducatum Lotheringiae filio suo Coun-
rado, marcham vero quae dicitur Antwerpha Gotefrido, consobrino Gozelonis
ducis, filio Eustachii comitis . . . tradidit'. Lampert, p. 350, tr. p. 310.

30 'dux Gotifridus . . . Cuius marcham sororis suae filius equivocus illius quadraginta libris auri vix emptam a rege possedit, ducatu, quem sibi iam avunculus
prestitum ab eo [Henry] acquisivit, iniuste privatus. Cui filium suum vix bien-
nem rex presidere fecit'. Berthold II, pp. 102–4, tr. p. 146.

31 Robinson, *Henry IV*, pp. 147–8; Andressohn, *Godfrey*, p. 33.

32 Robinson, *Henry IV*, p. 148, n. 27.

33 Breysig, 'Gottfried', p. 181; Dorchy, 'Godefroid', p. 963.

34 Robinson, *Henry IV*, pp. 35–6. Henry's mother also appointed Rudolf of Rheinfelden duke of Swabia in 1057, and Berthold of Zähringen duke of Carinthia in
1061. Both of these men would rebel against her son in 1077.

35 Weinfurter, *Salian Century*, p. 149.

36 Dorchy, 'Godefroid', pp. 963–4; Robinson, *Henry IV*, p. 148; MvK, vol. 2, p. 659,
n. 66.

37 See above, p. 32.

38 *AAM*, p. 49; Herman, p. 133, tr. pp. 97–8.

39 Robinson, *Henry IV*, p. 253.

40 The document, concerning the church of St Peter in Liège, is dated 'tempore
Henrici imperatoris, Henrico Leodiensi episcopo, comite Namurcensi Alberto
principatum vice ducis tenente'. See: *Analectes pour servir à l'histoire ecclésiastique
de Belgique*, 36 (1910), p. 347 (no. 1).

41 Dorchy, 'Godefroid', pp. 965–6; Aubé, *Godefroy*, p. 83.

42 After this, Godfrey is generally described as 'Margrave Godfrey'. See e.g. the reference to 'Godefridus marchio' in *Cantatorium*, p. 91.

43 Murray, *Crusader Kingdom*, pp. 24–5.

44 Robinson, *Henry IV*, p. 148, suggests that Henry may have granted the march of Antwerp to Godfrey 'as an earnest of future generosity', while Murray, *Crusader Kingdom*, p. 21, describes the grant as 'a consolation prize'. Andressohn, *Godfrey*, p. 33, surmises that Henry IV and Godfrey came to a mutually beneficial arrangement whereby the ducal office was placed under royal protection until such time that the latter came of age and could fulfil all the duties expected of its duke.

45 On the dynastic lands at the time of Godfrey of Bouillon's accession, see: Murray, *Crusader Kingdom*, pp. 8–16; Andressohn, *Godfrey*, pp. 30–3. These are not to be confused with the lands associated with the ducal office, on which see: Christian Dupont, 'Les domains des ducs en Basse-Lotharingie au XIe siècle', *PSHIGL* 95 (1981), 217–40.

46 On Bouillon and its associated properties, see: Murray, *Crusader Kingdom*, pp. 10–12; Léon Saur, 'Entre Bar, Namur et Liège: Bouillon, place stratégique', *PSHIGL* 95 (1981), 258–82; Michel Ozeray, *Histoire de la ville et du duché de Bouillon*, 2nd edn (Brussels, 1864).

47 Ozeray, *Histoire*, p. 11; Andressohn, *Godfrey*, pp. 30–1.

48 See above, pp. 26–7.

49 *Cantatorium*, pp. 244–5. On this fief, see: Murray, *Crusader Kingdom*, pp. 11–12; *Actes des Comtes de Namur de la première race (946–1196)*, ed. Félix Rousseau (Brussels, 1937), p. lxxxv.

50 'duci . . . Godefridi, ecclesiastici advocati', *Cantatorium*, p. 121.

51 Murray, *Crusader Kingdom*, pp. 12–14.

52 Murray, *Crusader Kingdom*, p. 15, citing *MGH DD H IV*, no. 373 (Metz, 1 June 1085) which records Matilda's claim on Stenay and Mouzay.

53 Murray, *Crusader Kingdom*, pp. 15–16.

54 Murray, *Crusader Kingdom*, pp. 9–10.

55 On the various claimants see: Murray, *Crusader Kingdom*, pp. 16–20.

56 See above, n. 52 in this chapter.

57 See above, p. 58.

58 'junior Godefridus marchio . . . consilio et hortatu optimatum suorum episcopo cessit, et quod suum erat beato Huberto voluntarie recognavit'. *Cantatorium*, p. 92.

59 'Dominica autem que dicitur in Palmis, post sollempnem ejus diei processionem, prosequentibus nobilibus suis, uterque accessit ad majus altare beati Petri apostoli, et baculum suum pastoralem tenente episcopo, dextera ejus dexteram suam Godefridus supposuit, et cum eo predictum allodium super illud absque ulla calumpnia reposuit. Imposita etiam sibi episcopus stola sacerdotali, ne quis illud amplius ecclesie subduceret, sub obtestatione divini nominis interdixit, et imprecatione eterni anathematis excommunicavit. Godefridum vero culpam suam suorumque antecessorum humiliter fatentem absolvit, et, facto publice privilegio hujus recognitionis, sua illud et suorum astipulata assignatione confirmavit'. *Cantatorium*, p. 92.

60 'inter illum [Godfrey] et Albertum Namuscensem comitem orta est gravissima dissensio pro castello Bulloniensi'. *Cantatorium*, 100.

61 *Cantatorium*, pp. 99–102; Aubé, *Godefroy*, pp. 84–5.

62 'Post mortem vero Ducis Godefridi, annuente ipsius uxore domna Mathilde, cui haereditario jure Comitatum Virdunensem reddidi, favente etian Namurcensi Comite Alberto, qui ipsum beneficium ab ea receperat'. Augustin Calmet, *Histoire de Lorraine*, 7 vols, new edn (Nancy, 1747–57), vol. 3, Preuves, cols 7–9. On this, see: MvK, vol. 2, p. 657, n. 61; Overmann, p. 195; Andressohn, *Godfrey*, p. 33; Aubé, *Godefroy*, pp. 81–4.

63 *Cantatorium*, p. 108; Overmann, *Reg. Mat.* no. 27d; Hay, *Military Leadership*, p. 67.
64 Andressohn, *Godfrey*, p. 36; Murray, *Crusader Kingdom*, p. 19.
65 Mayer, 'Baudouin Ier', p. 24.
66 'et auxilium ac receptus meos promitto fideliter et promisi, et de reiciendo G. et recipiendo comite A. quidquid ipsa quaesierat paratus sum exequi'. Hugh of Flavigny, *Chronicon*, *MGH SS*, vol. 8, pp. 285–502 (Manasses' letter is at pp. 419–20), tr. in Andressohn, *Godfrey*, p. 34. Though Hugh of Flavigny copied this letter into his account some time later, there is no reason to doubt its authenticity. On this chronicler, see: Patrick Healy, *The Chronicle of Hugh of Flavigny: Reform and the Investiture Contest in the Late-Eleventh Century* (Aldershot, 2006).
67 On Manasses I's conflict with Gregory VII, see: John S. Ott, ' "Reims and Rome are Equals": Archbishop Manasses I (c.1069–1080), Pope Gregory VII, and the Fortunes of Historical Exceptionalism', in Sigrid Danielson and Evan A. Gatti (eds), *Envisioning the Bishop: Images and the Episcopacy in the Middle Ages* (Turnhout, 2014), 275–302.
68 Gregory VII, *Register*, pp. 538–9 (no. 8.17), tr. pp. 382–3, records that Gregory deposed Manasses from the office of archbishop in December 1080.
69 Aubé, *Godefroy*, p. 82.
70 *Die Urkunden und Briefe der Markgräfin Mathilde von Tuszien*, ed. Elke Goez and Werner Goez (Hannover, 1998), p. 412, Dep. 33; Hay, *Military Leadership*, p. 86.
71 *MGH DD HIV*, no. 385 (Worms, 14 January 1086), records the confiscation of some of Matilda's lands. On this, see: Hay, *Military Leadership*, p. 98; Robinson, *Henry IV*, pp. 215–16.
72 'Godefridus Theodericum comitem cepit, qui filius Gerardi Flamensis, regi etiam Henrico admodum familiaris, in quibus poterat adversabatur juveni'. *Cantatorium*, pp. 104–5. For comment, see: Dorchy, 'Godefroid', pp. 968–70; Andressohn, *Godfrey*, p. 38.
73 'Increscentibus autem inimicitiis inter Albertum Namucensem et Godefridum Bulloniensem, Albertus pro werra Bulloniensi Mirvoldense castrum latenter refirmare disposuit'. *Cantatorium*, p. 106.
74 For comment on this episode, see: Dorchy, 'Godefroid', p. 967; Andressohn, *Godfrey*, pp. 38–9; Aubé, *Godefroy*, pp. 85–6; Jean Baudhuin, 'Les relations entre le comte de Namur Albert III et l'abbaye de Saint-Hubert', in Joseph Balon (ed.), *Études d'histoire et d'archéologie namuroises dédiées à Ferdinand Courtoy*, 2 vols (Namur, 1952), vol. 1, pp. 327–34, at p. 331; Mayer, 'Baudouin Ier', pp. 23–30. On Mirwart, see: André Matthys, 'Les châteaux de Mirwart et de Sugny, centres de pouvoirs aux Xᵉ et XIᵉ siècles', in Jean-Marie Duvosquel and Alain Dierkens (eds), *Villes et campagnes au moyen âge: mélanges Georges Duby* (Liège, 1991), pp. 465–502.
75 'Id cum Henricus episcopus deprehendisset, tum quia Godefrido omnimodis favebat, tum etiam quia per hoc vexandum episcopium timebat, anticipavit prevenire intentionem Alberti'. *Cantatorium*, p. 106.
76 'ipsum castrum . . . legaliter habendum tradidit ecclesie'. *Cantatorium*, p. 107.
77 For an overview, see: H. E. J. Cowdrey, 'The Peace and the Truce of God in the Eleventh Century', *Past and Present*, 46 (1970), 42–67.
78 On the Liège Peace assembly, see: Herman Vanderlinden, 'Le tribunal de la Paix de Henri de Verdun et la formation de la principauté de Liège', in Herman Vanderlinden, François-Louis Ganshof and Gaston G. Dept (eds), *Mélanges d'histoire offerts à Henri Pirenne par ses anciens élèves et ses amis à l'occasion de sa quarantième année d'enseignement à l'Université de Gand, 1886–1926*, 2 vols, c.p. (Brussels, 1926), pp. 589–96; André Joris, 'Observations sur la proclamation de la Trêve de Dieu à Liège à la fin du XIe siècle', in his *Villes-Affaires-Mentalités. Autour du pays mosan* (Brussels, 1993), pp. 313–44; *MGH Const.*, vol. 1, p. 603, n. 1; Kupper, *Liège et l'Église impériale*, p. 459, n. 76; MvK, vol. 2, pp. 467–9; Maquet, *'Faire Justice'*, pp. 185–219.

79 Godfrey's involvement is mentioned briefly, and without discussion, in Andressohn, *Godfrey*, p. 36, and Dorchy, 'Godefroid', pp. 969.
80 For a discussion of the date, see: Joris, 'Observations'.
81 Giles of Orval, *Gesta episcoporum Leodiensium, MGH SS*, vol. 25, pp. 1–129, at pp. 89–90; Idem, *Gesta episcoporum Leodensium abbreviata, MGH SS*, vol. 25, pp. 129–35, at p. 131.
82 *MGH Const.*, vol. 1, pp. 602–5 (no. 424); Robinson, *Henry IV*, pp. 249–50.
83 Vanderlinden, 'Le tribunal', p. 592, notes the 'analogies frappantes'.
84 *MGH Const.*, vol. 1, pp. 605–8 (no. 425).
85 Robinson, *Henry IV*, p. 250.
86 Giles of Orval, *Gesta episcoporum Leodiensium*, p. 90; Vanderlinden, 'Le tribunal', p. 593; Joris, 'Observations', pp. 315–16.
87 Giles of Orval, *Gesta episcoporum Leodiensium*, p. 90; Vanderlinden, 'Le tribunal', p. 593.
88 Giles of Orval, *Gesta episcoporum Leodiensium*, p. 90.
89 Several of the participants are mentioned not by name, but by their office. Hence, Herman II is listed simply as 'comes palatinus', while Godfrey of Bouillon is described only as 'marchio'. Giles of Orval, *Gesta episcoporum Leodiensium*, p. 90.
90 On Henry IV's Italian campaign, see above, pp. 71–2.
91 Robinson, *Henry IV*, p. 253.
92 See: *Cantatorium*, pp. 120–2.
93 'coram episcopo et duce Godefrido conventio condicta de Caviniaco'. *Cantatorium*, p. 121.
94 *Cantatorium*, p. 121. The text states that Chévigny was transferred 'by turf and by branch' (*per cespitem et ramum*), which seems to denote a ritual gesture.
95 *Cantatorium*, p. 121.
96 In this part of his account, the author of the *Cantatorium* described Godfrey as 'duke'. Rather than denote an elevation in Godfrey's status, however, this was no doubt a result of the author's confused chronology. Cf. Dorchy, 'Godefroid', pp. 981–2, which cites this passage in support of the argument that Godfrey had effectively acquired the ducal authority by 1084.
97 This is recorded in *MGH DD H IV*, no. 373 (Metz, 1 June 1085).
98 Louis Clouet, *Histoire de Verdun et du pays Verdunois*, 3 vols (Verdun, 1867–70), vol. 2, pp. 146–8.
99 Mayer, 'Baudouin Ier', p. 25, n. 43; Rousseau, *Actes des Comtes de Namur*, p. lxxxix; Robinson, *Henry IV*, pp. 252–4; Cf. Aubé, *Godefroy*, p. 94.
100 Mayer, 'Baudouin Ier', pp. 25–7. Mayer suggests that it is more likely that Godfrey was made count of Verdun when he was appointed duke of Lower Lotharingia in 1087.
101 *Cantatorium*, pp. 126–7.
102 See above, p. 59.
103 See, among others: Steven Runciman, *A History of the Crusades*, 3 vols (Cambridge, 1951–4), vol. 1, pp. 145–6; Jean Richard, *The Crusades, c.1071–c.1291* (Cambridge, 1999), p. 9; Asbridge, *First Crusade*, p. 61; Tyerman, *God's War*, p. 48; Jonathan Phillips, *Holy Warriors: A Modern History of the Crusades* (London, 2009), p. 11; Jonathan Riley-Smith, *The Crusades: A History*, 3rd edn (London, 2014), pp. 50–1.
104 Lampert, pp. 214–15, tr. p. 205–6; Robinson, *Henry IV*, p. 94.
105 On the Tribur assembly, see: Cowdrey, *Gregory VII*, pp. 150–3; Robinson, *Henry IV*, pp. 155–8.
106 Bonizo, p. 609, tr. p. 239.
107 Cowdrey, *Gregory VII*, p. 153.

108 On Canossa, see the essays collected in Christoph Stiegemann and Matthias Wemhoff (eds), *Canossa 1077: Erschütterung der Welt. Geschichte, Kunst und Kultur am Aufgang der Romanik,* 2 vols (Munich, 2006).

109 On the Forchheim assembly and the appointment of Rudolf of Swabia, see: Robinson, *Henry IV,* pp. 165–71.

110 On this campaign, see: Robinson, *Henry IV,* pp. 171–210.

111 Frutolf, p. 94, tr. pp. 119–20; *Vita Heinrici IV. Imperatoris, Q H IV,* pp. 407–67, at p. 424.

112 Bruno, pp. 390–2.

113 Robinson, *Henry IV,* p. 204.

114 Henry issued this diploma on the eve of the battle (14 October) in his camp by the river Elster. See: *MGH DD H IV,* no. 325. The document does not list Godfrey of Bouillon as present at that point, though it should be noted that the list of testators includes only Henry's ecclesiastical supporters, and none of his allies among the secular nobility.

115 William of Apulia, *Gesta Robertii Wiscardi, MGH SS,* vol. 9, pp. 239–98, at p. 280.

116 Bruno, p. 392; Robinson, *Henry IV,* pp. 203, 269.

117 See: Henri Glaesener, 'Godefroy de Bouillon et la bataille de l'Elster', *Revue des études historiques,* 105 (1938), 253–64, which examines the later evidence connecting Godfrey to the battle of the Elster. Note, however, that Glaesener draws the conclusion that Godfrey fought in the battle.

118 Breysig, 'Gottfried', p. 188; Andressohn, *Godfrey,* pp. 38–9; Aubé, *Godefroy,* pp. 83–4.

119 Dorchy, 'Godefroid', pp. 972–6, sifts the later evidence in detail. See also: MvK, vol. 3, p. 648, n. 14.

120 Gregory VII, *Register,* pp. 479–87 (no. 7.14*a*), tr. pp. 340–4.

121 Cowdrey, *Gregory VII,* p. 194; Robinson, *Henry IV,* pp. 194–6.

122 On the Italian campaign, see: Robinson, *Henry IV,* pp. 211–35.

123 Henry was consecrated on Easter Sunday, and crowned on the following day. See: Robinson, *Henry IV,* pp. 229–31.

124 'Godefridus dux, memor quam quoniam persimili clade olim Rome est tactus in expeditione quam egit cum Heinrico rege quarto . . . quingenti fortissimo milites et plures nobiles obierint, pluresque exterriti cum ipso cesare ab urbe recesserint'. AA, pp. 354–5. On the siege of Antioch, see below, pp. 136–46.

125 Frutolf, p. 96, tr. pp. 121–2.

126 *MGH DD H IV,* from no. 333 (Rome, 3 June 1081) to no. 366 (Verona, 18 June 1084).

127 *Cantatorium,* p. 106. Dorchy, 'Godefroid', pp. 976–7, cites this passage as evidence that in *c.*1082 Godfrey was in Lotharingia rather than Italy.

128 *Cantatorium,* p. 153.

129 Andressohn, *Godfrey,* pp. 38–9, and Breysig, 'Gottfried', pp. 189–90, both conclude that Godfrey played a role in the Italian campaign, while Dorchy, 'Godefroid', pp. 976–7, and MvK, vol. 4, p. 513, n. 73, assert that Godfrey remained in Lotharingia while Henry IV was in Italy.

130 *Cantatorium,* p. 121; Breysig, 'Gottfried', pp. 190–2; Dorchy, 'Godefroid', pp. 967, 982.

131 Despy, 'La date de l'accession', esp. pp. 1277–81. On the mistakes in chronology in the *Cantatorium,* see Hanquet, *Étude critique,* pp. 109–21. Aubé, *Godefroy,* p. 93, n. 1, asserts that Despy's argument has gained universal acceptance, while Mayer, 'Baudouin Ier', p. 22, n. 34, states that Despy makes his argument about Godfrey's acquisition of the ducal office in 'a conclusive manner'.

132 Despy, 'La date de l'accession', p. 1284. See also: Vanderlinden, 'La date de la nomination', pp. 189–92, and Andressohn, *Godfrey,* p. 41.

133 *MGH DD H IV*, no. 395. See also: Robinson, *Henry IV*, pp. 262–3; Despy, 'La date de l'accession', pp. 1275, 1283–4, n. 1; MvK, vol. 4, p. 160.

134 'Cuonradus puer, filius Heinrici imperatoris, Aquis sublimatur in regem. Marchio Godefridus in ducem'. *Annales S. Iacobi Leodiensis*, p. 639.

135 'Godefridi ducis et ejusdem ecclesiae [St Hubert] advocati'. *Chartes Saint-Hubert*, vol. 1, pp. 56–7 (no. 46); Despy, 'La date de l'accession', pp. 1277–8.

136 'Godefrido ... ducibus'. *ODEH*, vol. 3, pp. 564–5; Wauters, vol. 1, pp. 565–6.

137 'Gotefrido, duce'. *Cartulaire de l'abbaye de Saint-Trond*, ed. Charles Piot, 2 vols (Brussels, 1870–1874), vol. 1, pp. 27–8 (no. 20).

138 'Godefrido duce' *Cantatorium*, p. 134.

139 'nunc est dux Lotharingiae'. *Genealogia Comitum Buloniensium*, p. 301.

140 'Godefrido, Godefridi Gimbosi ex sorore nepoti, tandem datur ducatus Lotharingiae'. Sigebert, p. 366.

141 MvK, vol. 4, pp. 159–60, n. 4; Robinson, *Henry IV*, p. 271, n. 187.

142 For instance, Sigebert asserts that William the Conqueror died in 1092, some five years after he actually died: Sigebert, p. 366.

143 For examples, see: Despy, 'Les actes', p. 71 (nos. 13 and 14).

144 The document is edited in *ODEH*, vol. 1, pp. 77–8. It is discussed in more detail below, p. 106.

145 Pierre de Ram, 'Notice sur un sceau inédit de Godefroi de Bouillon', *Bulletin de l'académie royale des sciences, des lettres et des beaux-arts de Belgique*, 13 (1846), 355–60.

146 Mina Martens, 'Une reproduction manuscrite inédite du sceau de Godefroid de Bouillon', *Annales de la société royale d'archéologie de bruxelles*, 46 (1942–1943), 7–27.

147 On the use of martial imagery on aristocratic seals in this era, see: Brigitte Bedos-Rezak, 'Medieval Seals and the Study of Chivalric Society', in Howell Chickering and Thomas H. Seiler (eds), *The Study of Chivalry: Resources and Approaches* (Kalamazoo, 1988), pp. 313–72; Pierre Bony, 'L'image du pouvoir seigneurial dans les sceaux: codification des signes de la puissance de la fin du XIe au début du XIIIe siècle dans les pays d'Oïl', in *Seigneurs et seigneuries au moyen âge: actes du 117e congrès national des Sociétes savantes, Clermont-Ferrand 1992* (Paris, 1995), pp. 489–523.

148 On William the Conqueror's seal, see: Bates, *William the Conqueror* (2004), pp. 172–4.

149 Robinson, *Henry IV*, p. 271.

150 *MGH DD H IV*, no. 402.

151 Aubé, *Godefroy*, p. 104, notes that this phase of Godfrey's life finds him 'au mileu d'un veritable desert documentaire'.

152 'ducatum amministrante Godefrido'. *Table chronologique*, vol. 7, p. 170.

153 *Cantatorium*, pp. 133–4. The agreement reached by Thierry and Count Baldwin is recorded in a charter issued by the latter, for which see: *Chartes Saint-Hubert*, vol. 1, pp. 77–8 (no. 60).

154 *Cantatorium*, pp. 144–5; Dorchy, 'Godefroid', p. 988. Though the author of the *Cantatorium* dated the negotiations at Prüm to 1083, Hanquet, *Étude critique*, p. 116, asserts that 1088 is the correct date.

155 'Documents relatifs à l'abbaye de Flône', ed. M. Evrard, *Analectes pour servir à l'histoire ecclésiastique de belgique*, 23 (1892), 273–504, with Henry of Liège's charter at pp. 282–5 (no. 1).

156 Germain Morin, 'Lettre inédite a A[nselme de Cantorbéry] a G[odefroy de Bouillon] ?', *Revue Bénédictine*, 34 (1922), 135–46.

157 Germain Morin, 'Godefroy de Bouillon et Adalbéron, Abbé de Saint-Vincent de Laon. A propos du manuscrit Rh. CVIII de Zurich', *Revue Bénédictine*, 42 (1930), 273–5.

158 See the discussion in Robinson, *Henry IV*, pp. 239–41.
159 Robinson, *Henry IV*, pp. 275–95. Henry remained in Italy until his return to Germany in spring 1097.
160 *Cantatorium*, pp. 152–5. On Otbert and his episcopate, see: Jean-Louis Kupper, 'Otbert de Liège: les manipulations monétaires d'un évêque d'Empire à l'aube du XIIe siècle', *Le moyen âge*, 35 (1980), 353–85; Cauchie, *Querelle*, vol. 2, pp. 7–17.
161 On Godfrey's involvement in the episode, see: Georges Despy, 'Godefroid de Bouillon et l'abbaye de Saint-Hubert en 1095', *Saint-Hubert d'Ardenne: Cahiers d'histoire*, 1 (1977), 45–50; Andressohn, *Godfrey*, pp. 42–6; Aubé, *Godefroy*, pp. 103–9.
162 *Cantatorium*, pp. 156–7.
163 'abbas . . . malle se Otbertum offendere quam Deum'. *Cantatorium*, pp. 158–9.
164 *Cantatorium*, p. 176.
165 *Cantatorium*, pp. 182–3.
166 *Cantatorium*, p. 184. Henry died in mid-1095, and was succeeded as count by his son Godfrey.
167 *Cantatorium*, p. 174.
168 *Cantatorium*, pp. 185–6.
169 See: *Annales Mosomagenses*, *MGH SS*, vol. 3, pp. 160–6 (at p. 162), which refers to the destruction of the castle of Mouzon under the year 1092.
170 'sicque malignante impietate cum avaritia, oppressa est elimande veritatis experientia'. *Cantatorium*, pp. 191–2.
171 'Otberti et ducis spes eorum frustrate esset'. *Cantatorium*, p. 193.
172 'Quod et hoc modo divina disponente clementia processit'. *Cantatorium*, pp. 193–4.
173 'Epistola Urbani II ad Beringerum abbaterm S. Laurentii Leodiensis', *PL*, vol. 151, cols 395–7; JL 4145.
174 On the date of Otbert's assault on Clermont-lez-Nandrin, see: *Cantatorium*, p. 194, n. 1.
175 'Quod . . . o commilitones, a Deo auxilium sperabimus, qui ejus ecclesiis depereuntibus, non solum defensionem non impendimus, sed et liberam vocem contradictionis subtrahimus? Scilicet hoc de nobis promeruit benignissima dispositio Creatoris, qui nos ministros sue publice rei constituit, ut pro sua quisque persona, nostrum illi negemus servitium, quos pro tuendo jure suo hoc nostro tempore elegit ejus generale dominium'. *Cantatorium*, p. 195. The translation is adapted from that in Andressohn, *Godfrey*, p. 45.
176 *Cantatorium*, pp. 195–7.
177 'coram duce Godefrido itermque primoribus civitatis'. *Cantatorium*, p. 198.
178 At this point, Thierry II reportedly attempted to recover some of the treasures of St Hubert which, before his exile from the abbey, he had sent to one Rudolf of Villance for safe-keeping. These included three ivory horns given to St Hubert by Godfrey the Bearded. *Cantatorium*, pp. 199–200.
179 'consilio Godefridi ducis aliorumque sapientium virorum'. *Cantatorium*, p. 201.
180 Aubé, *Godefroy*, p. 107.
181 Cauchie, *Querelle*, vol. 2, pp. 70–1.
182 *Cartulaire Gorze*, pp. 242–4 (no. 139); *ODEH*, vol. 1, p. 360; *Table chronologique*, vol. 1, p. 581; *Les Chartes du Clermontois, conservées au musée Condé, à Chantilly*, ed. André Lesort (Paris, 1904), pp. 56–8 (no. 2). The same confirmation was recorded again in a charter which purports to have been drawn up at Stenay in 1096, though this latter document appears to be a forgery. See: *ODEH*, vol. 1, pp. 365–6. Godfrey's brother Baldwin is one of the witnesses named in this document.

183 'Godefridus, legitimus successor & heres Ducis Godefridi Barbati, filiique ejus potentissimi & justissimi Ducis Godefridi, avunculi mei'. *ODEH*, vol. 1, pp. 76–7. On Godfrey the Bearded's donation of the priory to St Hubert, see above, pp. 26–7.

184 'Documents relatifs à l'abbaye de Flône', ed. Evrard, pp. 285–6 (no. 2).

185 'Godefrido regni Lotharingorum ducatum et marchiam procurante et ipso presente'. Anne-Marie Bonenfant-Feytmans, 'Le plus ancien acte de l'abbaye d'Andenne', *Etudes d'histoire dédiées à la mémoire de Henri Pirenne: par ses anciens élèves* (Brussels, 1937), pp. 19–33, esp. pp. 32–3, for the act itself. Previous scholarship had dated the act to 1105, but Bonenfant-Feytmans makes a convincing case for the earlier date.

186 'dux Godefridus Buliensis filius Eustacii de Bulengiis'. *Recueil des chartes de l'abbaye de Stavelot-Malmédy*, ed. Joseph Halkin and Charles G. Roland, 2 vols (Brussels, 1909), vol. 1, pp. 264–6 (no. 129); *Table chronologique*, vol. 1, p. 594; Maquet, *'Faire Justice'*, p. 404.

3 The coming of the First Crusade, 1095–1096

Pope Urban II's call for the First Crusade

The origins of the First Crusade have been much discussed in modern scholarship. It is therefore necessary only to sketch a few details here. In March 1095, at the council of Piacenza, an embassy from the Byzantine Emperor Alexios Komnenos (1081–1118) reached Pope Urban II and reported on the situation in the Near East.[1] These messengers informed those present at Piacenza that the powers of Asia Minor, Palestine, and Egypt were divided and weakened. They beseeched the pope to send military assistance there to help recover some of the Byzantine territory which had been lost in the late eleventh century.[2] The Byzantine assessment of the Near East was accurate. In the mid-1090s, the Shi'ites of Fatimid Egypt were firmly divided from the predominantly Sunni powers of Palestine, which in theory was part of the Abbasid Caliphate centred upon Baghdad. Moreover, the political map of Palestine itself was extremely fragmented. Asia Minor had slipped out of Baghdad's ambit into the hands of local rulers.[3]

The Byzantine appeal seems to have prompted Urban to instigate a plan he had already been formulating. In August 1095, he crossed the Alps and embarked on a year-long tour of southern and central France (as a result of a dispute with King Philip I of France (1059–1108), he only travelled as far north as Le Mans). He was the first reigning pope to visit France for half a century. During his time there, he visited a number of towns, consecrated churches, and held several reforming councils. He also passed legislation aimed at extending the Peace of God to the areas he visited.[4] On the penultimate day of the council he held at Clermont (18–28 November 1095), Urban called for an armed expedition to go to the East to free the Holy Sepulchre in Jerusalem and the other holy places from Muslim hands, and bring aid to the Christians who lived there. The pope apparently framed the enterprise as a pilgrimage to the Holy City, and instructed participants to distinguish themselves by adopting the sign of the cross. He told participants to depart on the feast of the Assumption (15 August) 1096, so that their journey east would coincide with the gathering of the harvest at the end of summer.[5] The movement that resulted from Urban's appeal became known as the First Crusade.

Urban made a compelling promise to those who agreed to take part in the expedition. The canons of the council of Clermont indicate that he offered to would-be participants a spiritual reward, namely, the remission of penance for properly confessed sins.[6] In popular perception, this indulgence was often interpreted as the remission of sin itself.[7] Yet, while Urban packaged the expedition as a penitential endeavour, it was clear from the outset that it would also be a military enterprise. In his letter of December 1095 to the people of Flanders, he referred to the expedition as a 'military undertaking' (*procinctum*).[8] In a missive that he sent the following October to the monks of Vallombrosa (near Florence), he spoke of 'the Jerusalem expedition' (*Jherosolimitana expeditio*).[9] As a result, then, participants would have understood that they were embarking on a spiritual enterprise, but that they were doing so as part of an army.[10] Would-be crusaders could therefore interpret the pope's appeal as an opportunity to attain spiritual rewards by exacting violence upon God's enemies in His name. After the council of Clermont, Urban continued his tour of France, holding further councils at Tours (March 1096) and Nîmes (July 1096), before returning to Italy in September. During his time in France, he continued to promulgate the call for the expedition, and encouraged ecclesiastics whom he met to do likewise.[11] The pope also despatched letters promoting the crusade to regions he was unable to reach in person. News of the expedition spread quickly. In his above-mentioned letter to Flanders, written perhaps a month after Clermont, Urban affirmed that the appeal he had made at that council was already widely known.[12]

The reaction to Urban's appeal astonished contemporaries.[13] Indeed, the pope himself seems to have been surprised by the scale of the response.[14] In total, perhaps around 100,000 people took the cross in 1095–1096.[15] Almost from the moment that Urban made his appeal, observers have sought to explain why so many responded positively to it. A number of modern scholars have concluded that the papal message stimulated such a widespread response because it keyed into the spiritual concerns of late-eleventh-century aristocratic armsbearers. In a seminal study, Erdmann analysed the process through which Christian thinkers had infused ideas of Holy War into the consciousness of Latin Christendom.[16] Riley-Smith carried out a study of a wide body of charters prepared for departing crusaders, and argued that Urban's message was transmitted essentially intact to those armsbearers, to whose religious sensibilities it had a profound appeal.[17] Bull has asserted that the wide uptake of Urban's call was possible because over the course of the eleventh century religious communities had built strong connections with aristocratic families. He suggests that the Church had successfully conditioned noble warriors to respond to its messages about sin, punishment, and judgement.[18] More recently, Purkis has suggested that monastic spiritual practices shaped how contemporaries framed the piety of crusaders.[19] But while the spiritual concerns of the armsbearing classes clearly lay at the heart of the response to Urban's appeal, socio-political factors should not be entirely discounted. France has asserted that in the aftermath of Clermont, some may have been pressured to take the cross because they were connected by bonds of homage to aristocrats who had already done so.[20] Crucially, Urban had formulated his appeal in a way which made it possible to take a range of concerns into consideration alongside each other. In short, a complex and interrelated array of impulses lay behind the immense response to Urban's appeal.

In late 1095 and early 1096 bands of crusaders crystallised under the leadership of the curious figure of Peter the Hermit. Historians generally describe these forces as the People's Crusade.[21] Peter was a charismatic preacher who had reportedly received divine encouragement to set out for Jerusalem. His activities seem to have been autonomous from Urban's, and they were at no point sanctioned by any ecclesiastical authority. By the end of 1095 Peter was preaching the expedition in Berry in northern France. He then crossed into Lotharingia, where he continued to recruit followers. The People's Crusade departed for Jerusalem in March 1096 – five months before the departure date specified by the pope – and reached Constantinople at the start of August. Alexios found them too unruly to deal with, however, and he soon had them transported across the Bosporus into Asia Minor, where they were all but wiped out by the Turks in October. In early 1096, further premature contingents of crusaders crystallised in Germany around figures including Count Emicho of Flonheim and Count Hartmann of Dillingen. These forces passed eastwards through the kingdom of Germany. Between May and July 1096, some of their number perpetrated attacks on Jewish communities in towns in the Rhineland.[22] These bands of crusaders travelled a few months behind the People's Crusade, but did not even reach Constantinople. They encountered difficulties and disintegrated in the kingdom of Hungary in August 1096.[23]

A number of high-ranking figures in the West responded to Urban's appeal and assembled armies for the expedition. Urban appointed Adhémar of Monteil, bishop of Le Puy, as his legate on the expedition.[24] The largest contingent was led by Raymond of St Gilles, count of Toulouse. He was the richest and most distinguished of all the crusaders.[25] Notable participants from northern France included Robert Curthose, duke of Normandy, Count Robert II of Flanders, and Count Stephen II of Blois.[26] Bohemond, a south-Italian Norman, also took the cross, and led a force on the First Crusade which included his nephew, Tancred of Hauteville.[27] Bohemond's decision to participate came as something of a surprise, since relations between the papacy and the Normans of southern Italy had often been extremely strained during the eleventh century.[28] Moreover, Bohemond had participated in his father Robert Guiscard's unsuccessful attack on the Byzantine Empire in 1081–4.[29] While ambition may well have played a part in his decision to take the cross, his choice underlines the immense appeal of the pope's call for the First Crusade.

Godfrey's response to the call for the First Crusade

It has sometimes been suggested that Urban aimed to confine his crusade appeal to France, and that he originally had no intention of stimulating participation in the kingdom of Germany.[30] This may not necessarily have been the case. From 1084 to Gregory VII's death in 1085 – that is, soon before Urban's own appointment as pope in 1088 – Urban had acted as Gregory's legate in Germany. He was thus familiar with politics there.[31] It is true that after Urban was appointed pope his influence in the German Church was limited as a result of the dispute with Henry IV. Henry's policy of appointing loyal allies to bishoprics in the 1080s and 1090s had served gradually to erode papal support there. From the outset of his pontificate, then, Urban's contact with the clergy in the kingdom of Germany was sporadic.[32] Yet, that contact was not entirely cut off. In the period leading up to the launch of the First Crusade, Urban was in communication with prelates in both Upper and Lower Lotharingia. In 1095, he wrote to the diocese of Cambrai (in Upper Lotharingia) about its dispute with the bishopric of Arras.[33] As noted in the previous chapter, early in 1095, possibly at the council of Piacenza in March of that year, Urban wrote to Abbot Berenger of St Laurent in connection with Bishop Otbert's activities in the diocese of Liège.[34] On the eve of the First Crusade, then, Urban must have possessed fairly up to date knowledge of affairs in Lotharingia. Moreover, while most of the clergy of the kingdom of Germany did stay away from the council of Clermont, some from Lotharingia did attend. A large delegation from Cambrai was present at the council, albeit to deal with affairs pertaining to that diocese.[35] Moreover, representatives from all the dioceses of the archbishopric of Rheims were present at Clermont.[36] The official papal message regarding the crusade was thus transmitted to dioceses in Rheims that were adjacent to Lotharingia, and this surely provided one route for word of the crusade to reach the westernmost part of the kingdom of Germany. Indeed, as noted in the previous chapter, Godfrey himself had visited Rheims in the first part of 1095 to confer with its archbishop, Renaud du Bellay, so he clearly spent time there during his career as duke.[37] Urban would surely have devoted thought to the regions which he hoped might respond to his appeal, and which areas he did not intend to contribute. It is noteworthy that he attempted to circumscribe the response which greeted his call in Spain. At some point in the first half of 1096, Urban wrote a letter exhorting Catalonian nobles not to depart for Jerusalem, but instead to stay and fight Muslims in Spain.[38] There is no evidence that suggests that Urban ever wished to contain the fervour for the expedition that coalesced in Lotharingia.

While calls to go to Jerusalem permeated Lotharingia quickly in 1095–1096, however, it was not only Urban's message that was transmitted.[39] As noted above, Peter the Hermit's preaching – which was independent of the pope's strategy – struck a chord with many in Lotharingia. Indeed, Albert of Aachen believed that Peter rather than Urban was the originator of the movement.[40] Sigebert of Gembloux emphasised the widespread attraction to the crusade throughout different sections of Western society, and identified Lotharingia as one of the many regions which responded enthusiastically to the call for the expedition. He did not, however, ascribe the crusade's origin to Urban II.[41] As the crusade appeal came at a time of long-standing enmity between Henry IV and the papacy, it is not surprising that some authors who wrote in Germany neglected to mention – or were simply ignorant of – Urban's role in the origin of the expedition. Nevertheless, it is clear that a number of observers in Germany received word of the First Crusade through official channels. Bernold of St Blasien, who wrote in Swabia, explicitly described Urban as 'the foremost author' of the crusade.[42] The most revealing report of how the pope's message permeated Lotharingia is provided by Frutolf of Michelsberg's 1106 continuator. This author identified Urban as the instigator of the First Crusade, and then proceeded to describe in considerable detail how messengers carried word of the expedition throughout the Latin world. Frutolf's continuator stated that there was a great uptake throughout much of the West, including France, Flanders, and Lotharingia. He then commented that there was a much more muted response in the other duchies of the kingdom of Germany, on account of the dispute between pope and emperor.[43] In explaining the response to the First Crusade, the continuator asserted that Lotharingia had responded with more enthusiasm than the rest of the kingdom of Germany. He aligned Lotharingia with other areas where Urban's message spread rapidly and – in some localities at least – fairly coherently.

Modern historians have sometimes expressed surprise that Godfrey of Bouillon responded positively to the call for the First Crusade. As noted in the previous chapter, it has been widely accepted that Godfrey was a supporter of Henry IV. On that basis, historians have suggested that he would not have been automatically attuned to the prospect of participating in a papal enterprise. Asbridge, for example, characterised Godfrey as an 'avowed [enemy] of the reform papacy', and noted that he 'stood entirely outside the network of papal supporters who formed the backbone of crusade recruitment. He had no history of collaboration with the reform party, nor any known connections to the *fideles beati Petri*'.[44] In the pages that follow, a rather different interpretation of Godfrey's response to the crusade appeal is offered. It will be suggested here that in fact Godfrey's dynastic background and his formative experiences and political allegiances in the West potentially played a significant role in priming his response to the crusade appeal.

Before Urban II launched his appeal for the First Crusade at Clermont, he had already secured the participation of several key figures. Soon after he crossed into France he must have discussed his plans with Adhémar of Le Puy and Raymond of Toulouse, as both were among the first publicly to commit to take part in the expedition.[45] While Urban would almost certainly not have had Godfrey in mind as a potential participant, as he probably did Adhémar and Raymond, the pope would surely not have been profoundly shocked when he discovered that Godfrey had taken the cross. Urban would have known who Godfrey was, and, more importantly, that his predecessors had been associated with the reform papacy. There was a significant degree of institutional continuity in the papal curia in the eleventh century. As noted above, Urban had earlier in his career been a prominent ally of Gregory VII, serving as his legate in Germany in 1084–1085.[46] When Urban was elected pope in 1088, he self-consciously cast himself as the continuator of Gregory's pontificate. In one of his first letters, sent to announce his appointment to bishops in Germany, Urban declaimed that he would uphold Gregory's policies: everyone Gregory had damned, Urban asserted, he damned too.[47] It is plausible that, like Gregory, Urban knew that Godfrey the Bearded, Godfrey's grandfather, had been the most prominent secular supporter of the papacy in Italy in the mid-eleventh century. If Urban had consulted Gregory's register, he would have known that soon after Gregory was appointed pope in 1073 he had written to Godfrey the Hunchback, warmly addressing him as a 'most beloved son of St Peter'.[48] Urban would also have been able to discern Gregory's hope that Godfrey the Hunchback would participate in his planned military expedition to Jerusalem in 1074.[49] A sense of Urban's reaction to the news of Godfrey's decision to participate in the First Crusade is conveyed in a letter the pope sent to Alexios Komnenos at some point in 1096. The purpose of the letter was to inform Alexios that a number of armies were marching toward Constantinople. In it, Urban described his original call for the expedition at Clermont, before noting that the first to set out was Peter the Hermit, who led an immense multitude. Urban then affirmed that 'the brothers Godfrey, Eustace and Baldwin, the counts of Boulogne', led an even greater army, which they had combined with Peter's force.[50] The information in this letter is rather garbled, attributing to Godfrey and Baldwin the comital title which only their brother Eustace held. Nevertheless, it yields significant evidence. Urban sought to convey in this missive to Alexios the sense that Godfrey – and Peter the Hermit for that matter – formed part of his wider plan for the expedition. While this was an effort to impose retrospective cohesion on the crusade, it does indicate that Urban quickly factored Godfrey's participation into the arrangements for the expedition.

As discussed above, some crusading activity which took shape in Lotharingia in the aftermath of the council of Clermont was stimulated by Peter the Hermit rather than through ecclesiastical channels which originated with Urban. It is worth considering which version of the appeal reached Godfrey. Several contemporaries did draw connections between Peter and Godfrey; Urban II himself linked Godfrey's crusade army to that of Peter in his 1096 letter to Alexios.[51] The author of the *Gesta Francorum* believed that the two armies had travelled together to Constantinople.[52] Some individuals whom Peter inspired to take the cross ended up joining Godfrey's contingent.[53] Nevertheless, it is clear that Godfrey and the associates who formed the kernel of his army were inspired by the message of Urban II.[54] Crucially, Godfrey had access to several communication networks along which the papal appeal could have reached him. Several of these networks were dominated by ecclesiastical figures. It has already been noted that prelates from parts of Lotharingia and adjacent dioceses in the archdiocese of Rheims were present at the council of Clermont. Those prelates would have brought word of the crusade back to their localities, from where they could easily permeate Godfrey's homelands. Moreover, Urban maintained direct epistolary contacts with ecclesiastics based in Lotharingia, including Abbot Berenger of St Laurent in Liège. It was demonstrated in the previous chapter that Godfrey had close dealings with Berenger on the eve of the First Crusade.[55] In the first chapter of this book, it was noted that during the latter part of the eleventh century Archbishop Anselm of Canterbury had sustained epistolary contact with Godfrey's mother Ida. Through Ida, Anselm's communications could surely have reached other members of the comital house of Boulogne. In a letter sent to the bishop of Salisbury in 1096, Anselm indicated that he had received news about the call for the expedition, and he would have been able to convey that news on to Ida and her family.[56] Each of these ecclesiastical connections could have provided a route for reports of the First Crusade to reach Godfrey in Lotharingia.

Godfrey could also have received word of the appeal through his dynastic connections to the aristocracy of northern France and the wider Anglo-Norman world. In his study of the response to Urban II's appeal for the crusade, Riley-Smith emphasised the importance of these dynastic ties in stimulating participation. He identified several chains of recruits who were bound together by kinship, and posited that these chains may have provided an infrastructure which allowed Urban's message to spread more rapidly than it could through clerical preaching.[57] Crucially, while Godfrey had been in Lotharingia for about twenty years by 1095, he remained part of a wider aristocratic nexus which encompassed Boulogne and other regions of northern France. These ties bisected the notional frontier between the kingdom of France and the Lotharingian duchies of the kingdom of Germany. Eustace, Godfrey, and Baldwin all committed to go on the First Crusade, and, though it is impossible to determine which of them took the decision first, it is incontrovertible that their decisions would have been linked.[58]

Eustace and Baldwin were both politically affiliated to aristocrats in regions where there was strong enthusiasm for the crusade. As count of Boulogne, Eustace was a vassal of William Rufus, king of England.[59] Though William did not himself take the cross, his brother Robert Curthose, duke of Normandy, did.[60] Eustace was also a vassal of Robert of Flanders, another figure who committed to participate in the expedition. Though Robert's father (Robert I) had been implicated in the attack on Godfrey the Hunchback in 1076, this dynastic enmity did not create any apparent difficulties between Robert II and Godfrey of Bouillon during the First Crusade itself. Indeed, at one point in his account, Albert of Aachen noted that Godfrey and Robert II were 'allied one to the other as beloved friends and comrades'.[61] Eustace seems to have set out on the First Crusade from northern France in the company of the two Roberts, only joining up with his brothers Godfrey and Baldwin at Constantinople.[62] Baldwin also held aristocratic connections which may have conditioned his – and perhaps his brothers' – response to the crusade appeal. For some time before the First Crusade, Baldwin had been married to Godehilde, the daughter of the Norman lord Ralph of Tosny.[63] Godehilde's first cousin was Emma of Hereford, who accompanied her husband Ralph of Gael on the crusade in Robert Curthose's army.[64] Baldwin was closely associated with Godfrey in the lead up to the departure of the crusade. At some point in 1095–1096, Baldwin travelled to Lotharingia and played a role in Godfrey's preparations. During his career in Lotharingia, Godfrey also established further associations which came into play in the run up to his departure on the First Crusade. For example, Godfrey was accompanied on the crusade by Baldwin of Mons, count of Hainaut. Baldwin was the son of Richilde of Mons, and Godfrey had encountered him several times in the 1080s while acting as advocate of St Hubert.[65] Murray has shown that Godfrey's crusade army incorporated a range of lords from Lotharingia and France who were connected to him by ties of kinship. Among these figures was Baldwin of Bourcq, the son of Count Hugh of Rethel.[66]

It is also worth considering when Godfrey heard about the papal call for the First Crusade. His access to a number of ecclesiastical and dynastic networks provided several routes by which news of the appeal could have reached him soon after the council of Clermont. It is of interest that one of Godfrey's crusade companions, Warner of Grez, appears to have been making preparations for the expedition at the very end of 1095. A charter drawn up to record Warner's sale of the allod of Vaux to the abbey of Fosses is dated 1095, and includes the statement that Warner planned to go to Jerusalem 'with Duke Godfrey as well as other princes of the realm'.[67] If this document is genuine and its date accurate, then reports that Godfrey had joined the First Crusade must have begun to spread within a few weeks of the council of Clermont, before the end of 1095. Significantly, contemporary sources indicate that it was indeed the papal message concerning the expedition that inspired Godfrey to participate. The author of the *Cantatorium*, writing in the diocese of Liège, recorded that Urban originated the expedition, and that when word of it reached Godfrey, he decided to participate.[68] Evidence which details Godfrey's preparations for the First Crusade – which will be assessed more fully later in the chapter – also indicates that he responded to the papal call. In a charter drawn up at the behest of Ida of Boulogne in 1098, it is explicitly stated that by that time her three sons had departed on the First Crusade 'on Apostolic command'.[69] Moreover, the fact that Godfrey departed on the crusade on or very close to 15 August 1096, the departure date specified by Urban, suggests that he drew up his plans for departing with the pope's instruction in mind.[70] No contemporary source describes the precise circumstances in which Godfrey formally committed to participate in the First Crusade. Participants usually assumed the cross as a 'large, noisy, hysterical assembly', and this may have been Godfrey's experience.[71]

As well as considering how the appeal for the First Crusade reached Godfrey, it is also important to discuss why he responded positively to it. On this subject, a constellation of factors must be addressed. His considerations must have been influenced by a range of spiritual, dynastic, and political impulses. Like many of those who heard the call in 1095–1096, Godfrey would surely have been attracted by the prospect of carrying out a penitential expedition to Jerusalem, in return for spiritual rewards. Certainly, he would have been familiar with the devotional practice of making a pilgrimage to the Holy City. In the latter half of the eleventh century a number of figures from Lotharingia and nearby regions had gone there as pilgrims.[72] In 1064–1065, a band of between 7,000 and 12,000 German pilgrims reached Jerusalem.[73] Robert I of Flanders – the father of Robert II, and the adversary of Godfrey the Hunchback – was away from the West between 1086 and 1089 on pilgrimage to the Holy City.[74] The author of the *Cantatorium* provided a brief account of Godfrey's response to the crusade appeal which highlights the appeal of journeying to Jerusalem. This author states that after Urban exhorted Christians to go to Jerusalem armed, a wide range of peoples rushed to join the expedition, and 'swap the uncertain for the certain' (*incerta pro certis*). Godfrey, the author reports, disposed to go with them.[75] Albert of Aachen sought to emphasise Godfrey's ambition to visit Jerusalem. According to Albert, throughout Godfrey's career in the West he 'would often sigh deeply, [and recount that] before all things his heart's desire was to visit the holy town of Jerusalem and to see the Lord Jesus' Sepulchre'.[76] This claim has to be taken seriously; the Holy City held a profound spiritual appeal to Christians in this era. However, Albert included this passage just after the point at which he had outlined the circumstances in which Godfrey had been appointed ruler of Jerusalem in the aftermath of the First Crusade in July 1099. On balance, then, this passage was probably intended to justify why it was Godfrey who had been chosen, rather than to provide an accurate reflection of Godfrey's state of mind in the era before the expedition. But even if Albert's assertion does not reflect Godfrey's own sentiments, it is nevertheless significant that his intentions could be interpreted in the light of contemporary expectations about participation in the First Crusade.

Previous scholarship has neglected to recognise that during Godfrey's time in Lotharingia, local ecclesiastical figures shaped his ideas about aristocratic conduct and spirituality. These formative influences must have informed how he interpreted the call for the First Crusade. Bull asserted that religious houses shaped the spiritual concerns of aristocratic armsbearing families over the course of several generations during the eleventh century, creating the conditions which made it possible for those armsbearers to comprehend Urban's call for the expedition.[77] The foregoing study of the careers of Godfrey, his uncle Godfrey the Hunchback, and his grandfather Godfrey the Bearded has suggested that St Hubert exerted this influence upon successive members of the house of Ardennes-Bouillon. At various points in the mid- to late eleventh century, abbots of St Hubert instructed all three about sin and the necessity of heeding the Church's instructions on attaining penitence.[78] This dynastic conditioning may well have helped to create a setting in which Godfrey could grasp the devotional dimensions of the First Crusade appeal.

Historians have also overlooked the possibility that Bishop Henry of Liège's institution of the Peace of God in his diocese in about 1082 had a formative influence on Godfrey. (Bishop Henry, it is worth reiterating, was a kinsman of Godfrey.) Bull has argued that the Peace played a minor role in shaping the response to the First Crusade, whilst acknowledging that there may have existed regional variations on this point. Bull's argument was based on a study of evidence from the Limousin and Gascony.[79] In contrast, others, including Flori, have continued to stress the importance of the Peace of God movements for priming the mindsets of the figures who responded to Urban's call in 1095–1096.[80] Godfrey participated in the institution of the Peace in Liège, and it is difficult to imagine that his ideas about ecclesiastical teachings on licit violence and spiritual punishment would have gone unaltered as a result. His exposure to the Peace pronounced in Liège may have helped equip him to grasp Urban II's message in 1095–1096.

In his study of the response to the appeal to the First Crusade, Riley-Smith noted that families which had traditions of supporting the reform papacy exhibited a greater tendency to take the cross.[81] The same scholar also asserted that Godfrey had served in Henry IV's military campaigns and that he had been an opponent of reform. He made no suggestion that the house of Ardennes-Bouillon had a tradition of assisting the papacy, and that this tradition may have shaped Godfrey's response to the papal call in 1095–1096.[82] While Godfrey himself does not appear to have had any direct connections to the reform papacy, his considerations may nevertheless have been influenced by dynastic precedent. He may have known that Godfrey the Bearded had been the papacy's principal supporter in Italy in the mid-eleventh century, and that his brother – Godfrey of Bouillon's great uncle – Frederick of Lotharingia, had held the papal office as Stephen IX in 1057–1058. He may also have been aware that Godfrey the Hunchback enjoyed a cordial relationship with Gregory VII at the outset of his pontificate, and that though the pope's opinion of his uncle had declined in 1074, it had not been irrecoverably damaged when he died in 1076.[83] Knowledge of these connections to the reform papacy could well have had a bearing on how Godfrey responded to the call for the First Crusade.

As well as considering the potential influence of the careers of Godfrey's maternal ancestors upon his state of mind in 1095–1096, the activities of his father, Eustace II of Boulogne, are also worth discussing in this connection. While the Norman Conquest of England and the First Crusade were different in nature, and a comparison of the factors which motivated individuals to participate in the two expeditions must take into account their distinct spiritual and devotional characters, it is not inconceivable that Godfrey may have seen in his father's activities in support of William the Conqueror in 1066, and his subsequent acquisition of the Honour of Boulogne, the possibilities – and rewards – that could result in participating in an expedition which had the support of the papacy.[84] The fact that Godfrey's career as duke of Lower Lotharingia was comparatively undistinguished may also have influenced his decision to join the First Crusade. Modern historians agree that Godfrey wielded considerably less authority as duke than his predecessors.[85] As noted in the opening chapter, the eleventh-century kings of Germany pursued policies which seem to have weakened ducal authority and strengthened episcopal power in the kingdom.[86] The authority associated with the office of duke of Lower Lotharingia had begun to decline long before Godfrey's appointment in 1087. Godfrey the Bearded's rebellions against Henry III had provoked reprisals which had served to sap the duke's power.[87] Moreover, for a duke to wield meaningful authority in his duchy, he needed to possess substantial land and holdings within its confines. Godfrey of Bouillon did not enjoy this advantage in Lower Lotharingia. It is also the case that the most influential dukes of the kingdom of Germany were able to exert their authority beyond their own duchy. Godfrey the Bearded's rebellions had shaken the political foundations of the Empire. Godfrey the Hunchback had loyally served in Henry IV's campaigns in Saxony, and been the king's most vocal secular supporter in his dispute with Gregory VII. In contrast, Godfrey of Bouillon's activities were largely confined to scuttling around the Middle Meuse attempting to safeguard Bouillon and other parts of his personal inheritance. As already noted, as late as 1094 Godfrey was asserting his status as the legitimate successor of Godfrey the Hunchback and Godfrey the Bearded.[88] The very fact that some contemporaries referred to Godfrey as 'Godfrey of Bouillon' might be interpreted as a sign that they were aware his activities were largely confined to the region surrounding his main stronghold.[89] While his two immediate predecessors who shared his name also used Bouillon as their main residence in the region, his association with that place was sufficiently notable in the eyes of his contemporaries for that place to form the basis of his distinguishing cognomen.

A clear indication of how far the authority of the duke of Lower Lotharingia had diminished by 1095 is the fact that Godfrey retained the office while he was on the First Crusade. It was not until Christmas 1101 – over five years after Godfrey's departure in August 1096 and about a year and a half after his death in Jerusalem in July 1100 – that Henry IV appointed a new duke.[90] In the late eleventh century, Henry IV seems to have regarded the count palatine of Lotharingia – rather than either of its dukes – as his main source of support in the region.[91] Ducal authority diminished in the late eleventh century in part because it was usurped by the bishops of Liège, namely Henry and his successor Otbert. Developments such as Bishop Henry's Peace assembly in *c.*1082 served to weaken ducal power and bolster episcopal authority.[92] While Godfrey was duke, Otbert conducted military campaigns and commanded troops in the manner of a secular prince.[93] Godfrey's departure on the First Crusade permitted Otbert further to increase episcopal influence in the region, and he subsequently attained a level of authority that previously had been associated with the ducal office.[94] Other ecclesiastical authorities proved inimical to Godfrey's authority as duke. As discussed in the previous chapter, in the early 1090s he became embroiled in the conflict which arose between Otbert and Abbots Berenger of St Laurent and Thierry II of St Hubert. At one point during that episode, Berenger had publicly rebuked Godfrey for failing to support them against Otbert. While the background of the 'Investiture Conflict' made it difficult for most secular lords to maintain friendly relationships with reform-orientated monasteries, the example of Robert II of Flanders – who succeeded in cultivating close ties with prominent houses located in his comital ambit – proves that it was not impossible.[95] In contrast to figures like Robert, Godfrey had more ambivalent relationships with monastic reformers in his locality. Modern historians who believe that Godfrey was closely affiliated with Henry IV have generally expressed surprise at his decision to participate in the First Crusade. The foregoing, however, has established that his decision might have relied on earlier developments and impulses. His career in Lotharingia was not as closely aligned with Henry as modern historians have generally supposed. While Godfrey did owe his appointment as duke of Lower Lotharingia in 1087 to Henry, contemporary evidence does not cast him as a close associate of the emperor. Moreover, during his career in Lotharingia, Godfrey was oftentimes in dispute with Henry's allies, including Bishop Otbert of Liège, Bishop Thierry of Verdun, and Count Albert of Namur. Godfrey can hardly thus be described as an avowed and unalloyed supporter of the imperial cause. He had no connection to Henry IV which created a potential barrier to his participation in the crusade. It should also be noted that Henry himself had no concerns with Godfrey taking part in the First Crusade. Frutolf of Michelsberg and, following him, his 1106 continuator indicate that before Godfrey set out on the crusade, he secured Henry IV's assent to depart, relating that Godfrey passed through Bohemia and Hungary 'with the permission of Emperor Henry'.[96] Admittedly, had Henry been implacably opposed to Godfrey participating in the crusade, there was probably not a great deal that he could have done in 1095–1096 to prevent it. The emperor had left Germany in March 1090 to campaign in Italy.[97] Matilda of Tuscany's marriage to Duke Welf of Bavaria had served to cut Henry off from the Alpine passes, preventing him from returning to Germany. As a result, in the years that followed, Henry was contained in north-east Italy, in the vicinity of Verona. Bernold of St Blasien explicitly states that at the time of the council of Piacenza in March 1095, Henry was confined in Italy.[98] Henry only returned to Germany in May 1097, by which point Godfrey and the rest of the crusaders from Germany had long since departed.[99] At Grone in July 1097, soon after his return to Germany, Henry issued a diploma in which he briefly mentioned the First Crusade and the departed Godfrey. In that document, he referred simply to the 'departure for Jerusalem, which came to be in our days on account of Duke Godfrey'.[100] This rather neutral description conveys no sense that Henry held any animosity toward Godfrey for departing Germany and the Empire to participate in the First Crusade.

Godfrey's decision to participate in the First Crusade, then, would have been shaped by a range of factors. He had access to channels of communication which would have enabled the papal message to reach him. He possessed dynastic ties to aristocrats based in regions beyond Lotharingia who took the cross, the most significant of whom were his brothers. The appeal to Godfrey (or for that matter any other inhabitant of the West in the late eleventh century) of visiting Jerusalem, on an expedition framed as a pilgrimage, should not be discounted. His response may have been conditioned by his father's exploits on the Norman Conquest and his maternal family's historic connections to the reform papacy, his involvement in his kinsman Henry of Liège's Peace assembly, and the influence of the teachings of the abbot and monks of St Hubert. The authority associated with his office of duke of Lower Lotharingia had declined in the eleventh century, and no hindrance to his participation was posed by Henry IV. While it is tempting to deliberate which of these factors had the most significant bearing on Godfrey's decision, it must be remembered that crusade motivation was in no sense a zero-sum issue. These factors were not mutually exclusive: they must have combined to heighten the overall appeal of the crusade message to Godfrey.

Godfrey's preparations for the First Crusade

After Godfrey had committed to go on the First Crusade, he began to prepare for his departure by raising funds. In an influential study, Riley-Smith estimated that at this time a crusader needed to amass resources equating to about four times his annual income to fund their expedition.[101] Participants thus had to make careful arrangements before setting out. In 1095–1096 Godfrey and other members of his family sold lands and property in order to accumulate collateral. The details of some of these transactions are described in contemporary evidence, including a number of charters. Modern historians have expressed differing views on the value of these documents for assessing the motivations of the individuals mentioned in them. Riley-Smith has argued that these documents provide a fair reflection of the named individuals' state of mind in advance of their departure on crusade.[102] Flori, in contrast, has suggested that this material demands a more critical interpretation. He stresses the role of clerics in drawing charters up, and questions how far these documents actually illuminate the ideas of the secular aristocrats whose financial exchanges they record.[103] The following analysis of the charters which detail Godfrey's preparations for the First Crusade leans towards the approach espoused by Flori. Crucially, these documents were created *after* the individual had decided to go on crusade, when they were at the stage of making preparations. These texts cannot therefore be used uncritically to deliberate what motivated that individual to make those decisions. Yet, these charters still provide highly significant evidence relating to the individuals named within them, as they convey a sense of how those individuals and their families wanted their attitudes to be *perceived* by their contemporaries.

Between taking the decision to go on the First Crusade and his departure in August 1096, Godfrey was engaged in a range of activities to accumulate funds for his expedition. The *Cantatorium* relates that soon after Godfrey had made his decision, he began to discuss the sale of the castle of Bouillon to Bishop Otbert of Liège, who, it is claimed, coveted Bouillon because he always strove to enhance his renown.[104] The text states that Godfrey's mother Ida came to Bouillon to help resolve the discussions.[105] Otbert then reportedly paid 1,500 silver marks for Bouillon to Godfrey.[106] This formed the bulk of his crusading funds. He apparently minted at least some of the resources he accumulated in advance of his departure. Coins seemingly manufactured on his behalf have turned up in hoards unearthed in Russia, one of which has been closely studied by modern scholars. The coin in question resembles derniers struck in Liège by Bishop Otbert, which provides an indication that it originated in Godfrey's locality. The obverse of the coin appears to hold the inscription *GODEFRIDUS IEROSOLIMITANUS*, which might be translated as 'Godfrey the Jerusalemite' or 'Godfrey the Jerusalem pilgrim'. It depicts a man with long curly hair, flanked on the left by the image of a raised sword and on the right by a *gonflamon* or war banner. The reverse of the coin bears the image of a cross.[107] Murray has suggested that while Godfrey may have carried low denomination coins so as to procure supplies on the march, he probably transported most of his silver in the form of ingots.[108]

The author of the *Cantatorium* claims that in order to raise the necessary funds to buy Bouillon, Otbert despoiled a number of religious houses of the diocese, and made a particular point of targeting St Hubert's resources. Otbert's agents reportedly took from St Hubert the golden table of the high altar, and destroyed three golden crosses so that they could take away the precious stones which adorned them.[109] The departure of Godfrey and other secular lords created in the diocese of Liège a power vacuum from which Otbert sought to profit. On 14 June 1096, he bought the castle of Couvin from Baldwin of Mons. In the document recording the purchase,

Otbert stated that his aim in obtaining Couvin was 'to ensure perpetual peace and tranquillity, because evildoers living in that place were lamentably vexing the diocese by plundering, robbing and other molestations'.[110] Another charter of 1096 records Otbert's acquisition of two mills – which had, incidentally, formerly been owned by Godfrey – from the church of Our Lady of Maastricht. In that document, Otbert asserted that he had purchased that property in order to protect the people of his diocese by keeping order while 'the most noble' (*nobilissimus*) Godfrey and other local secular lords were away on crusade.[111]

After noting that Ida arrived in Lotharingia to help discuss the sale of Bouillon to Otbert, the author of the *Cantatorium* recounted an episode which sheds important light on Godfrey's preparations for the First Crusade.[112] The author of this text relates that when Ida reached Bouillon, she found to her sorrow that, with the consent of her son, the priory of St Peter at Bouillon had been liquidated, and its monks had been sent to St Hubert, their mother house. (If Godfrey had been absorbing the revenues of the priory on the eve of the First Crusade, it is possible that he intended to use those revenues to finance his crusade.[113]) Knowing that the priory had been founded through the charity of her father, Godfrey the Bearded, Ida summoned Abbot Thierry II and asked what had happened. The abbot informed her that her brother, Godfrey the Hunchback, and her son, Godfrey of Bouillon, had ruined the priory by taking its revenues. The abbot adroitly reminded Ida that St Hubert possessed a bull of Pope Alexander II which confirmed that anyone who injured the abbey would be placed under excommunication. Ida was reportedly anxious to ensure the salvation of her father and the absolution of her brother and son. She tearfully beseeched Thierry to send the monks back to the priory, and absolve her brother and son, who had sinned in the eyes of God and her father. The abbot replied that he did not possess the power to do so, and that she would have to persuade her son to make restitution to St Hubert. To that end, Thierry informed Ida that Godfrey should offer to St Hubert the church of Sensenruth with its subject chapels, and the chapel of St John – which was probably in Bouillon itself – and the costs of maintaining the brethren in that place, as Godfrey the Bearded had formerly prescribed. Thierry's subtle threat of excommunication spurred Godfrey into action. The author states that Godfrey formally committed to the proposed agreement in front of an audience which included his nobles, and that he promised not to retract or contradict the gesture. Ida then donated to St Hubert the church of Baisy (near Nivelles in Brabant), for the safety of the souls of her father, brother, and son. A document, endorsed by legitimate witnesses, was drawn up to record St Hubert's acquisition of the church.

The author of the *Cantatorium* recounted Godfrey's actions regarding the priory of St Peter without passing explicit judgement on them. It might at first seem paradoxical that an individual should seek to raise funds for a devotional endeavour by despoiling a religious house. But

Godfrey's reputed actions in relation to the priory of St Peter could hardly be described as atypical of his age. It was possible for secular aristocrats at the time of the First Crusade to see no inconsistency between possessing a profound devotion to their faith and being sufficiently vigorous in military matters that they thought to target religious houses. As Riley-Smith put it, lords in Godfrey's age could be 'both rough and pious'.[114]

In the build up to Godfrey's departure, he and his mother Ida made a number of sales and donations to local ecclesiastical institutions. Ida continued in this vein after her three sons had departed on the crusade. A charter drawn up at some between January and August 1096 records that Ida relinquished the rights to a number of holdings around Tongres to the abbey of Munsterbilzen. This donation was made with Godfrey's consent, and he is listed among the witnesses.[115] Another charter records that Ida donated land in the region of Genappe to the abbey of Affligem in 1096 'for the safety of my soul, my father's, and those of my sons Duke Godfrey and Count Eustace'.[116] The same document records that Godfrey had previously made a donation of land in the same area to this abbey.[117] At one point in 1098 – about two years after her sons had departed – Ida made a bequest to the monastery of St Bertin. The document recording the exchange explains that she did so 'for the safety of my soul and for the souls of my husband Count Eustace, and for the safety of my sons, Eustace, Godfrey and Baldwin, who are fighting against the pagans, having gone to Jerusalem on Apostolic command'.[118] Further illuminating evidence is contained in a charter recording Ida's donation of the fiefs of Genappe and Baisy to the abbey of Nivelles in 1096. Though the original charter is lost, its content was incorporated into a diploma of confirmation issued to Nivelles by Henry IV in February 1098. At one point the diploma notes that 'the son of . . . countess [Ida], Duke Godfrey, and his brother Baldwin' had approved the donation to Nivelles, and states that at the time that it was made, the two brothers had been 'moved by the hope of an eternal inheritance and by love, [and] are preparing to fight for God in Jerusalem [after having] sold and relinquished all their things'.[119] The Nivelles document attributes to Godfrey and Baldwin the hope of an 'eternal inheritance'. If this denotes a secular rather than spiritual reward, then it seems especially applicable to Baldwin, given that he was a third son without land or title. Yet, the verbs *vendebant* and *relinquebant* are both formed in the third person plural, making it clear that the assertion also applied to Godfrey. However, the document also records that Godfrey and Baldwin had gone on the crusade in order to 'fight for God in Jerusalem', a phrase clearly intended to impute spiritual motives to them. Riley-Smith interpreted the information provided in these two charters as evidence that Godfrey had taken the cross out of spiritual concerns and in accordance with the papal message.[120] Similar ideas are expressed in charters drawn up on behalf of other prominent crusaders.[121] While the evidence provided in the St Bertin and Nivelles charters is significant, it is debatable how far they yield insight into Godfrey's state of mind. The information recorded in these documents relates chiefly to the activities of Ida. Godfrey's involvement in the Nivelles transaction is uncertain, and he had already departed by the time of the St Bertin bequest. At the very least, though, these documents show that ecclesiastics in Godfrey's locality interpreted his actions in the light of contemporary expectations and ideas about the First Crusade.

Modern historians have debated whether Godfrey intended to return to Lotharingia after the conclusion of the First Crusade. Mayer argued forcefully that it was Godfrey's intention to return to Europe.[122] In contrast, others have concluded that Godfrey departed on the First Crusade without the aim of returning.[123] A study of the material which details Godfrey's disposal of his lands and rights in 1095–1096 supports the latter view. Godfrey would surely have known that alienating his principal holdings would have made it almost impossible to resume the career that he had known in Lotharingia before 1095. The overall sense conveyed by this material is of an individual who had little inclination to return to the West. Crucially, participants in the First Crusade who possessed serious intentions of returning to the West could ensure that they had the option of doing so. Some of the written agreements of property disposals prepared for departing crusaders include clauses which permitted those individuals to reclaim property (or part of it) in the future. A crusader named Bernard Morel, for example, pledged a farm to the nuns of Marcigny (halfway between Lyon and Bourges), and the document drawn up to record that exchange indicates that Bernard retained the right to reclaim half of that farm if he returned.[124] No source written while Godfrey lived or within a few years of his death indicates that he made any kind of contingency plan that would have enabled him to resume his career in Lotharingia after the conclusion of the crusade. It is significant that the author of the *Cantatorium* described him as one of the many who upon hearing the call for the First Crusade resolved to 'swap the uncertain for the certain'.[125] Likewise, Frutolf states that in advance of his departure Godfrey 'converted virtually all his possessions into money'.[126] If the coins unearthed in Russian hoards were indeed minted for Godfrey in advance of his departure on the First Crusade, then they can be regarded as evidence that in 1095–1096 'Godfrey the Jerusalemite' saw his future not in the West but in the East.[127]

The composition of the army at whose head Godfrey departed Lotharingia also sheds light onto his preparations for the First Crusade. As previously indicated, Riley-Smith emphasised the importance of dynastic connections in explaining how participants were recruited to the First Crusade.[128] Murray's prosopographical work on Godfrey's contingent shows that ties of kinship bound him to many of those who accompanied him on the expedition.[129] The core of Godfrey's army was formed by his personal household, which included figures such as Baldric, the seneschal (*dapifer*),[130] Stabelo, the chamberlain (*camerarius*),[131] and, possibly, Ruthard, the steward (*prouisore*), who was in his company during the latter stages of the First Crusade.[132] Godfrey's household also included warriors who were dependent on him. Albert of Aachen refers at one point to Godfrey being accompanied by his *sodales*, a term which denotes household knights.[133] Elsewhere Albert refers directly to 'knights of Duke Godfrey's household'.[134] Godfrey's personal household formed a core around which other elements crystallised in 1095–1096. One of these elements consisted of individuals from Bouillon and nearby territories around the Middle Meuse, including figures such as Heribrand, the castellan of Bouillon.[135] A second element was formed by a number of lords from other parts of Lower Lotharingia, and a third comprised figures from Upper Lotharingia, the other German duchies, and northern France.[136] Albert of Aachen sought to emphasise the German character of Godfrey's army, noting at one point that alongside Lotharingians, his contingent included men from Saxony, Swabia, and Bavaria. He also referred at one point to the force under Godfrey as a 'Germanic company' (*Theutonicorum comitatus*).[137] Likewise, the author of the 'Bartolf' text stated that Godfrey went on the crusade accompanied by Swabians, Saxons, and Germans.[138] The author of the *Cantatorium* stated that when Godfrey departed on the First Crusade he took 'many nobles and clerics with him'.[139] This statement is somewhat misleading in the sense that only a few clerics are attested as being part of his army, at least at the time of his departure.[140] The wider background of the ongoing conflict between Henry IV and the papacy would have made it difficult for most prelates in Lotharingia and elsewhere in the kingdom of Germany to leave their offices.[141] Godfrey's army also provided a nucleus around which a number of poor non-combatant participants coalesced. Like their noble counterparts, these lower-ranking individuals had been inspired by the appeal for the crusade. By leading his force out of Lotharingia and through Germany, Godfrey provided such figures with the opportunity to join in the enterprise.

Contemporary evidence affords glimpses into the activities of the men who subsequently joined Godfrey's contingent. The charter of Ida's donation of Genappe and Baisy to Nivelles (as recorded in Henry IV's diploma of 1098) was witnessed by Godfrey, his brother Baldwin, and six other men who subsequently accompanied him on the First Crusade.[142] As Murray notes, occasions such as this no doubt provided an opportunity to discuss plans for the First Crusade.[143] Based on a study of the documents which detail Godfrey's preparations, Murray has also suggested that Godfrey had nominated Baldwin as his heir before they departed Lotharingia.[144] Contemporaries were impressed by Godfrey and his army. As noted above, Urban wrote in his 1096 letter to Alexios that Godfrey and his brothers led an army that surpassed that of Peter the Hermit.[145] Sigebert of Gembloux described the armies which comprised the First Crusade, before asserting that 'in the host of God, Godfrey, duke of Lotharingia, and his brothers Eustace and Baldwin, shone forth'.[146] Frutolf stated that Godfrey set out 'fortified with no little faith and many knights'.[147]

Notes

1 On Urban II and his pontificate, see: Alfons Becker, *Papst Urban II. (1088–1099)*, 3 vols (Stuttgart, 1964–2012).

2 The Byzantine embassy at the council of Piacenza is described in Bernold, p. 412, tr. p. 324. On the council, see: Robert Somerville, *Pope Urban II's Council of Piacenza* (Oxford, 2011). On the situation in Byzantium in the period leading up to the First Crusade, and the contacts between the Byzantines and the West, see: Peter Frankopan, *The First Crusade: The Call From the East* (London, 2012), esp. pp. 13–100.

3 On the Muslim world of the Near East on the eve of the First Crusade, see: Paul M. Cobb, *The Race for Paradise: An Islamic History of the Crusades* (Oxford, 2014), pp. 1–103; Carol Hillenbrand, *The Crusades: Islamic Perspectives* (Edinburgh, 1999), pp. 33–50. On Western conceptions of the Muslim world at this time, see: Nicholas Morton, *Encountering Islam on the First Crusade* (Cambridge, 2016).

4 Robert Somerville, *The Councils of Urban II: I Decreta Claromontensia* (Amsterdam, 1972), p. 143.

5 On Urban's plan for the crusade, see: Riley-Smith, *First Crusade*, pp. 13–30; Georg Strack, 'Pope Urban II and Jerusalem: A Re-Examination of His Letters on the First Crusade', *The Journal of Religious History, Literature and Culture*, 2 (2016), 51–70; Idem, 'The Sermon of Urban II in Clermont and the Tradition of Papal Oratory', *Medieval Sermon Studies*, 56 (2012), 30–45.

6 Somerville, *The Councils of Urban II*, p. 74.

7 On the First Crusade indulgence, see: Riley-Smith, *First Crusaders*, pp. 68–70. On crusade indulgences more generally, see: Ane L. Bysted, *The Crusade Indulgence: Spiritual Rewards and the Theology of the Crusades, c.1095–1216* (Leiden, 2015).

8 *DK*, pp. 136–7 (no. 2); JL 5608.

9 'Papsturkunden in Florenz', ed. Wilhem Wiederhold, *Nachrichten von der Gesellschaft der Wissenschaften zu Göttingen. Philosophisch-historische Klasse*, 3 (1901), 306–25, at pp. 313–14.

10 Riley-Smith, *First Crusaders*, pp. 67–9.

11 On Urban's tour of France in 1095–1096, see: René Crozet, 'Le voyage d'Urbain II et ses négociations avec le clergé de France (1095–1096)', *Revue Historique*, 179 (1937), 271–310; Becker, *Papst Urban II.*, vol. 2, pp. 435–57; H. E. J. Cowdrey, 'Urban II's preaching of the First Crusade', *History*, 55 (1970), 177–88; Riley-Smith, *First Crusaders*, pp. 53–80; Penny J. Cole, *The Preaching of the Crusades to the Holy Land, 1095–1270* (Cambridge, MA, 1991), pp. 1–36.

12 *DK*, p. 136.

13 For an overview of the response, see: Jean Flori, 'Ideology and Motivation in the First Crusade', in Helen J. Nicholson (ed.), *Palgrave Advances in the First Crusade* (Basingstoke, 2005), pp. 15–36.

14 Evidently, some took the cross whom Urban did not wish to go. In late 1096, he wrote to the people of Bologna, and instructed clerics not to set out on the expedition: *DK*, pp. 137–8 (no. 3).

15 On the number of participants in the First Crusade, see: France, *Victory*, pp. 122–42; Jonathan Riley-Smith, 'Casualties and the Number of Knights on the First Crusade', *Crusades*, 1 (2002), 13–28.

16 Carl Erdmann, *The Origin of the Idea of the Crusade*, tr. Marshall W. Baldwin and Walter Goffart (Princeton, 1977). For critiques, see: John T. Gilchrist, 'The Erdmann Thesis and the Canon Law, 1083–1141', in Peter Edbury (ed.), *Crusade and Settlement: Papers Read at the First Conference of the Society for the Study of the Crusades and the Latin East and presented to R. C. Smail* (Cardiff, 1985), pp. 37–45; John France, 'Holy War and Holy Men: Erdmann and the Lives of the Saints', *EC1*, pp. 193–208.

17 Riley-Smith, *First Crusaders*, pp. 81–143.
18 Bull, *Knightly Piety*.
19 William J. Purkis, *Crusading Spirituality in the Holy Land and Iberia, c.1095–c.1187* (Woodbridge, 2008), pp. 30–58.
20 John France, 'Patronage and the Appeal of the First Crusade', in *FCOI*, pp. 5–20. Riley-Smith, *First Crusaders*, p. 84, asserts that many dependants must have accompanied their lord willingly.
21 AA, pp. 2–45. For modern analysis, see: E. O. Blake and Colin Morris, 'A Hermit Goes to War: Peter and the Origins of the First Crusade', *SCH*, 22 (1985), pp. 79–107; Jean Flori, *Pierre l'Ermite et la première croisade* (Paris, 1999).
22 Robert Chazan has published a number of studies on the attacks on the Jewish communities of the Rhineland in 1096. See most recently his *God, Humanity, and History: The Hebrew First Crusade Narratives* (Berkeley, 2000). See also: Jeremy Cohen, *Sanctifying the Name of God: Jewish Martyrs and Jewish Memories of the First Crusade* (Philadelphia, 2004).
23 *CPC*, nos. 49–50, 64.
24 James A. Brundage, 'Adhemar of Puy: The Bishop and His Critics', *Speculum*, 34 (1958), 201–12. On papal legates at this time, see: I. S. Robinson, *The Papacy, 1073–1198: Continuity and Innovation* (Cambridge, 1990), pp. 146–78.
25 John H. Hill and Laurita L. Hill, *Raymond IV, Count of Toulouse* (Syracuse, 1962).
26 William M. Aird, *Robert Curthose, Duke of Normandy* (Woodbridge, 2008); M. M. Knappen, 'Robert II of Flanders on the First Crusade', in L. J. Paetow (ed.), *The Crusades and Other Historical Essays* (New York, 1968), pp. 79–100; James A. Brundage, 'An Errant Crusader: Stephen of Blois', *Traditio*, 16 (1960), 380–95.
27 Ralph B. Yewdale, *Bohemond I, Prince of Antioch* (Princeton, 1924); Jean Flori, *Bohémond d'Antioche: chevalier d'aventure* (Paris, 2007); Nicholas L. Paul, 'A Warlord's Wisdom: Literacy and Propaganda at the Time of the First Crusade', *Speculum*, 85 (2010), 534–66; Robert L. Nicholson, *Tancred: A Study of His Career and Work in Relation to the First Crusade and the Establishment of the Latin East* (Chicago, 1940).
28 On eleventh-century relations between the papacy and the Normans of southern Italy, see: Robinson, *Papacy*, pp. 367–97; Graham A. Loud, *The Age of Robert Guiscard: Southern Italy and the Norman Conquest* (Harlow, 2000), pp. 186–233.
29 On Guiscard's campaign, see: Loud, *The Age of Robert Guiscard*, pp. 209–23; Georgios Theotokis, *The Norman Campaigns in the Balkans, 1081–1108* (Woodbridge, 2014), esp. pp. 137–84.
30 See, for example: France, *Victory*, p. 5.
31 Becker, *Papst Urban II.*, vol. 2, pp. 62–77; Cowdrey, *Gregory VII*, p. 234.
32 See, in general: Alfons Becker, 'Urban II. und die deutsche Kirche', in Josef Fleckenstein (ed.), *Investiturstreit und Reichsverfassung* (Sigmaringen, 1973), pp. 241–75.
33 *PL*, vol. 151, col. 406; JL 4153.
34 *PL*, vol. 151, cols 295–7; JL 4145.
35 Robert Somerville, 'The Council of Clermont (1095) and Latin Christian Society', *Archivum Historiae Pontificiae*, 12 (1974), 55–90, p. 67; Murray, *Crusader Kingdom*, p. 37. The affairs relating to Cambrai were settled at Clermont. See Urban's letter to the diocese: *PL*, vol. 151, col. 437; JL 5598.
36 Somerville, 'The Council of Clermont', p. 67. Urban's letter of December 1095 to the people of Flanders is no doubt typical of other missives that have not survived.
37 See above, pp. 78–9.
38 *Papsturkunden in Spanien: I Katalonien*, ed. Paul Kehr (Berlin, 1926), pp. 287–8.
39 On the spread of oral reports in Lotharingia, see: Flori, *Pierre l'Ermite*, pp. 62–3.

40 AA, pp. 4–5.
41 Sigebert, p. 367.
42 'domnus papa maximus auctor fuit'. Bernold, p. 420, tr. p. 329. When Urban vis-
    ited Germany as Gregory VII's legate in 1084–1085, the future pope had raised
    Bernold to the priesthood, and this may have influenced how this chronicler
    reported the origin of the First Crusade.
43 Frutolf 1106, pp. 136–44, tr. pp. 146–9.
44 Asbridge, *The First Crusade*, p. 61. See also: Riley-Smith, *First Crusaders*, p. 96;
    France, *Victory*, p. 5.
45 Riley-Smith, *First Crusaders*, p. 55.
46 See above, p. 94.
47 *PL*, vol. 151, cols 283–4; JL 5348.
48 'karissimo sancti Petri filio'. Gregory VII, *Register*, pp. 13–15 (no. 1.9), tr.
    pp. 9–10. On how popes used their predecessors' registers at this time, see: Uta-
    Renate Blumenthal, 'Papal Registers in the Twelfth Century', in Peter Linehan
    (ed.), *Proceedings of the Seventh International Congress of Medieval Canon Law (Cam-
    bridge, 23–27 July 1984)* (Vatican City, 1988), pp. 135–51.
49 Gregory VII, *Register*, pp. 69–71 (no. 1.46), tr. pp. 50–1. See above, pp. 34–5.
    Some in the early-twelfth-century curia believed that Gregory's 1074 plans had
    foreshadowed the First Crusade. See: Riley-Smith, *First Crusaders*, p. 50.
50 'Primus omnium Petrus eremita innumerabilibus se ducem praebuit, cui Gode-
    fridus, Eustachius et Balduinus fratres, Bolonii comites, se addiderunt, majores
    etiam copias paraverunt'. *PL*, vol. 151, col. 485.
51 For the letter, see the previous footnote.
52 *GF*, p. 6.
53 Such figures included Count Hartmann of Dillingen and Wicher the Swabian.
    See: Murray, *Crusader Kingdom*, pp. 208–9, 235–6.
54 On this point, see also the discussion at pp. 98–9.
55 See above, pp. 77–81.
56 Anselm, *Opera*, vol. 4, pp. 85–6 (no. 195), tr. vol. 2, pp. 126–7.
57 Riley-Smith, *First Crusaders*, pp. 81–105.
58 As already indicated, Urban himself associated Godfrey with his brothers when
    describing their participation in the First Crusade. See above, p. 96.
59 It was noted in Chapter 1 that in 1088 Eustace participated in a failed rebel-
    lion in support of Robert Curthose against William Rufus, after which he had
    been deprived of the Honour of Boulogne. This remained the situation in
    1095, meaning that Eustace could not draw on the family's lands in England
    to raise funds for the First Crusade. Nevertheless, Eustace's relationship with
    the English crown was not irreparably damaged. In 1101, Henry I (1100–1135)
    restored Eustace to his English lands, and in the years that followed the count of
    Boulogne regularly attended the royal court. Tanner, 'In his brothers' shadow',
    p. 84; Eadem, *Families*, pp. 132–3, 145–7.
60 Riley-Smith, *First Crusaders*, pp. 91–2.
61 'adinuicem dilectissimi amici et consocii federati erant'. AA, pp. 262–3.
62 AA, pp. 92–3; Murray, *Crusader Kingdom*, p. 193.
63 AA, pp. 182–3; Murray, *Crusader Kingdom*, p. 203; Mayer, 'Baudouin Ier',
    pp. 32–42. Mayer dates the marriage of Baldwin to Godehilde to *c*.1090.
64 Riley-Smith, *First Crusaders*, pp. 91, 93.
65 AA, pp. 72–3. On their meetings in the 1080s, see above, pp. 68, 75. On Baldwin
    of Mons, see: Murray, *Crusader Kingdom*, pp. 186–7; Idem, 'The Army of Godfrey
    of Bouillon', p. 307. Robert I had usurped Baldwin's family as count of Flanders,
    and it was no doubt for this reason that Baldwin did not wish to accompany

Robert II of Flanders on the First Crusade. Baldwin was killed on the expedition in 1098.

66 Murray, 'The Army of Godfrey of Bouillon', pp. 303–9; Idem, *Crusader Kingdom*, pp. 46–51.

67 'cum duce Godefrido, nec non et aliis regni principibus'. 'Documents extraits du cartulaire du chapitre de Fosses', ed. J. Barbier, *Analectes pour servir à l'histoire ecclésiastique de la Belgique*, 4 (1867), 396–422, at pp. 396–8 (no. 1). See also: Murray, *Crusader Kingdom*, pp. 47–8, 234–5.

68 *Cantatorium*, p. 203.

69 'ex praecepto Apostolico'. *ODEH*, vol. 1, p. 79.

70 AA, pp. 60–3; *CPC*, no. 67; MvK, vol. 4, pp. 519–20.

71 Riley-Smith, *First Crusaders*, p. 81.

72 Riley-Smith, *First Crusaders*, pp. 25–33. On pilgrimage to Jerusalem in the era before the First Crusade, see: Matthew Gabriele, *An Empire of Memory: The Legend of Charlemagne, the Franks, and Jerusalem Before the First Crusade* (Oxford, 2011), pp. 73–93.

73 Einar Joranson, 'The Great German Pilgrimage of 1064–1065', in Louis J. Paetow (ed.), *The Crusades and Other Historical Essays: Presented to Dana C. Munro by His Former Students* (New York, 1928), pp. 3–43; Fritz Lösek, ' "Et bellum inire sunt coacti": The Great Pilgrimage of 1065', in Michael J. Herren, C. J. McDonough, and Ross J. Arthur (eds), *Latin Culture in the Eleventh Century: Proceedings of the Third International Conference on Medieval Latin Studies* (Turnhout, 2002), pp. 61–72.

74 Verlinden, *Robert Ier*, pp. 151–9; France, *Victory*, p. 101.

75 'Huic expeditioni non solum diverse etatis populares, sed etiam ipsi provincirarum consenserant principes, et sponte posthabitis uxoribus et filiis, honoribus quoque et patrimoniis aut omnino relectis aut precio distractis, festinabant captare incerta pro certis. Cum his Godefridus dux ire disposuerat'. *Cantatorium*, p. 203.

76 'Ante huius uie initium cum sepe idem dux suspira traheret, et sui animi optio ante omnia esset uisitare ciuitatem sanctam Ierusalem, et uidere sepulchrum Domini Iesu, et sepe priuatis famulis animi sui intentionem aperiret'. AA, pp. 436–7.

77 Bull, *Knightly Piety*, esp. pp. 155–203.

78 See above, pp. 26–7, 28–9, 30–1.

79 Bull, *Knightly Piety*, pp. 21–69. Urban preached the Peace at Clermont and continued to do so during his subsequent tour of France.

80 Jean Flori, 'De le paix de Dieu à la croisade? Un réexamen', *Crusades*, 2 (2003), 1–23; Idem, *La Guerre Sainte. La formation de l'ideé de croisade dans l'Occident chrétien* (Paris, 2001).

81 Riley-Smith, *First Crusaders*, p. 94.

82 Riley-Smith, *First Crusaders*, p. 96.

83 See above, p. 38.

84 On William the Conqueror's efforts to secure papal support for his invasion of England in 1066, see Bates, *William the Conqueror* (2016), pp. 221–3.

85 Maquet, *'Faire Justice'*, pp. 503–23; Despy, 'La fonction ducale en Lotharingie', pp. 107–9; Mayer, 'Baudouin Ier', p. 20. In contrast, Dorchy, 'Godefroid', p. 998, and Laret-Kayser, 'La function et les pouvoirs', reject the argument that Godfrey was a weak duke, suggesting that he retained significant authority in the duchy.

86 See above, p. 16.

87 Robinson, *Henry IV*, p. 24.

88 *ODEH*, vol. 1, pp. 76–7.

89 As previously noted, the author of the *Cantatorium* referred several times to Godfrey as 'Godfrey of Bouillon': *Cantatorium*, pp. 106, 126–7. The account of

the judicial duel written by the abbot of Stavelot in 1095 also refers to him in this way: *Recueil des chartes de l'abbaye de Stavelot-Malmédy*, vol. 1, pp. 264–6 (no. 129).

90 The appointee at that time was Henry, count of Limburg, the grandson of Frederick of Luxemburg, who had held the office of duke between 1045 and 1065: Sigebert, p. 368.

91 Robinson, *Henry IV*, pp. 314–15; Murray, *Crusader Kingdom*, p. 26.

92 Kupper, *Liège et l'Église impériale*, pp. 464–70, esp. pp. 467–8; Werner, 'Der Herzog von Lothringen', pp. 445–6.

93 See above, pp. 77, 79–80.

94 Kupper, 'La Maison d'Ardenne-Verdun', p. 213.

95 Steven Vanderputten, *Monastic Reform as Process: Realities and Representations in Medieval Flanders, 900–1100* (Ithaca, 2013), pp. 176–8.

96 'tam imperatoris Heinrici . . . permissione'. Frutolf, p. 108, tr. p. 131; Frutolf 1106, p. 126, tr. p. 139. Functionally, permission to traverse Bohemia and Hungary amounted to permission to depart on the expedition. Some crusaders at this time requested permission to depart from their overlords before setting out; Rainald III of Château-Gontier departed in 1097 after receiving the consent of Count Fulk IV of Anjou: *Chroniques des comtes d'Anjou et des seigneurs d'Amboise*, ed. Louis Halphen and René Poupardin (Paris, 1913), p. 149; Riley-Smith, *First Crusaders*, p. 88.

97 Robinson, *Henry IV*, pp. 275–96; MvK, vol. 4, p. 1.

98 Bernold, pp. 408, tr. p. 323.

99 Indeed, by that point, the forces of the First Crusade had already reached Constantinople and had crossed into Asia Minor. See below, 125–7.

100 'ad profectionem Ierosolimorum, quę facta est in diebus nostris duce quodam Godefrido'. *MGH DD H IV*, no. 457 (Grone, 26 July 1097).

101 Jonathan Riley-Smith, 'First Crusaders to the East and the Costs of Crusading, 1095–1130', in Michael Goodich, Sophia Menache and Sylvia Schein (eds), *Cross Cultural Convergences in the Crusader Period* (New York, 1995), pp. 237–57; Giles Constable, 'The Financing of the Crusades in the Twelfth Century', in Kedar, Mayer and Smail (eds), *Outremer*, pp. 64–88.

102 Riley-Smith, *First Crusaders*, pp. 2–5.

103 Flori, 'Ideology and Motivation', p. 21.

104 'Otbertus glorie sue students, predictum castrum oblatum sibi concupivit'. *Cantatorium*, p. 206.

105 *Cantatorium*, p. 204.

106 'Otbertus . . . mille quingentas argenti libras pro eo duci condixit'. *Cantatorium*, p. 206. Kupper, *Liège et l'Église impériale*, p. 429, describes this as 'une somme fabuleuse'.

107 For the coin, see: Victor Tourneur, 'Un denier de Godefroid de Bouillon frappé en 1096', *Revue belge de numismatique et de sigillographie*, 83 (1931), 27–30. On the hoard, see: N. Bauer, 'Der Fund von Spanko bei St. Petersburg', *Zeitschrift für Numismatik*, 36 (1926), 75–94, esp. pp. 78–9.

108 Alan V. Murray, 'Money and Logistics in the Forces of the First Crusade: Coinage, Bullion, Service, and Supply, 1096–99', in John H. Pryor (ed.), *Logistics of Warfare in the Age of the Crusades* (Aldershot, 2006), pp. 229–49, at pp. 239–41.

109 *Cantatorium*, pp. 208–6.

110 'propter pacem et tranquillitatem perpetuo habendam, quia malefactores ibidem commorantes rapinis et predis aliisque molestiis miserabiliter vexabant episcopatum'. *Cartulaire de la Commune de Couvin*, ed. Stanislas Bormans (Namur, 1875), pp. 1–5 (no. 1), at p. 1. On Otbert's acquisition of Couvin, see: Kupper, 'Otbert de Liège', pp. 372–4; Murray, *Crusader Kingdom*, pp. 186–7.

111 *Diplomata belgica ante annum millesimum centesimum scripta*, ed. M. Gysseling and A. C. F. Koch (Brussels, 1950), pp. 393–4 (no. 236). For comments on Otbert's acquisition of Bouillon and other properties around the time of Godfrey's departure, see: Kupper, 'Otbert de Liège', pp. 372–9; Riley-Smith, *First Crusaders*, pp. 125–6.

112 *Cantatorium*, pp. 204–6.

113 Murray, *Crusader Kingdom*, p. 38.

114 Riley-Smith, *First Crusaders*, p. 42.

115 *Diplomata belgica*, pp. 376–7 (no. 225).

116 'pro salute animae meae, patris quoque mei ducis Godefridi & Comitis Eustathii'. *ODEH*, vol. 1, pp. 77–8.

117 *ODEH*, vol. 1, p. 77.

118 'pro incolumitate filiorum meorum Eustathii, Godefridi & Balduini . . . qui contra Paganorum incursus, ex praecepto Apostolico Hierosolymam profecti sunt'. *ODEH*, vol. 1, p. 79.

119 'dux Godefridus et frater eius Balduinus . . . eterne hereditatis spe et amore concepto Hierosolimam deo militatum ire parantes sua quoque omnia vendebant et relinquebant'. *MGH DD H IV*, no. 459 (Aachen, February 1098).

120 Riley-Smith, *First Crusaders*, pp. 63, 70.

121 A charter of Robert of Flanders issued toward the end of 1096, for example, states that he had been spurred by apostolic command to go to Jerusalem to liberate the Church of God ('auctoritate apostolicę sedis promulgato, iturus Jherusolimam, ad liberandam Dei ęcclesiam'. *Actes des comtes de Flandre, 1071–1128*, ed. Fernand Vercauteren (Brussels, 1938), pp. 62–3 (no. 20).

122 Mayer, 'Baudouin Ier', pp. 43–8. It should be noted that some of those who conclude that Godfrey intended to return based their judgements on mid–twelfth-century evidence which suggests that he and his brother Eustace retained an option to redeem Bouillon from the bishopric of Liège. Since that evidence is not contemporary it is not considered here.

123 See, for example: Robinson, *Henry IV*, p. 314; Murray, *Crusader Kingdom*, p. 39.

124 *Le Cartulaire de Marcigny-sur-Loire, 1045–1144*, ed. Jean Richard (Dijon, 1957), p. 164; Riley-Smith, *First Crusaders*, p. 116.

125 'incerta pro certis'. *Cantatorium*, p. 203.

126 'Gotefridus . . . qui priori anno cunctis quę possidebat in precium redactis'. Frutolf, 126, tr. p. 131. The passage was repeated by Frutolf's continuator: Frutolf 1106, p. 126, tr. p. 139.

127 See above, p. 104. The term 'Jerosolimitanus' became particularly associated with participants in the First Crusade. A number of veterans of the expedition acquired the sobriquet upon their return to the West. See: Riley-Smith, *First Crusaders*, p. 149.

128 Riley-Smith, *First Crusaders*, p. 86.

129 Murray, *Crusader Kingdom*, pp. 37–55; Idem, 'The Army of Godfrey of Bouillon'.

130 AA, pp. 62–3, 300–1; Murray, *Crusader Kingdom*, p. 184.

131 AA, pp. 62–3, 436–9; Murray, *Crusader Kingdom*, p. 229.

132 AA, pp. 436–7; Murray, *Crusader Kingdom*, p. 80; Idem, 'The Army of Godfrey of Bouillon', p. 302.

133 AA, pp. 134–5; France, *Victory*, p. 19.

134 'milites de domo ducis Godefridi'. AA, pp. 538–9.

135 AA, pp. 100–1, 352–3; Murray, *Crusader Kingdom*, pp. 209–10.

136 Murray, *Crusader Kingdom*, pp. 46–51; Idem, 'The Army of Godfrey of Bouillon', pp. 303–10.

137 AA, pp. 200–1, 210–11.

138 Bartolf, p. 493.

139 'multos secum nobiles et religiosos'. *Cantatorium*, p. 208.
140 The two securely attested prelates are Louis, archdeacon of Toul, and Adalberon, archdeacon of Metz. See: Murray, *Crusader Kingdom*, pp. 178–9, 217.
141 Murray, *Crusader Kingdom*, pp. 50–1.
142 Those seven witnesses are: Godfrey's brother Baldwin, Cono of Montaigu, Warner of Grez, Henry and Godfrey of Esch, and Heribrand and Walter of Bouillon. See: *MGH DD H IV*, no. 459; Murray, 'The Army of Godfrey of Bouillon', pp. 306–7.
143 Murray, 'The Army of Godfrey of Bouillon', pp. 306–7.
144 Murray, *Crusader Kingdom*, p. 34.
145 See above, p. 96.
146 'Eminebant in hoc Dei hostico dux Lotharingiae Godefridus et fratres eius Eustatius et Balduinus'. Sigebert, p. 367.
147 'militibus copiosis fideque non modica instructus'. Frutolf, 108, tr. p. 131, repeated by the continuator: Frutolf 1106, p. 126, tr. p. 139.

4   The First Crusade, 1096–1099

Lotharingia to Constantinople, August–December 1096

With his departure on the First Crusade, Godfrey of Bouillon emerged from the relative obscurity that had characterised his career in Lotharingia. From this point in his career on, Albert of Aachen's account is indispensable. This author made Godfrey – whom he described as 'duke of the realm of Lotharingia [and] a most noble man' – the chief protagonist of his account of the First Crusade.[1] Of all the Latin chroniclers of the expedition, only Albert accumulated significant information regarding Godfrey's march to Constantinople.[2] According to Albert, Godfrey departed on 15 August 1096 or within a few days of it, stating that he and his contingent were on the road to Jerusalem by mid-August (Map 4.1).[3]

Albert, however, provides no information on the first few weeks of Godfrey's journey to Constantinople. In contrast, a Hebrew text seems to record that in that period, Godfrey threatened violence against Jewish communities in Germany. The account – known to modern historians as the *Solomon bar Simson* chronicle – describes the various attacks perpetrated by the bands of crusaders who set out prematurely, before accusing Godfrey of committing a further crime:

> It was as this time that Duke Godfrey [of Bouillon], may his bones be ground to dust, arose in the hardness of his spirit, driven by a spirit of wantonness to go with those journeying to the profane shrine, vowing to go on this journey only after avenging the blood of the crucified one by shedding Jewish blood and completely eradicating any trace of those bearing the name 'Jew,' thus assuaging his own burning wrath.[4]

The author states that one member of the Jewish community of Mainz despatched a messenger to Henry IV in Italy, who sent letters to Godfrey and various other figures in Germany, both secular and ecclesiastical, demanding that they do no harm to the Jewish communities.[5] The author asserted that

> the evil duke then swore that he had never intended to do them harm. The Jews of Cologne nevertheless bribed him with five hundred *zekukim*

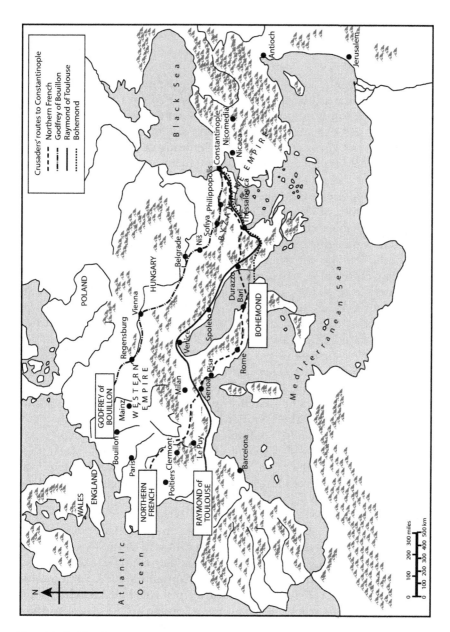

Map 4.1 Godfrey's route to Constantinople

of silver, as did the Jews of Mainz. The duke assured them of his support and promised them peace.[6]

According to this author, then, Godfrey capitalised on the earlier attacks on the Jewish communities of Mainz and Cologne by extorting money from them.

It is important to note, however, that the authenticity of the claim in the *Solomon bar Simson* text is far from secure. While Albert noted that some of the premature bands of crusaders had persecuted Jewish communities in the kingdom of Germany, he made no mention of Godfrey in connection to those attacks.[7] Moreover, the Hebrew lettering of the sole extant manuscript of the *Solomon bar Simson* text is such that it is debatable whether the 'evil duke' was indeed intended to denote Godfrey of Bouillon.[8] Hiestand has highlighted inconsistencies in the chronology of the account, noting that earlier bands of crusaders had destroyed the Jewish communities in Mainz and Cologne months before Godfrey had set out on the crusade, and it is difficult to imagine that many Jews would have remained in those places up until the time he departed.[9] Moreover, the passage which purportedly concerns Godfrey appears to date to the middle of the twelfth century, some fifty years or so after the First Crusade. Chazan, who has studied the various Hebrew First Crusade texts at length, has posited that the passage in question may have been inserted into the *Solomon bar Simson* text by a later interpolator.[10] Murray suggests that Godfrey's posthumous reputation as one of the leading heroes of the First Crusade may have induced the author of the *Solomon bar Simson* text (or its interpolator) to level this accusation of extortion against him.[11] On the other hand, it is possible that the text accurately describes how Godfrey dealt with Jewish communities soon after he departed. Like those earlier bands of crusaders who had already carried out attacks on Jewish communities, Godfrey may have sought to target perceived enemies of Christianity close to home. If he did extract these funds in the manner described, he would have significantly bolstered the resources he had collected for the expedition before August 1096. Murray has calculated that a thousand *zekukim* of silver amounted to between 8,000 and 12,000 ounces of silver, that is, between 1,000 and 1,500 marks.[12]

Godfrey's route to Constantinople began on the well-trodden pilgrim road which straddled the Danube through southern Germany before passing into the kingdom of Hungary. This was the same route along which Peter the Hermit's forces had travelled to Constantinople several months earlier (see Map 4.1).[13] Peter and Godfrey probably both marched south along the Rhine to reach the Danube. According to the dates provided by Albert of Aachen, Godfrey's force passed through southern Germany quickly. After noting that Godfrey's army set out on the crusade in mid-August, he relates that it camped at the city of Tulln, about twenty-five miles west of Vienna, for three weeks in September.[14] The journey to Tulln from Lotharingia must therefore have taken only a few weeks during the second half of August and early September.[15] While Godfrey's forces were camped at Tulln, they discovered that some of the crusaders who had reached the kingdom of Hungary earlier in the year had suffered at the hands of its king, Coloman (1095–1116).[16] Albert relates that the most prominent figures in Godfrey's contingent debated how they should deal with Coloman. They concluded that they should not send any of the most renowned men in the army to speak to the king in person, except Godfrey of Esch, who, the chronicler claims, had met Coloman long before, for he had previously been sent to Hungary on a diplomatic mission by Godfrey of Bouillon.[17] Albert's suggestion that Godfrey of Bouillon had been in contact with Coloman many years before 1096 is implausible, as Godfrey would have had no reason to contemplate passage through Hungary before the time of the First Crusade. If Godfrey of Esch had previously met Coloman, though, it would have made good sense to send him as a representative. Godfrey of Esch was accompanied on his mission to Coloman with a dozen members of Godfrey of Bouillon's household, including Baldric the seneschal and Stabelo the chamberlain. These representatives enquired of Coloman why he had created such difficulties for the earlier bands of Christians, to which the king replied that those contingents had been unruly and ill-disciplined, and so had brought the problems that beset them in Hungary upon themselves. Coloman sent Godfrey's representatives back to the army with the message that he had heard that Godfrey was a powerful lord and trustworthy man, and so, wishing to meet in person, the king invited him to join him at his castle at Sopron.[18]

Leaving Baldwin in charge of his army, Godfrey departed the camp to meet Coloman at the suggested place. During that encounter at Sopron, Coloman assured Godfrey of his friendship, and this persuaded Godfrey to travel on to Pannonhalma, where the king entertained him for eight days. Albert claims that many Hungarian nobles had learned that Godfrey was a renowned warrior, and so flocked to Pannonhalma to meet him. During the discussions in that place, Godfrey secured from Coloman safe passage through Hungary and markets for his army. For his part, Godfrey sealed the agreement by committing to send to Coloman hostages including Baldwin, along with his wife Godehilde and household, and other high-ranking figures from his army. With this agreement in place, Godfrey ordered the rest of his force to move up to Sopron.[19] When Godfrey returned to his army there, he announced that all were to pass through Hungary peacefully, and informed Baldwin that he was to be sent as a hostage to Coloman until the army had left the kingdom. At one point after this, Baldwin violently argued against the arrangement, and only assented to act as a hostage when Godfrey declared that he himself would go if Baldwin would not. According to Albert, Baldwin finally consented to the plan in order to protect the rest of the army. After Baldwin had entered the king's custody, Godfrey brought his army up to Pannonhalma, and instructed his force not to plunder or commit violence in Hungary upon pain of death. Coloman maintained his part of the agreement, and arranged for markets to be set up for Godfrey's men, who were then able to procure essential supplies at a fair price.[20]

Godfrey's force crossed the river Drava (which meets the Danube near modern Osijek in Croatia), shadowed by Coloman and a force of cavalry, and marched on to Francavilla, where they stayed for three days, during which time they acquired more supplies. Albert states that the army then moved on to Zemun (close to Belgrade), and passed five nights on the bank of the Sava. The Sava, which flows into the Danube at Belgrade, was a significant frontier marker, for it divided the kingdom of Hungary from Bulgaria, which was part of the Byzantine Empire.[21] The chronicler states that it was at Zemun that Godfrey and his chief associates learned that Byzantine troops were blocking the path onwards through Bulgaria. In response, they sent a force of warriors across the Sava to ward off the Byzantines, and this enabled the rest of the contingent to follow behind. At this point Coloman sent Baldwin and the other hostages back to Godfrey, and then turned back into Hungary. Godfrey's army camped for a night in Belgrade – which lay on the opposite bank of the Sava to Zemun – before departing the next morning. Instead of continuing to straddle the Danube further east, though, they left the banks of the river and headed south into the vast Bulgarian forest. Soon, they encountered legates bearing a message from Alexios Komnenos imploring Godfrey to prevent his troops plundering Byzantine territory, in exchange for fair and secure markets. Albert claims that when Godfrey 'learnt of the emperor's goodwill, he promised to obey the emperor's commands in all things', and had it announced that all were to keep the peace.[22] Andressohn interpreted Albert's claim as evidence that Godfrey possessed a 'conciliatory nature'.[23] However, a likelier explanation is that Albert sought with this assertion to convey the impression that Godfrey had begun the First Crusade favourably disposed toward Alexios and the Byzantines. Albert would not have wanted to suggest that Godfrey was at all culpable for the subsequent breakdown in relations between the Byzantines and the crusaders.

Godfrey led his army southward through Byzantine territory in peace to the imperial fortress of Niš. They camped there for four days 'in great plenty and enjoyment', having received gifts of supplies and access to markets.[24] The army then moved on to Sofiya, where it camped for several days, and received yet more supplies from Alexios.[25] They then moved on to the city of Philippopolis, and it was there that Godfrey received the news that Alexios was holding captive a number of Western nobles, including Hugh of Vermandois, the younger brother of King Philip I of France.[26] Godfrey was greatly angered by these reports, and he sent an embassy to Alexios requesting that the emperor free those men, and warning that if he did not do so, he would forfeit Godfrey's trust and friendship. It was at this point that Baldwin of Mons and Henry of Esch secretly departed Godfrey's army, so that they could arrive at Constantinople before Godfrey's embassy reached Alexios. They believed that Godfrey's demand regarding the captives would displease Alexios, and so wanted to reach the city before Godfrey's representatives so that they could receive more gifts from the emperor. According to Albert, Godfrey reacted to the news of Baldwin and Henry's furtive departure with displeasure and anger, which he strove to conceal.[27] Godfrey moved his army on to Adrianople, but found that the inhabitants had barred the bridge over the river. They departed that place quickly and moved on to Salabria, located on the sea of Marmara about forty miles west of Constantinople. Godfrey's messengers returned from the Byzantine capital and reported that Alexios had yet to release his captives. Albert states that this news angered Godfrey, and prompted him to curtail friendly relations with the emperor. Godfrey also gave his army permission to plunder, and for a period of eight days they devastated the region around Salabria. When Alexios heard about this development, he sent a number of Westerners who were in his service to Godfrey, requesting that he bring his army back under control. The emperor also promised to release the men he was holding captive. Godfrey assented to the request, and set out on the short march to Constantinople.[28] During the very last stages of Godfrey's march to the Byzantine capital, then, relations between his army and the Byzantines were extremely tense.

Constantinople, December 1096–April 1097

Godfrey's army reached Constantinople just before Christmas 1096.[29] The plan for the expedition as a whole was for the various armies to muster at Constantinople before crossing the Bosporus into Asia Minor as one. Hence, in the months after Godfrey's arrival, the forces led by Raymond of Toulouse, Bohemond, Stephen of Blois, Robert of Normandy, and Robert of Flanders would assemble there. The author of the *Gesta Francorum* asserted that Godfrey's 'great army' had marched to Constantinople along a route that Charlemagne had taken centuries earlier, and that Godfrey and Peter the Hermit had travelled together.[30] While Peter had taken the same route, he had done so several months before Godfrey. This error might reflect misinformation that circulated in Bohemond's contingent during the expedition.

The arrival of the crusader armies at Constantinople in late 1096 and early 1097 made Alexios wary.[31] He had good reason to be. Earlier in 1096, the forces led by Peter the Hermit had wreaked havoc in Byzantine territory. When Alexios had originally contacted Urban II to request military assistance, the emperor had envisaged gaining help from a specialist military force. There can be little doubt that he would have been perplexed and unnerved to discover that vast armies containing large numbers of non-combatants were wending their way to his capital. Moreover, the fact that one of those armies was under the command of Bohemond would have caused the emperor particular anxiety. As previously noted, in 1081 Bohemond and his father Robert Guiscard had led an invasion of the western flank of the Byzantine Empire.[32] Anna explicitly states that Bohemond's participation caused apprehension among many Byzantines at this time.[33] In the run up to the crusaders' arrival, Alexios also had to grapple with the logistical difficulties of supplying such vast contingents. Though Urban had warned Alexios that the crusaders were heading to Constantinople, the task of preparing adequate provisions nevertheless remained mountainous.[34] The emperor's plan for dealing with the crusaders was to keep the forces apart from each other and monitor communications between the leaders, and thereby prevent them from uniting and attacking his capital.[35] By manipulating the supply of provisions and halting markets when necessary, and by bestowing gifts of precious metals and fabrics, he sought to compel each of the leaders to take an oath to him. Under the terms of that oath – which seems to have been framed as an oath of vassalage of the kind with which the crusaders would have been familiar in the West – the leaders agreed to prevent their armies from plundering imperial land, and to hand over to the emperor any former Byzantine territory that they captured during the course of the expedition.[36] For his part, Alexios agreed to provide support to the crusaders.

Assessing the interactions between Alexios and the crusaders at Constantinople in 1096–1097 is no easy task. The sources which detail these discussions were coloured by hindsight, and above all, the knowledge that the crusaders and the Byzantines became estranged over Bohemond's refusal to relinquish Antioch to Alexios after its capture in 1098. The Latin sources – above all, those of the *Gesta Francorum* tradition – portray Alexios as a perfidious villain; a traitor who sought from the outset only to undermine the First Crusade.[37] Anna Komnene, in contrast, sought to safeguard her father's reputation, asserting that he had adopted the correct strategy in his dealings with the crusaders.

Godfrey's army remained at Constantinople from December 1096 to April 1097.[38] For much of that period, relations with the Byzantines were strained, and there were several armed confrontations. The dynamic which underpinned these hostilities was Alexios' concerted effort to secure from Godfrey the oath, and his manipulation of markets to that end. As Godfrey and his army neared Constantinople just before Christmas Day 1096, they were greeted by Hugh of Vermandois and the other captives whom Alexios had – true to his word – released. At this point, a group of Byzantine legates asked Godfrey to leave his army behind outside the city walls, and take some of his most prominent companions with him into the city to meet the emperor. Almost immediately after Godfrey received this request, 'certain strangers from the land of the Franks' emerged from Constantinople and went to his camp, in order to counsel him to avoid meeting Alexios in person. They warned Godfrey that if he did come face-to-face with Alexios, he would inevitably succumb to the emperor's tricks and deceit.[39] Godfrey heeded this advice, and refused to meet Alexios. Godfrey's reluctance to meet piqued the emperor, and to signal his displeasure he closed the markets to Godfrey's army. Following Baldwin's suggestion, the army secured the requisite supplies by looting the region surrounding their camp. They continued plundering until Alexios relented and restored the markets. Their restoration coincided with Christmas Day, and for the next four days, peace was observed on both sides.[40]

On 29 December, Alexios sent messengers to Godfrey, requesting that he relocate his army to a part of the city which straddled the sea.[41] This was the area outside the city wall near the northern part of the Golden Horn. Nearby, on the other side of the wall inside the city, was Alexios' Blachernae Palace.[42] Godfrey shifted his camp to the specified location, and in that place his army continued to receive supplies from the Byzantines. Soon after, another imperial legation visited Godfrey and again asked him to meet with Alexios in person. Godfrey again refused the request, and instead sent a group of associates including Baldwin of Bourcq to speak with the emperor. Those messengers returned to Godfrey and reported that Alexios had promised friendship and good faith to him, but Godfrey remained unconvinced. For the next fifteen days messages passed back and forth between him and Alexios.[43] Finally, the emperor's patience wore thin and he once again cut off the markets. Albert also states that Alexios sent a force of Turcopoles to menace Godfrey's contingent. The Turcopoles reportedly shot arrows at the camp, killing some and wounding others. In response, Godfrey drew up his military forces and destroyed some of the buildings near their camp. He also became concerned that Alexios would attempt to seize the bridge which provided access from Constantinople to his camp. He thus instructed Baldwin to take a force and seize the bridge pre-emptively. Baldwin remained stationed with that force on the bridge from dawn to dusk, and in that time they skirmished against Alexios' Turcopole troops. Baldwin's efforts enabled the rest of the contingent to cross the bridge and set up camp on the side next to the city. At night, Godfrey had his brother stand down, and he then restored peace with the Byzantines.[44] That peace was short-lived, however; at sunrise the next morning, Godfrey gave the order for everyone in his contingent to rise up and plunder the surrounding area, and they did so for the next five or six days.[45] These hostilities prompted Alexios to send yet another message to Godfrey, asking him to restore his army to peace, and to come and confer in person. Godfrey agreed to this on the condition that Alexios sent him high-ranking hostages as assurance.[46] Anna Komnene later wrote that at some point in this period in which Godfrey steadfastly rebuffed repeated requests to meet Alexios, the emperor asked Hugh of Vermandois to visit Godfrey and persuade him to come to terms. Anna states that Godfrey firmly rejected Hugh's plea.[47] While no other source attests that Alexios tasked Hugh with speaking to Godfrey, the claim is not out of keeping with the rest of her father's varied efforts to manipulate Godfrey into meeting in person.

Just as Godfrey sent his messengers to Alexios confirming his assent to a meeting in person, Bohemond and his force of Normans approached

Constantinople. Bohemond had crossed the Adriatic from southern Italy, and had marched at an easy pace along the Via Engatia, delaying his arrival at the Byzantine capital in order to see how events unfolded.[48] According to Albert of Aachen, as Bohemond neared Constantinople, he sent Godfrey a message in which he suggested that they should unite their forces and attack the Byzantines.[49] There may be truth in Albert's claim. Anna Komnene wrote that after her father discovered that Bohemond and Godfrey intended 'to fulfil their dream of taking Constantinople' and that they 'planned to dethrone [him] and seize the capital', he ensured that messages sent between the two men were intercepted.[50] Modern historians including France and Flori have concluded that Bohemond did make this proposal to Godfrey.[51] Such a proposal would certainly have been in keeping with the aggressive and acquisitive approach that Bohemond generally adopted. Crucially, however, whether or not Bohemond did suggest this course of action, Albert seized upon it to emphasise Godfrey's admirable motivation for joining the crusade and his honourable intentions towards the Byzantines. According to Albert, Godfrey mulled over Bohemond's proposition for a night, and took counsel with his men, but then refused it because

> he had not left his homeland and family for the sake of profit or for the destruction of Christians, but had embarked on the journey to Jerusalem in the name of Christ, and he wished to complete the journey and to fulfil the intentions of the emperor, if he could recover and keep his favour and goodwill.[52]

In this passage, the chronicler draws an implicit contrast between Godfrey and Bohemond in order to cast the former in a more favourable light.

A crucial indication that Bohemond did contact Godfrey with the suggestion that they unite against the Byzantines is that just before the former arrived at Constantinople, Alexios renewed his efforts to persuade Godfrey to meet him in person to take the oath. The emperor promised to grant supplies and markets, and to send his son John (the future Emperor John II Komnenos) as a hostage. Godfrey ordered Cono of Montaigu and Baldwin of Bourcq to take custody of the boy. Alexios' efforts paid dividends; around 20 January, Godfrey proceeded with some of his most prominent companions – but not his brother Baldwin – to the emperor's palace for a conference.[53] Albert reports that Godfrey and his retinue appeared before Alexios 'in splendour and adorned with expensive clothing, lavishly fringed with both purple and gold, snow-white ermine, and grey and variegated marten fur, which the princes of Gaul use in particular'.[54] Alexios, Albert reports, was impressed by Godfrey and his men, and received them all with the kiss of peace, though he remained seated on his throne instead of rising from it. Alexios reportedly then greeted Godfrey with the following words:

> I have heard about you that you are a very powerful knight and prince in your land, and a very wise man and completely honest. Because of

this I am taking you as my adopted son, and I am putting everything I possess in your power, so that my empire and land can be freed and saved through you from the present and future multitudes.[55]

Since Alexios' strategy was to compel Godfrey into swearing an oath to him, the emperor may well have deployed flattery of this kind at their meeting. Albert states that Godfrey was pleased by the emperor's words, and that he then 'not only gave himself to [Alexios] as a son, as is the custom of that land, but even as a vassal with hands joined, along with all the nobles who were there then, and those who followed afterwards'.[56] This seems to describe an oath of vassalage of the kind which the leading crusaders would often have performed in the West. Alexios then bestowed fine gifts upon Godfrey and his companions, thereby establishing 'an unbreakable chain of complete trust and friendship'.[57] A few passages later in his account, Albert states that as part of the agreement between Bohemond and Alexios, the former 'became the emperor's man', and promised not to retain any former part of the Byzantine Empire unless Alexios permitted it.[58] Though Albert is not explicit on this point, these terms clearly also applied to the accord between Godfrey and the emperor. Anna Komnene, in contrast, reports outright that Godfrey 'swore on oath as he was directed that whatever towns, lands or forts he might in future subdue that had in the first place belonged to the [Byzantine] Empire would be handed over' to her father.[59] In short, then, Godfrey entered into the agreement with Alexios, and did so on the emperor's terms.

After Godfrey took the oath to Alexios, relations between the two were congenial. Albert states that every week from the time they reached their agreement at the start of 1097 to just before Pentecost (fifty days after Easter), four Byzantine envoys brought stacks of gold coins to Godfrey's camp, for distribution to his army.[60] The day after Godfrey returned to his army after reaching his accord with Alexios, he ordered that 'peace and honour should be shown to the emperor and all his men', while the emperor for his part instructed his men to provide fair markets to the crusaders, and even ordered prices to be lowered.[61] At the beginning of Lent, Alexios summoned Godfrey to another face-to-face meeting, and enjoined him to move his army across the Bosporus into Asia Minor. Albert states that Godfrey assented to the request and had his army set up camp on the opposite side of the Bosporus at the northern tip of Asia Minor, although he subsequently had to return and meet the emperor several times to ensure the Byzantines maintained fair market rates.[62]

Albert of Aachen's treatment of events at Constantinople during the winter of 1096–1097 serves to emphasise Godfrey's noble qualities and cast him as the chief protagonist of the *Historia*. Significantly, in contrast, Anna Komnene paid very little attention to Godfrey in her treatment of these events. That author instead focussed her attention firmly on Bohemond, who occupies the role of anti-hero not just in her account of the First Crusade, but in her *Alexiad* as a whole.[63] Anna's treatment of the discussions at

Constantinople conveys a sense of how the Byzantines perceived the relative status of Godfrey and Bohemond while the two were camped at Constantinople; they clearly regarded the latter as the more serious threat.[64]

After concluding the agreement with Godfrey, Alexios deployed similar tactics to compel the other leading crusaders to take oaths to him. Albert reports that Bohemond arrived at Constantinople around Easter Sunday (5 April), and that, at Alexios' request, Godfrey met him and escorted him to a meeting with the emperor. The chronicler states that Godfrey negotiated at length with Alexios on Bohemond's behalf, and persuaded him 'with very many coaxing words' to meet the emperor face-to-face, at which point he took the oath.[65] Anna Komnene paints a rather different picture of the interactions between Bohemond and Alexios. She claims that Bohemond requested to be appointed to the office of *Domestikos* of the East, but that her father astutely demurred instead of giving him a definitive answer.[66] In the ensuing weeks, the remaining groups of crusaders reached Constantinople. Robert of Flanders was the next to arrive. Upon learning that Bohemond and Godfrey had taken oaths to the emperor, Robert quickly followed suit.[67] Robert of Normandy, Stephen of Blois, and Eustace of Boulogne – Godfrey and Baldwin's elder brother, who had travelled to the Byzantine capital with the other forces from northern France – then did likewise.[68] Raymond of Toulouse's army skirmished with Byzantine troops during its approach to Constantinople in late April, and this made discussions with Alexios difficult. The other leaders had to convince Raymond not to attack the city in retribution. Raymond, for his part, had no intention of swearing an oath to the emperor. Bohemond, who was now striving to convey the image of a stalwart ally of Alexios, threatened violence against Raymond to compel him to come to terms with Alexios. Raymond only did so after intense discussions, and after the emperor permitted Raymond to take a modified oath of the kind often sworn in southern France, in which he promised to do the emperor no harm.[69] While Alexios managed to secure oaths from most of the prominent crusaders, some – principally Tancred and Baldwin – managed to slip across the Bosporus without doing so.[70] With most of the princes now bound to him by their oaths, though, Alexios was eager for the crusaders to leave Constantinople and cross the Bosporus to Asia Minor. All did so except Raymond of Toulouse, who remained behind at the Byzantine capital for further discussions with the emperor.

Writing in hindsight, the author of the *Gesta Francorum* asserted that the crusaders had taken oaths to Alexios out of 'desperate need', and that they had been deceived by his 'fraud and cunning'.[71] But this misrepresents the true nature of the agreements reached between the emperor and the crusaders in 1097. The leaders swore oaths to Alexios because they knew that Byzantine aid and advice would be essential if the crusade was to stand any chance of succeeding.[72] It is clear that at the time the agreements with the emperor were made, relations were generally friendly; Stephen of Blois wrote to his wife in 1097 and spoke warmly about how Alexios had treated the crusaders.[73]

The gathering of the crusader forces at Constantinople must have pre-cipitated discussions among the chief participants over the leadership of the expedition. Urban explicitly noted in his letter to Flanders that he had appointed Adhémar as the leader of the expedition, but the bishop of Le Puy was hardly likely to have been capable of directing military affairs.[74] That responsibility was not assumed by a single individual. Although Godfrey – along with Robert of Normandy – possessed the title of duke and so technically held the highest secular office among the participants of the expedition, in practice, the crusade was directed by a council of its leading figures. During the initial stages of the expedition, at least, these figures managed to reach agreements on most issues.[75] At various points in his account, Albert provides an insight into this process. In one passage, he states lucidly that the leaders of the crusade 'took counsel together and led as equals'.[76] He also refers to the leaders holding councils and reach-ing decisions by consultation during the early stages of the crusade.[77] It is also important to note, however, that at many points during the cru-sade, the leading figures had to respond to the wishes of the rank and file participants.[78]

Asia Minor, May–October 1097

Godfrey's force set out from their camp at the northern point of Asia Minor toward Nicaea at the start of May. Heading south, they soon arrived at Nicomedia (see Map 4.2). Several of the other crusader armies joined him there, including those from northern France. It was at that place that the crusaders encountered Peter the Hermit and the remnants of the People's Crusade. At this point, the objective of the crusaders was to recapture the former Byzantine city of Nicaea, which was held at that time by Kilij Arslan, the sultan of Rhum.[79] Godfrey sent ahead from Nicomedia a force of 3,000 men to clear a path through the dense forest to Nicaea. Those men placed crosses along the newly cleared road so that the rest of the crusaders knew which route to take.[80] The armies reached Nicaea on 6 May, and Godfrey's force set up camp next to the city's eastern gate.[81] Albert explicitly notes that Eustace and Baldwin also took up positions outside the city wall, indicating that the three brothers had by this stage linked up.[82] Thereafter throughout the crusade, Eustace would work closely with Godfrey.[83]

On 14 May Bohemond reached the city, and his force immediately invested the northern gate. Although the city's southern gate remained open – in anticipation of Raymond of Toulouse's arrival from Constantinople – the crusaders began operations on the city.[84] Albert describes the disposi-tion of the crusader forces around Nicaea. He identified a number of fig-ures present in Godfrey's contingent, including Warner of Grez, Baldwin of Mons, and Baldwin of Bourcq.[85] Albert also states that in the period fol-lowing Bohemond's arrival, the crusaders captured an enemy spy, against whom Godfrey and others encouraged the use of torture. The prisoner was

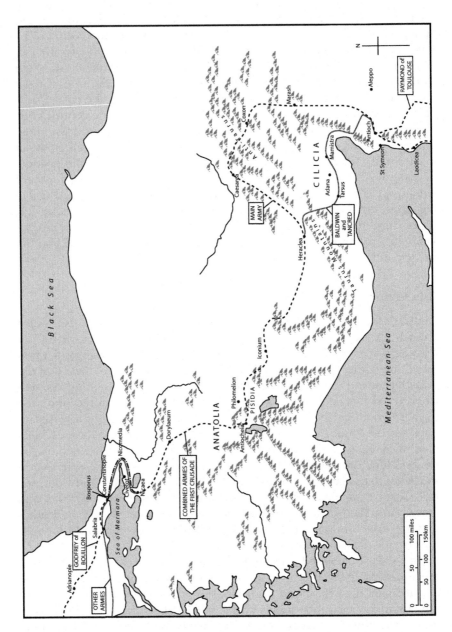

Map 4.2 The route of the First Crusade across Asia Minor

then compelled by the crusaders to convert to Christianity. He also revealed to the crusaders that a relief army under Kilij Arslan was nearby and poised to attack. This prompted the leaders at Nicaea to send a message to Raymond of Toulouse, who was en route from Constantinople, asking him to hurry on to the city as fast as he could.[86]

Raymond marched his army through the night to Nicaea. His men were setting up their camp outside the city when Kilij Arslan's force struck. Raymond of Aguilers provides an account of the ensuing encounter, relating that Arslan's force divided into two, with one group attacking Godfrey's camp and the other seeking to enter through the unguarded south gate. According to this chronicler, Raymond of Toulouse resisted Arslan's force while Godfrey and Bohemond attacked from the east.[87] Albert of Aachen describes how at one point Godfrey and Bohemond sped to enter the combat:

> Duke Godfrey and Bohemond did not curb their horses but let them have their heads and flew through the midst of the enemy, piercing some with lances, unsaddling others, and all the while urging on their allies, encouraging them with manly exhortations to slaughter the enemy.[88]

France, trusting more in Albert's account than that of Raymond of Aguilers, concludes that Godfrey and Bohemond rallied their men well in this encounter.[89]

After the crusaders repelled Kilij Arslan's attack, the siege entered a stalemate. They attempted a range of strategies, including the deployment of siege engines. Albert asserts that during this time Godfrey's associates Henry of Esch and Hartmann of Dillingen paid out of their own pockets for the construction of a siege device.[90] For a period of about a month, the crusaders made no progress because they were unable to enforce an effective blockade of the city. Crucially, Nicaea backed onto a lake from where supplies could be delivered to the garrison in defiance of enemy forces camped outside the city wall. Albert writes that at some point during this period of deadlock Godfrey carried out a notable feat of arms. The chronicler states that a Turkish archer stationed on the walls of Nicaea was inflicting heavy casualties upon the crusaders camped outside the city. He relates that to eliminate this threat 'Duke Godfrey . . . seized his crossbow, and, standing behind the shields of two of his comrades, he struck that Turk through the vitals of his heart'.[91] The decisive moment in the siege of Nicaea came on 18 June. On that day, the crusaders used a siege engine to destroy a wall tower, while, at the same time, Byzantine ships took control of the lake behind the city. These attacks compelled the garrison finally to surrender.[92] Alexios arrived shortly after and took possession of Nicaea. On 22 June at Pelekanum, Alexios met with most of the leading crusaders. There, they renewed their oaths to him, and he most probably provided to them advice on attacking Antioch, the crusaders' next target.[93]

On 26 June, the crusaders began to depart Nicaea. They started to march across Asia Minor in the direction of Dorylaeum, an old Byzantine fortress. A few days into the march, the crusaders became divided into two. The contingents under Bohemond and others including Robert of Normandy and Stephen of Blois ended up two miles further ahead from the forces led by Godfrey, Robert of Flanders, and Raymond of Toulouse.[94] Albert of Aachen suggests that the forces parted deliberately, to make it easier to procure supplies and so that the crusaders did not have to camp too close together.[95] In contrast, Fulcher of Chartres, who was present at this time, noted that 'Godfrey [and the other leaders] had been absent from us for two days. They had for some reason, I know not what, separated from us with a large number of men'.[96] The author of the *Gesta Francorum* suggests that the separation of the crusaders was unintended, and that it took place during the hours of darkness when they were unable to see each other and maintain unity.[97] Early in the morning on 1 July, forces under Kilij Arslan pounced on the crusaders' exposed vanguard.[98] Bohemond, in command of that beleaguered force, despatched a request for assistance to Godfrey and the others, who were further back along the road. The forces under Bohemond resisted the attack, anticipating that their fellow crusaders would soon come to their aid. Raymond of Aguilers describes how Bohemond requested assistance from Raymond of Toulouse and Godfrey, who then sped to the battle.[99] Albert provides a more dramatic rendition of this phase in the battle, recounting how Bohemond's messenger reached Godfrey and informed him of the attack. Godfrey, the chronicler asserts, immediately called upon all those in his camp to take up their arms, before he and his comrades flew to the battle without delay, 'just as if they had been called to a party offering every sort of pleasure'.[100] The chronicler then provided a vivid description of Godfrey's troops as they rushed to help the force under Bohemond:

> Already a very clear day had dawned, the sun was shining with brightest rays, and its splendour glittered on the golden shields and the iron mail; the standards and flags, bright with jewels and purple, raised high and fixed on spears, were fluttering. The swift horses were urged on with spurs, they pressed on their way, nobody waiting for companion or friend, but each going as fast as he could to the assistance and revenge of the Christians.[101]

Godfrey and his relief force arrived at the battle and immediately launched into the fray. After a period of sustained and intense combat, Kilij Arslan's men began to flee. Albert devoted particular attention to Godfrey's role in the combat. According to this chronicler, after Arslan's forces began to turn away from the battle, Godfrey and fifty of his household warriors (*sodales*) pursued them for six miles and captured much plunder.[102] The author of the *Gesta Francorum* says little about the battle, but does note that Godfrey had fought with distinction, proving himself to be *audax et fortis*, a phrase which Hill rendered as 'reckless and brave'. It is doubtful, however, that the author intended this phrase to have any negative connotations. Following the *Gesta*, Tudebode stated that Godfrey fought in the battle in exactly the same terms, which the modern editors of his account translated as 'splendid and brave'.[103] As France notes, Albert's customary preference for Godfrey led the chronicler to emphasise his role in the encounter, even though it is clear that the other leaders who rushed to assist the vanguard also fought well.[104] Nevertheless, the fact that the author of the *Gesta Francorum* and Tudebode also mentioned Godfrey's role in the battle suggests that he did indeed distinguish himself in the clash.

While the defeat of Kilij Arslan's army removed the last major military obstacle to the crusaders' passage through Asia Minor, the remainder of their journey was far from trouble-free; the summer climate and harsh conditions claimed many lives during the march.[105] At the end of July the crusaders reached Antiocheia (Antioch in Pisidia). Albert of Aachen alone recounts a story that took place soon after their arrival. The chronicler relates that because the crusaders had suffered so badly during the march, they resolved to pause in that place to recuperate. He states that the nobles present in the army were pleased when they discovered that nearby were meadows and woods which were suitable for hunting. The leaders reportedly spread out in the forest to hunt. At this point, Godfrey happened upon a crusader who was attempting to flee the attack of a wild bear. According to Albert, Godfrey sped to the aid of the unfortunate crusader by engaging the beast in single combat:

> The duke, then, as he was accustomed and ready to help his Christian comrades at all times of misfortune, hastily drew his sword, vigorously spurred his horse and swooped down upon the wretched man . . . When the bear saw [Godfrey] bearing down on it at a gallop, trusting its own fierceness and the rapacity of his claws, met the duke face to face with no less speed, opened its jaws to tear his throat, raised up his whole body to resist – or rather to attack, unsheathed its sharp claws to rip him to pieces; it drew back its head and forepaws, carefully guarding against a blow from the sword . . . The duke, reflecting that the cunning and evil animal would oppose him with bold savagery, was keenly provoked and violently angry, and with the point of his sword turned towards it he approached the brute in a rash and blind attack, to pierce its liver. But by an unlucky chance, as the beast was escaping the blow of the sword it suddenly drove its curved claws into the duke's tunic, the duke fell from his horse, brought down to the ground embraced in his forepaws, and it wasted no time before tearing his throat with its teeth.

The chronicler then recounted how Godfrey reacted to the beast's ferocious attack:

> The duke therefore, in great distress, remembering his many distinguished exploits and lamenting that he who had up to now escaped splendidly from all danger was now to be choked by this bloodthirsty beast in an ignoble death, recovered his strength; he revived in an instant and was on his feet, and, seizing the sword . . . he held it by the hilt and aimed swiftly sat the beast's throat, but mutilated the calf and sinews of his own leg with a serious cut.[106]

A modern scholar with medical expertise has assessed Albert's report of Godfrey's self-inflicted wound, and tenuously diagnosed a ruptured artery.[107] According to Albert, it was only the intervention of a man named Husechin, who happened to be nearby, that prevented the bear from killing Godfrey. Though Godfrey's strength had begun to wane from the blood loss caused by the wound to his leg, he and Husechin together attacked the beast with their swords, and managed finally to kill it.[108] Godfrey, gravely wounded, was carried on a litter back to the crusaders' camp. Godfrey was reportedly so stricken by his injuries that his army was forced to march at a slower rate behind him.[109]

Albert's account of the bear fight can be interpreted in several ways. On one hand, it can be taken at face value as a description of an incident which actually unfolded. Wild bears seem to have inhabited the forested areas of Asia Minor in the eleventh century, so it is possible that the crusaders encountered such beasts during their march.[110] According to this chronicler, Godfrey was not the only crusader to enter combat against a ferocious wild animal. Later in his account, Albert claims that Godfrey's associate Wicher the Swabian distinguished himself in the vicinity of Jaffa by single-handedly killing a lion.[111] At a later point in his account, Albert asserts that Godfrey had completed his recovery from this injury early in 1098.[112] The fact that almost no mention is made of Godfrey in relation to events which took place from the summer of 1097 until that time suggests that some unfortunate incident probably did befall him. Moreover, as no other chronicler provides any other information on Godfrey's absence, Albert's account of the incident cannot simply be dismissed.

Accepting Albert's description of the bear fight at face value does raise a question about authorial intention, however. Throughout the rest of his *Historia* Albert was careful to emphasise Godfrey's credentials as a warrior. It may be that he intended in this passage to outline Godfrey's noble character rather than his military abilities, and it is the case that the former does become more sharply defined when juxtaposed with the bear's evil ferocity. Nevertheless, it remains perplexing that Albert should suggest that Godfrey's own shortcomings were in part responsible for the outcome of the fight. The implication of the passage is that Godfrey was overconfident in his own abilities, and so acted rashly by attempting to fight the animal. Moreover, to inflict an injury upon himself with his own sword in the manner described would have been an act of extreme clumsiness. If Albert had intended to showcase Godfrey's military skill in this passage, he would surely have omitted any suggestion of a self-inflicted injury.

As well as approaching the passage as a treatment of an historical incident, it is also useful to interrogate its narrative function within Albert's *Historia.* The story bears the hallmarks of a micronarrative of the kind that circulated in spoken form widely both during and after the First Crusade.[113] The story may have been designed to convey particular meanings. As Hodgson has argued, in medieval literature bears could create connotations of royalty and regnal authority.[114] Moreover, Albert's account of Godfrey's fight with the bear stands comparison with analogous scenes recounted in the *chansons de geste* in which Christian protagonists enter combat against wild animals. At one point in the *Chanson de Roland,* for instance, Charlemagne experiences a dream in which he fights a series of wild beasts, including a bear. This dream foreshadows Roland's death and the impending battle between Charlemagne's army and the Islamic Moors.[115] A study of Albert's *Historia* suggests that the passage had a particular purpose within his rendition of a wider series of events. For about seven months after the point at which Albert claims this incident took place, Godfrey was conspicuously absent from events. None of the sources of the *Gesta Francorum* tradition provide information on his whereabouts or explain in detail his absence during this period. He simply slips out of the narrative of these accounts, only to reappear in an event which took place in February 1098 during the siege of Antioch. Whether or not the incident unfolded as Albert suggests, then, the chronicler clearly used the story to account for Godfrey's absence during this crucial phase of the crusade. Albert asserts that the entire army 'was thrown into confusion by the wicked news' of Godfrey's incapacitation.[116] It is at this point in his narrative that the chronicler also describes Godfrey as a 'brave champion and man of wisdom, [and] head of the pilgrims'.[117] This passage therefore serves to reinforce Godfrey's importance to the expedition, just at the point at which he disappears from the thick of events.

The crusaders pressed on from Antiocheia and reached Heraclea by the end of August 1097. Nearing the end of their march across Asia Minor, they began to plan for their assault on Antioch. The main armies of the crusade departed Heraclea around 14 September, but rather than taking the most direct route to Antioch south through the Cilician Gates and across the Taurus Mountains and Cilicia, they instead turned north and travelled as far as Caesarea in Cappadocia before turning back southwards and making for Antioch. The purpose of this considerable detour was to cultivate alliances with local Armenian Christians, in anticipation of their attack on Antioch.[118]

From Heraclea, Baldwin and Tancred departed the main army and each took a force of men through the Taurus Mountains into Cilicia, apparently also with the aim of creating links with the native Armenians.[119] From this point, Baldwin's retinue began to grow. Members of Godfrey's household, including Baldwin of Bourcq, now switched to that of Godfrey's younger brother.[120] Albert, who provides the fullest account of these developments, wrote that Tancred soon arrived at the town of Tarsus, and, after issuing various promises and threats of reprisals from his uncle Bohemond, seemed poised to accept the town's surrender. This was signified when the townsfolk flew Tancred's flag atop the citadel. At this point, Baldwin and his following arrived, causing a brief moment of confusion as both Baldwin and Tancred's contingents mistook the other for an enemy force. The next day, Baldwin discovered Tancred's flag flying atop Tarsus, causing a dispute that nearly resulted in blows being traded. Baldwin then informed the inhabitants of Tarsus that if they instead surrendered to him they would be allied to Godfrey rather than Tancred and Bohemond. The people of Tarsus responded that they preferred to stay loyal to Tancred. According to Albert, Baldwin angrily countered that an agreement with himself and Godfrey would be more advantageous to the townsfolk of Tarsus. With the help of an interpreter, he spoke to the inhabitants as follows:

> You should not believe that Bohemond and this Tancred whom you so respect and fear are in any way the greatest and most powerful chiefs of the Christian army, nor that they bear comparison with my brother Godfrey, duke and leader of the soldiers from all Gaul, or any of his kin. For this same prince, my brother Godfrey, is duke of a realm of the great and earliest Roman emperor Augustus by hereditary right of his noble ancestors; he is esteemed by the whole army, and great and small do not fail to comply with his words and advice on all matters because he has been elected and appointed chief and lord by everyone.[121]

According to Albert, Baldwin's oration had the intended effect, for the inhabitants of the town soon resolved to come to an accord with him, which they sealed by removing Tancred's banner from the citadel and putting Baldwin's in its place.

It is possible that Baldwin actually uttered this hyperbole to the people of Tarsus. If he had been attempting to outmanoeuvre Tancred as Albert suggests, he may well have extolled his brother in such terms. By describing Godfrey as 'duke and leader of the soldiers from all Gaul' and emphasising the significance of his holding the ducal office, Baldwin may have sought to convey the sense that his brother outranked Bohemond. Even though Albert elsewhere wrote that the leaders of the crusade 'took counsel together and led as equals', the chronicler also seized upon the episode once again to underline Godfrey's superior authority among the rest of the leaders.[122] He did so by casting the struggle between Tancred and Baldwin at Tarsus as a symptom of a larger conflict that was unfolding at this time between Bohemond and Godfrey. Intriguingly, one of Albert's claims is that although Godfrey held the title of duke, it was on the First Crusade that he made his name, in contrast to Bohemond, whose reputation was already established. Albert thus wrote that as a result of Baldwin's efforts at Tarsus, 'Godfrey's name glittered for the first time'.[123] It should be noted that in contrast, the author of the *Gesta Francorum* portrays the events at Tarsus as nothing more than a personal rivalry between the two younger men.[124] Fulcher of Chartres, who was with Baldwin at this point, gives no indication that the names of Godfrey and Bohemond were invoked at Tarsus.[125] It seems that the confrontation at Tarsus resulted from a rivalry between two ambitious young men, who both invoked the name of their powerful relative to threaten the other as tensions escalated.[126]

Albert asserts that Tancred realised that Baldwin had the upper hand at Tarsus, and so departed to seek opportunities elsewhere. Baldwin was given partial control over Tarsus, but trouble arose after he refused entry to 300 members of Bohemond's army who arrived there, forcing them to camp outside the town walls. After Bohemond's men were attacked by a force of Turks, Baldwin faced recriminations from his men, but he succeeded in exonerating himself.[127] Tancred departed Tarsus and soon reached the nearby town of Adana, but he found that it was occupied by the Turks, and so moved on to the town of Mamistra, which he quickly captured and garrisoned. Baldwin soon followed Tancred to Mamistra and camped next to the city. Tancred, still fuming over what had transpired at Tarsus, sped to engage Baldwin's forces in combat. In the resultant skirmish, a number of crusaders were wounded and some were killed. As the repercussions of the dispute became clear, both sides sought peace, and this was duly concluded. Baldwin's solo exploits did not cease at this point. however. Acting on the advice of a 'certain Armenian soldier' named Pakrad, Baldwin captured Turbessel and Ravendel and expelled the Turkish garrisons of those places with the aid of the Armenian inhabitants. Pakrad, whom Baldwin briefly placed in charge of Ravendel, proved duplicitous and so was removed from the office.[128]

While Baldwin and Tancred were in Cilicia, the main army carried out its detour to Caesarea in Cappadocia and on about 10 October reached Marash, at the foot of the Taurus Mountains.[129] It was there a few days later that Baldwin's wife Godehilde died.[130] Baldwin briefly returned to the main army at Marash, but he soon departed once again to seek alternative opportunities. It was at this point that the chronicler Fulcher of Chartres joined Baldwin's following.[131] Baldwin's reputation had apparently circulated far and wide. The Armenian ruler of Edessa, Thoros, invited him to come to the city. After Baldwin travelled there in February 1098, Thoros adopted Baldwin as his son. About a month later the population turned on Thoros, a development which Baldwin seems to have unscrupulously seized upon in order to acquire Edessa for himself. In this way, Baldwin founded the first Latin state in the Holy Land.[132]

Antioch, October 1097–June 1098

The main crusader force departed Marash on 16 October and arrived at
Antioch five days later. The city had been held by the Turks since they captured it from the Byzantines in 1084. From a military standpoint, Antioch
was a formidable proposition. It was protected by extensive man-made fortifications and by nature, situated as it was on the steep slopes of mounts
Staurin and Silpius (see Map 4.3). As soon as the crusaders arrived, they

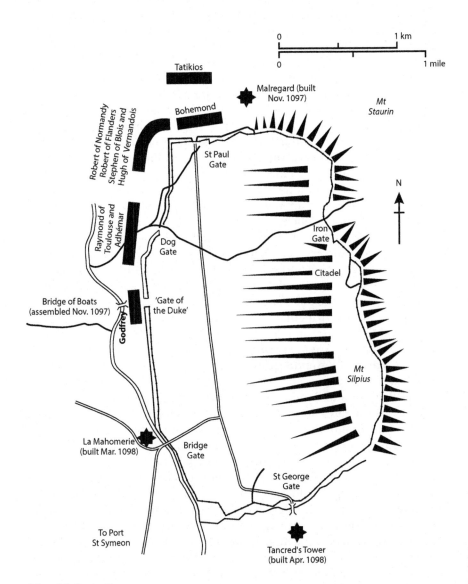

Map 4.3 Antioch

began their siege operation. However, the walls of the city were so extensive that they could only implement a partial blockade. Bohemond, Robert of Flanders, Robert of Normandy, Hugh of Vermandois, and Stephen
of Blois camped in the vicinity of the St Paul Gate. Raymond of Toulouse
and Adhémar camped outside the Dog Gate. Godfrey's force was stationed
outside a portal which later became known as the 'Gate of the Duke'. The
crusaders were, however, unable to blockade the Bridge Gate – so named
because it was placed directly beyond a bridge which jutted immediately
out from the gate over the Orontes river – and the St George Gate, situated
on the slopes at the southernmost point of the city.[133] The siege quickly settled into a stalemate, and this was how it remained during the initial few
months. Since the crusaders had left some of the gates unguarded, the garrison under the command of Yaghi Siyan, the city's governor, continued to
receive supplies. They were also able to sally out of the city and attack with
impunity. This opening period was characterised by frequent yet indecisive
military activity. As Albert of Aachen put it, 'a period of time was spent in
[the] sports of ever-present Mars, and in very frequent attacks'.[134]

In November, the crusaders fashioned a number of boats into a bridge
over the Orontes behind Godfrey's camp.[135] This makeshift bridge strengthened the crusaders' access to the nearby port of St Symeon. The arrival of
a fleet of Genoese ships in mid-November also provided the crusaders with
the materials they required to construct a counterfort – which they named
Malregard – on the slopes of Mount Staurin next to Gate of St Paul.[136] Of
the chroniclers who described the first months of the siege of Antioch, only
Albert provides any information regarding Godfrey's activities. According
to this chronicler, at one point Adalberon, a nobleman and archdeacon of
Metz, was having a liaison with a certain woman in an orchard near Godfrey's camp. Adalberon and the woman were both captured by the enemy
and decapitated. After the Turks launched their dismembered heads outside the city, they were reportedly retrieved and taken to Godfrey for identi-
fication.[137] Albert states that after another crusader, a knight named Arnulf
of Tirs, was mortally wounded in the same orchard, Godfrey ordered it to
be cut down.[138]

In December, the crusaders began to run short of supplies. This forced
them to seek provisions beyond the immediate vicinity of Antioch. At the
end of the month, they assigned Bohemond and Robert of Flanders to lead
a foraging expedition out in the direction of Aleppo. A few days after their
departure from Antioch they encountered an army led under Duqaq of
Damascus. Though the crusaders managed to escape largely unharmed
from the ensuing battle, they were unable to secure provisions before their
return to Antioch.[139] On 29 December, while Bohemond and Robert of
Flanders and their forces were still away from Antioch, the Muslim garrison
sallied out and attack the crusaders camped outside the city. The resistance
was led by Raymond of Toulouse, and the crusader forces sustained heavy
losses before Bohemond and Robert of Flanders returned just in time to tip

the balance in their favour.[140] These two men displayed decisive leadership at this time, with Raymond of Aguilers conveying the sense that Bohemond gained fame on account of his exploits.[141] This chronicler makes a point of noting that Godfrey was absent from these military confrontations in late December because he was 'gravely ill' (*dux maxime infirmabatur*).[142] While Raymond of Aguilers did not reveal the precise nature of Godfrey's malady, this author conveyed no sense that his absence was extraordinary. Other of the leaders were periodically incapacitated by illness during the First Crusade. Elsewhere, for example, this author noted that during the summer of 1097 Raymond of Toulouse was afflicted by 'a long and grave illness' which caused some to question his ability to fight.[143]

The crusaders' shortage of supplies became more acute in January and February 1098. As a result, the cost of food became greatly inflated.[144] Some began to despair of the situation, leading them to take drastic action. Louis, archdeacon of Toul, likely an associate of Godfrey's kinsman Count Rainald of Toul, led a force of 300 men away from Antioch in search of food, only to be attacked and wiped out by an army of Turks.[145] The circumstances at Antioch were so dire that in late January two prominent crusaders, Peter the Hermit and Walter the Carpenter, lord of Melun, attempted to flee, only to be intercepted and brought back to the camp by Tancred.[146] Raymond of Aguilers also claims that at some point around this time all the leaders of the crusade except Raymond of Toulouse agreed to grant Antioch to Bohemond, though it may be that the chronicler was thinking of discussions which took place a while later.[147]

Crucially, Albert brings Godfrey back to the fore of his narrative in relation to a development which took place in the first months of 1098. The chronicler explicitly notes that at this time Godfrey was 'now recovered from the illness caused by his wound', and so was sent 'with God's approval' on another foraging expedition.[148] This passage permits the establishment of a clearer picture of Godfrey's whereabouts during the first few months of the siege of Antioch. For that period, Albert only referred to Godfrey in relation to the incidents involving Adalberon of Metz and Arnulf of Tirs and does not ascribe to him any notable actions of his own. Albert's testimony, coupled with Raymond of Aguilers' explicit and independent assertion that Godfrey was seriously ill at the very end of 1097, makes it fairly conclusive that he was indeed incapacitated during this period.[149] Some mishap clearly befell Godfrey before the crusaders arrived at Antioch, and whether or not he had sustained serious injuries during a fight with a bear in Asia Minor as Albert had written, he remained in the background until early in 1098.

In early February, the crusaders learned that an army under Ridwan of Aleppo was marching to Antioch. On 8 February, the leaders held a council to decide on a strategy for facing Ridwan's forces. Albert reports that Adhémar suggested the crusaders should carry out a pre-emptive strike. The chronicler then has Godfrey – now very much restored to prominence – make a vocal contribution to the discussion. The chronicler uses Godfrey – whom he describes as 'always unflagging in the service of war' – to articulate the cause for which the crusaders would fight Ridwan:

> We are followers of the living God and Lord Jesus Christ, for whose name we serve as soldiers. [Ridwan's] men are gathered in their own strength: we are gathered in the name of God. Let us trust in his favour and not hesitate to attack the wicked and unbelieving foe, because whether we live or die we are the Lord's.[150]

In this passage, a very clear contrast is drawn between the crusaders and their enemy. While it is possible that Godfrey did make an intervention at the 8 February meeting, given that the passage invokes two scriptural passages (Psalms 19[20]:8 and Romans 14:8), the precise words used here are more likely to have been Albert's.

Putting aside Albert's customary predilection for his chief protagonist, it is clear that the most crucial development in the leaders' meeting was that for the first time the crusaders appointed a single commander: Bohemond.[151] It was he who directed the crusaders' strategy in the ensuing battle. The same day as the meeting, the crusaders divided their forces into two, with one staying at Antioch to guard the camp, and the other, led by Bohemond and including Godfrey, departing pre-emptively to attack the Aleppan force. Tudebode adds to the information found in the *Gesta Francorum* the detail that Adhémar, Robert of Normandy, and Eustace of Boulogne remained at the city to protect the camp.[152] The force led by Bohemond encountered the Aleppan force the following day (9 February). He orchestrated a daring cavalry attack which won the day for the crusaders.[153] While Godfrey was evidently following Bohemond's lead, Albert customarily attributed to Godfrey a prominent role in this encounter, writing that he was 'burning . . . with the desire to join the battle'.[154]

The arrival of an English fleet on 4 March at St Symeon instigated a new phase in the siege. The following day, the crusaders resolved to make use of the opportunity presented by the fleet's arrival by building a counterfort on the site of an old mosque outside Antioch's Bridge Gate. The intention was to increase the pressure on the garrison. Bohemond and Raymond led a force to St Symeon to collect the sailors and their materials and escort them back to Antioch. As they were returning to Antioch a few days later – most likely on 7 March – the garrison sallied out of the city and attacked them. A knight escaped from that melee to Antioch and reported what had happened to Godfrey, who, on Adhémar's orders, was crossing the bridge of boats near his camp in an effort at forcing the enemy back into the city. When he heard this news, according to Albert, Godfrey was visibly grief-stricken. Shortly afterwards, another messenger from Bohemond and Raymond reached Antioch and advised the crusaders there to withdraw into their camp to avoid the enemy's onslaught. According to Albert, this was not advice that Godfrey wished to heed. This author states that he

> was unafraid and thirsting for revenge for the destroyed Christians, and he refused absolutely to move from there or to desert this place out of any fear, but he declared with an oath that either he would today ascend the mountain [near the Bridge Gate] on which the fortress had been built, or he would lose his life with his men on that same mountain.[155]

Godfrey arrayed the crusader forces at the city into battle lines just as Bohemond and Raymond returned to the city. What followed was a fierce battle fought near the Bridge Gate.

Godfrey clearly carried out a notable feat of arms in that battle.[156] Raymond of Aguilers states that 'the duke of Lotharingia distinguished himself greatly there. He prevented the enemies [*hostes*] from reaching the bridge, and divided them in half as they climbed the stairs'.[157] The chronicler uses the plural noun *hostes* in this passage, indicating that he believed Godfrey's exploits in the battle had undermined the cohesion of a *group* of Muslim warriors. Albert of Aachen provides a somewhat different account of Godfrey's actions in this battle. This author relates that Godfrey sped to engage the enemy contingent, and, in the ensuing clash, carried out a feat of considerable martial skill and strength:

> Duke Godfrey, whose hand was very schooled in war, is reported to have cut off many heads there even though they were helmeted: this is said by those who were present and saw it with their own eyes. While he was thus exerting himself in the great labour of war and inflicting a great massacre in the midst of the enemy, amazingly he cut an armoured Turk who was threatening him with his bow into two parts with his very sharp sword. The half of the body from the chest upwards fell to the sand, the other half still grasped the horse with its legs and was carried onto the middle of the bridge in front of the city where it slid off and remained.[158]

This chronicler then noted that Godfrey's feat of arms prompted the rest of the crusaders to rejoice and renew their efforts in the battle. While Raymond of Aguilers' account conveys the sense that Godfrey's intervention had divided an enemy force in two, Albert has Godfrey cutting a single enemy soldier clean in two with a single blow of his sword. This chronicler no doubt asserted that he had heard about the incident from first-hand witnesses with the aim of authenticating his account.[159] Intriguingly, Albert attributes to Godfrey's associate Wicher the Swabian a similar feat at the same location, referring at one point in his *Historia* to the 'sword [Wicher] used to cut the Turk in half through hauberk and clothing on the bridge at Antioch'.[160] As previously noted, Albert also stated that Wicher bested a wild lion in combat.[161] It may be that the anecdotes concerning Godfrey and Wicher's exploits shared a common narrative basis.

Though Raymond of Aguilers and Albert of Aachen provide different versions of the feat, they both note that Godfrey distinguished himself in the Bridge Gate battle. As these two chroniclers wrote independently of one another, Godfrey must indeed have carried out a feat of repute during the clash. The differences in detail between the two accounts may indicate that the story became increasingly dramatic in the telling and retelling.[162] This supposition is supported by the fact that Godfrey's reputed feat became the subject of the most widely circulated micronarrative to emerge from the First Crusade. Albert's version of the feat shares stylistic similarities with examples of epic swordsmanship recounted in the *chansons de geste*, and this may provide a hint as to how the story circulated in the aftermath of the First Crusade.[163]

The crusaders' victory in the Bridge Gate battle permitted them to strengthen their grip on Antioch. They completed the construction of their fort, which they named *La Mahomerie*. Tudebode states that Raymond of Toulouse was appointed to hold the fort because, of all the leaders, 'he had more knights in his household than others and had more to give'.[164] This remark conveys a clear sense of how Raymond exerted his influence on the expedition. Raymond of Aguilers, on the other hand, reports that Raymond bought the rights to the fort. The chronicler states that over the previous summer Raymond had been periodically incapacitated by a debilitating illness, to the extent that some participants in the crusade had suggested he had had neither the stomach to fight nor the will to make donations to others. Evidently mindful of the need to safeguard his reputation, then, he was anxious to seize control of *La Mahomerie* and impress upon the rest of the crusaders his commitment to the cause.[165] The same chronicler also asserts that Raymond's strenuous efforts at this time caused the criticism of him to dissipate 'to the extent that he was called father and defender of our army by all', and noted that 'from that time, the count's name grew'.[166] Underpinning this claim is a crucial point about the dynamics of the First Crusade. It demonstrates not only that the opinions of the rank and file had a significant bearing upon the leaders' reputations, but also that those opinions rested on how the leaders acted.

In early April the leaders held a council, at which they appointed Tancred to fortify a monastery near the St George Gate. The other leaders subsidised this action, with Raymond of Toulouse contributing a quarter of the 400 marks of silver granted to him.[167] With this, the crusaders had established a blockade against all of Antioch's gates except the Iron Gate. The crusaders' blockade of the Bridge and St George gates precipitated another lull in proceedings, during which time food and supplies again became scarce. It was around this time that the crusaders began to receive assistance from Baldwin, the new ruler of Edessa.[168] Albert reports that Baldwin sent to the leaders 'very many talents of gold and silver', strong horses adorned with valuable reins and saddles, and costly weapons.[169] According to the same chronicler, in this period Nicusus, an Armenian prince from the region of Turbessel, sent a 'pavilion of wonderful handiwork and ornament' to Godfrey, 'in order to acquire favour and friendship'.[170] However, this gift was intercepted by Pakrad (Baldwin's erstwhile associate), who gave it instead to Bohemond. After Godfrey and his ally Robert of Flanders found out what had happened, they went to Bohemond to ask him to hand the pavilion over. The two men were angered when he refused, and requested the pavilion's return again, to which Bohemond retorted that he would never give it up. It was only after they threatened to visit Bohemond's camp with a band of men, and the other leaders intervened to advise him to relent, that he agreed to give up the pavilion. Albert states that Bohemond restored the pavilion, and that all concerned made peace and once again restored their friendship.[171] While Albert provides the only report of this incident, it is not out of keeping with other documented outbreaks of hostility between the leaders. Godfrey no doubt felt that the loss of the pavilion would be detrimental to his status. Moreover, there were important financial considerations at stake; in the context of the expedition's own internal economy, precious fabrics that could be folded and easily transported or exchanged were much sought after.[172] Albert reports that in the aftermath of this incident, the crusaders' privations at Antioch deepened. As a result, the chronicler states, Baldwin conferred onto Godfrey the revenues of Turbessel, in the form of corn, barley, wine, oil, and gold that totalled 50,000 bezants a year.[173] This was a crucial development. From this point Baldwin evidently provided substantial assistance only to his brother Godfrey to support him at Antioch.

Between April and July 1098 the leaders of the crusade sent to the West a letter, in which they described the course of the expedition up to that point.[174] In the missive, it is pointedly noted that the crusaders who had died in one battle were 'undoubtedly enjoying eternal life', while those who survived it had collected a vast amount of gold, silver, weapons, and precious garments.[175] The crusaders were fully aware that they needed reinforcements if they were to bring the siege of Antioch to a successful conclusion, and the intention underpinning these assertions was no doubt to highlight the rewards on offer to those who might join them in the East. Significantly, the order and manner in which the chief crusaders are listed in this letter is revealing of the power dynamics within the leadership of the expedition at that point. At the outset of the letter, the first three leaders are named as follows: 'Bohemond, son of Robert [Guiscard], and Raymond, count of St Gilles, and also [*simulque*] Duke Godfrey'.[176] The use of the term *simulque* serves slightly to subordinate Godfrey to Bohemond and Raymond of Toulouse, the two men listed first. Crucially, then, the manner in which the three men are presented at the outset of the letter encapsulates their relative status in the summer of 1098. Bohemond (owing to his military exploits) and Raymond (thanks to his riches and ability to buy influence) had established themselves as the two most prominent leaders, and in mid-1098, Godfrey remained in the shadow of those two men.[177]

In late May the crusaders were spurred into action when they received word that a large army under Kerbogha of Mosul was heading in their direction. Kerbogha had earlier attacked Edessa for about three weeks, and, having failed to capture it, turned his attention to the vulnerable army camped outside Antioch.[178] The crusaders' scouts confirmed his approach to Antioch on 28 May. At this point, Bohemond took a firm grasp of proceedings. At an emergency gathering of the leaders the next day, he announced that he had devised a plan for gaining access into the city before Kerbogha's forces arrived, but stipulated that he would only reveal it if the other leaders agreed to cede Antioch to him if the crusaders captured it. It is stated in the *Gesta Francorum* that all the leaders agreed to this, on the condition that if Alexios came to the crusaders' aid, the city should be returned to him.[179] (Albert suggests that the meeting comprised Godfrey, Robert of Normandy, Robert of Flanders, Raymond of Toulouse, Eustace of Boulogne, and Tancred, and claims that they all accepted Bohemond's proposal without condition.[180]) Bohemond proceeded to divulge his plan, relating that in the preceding weeks he had gained the confidence of a tower guard named Firuz, from whom he had secured an agreement to admit the crusaders into Antioch.[181] While some of the crusaders were heartened by this news, others continued to despair about the plight of the expedition. On 2 June, Stephen of Blois and a number of others departed Antioch, and they came to be regarded as deserters.[182]

It was also Bohemond who devised the military strategy by which the crusaders aimed to enter the city.[183] He directed the operation, with Godfrey and the rest of the leaders acting in accordance with his strategy. During the night of 2–3 June, Godfrey and Robert of Flanders led a force of about 700 knights eastwards away from Antioch, with the aim of giving the garrison the impression that they had gone to meet Kerbogha's approaching army head on. In fact, they circled around and returned to the west of the city, to a point at the wall close to Firuz' tower. Meanwhile, Bohemond took a force of infantry – including, it would appear, the author of the *Gesta Francorum* – to the same place. Albert states that when the crusaders at the foot of the wall expressed reluctance to be the first to ascend the ladder Firuz had lowered, Godfrey and Robert of Flanders sought to allay their concerns with a heartfelt speech in which they highlighted the rewards on offer to anyone who was killed: 'Most faithful soldiers of Christ, you do not run this risk for earthly recompense, but in expectation of His reward, who is able to grant to His own the prizes of eternal life after present death'.[184]

The first crusaders who ascended the ladder opened a postern gate to admit those stationed outside. As the crusaders overran the city, they killed many whom they encountered.[185] Albert states that as they entered the city, they sounded trumpets, which was the signal for Godfrey, Robert of Flanders, and others to attack a gate near the citadel. This suggests that they had been deputed to seize the citadel during the operation.[186] However, they failed in this task, for the garrison managed to retain hold of it. During Antioch's capture, both Bohemond and Raymond of Toulouse managed to capture different portions of the city and its fortifications, and this would have a significant bearing on the events that followed.[187]

On 4 June elements of Kerbogha's army began to arrive at Antioch. Over the course of next few days, he arrayed the rest of his forces around the city, focussing in particular on the part of the wall nearest the citadel. He soon attacked *La Mahomerie*, the crusaders' fort outside the Bridge Gate. The crusaders stationed there were unable to hold the fort, and so they burned it before hurrying in to the city.[188] A new deadlock had commenced, with the former besiegers now assuming the role of the besieged. According to Albert, at one point around this time, Godfrey attempted to break the impasse by leading a force out of the St Paul Gate. They encountered stiff resistance, though, and they were soon forced to flee back into the city. Albert states that 200 of them were killed, wounded, or captured.[189] As Kerbogha increased his stranglehold on the city in the week or so after his arrival, the crusaders' morale plummeted. This provoked further desertions. On 10 June, a number of crusaders lowered themselves down from the city wall and fled the city.[190] Rumours even began to circulate among the rank and file that the leaders planned to flee. Several authors state that this prompted Adhémar to encourage them to swear an oath that they would not take flight from Antioch.[191] Albert makes a similar claim, and credited Godfrey and Robert of Flanders along with Adhémar with encouraging the rest of the crusaders to remain at the city.[192] Trapped within the city walls, the crusaders were once again beset by a lack of food and supplies.[193] According to Albert of Aachen, even Godfrey felt the effects of these privations. He states that there was reliable testimony that Godfrey had to pay the inflated price of fifteen marks of silver for the flesh of a 'miserable camel', while his seneschal Baldric paid three for a she-goat.[194] It was also around this time that Godfrey took pity on Count Hartmann of Dillingen and Henry of Esch, two men who had become so destitute that they had been forced to sell all their weapons and armour and resort to begging. Albert states that Godfrey allocated food from his own store to Hartmann, giving him each day a loaf and a portion of meat or fish, as well as allowing Henry to eat at his own table.[195]

While the First Crusaders were trapped inside Antioch, some of their number experienced what many regarded as providential interventions.[196] The sources relate that several participants in the expedition experienced divine visions. A priest named Stephen of Valence reported to the rest of the crusaders that Christ had visited him and promised that He would aid the crusaders.[197] Another crusader, Peter Bartholomew, claimed that he had been visited by St Andrew and Christ, who informed him that the Holy Lance was concealed within Antioch, before revealing its location. On 14 June, a shard of metal was duly uncovered. Some accepted that the artefact was the Holy Lance, while others were more sceptical. Raymond of Toulouse became the relic's most ardent adherent, and so it became strongly associated with the southern French contingent.[198] In a letter of September 1098 – a document which will be considered in closer detail later in the chapter – the leaders of the expedition stated that the discovery of the Holy Lance galvanised the crusaders and strengthened their resolve to face Kerbogha's forces in battle.[199] This may not be the full story, however. A short time after the discovery of the relic, the leaders sent Peter the Hermit to Kerbogha's camp. The author of the *Gesta Francorum* records that Peter warned Kerbogha to leave Antioch, and suggested he convert to Christianity.[200] Albert cast Peter's mission in a different light, stating that he was sent to Kerbogha to seek an agreement to end the siege by having twenty men from both sides battle each other. Peter also reportedly promised that if Kerbogha's champions prevailed, the crusaders would depart Antioch and return to Europe. Kerbogha – not surprisingly – refused the proposal.[201] The implicit suggestion in this passage is that the crusaders sought from Kerbogha an agreement which allowed them to depart Antioch peacefully. The same chronicler reports that as soon as Peter the Hermit returned to Antioch and began to describe to the rest of the crusaders his discussions with Kerbogha, Godfrey interrupted him, before taking him to one side and asking him to refrain from describing what he had observed in the enemy camp to preserve morale. The failure of Peter's mission, Albert states, promoted the crusaders to settle on an all-or-nothing attack on Kerbogha, rather than wait to starve to death in Antioch.[202]

At this decisive moment, Bohemond again asserted himself on proceedings. On 28 June, he ordered the crusaders into four fighting divisions (one of which was placed under Godfrey's command) and led them out of Antioch's Bridge Gate to meet Kerbogha's army.[203] Since many of the knights had lost their horses and equipment by this point, these divisions mostly consisted of infantry. Albert reports that Godfrey's associate Hartmann of Dillingen rode a donkey into the battle, wielding a shield and sword captured from a Turkish warrior.[204] Even princes as prominent and influential as Godfrey and Robert of Flanders had no horses at this point. Raymond of Toulouse gave Godfrey a horse, and, while Albert says that Raymond gave the animal as a gift, the chronicler states that he only granted it after repeated requests. Robert of Flanders, Albert states, obtained a horse by begging.[205] Against the odds, the crusaders prevailed in the battle that followed. Kerbogha had divided his army up in order to blockade each of the city gates, allowing the crusaders to defeat his contingents one by one. The defeat of Kerbogha's forces compelled the garrison to surrender. Raymond of Toulouse, who had remained in the city, first attempted to take control of the citadel by having his banner flown atop its tower, only for the Muslim warrior in charge of the citadel to return it when Bohemond offered his own banner (and thus his protection).[206] After more than eight months punctuated by famine and almost daily military activity, the crusaders had finally taken Antioch.

Godfrey and his army contributed to the crusaders' victory at the battle of Antioch, but, once again, their efforts helped to fulfil a military strategy which had been devised by Bohemond. It should be noted, though, that in a letter of July 1098 Anselm of Ribemont – a participant in the battle – listed all the leading crusaders who took part in the battle, but omitted even to mention Godfrey's name.[207] This must have been a lapse in memory, however, for other sources make it clear that Godfrey took a prominent role in the encounter. The sources of the *Gesta Francorum* tradition record that Godfrey led one of the crusader contingents during the battle.[208] The *Gesta Francorum* itself highlights Godfrey's involvement at two stages in the battle; the first, when some of his men joined with those of Robert of Normandy to improvise a new battle line, and the second, when Godfrey and Robert of Flanders 'rode along the river bank, where the strongest Turkish force was stationed, and, defended by the Sign of the Cross, were the first to make a concerted attack upon the enemy'.[209] The 'Bartolf' text recounts how Godfrey lined up for the battle alongside 'many Lotharingian counts and a legion of swordsmen'.[210] Albert of Aachen, as is his custom, accords Godfrey a prominent role in the battle, giving scant indication that Bohemond was behind the crusaders' overall strategy. At one point, Albert reports, Godfrey was fighting 'and conquering in the name of Jesus son of the living God', before a messenger from Bohemond reached him and asked him to render assistance quickly.[211] The chronicler states that Godfrey led his force to the aid of Bohemond's company, and that the mere sight of their approach prompted some of the enemy troops to begin fleeing.[212] Albert also highlights the participation of Godfrey's brother Eustace in the fighting, placing him alongside Baldwin of Mons, Robert of Flanders, and Robert of Normandy.[213] As the *Gesta Francorum* and Albert independently drew attention to Godfrey's contribution to the victory, though, he clearly fought in the battle with distinction. While this was the case, it is clear that the most telling factor behind the defeat of Kerbogha's forces was Bohemond's exceptional leadership and tactical nous.[214]

Impasse, June 1098–May 1099

With Kerbogha defeated and Antioch firmly in the crusaders' possession, the path to Jerusalem seemed to be straightforward. The Holy City lay only a few weeks' hard march to the south, and there were no major military obstacles left in the way. Yet, neither Godfrey nor any other of the leaders exhibited any inclination to set out for Jerusalem immediately. Disagreements between the leaders came to the fore, causing the First Crusade to grind to a halt. It would be almost a year after the defeat of Kerbogha before the crusaders reached Jerusalem.[215] On 3 July, the leaders held a council at Antioch to discuss the situation, and they resolved to postpone the march to Jerusalem until 1 November. The author of the *Gesta Franco-rum* asserts the leaders reached this decision because they did not wish to enter enemy territory, and because they wanted to avoid marching in the summer heat.[216] Tudebode added to this the claim that everyone accepted this decision.[217] Raymond of Aguilers, however, was incensed by the decision to delay the march to Jerusalem, accusing the leaders of 'luxuriating in idleness and riches' and claiming that they had acted 'contrary to God's commands' by choosing to remain at Antioch. This chronicler asserted that if the crusaders had left for Jerusalem immediately after the defeat of Kerbogha, they would have reached the Holy City without encountering any opposition.[218]

   The leaders were at odds over the question of who should rule Antioch, and the connected issue of the alliance with Byzantium. The most serious dispute was between Bohemond (who had control of Antioch's citadel) and Raymond of Toulouse (who possessed the Bridge Gate and the nearby governor's palace).[219] Raymond apparently asserted that Antioch should be handed over to Alexios, in accordance with the oaths which the crusaders had sworn to the emperor at Constantinople in early 1097.[220] Bohemond, in contrast, argued that Antioch should be ceded to him, since he had originally engineered access into the city, and the Byzantines had failed to come to the crusaders' aid while they were besieging it.[221] Despite Raymond's opposition, Bohemond soon began to act as though he was already the undisputed ruler of Antioch. On 14 July he issued a charter in which he granted rights in the city to the Genoese. The document records that the Genoese agreed to support Bohemond against any aggressor except Raymond of Toulouse; clearly, the Genoese believed that there was a strong chance that violence would erupt between the two men.[222] Albert of Aachen states that at this time, Godfrey, Robert of Flanders, Robert of Normandy, and other of the leaders did not make any claims on the city, as they did not wish to violate their oaths to Alexios to return former imperial possessions.[223] These men may simply have been seeking to avoid becoming embroiled in the argument. By remaining neutral in the dispute, though, they were seen to show tacit support for Bohemond. Raymond of Aguilers seems to imply this when he noted that Bohemond had gone unpunished when he had managed to wrest control of Antioch's citadel from Raymond.[224]

   In early July, the crusaders sent a legation under Hugh of Vermandois and Baldwin of Mons to Constantinople to confer with Alexios. The sources make rather different assertions about the legation's purpose. The author of the *Gesta Francorum* reports that the legates were charged with asking Alexios to come to Antioch and take control of the city.[225] Albert of Aachen, on the other hand, states that the messengers' task was to inform the emperor that the oaths taken at Constantinople were void on account of his failure to assist the crusaders at Antioch.[226] Whatever its actual message, though, this legation had no bearing on ensuing discussions, for these representatives did not return to Antioch, nor did Alexios come to the city.

Bohemond's claim to Antioch would have been strengthened after the crusaders heard reports of what had happened around 20 June at Philomelion in Asia Minor, when Alexios had encountered Stephen of Blois and other crusaders who were fleeing Antioch siege. They reported to the emperor that the crusaders who remained at the city were about to be annihilated by Kerbogha's army. For that reason, Alexios turned back to Constantinople rather than proceed across Asia Minor to assist the crusaders.[227] Though there still remained some crusaders who advocated retaining ties to Alexios even after this – Raymond of Toulouse chief among them – news of Philomelion dealt a near-fatal blow to the alliance between the crusaders and the Byzantines. This set the First Crusade on a different course. After this, its participants could no longer rely on assistance from Byzantium, though they were also now freer to focus on what was now their undisputed goal: Jerusalem.

With no imminent resolution over Antioch likely, the leading crusaders resolved in July 1098 to leave the city for the summer. They took their contingents to different regions nearby, with the ostensible aim of relieving pressure on supplies. As the author of the *Gesta Francorum* put it, '[our] leaders separated and each went off into his own territory until it should be time to resume the march'.[228] Bohemond spent much time during this period in Armenian Cilicia. Raymond of Toulouse based himself at Rugia in the Orontes valley to the south of Antioch. As the following pages will discuss, Godfrey pursued interests in the Afrin valley, out towards Edessa, which his brother Baldwin now held.[229] All three had already been building interests in these respective areas. These men clearly regarded the postponement of the expedition until 1 November as a chance to pursue money and land in those areas. Occupied with these pursuits, they did not have the resumption of the march to Jerusalem foremost in mind.

In late July, a plague broke out at Antioch. Adhémar, who had remained at the city, contracted it and died on 1 August. His death exacerbated the divisions among the leadership of the crusade at this point.[230] Albert of Aachen records that this plague also claimed the lives of two prominent members of Godfrey's contingent, Henry of Esch and Reinhard of Hamersbach. He also claims that it was at this time that Godfrey was reminded of the privations suffered by Henry IV of Germany's forces during the siege of Rome.[231]

In the late summer and autumn of 1098, the First Crusade lacked clear leadership. As a result, the expedition fell into a state of inertia.[232] Only three men possessed sufficient authority to reinvigorate the expedition and lead its participants on to the Holy City: Bohemond, Raymond of Toulouse, and Godfrey. However, Bohemond and Raymond remained at odds over the issue of who should rule Antioch. Moreover, all three were busily pursuing their own interests in their burgeoning enclaves in the regions surrounding Antioch. The crusade's lack of direction is apparent in a letter sent by the leaders from Antioch on 11 September to Urban II.[233] In that missive, the crusaders exhorted Urban to come to the Holy Land and assume personal command of the expedition by leading them to Jerusalem. A postscript to the letter, seemingly added at Bohemond's behest, calls on Urban to terminate relations with Alexios. Significantly, the leading participants are once again listed in this letter in an order which probably reflects their relative standing at this time: Bohemond, then Raymond, and then Godfrey. It is also of interest that the letter to Urban names three other prominent figures: Robert of Normandy, Robert of Flanders, and Eustace of Boulogne.[234] This suggests that Godfrey's elder brother was regarded as part of the expedition's leadership group at this point.

Between about July and November 1098, then, Godfrey pursued his own interests in the Afrin valley. He based himself at the towns of Turbessel and Ravendel, which lay halfway between Antioch and Edessa (see Map 4.4). Baldwin had captured these towns and then transferred them to his brother when he went to take up the rule of Edessa.[235] Godfrey seems to have had an eye on carving out a lordship for himself in this region. Albert of Aachen, who was well-informed about Godfrey's activities at this time, recounted a long episode which commenced when a member of Godfrey's retinue, a knight named Folbert of Bouillon, was captured along with his wife during a journey to Edessa. While Folbert was killed, his wife was spared, and she was taken to the fortress at Azaz, whose lord was named Omar. Folbert's wife was soon married to a Turkish knight, whose spirits were greatly bolstered by the nuptials. The knight proceeded to exert himself in warfare against the surrounding potentates, and this incurred the wrath of Ridwan of Aleppo, who decided to lead a force to capture Azaz. The Turkish knight's new wife provided Omar of Azaz with a solution to this predicament:

> you will waste no time before pledging friendship by giving your right hand to Godfrey, duke of the Christian army, who powerfully took Antioch while [Kerbogha] had fled, and in this way you may be sure that you will acquire the whole assistance and alliance of the Christians in this emergency.[236]

This passage serves once again to outline Godfrey's importance to the First Crusade. The chronicler states that Omar heeded the woman's advice, and that he sent a Syrian Christian to Godfrey to request help against Ridwan. When the Syrian met Godfrey, Albert states, he employed flattering words, saying that he had heard that Godfrey was 'a man and a prince powerful in military strength'.[237] Godfrey was initially wary of trickery, but his concerns were assuaged when Omar sent his son as a hostage. This prompted Godfrey to agree to the alliance, and he promised to lead a force against Ridwan when he attacked Azaz. When Ridwan's assault duly came, both Godfrey and Baldwin brought troops to Azaz. Raymond of Toulouse and Bohemond, reputedly jealous of Godfrey's alliance with Omar, initially refused to participate. According to Albert, Godfrey reminded them of the need to

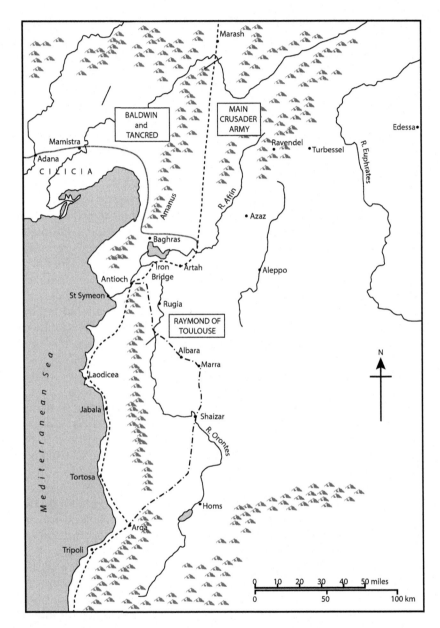

Map 4.4 Antioch and its region

help fellow Christians, and asserted that if they did not aid him, he would never lift a finger to assist them in the future. Suitably reproached, the two men agreed to accompany him to Azaz. The crusaders succeeded in repelling Ridwan, and they entered Azaz, where Godfrey and Omar formally secured their alliance.[238] This significant episode indicates that during the summer and autumn of 1098, Godfrey was interacting with local Muslim rulers in the Afrin valley. Albert's claim that the alliance incurred the envy of Bohemond and Raymond of Toulouse suggests that those interactions were beneficial to Godfrey's status among the crusaders. Most importantly, his willingness to make an alliance with one Muslim potentate against another demonstrates that he did not think that political allegiances could only be made with fellow Christians. In this regard, he seems to have adopted a pragmatic approach.[239]

After the expedition to Azaz, Godfrey exacted his revenge on Pakrad, the Armenian who had earlier incurred his anger by intercepting a pavilion gifted to him and sending it instead to Bohemond.[240] Albert states that Pakrad's soldiers had been harassing Armenian monks in Ravendel and Turbessel. The monks, regarding Godfrey as 'a peace-loving man and one devoted to justice', came to him and asked him for help. Godfrey was reportedly moved by the monks' plight. He had also remembered Pakrad's earlier conduct over the pavilion. Albert states that Godfrey took a force of fifty warriors and razed one of Pakrad's strongholds. He had twenty soldiers stationed there blinded, in revenge for the wrongs done to him and to the monks.[241] Godfrey then attacked and razed the citadel of Pakrad's brother.[242] Godfrey's strenuous attacks against Pakrad and his brother bear the hallmark of a man who intended to stamp his authority in the region. Albert was thus correct to characterise Godfrey's efforts as a 'military show of strength'.[243]

Albert of Aachen and Raymond of Aguilers also report another incident involving Godfrey. According to Raymond, Godfrey and a band of twelve knights were on their way to Antioch for a gathering of the leaders – perhaps that of 1 November – when he encountered a far larger force of 150 Muslim warriors. The chronicler relates that despite the difference in numbers, Godfrey was

> not the least bit hesitant, [and he] prepared his arms, exhorted his knights and courageously charged the enemy. The [Muslims were] impressed by the daredevil choice of death rather than safety in flight . . . during the long and violent melee, Godfrey's knights, equal in number to the twelve apostles and secure in their belief the Duke was God's vicar, bravely charged the enemy. God gave the Duke . . . a great victory.[244]

The chronicler then asserts that Godfrey carried the heads of the slain Muslims with him on to Antioch, which he entered in triumph. While this author generally reserved his praise for Raymond of Toulouse, he used this incident to laud Godfrey's military ability and the confidence his men had in him. There is a particular resonance in the description of Godfrey as 'God's vicar', and the assertion that his knights numbered the same as the apostles. Albert of Aachen described the confrontation in similar terms, though he states that Godfrey's band numbered forty and their opponents 100. This chronicler states the incident took place a few miles from Antioch, in a region known as 'Episcopate'. Albert notes that Godfrey vanquished the enemy force, and then went to Antioch, where he reported to the rest of the leaders what had happened.[245]

The leaders convened again at Antioch on 1 November for another round of discussions regarding the resumption of the march to Jerusalem. However, the same fundamental obstacle to an agreement persisted: Bohemond and Raymond of Toulouse could not come to a settlement over Antioch. Bohemond again sought recognition of his rights to Antioch, while Raymond reiterated his intention to maintain his oath to Alexios. Raymond of Aguilers states that the dispute became so severe that the two almost took up arms against each other.[246] The author of the *Gesta Francorum* asserted that Godfrey, Robert of Normandy, Robert of Flanders, and other leaders stood apart from Bohemond and Raymond of Toulouse so that they could pass judgement on the dispute. Yet, they were fearful of further delaying the march to Jerusalem, and so they refused to give a clear judgement on the matter.[247] (Tudebode made the same claim, but added Eustace of Boulogne to the list of leaders who deliberated on the dispute.[248]) Raymond of Aguilers criticised Godfrey and Robert of Flanders, stating that they 'took the Antioch quarrel lightly and secretly favoured Bohemond's possession', but that they would not say so in public for fear of being accused of violating their oaths to Alexios.[249] The same chronicler reports that in response to the leaders' failure to come to an agreement to resume the march, the rank and file began to complain, and mooted the possibility of electing 'some brave warrior' (*militibus aliquem fortem*) to lead them to Jerusalem.[250] These murmurings compelled Raymond of Toulouse and Bohemond to make peace – albeit a fragile one – and set a day to resume the march.[251]

When the appointed day for the departure from Antioch came a few weeks later, however, Raymond did not have the Holy City in mind as a destination. He was instead set on enhancing his burgeoning lordship around Rugia, where he had passed much of the summer. In September, while he had been awaiting the discussions with the other leaders at Antioch, Raymond had captured the town of Albara, installing one of his chaplains, Peter of Narbonne, as its bishop.[252] Albert suggests that Raymond was accompanied at Albara by Robert of Normandy, Robert of Flanders, and Eustace of Boulogne.[253] Albara provided Raymond with a platform from which he could further extend his interests in the area. So, when he led his army out of Antioch in November, he took his forces to Marra, a town close to Albara, arriving on 27 November.[254] Bohemond was concerned that he might miss out on capturing spoils at Marra, and so quickly brought his forces there too. Raymond of Aguilers, it is important to note, expressly states that Godfrey was not present at Marra at this time.[255] Albert, in contrast, says that Godfrey and several of the other leaders were present at Marra, but stayed there only for fifteen days, before leaving to return to Antioch.

Intriguingly, Albert notes that when Godfrey departed Marra, his brother Eustace remained there alongside Raymond of Toulouse, and continued to participate in the assault on the city.[256] A few passages later, Albert explicitly states that Eustace had helped to capture Marra.[257] These brief references to Eustace's activities at Marra shed light onto a significant dynamic of Godfrey's interactions with his brothers on the crusade. With the expedition beset by the lack of clear direction and Godfrey's focus locked onto his efforts in the Afrin valley, Eustace was able to explore opportunities elsewhere, much as Baldwin had earlier done.

The crusaders made a vigorous attack on Marra, and it fell to them on 11 December. Raymond and Bohemond managed to seize different parts of its fortifications, creating a stalemate like that which already existed at Antioch. Bohemond does not seem to have had serious designs on Marra, though; he was instead seeking to secure leverage for gaining the parts of Antioch that Raymond still possessed.[258] At this point, the knights and the people reportedly began to ask when the journey to Jerusalem would be resumed, only for Bohemond to reply that he would not set out before Easter. Peter of Narbonne, some nobles, and many of the rank and file went to Raymond of Toulouse in the latter part of December and asked him to 'make himself leader and lord of the army'. They acknowledged his status as custodian of the Holy Lance, but stated that if he did not wish to continue the march, he should hand over the relic to them so that they could take it on to Jerusalem. This forced Raymond's hand, and he stated that he would depart in two weeks' time, even though he feared that the other leaders would not follow.[259] This development reveals that popular sentiment – now firmly fixed on the Holy City – was starting to hold the key to the leadership of the crusade.

Raymond of Toulouse then asked the other leaders to meet him Rugia, halfway between Antioch and Marra. When they assembled there around 4 January 1099, they again could not resolve the dispute over Antioch.[260] Raymond tried a new approach, offering all the leading crusaders except Bohemond money to continue in his service. Raymond no doubt hoped that his efforts would undermine the others' tacit support for Bohemond's claims on Antioch, while underlining his own status as the leader of the expedition.[261] According to Raymond of Aguilers, Raymond offered Godfrey and Robert of Normandy 10,000 *solidi* each, and offered Robert of Flanders and Tancred 6,000 and 5,000 *solidi* respectively.[262] While the chronicler does not explicitly say whether or not these offers were accepted, the fact that Tancred and Robert of Normandy were present among Raymond's army in January 1099 suggests that they did take his money.[263] The picture is less clear in respect of Godfrey. While Raymond of Aguilers does not say whether Godfrey accepted the offer, it is possible that some point after this meeting he did so. It would have been impolitic, however, for the chronicler to record as much. Failing once again to secure an agreement to renew the march, the leaders left Rugia without plans to reconvene. Bohemond departed for Antioch, accompanied by Godfrey, Robert of Flanders, and Robert of Normandy, while Raymond returned to Marra.[264]

While Raymond had been away from Marra, the plight of the crusaders camped there had reached its nadir. They had endured a famine so severe that some apparently resorted to eating the flesh of Muslims killed during the assault on the city.[265] After the rank and file at Marra discovered that Raymond of Toulouse planned to garrison the city, tensions flared to the point of open rebellion. The crusaders began to tear down the city's walls in an attempt to spur Raymond into restarting the march.[266] This compelled him to relent, and on 13 January he led his forces away from Marra, with the aim of traveling to a region where there were plenty of supplies. Raymond himself departed Marra in a religious procession; Raymond of Aguilers records that he 'trudged along barefooted, calling out for God's mercy and the saints' protection'.[267] With him at this point were Tancred and Robert of Normandy – suggesting they had indeed accepted his money – and he must have hoped that the rest of the leaders would follow.[268] However, Bohemond – who had now seized all of Antioch's fortifications – Robert of Flanders, and Godfrey remained unmoved.[269]

As Raymond of Toulouse's force marched south from Marra, they faced no major opposition. Word of the crusaders' military prowess – coupled, no doubt, with reports of the cannibalism at Marra – had reached the inhabitants of towns which lay along their route, promoting them to conclude truces with the crusaders rather than suffer an attack by them.[270] The ruler of Shaizar quickly came to terms with Raymond's force, and even provided markets at which they were able to buy horses.[271] Other Muslim-held towns came to similar accommodations. In February, Raymond decided to launch a siege on the town of Arqa. This was probably intended as a stopgap activity to provide time for the other crusaders who were still at Antioch to catch up.[272] Given the popular clamour to reach the Holy City, though, this would prove to be an unwise decision. The crusaders besieged Arqa for the next three months, but made little progress in capturing it.[273]

Though Bohemond, Robert of Flanders, and Godfrey had stayed at Antioch, like Raymond, they found that the will of the rank and file could no longer be ignored. Albert of Aachen reports that members of the contingents which remained at Antioch began to grumble about the delay in the resumption of the march to Jerusalem. As a result, there was 'great discord among the people', with some crusaders even leaving Antioch to travel to Jerusalem, doubting the assurances of the three leaders that they would soon depart for the Holy City. Bohemond, Robert, and Godfrey placed guards at the seaports to prevent crusaders setting sail for home, and arranged a meeting for 2 February. The resolution of that meeting was to depart Antioch on 1 March, and travel south to the port of Laodicea, and from there, on to Jerusalem.[274] On the appointed day the three men duly assembled their forces and travelled to Laodicea, before continuing south to Jabala. It was at this point that Bohemond took his leave of Godfrey and Robert of Flanders, and he returned with his force to Antioch.[275] This was one of the most crucial moments in the entire course of the First Crusade. Up to this point, Bohemond's redoubtable military leadership had made him the most dominant figure on the expedition. By turning back to Antioch, he ruled himself out of contention to lead the crusade. As a result, the only viable candidates left to fulfil that role were Raymond of Toulouse and Godfrey.

Godfrey and Robert of Flanders began to besiege Jabala. Albert reports that they refused its inhabitants' offer of a large sum of money to break off their attack. Jabala's inhabitants are claimed to have instead turned to Raymond of Toulouse and offered their money to him if he would try to make Godfrey and Robert cease the assault. Raymond thus sent messengers to Godfrey and Robert informing them that an enormous Muslim army was gathering near Arqa, and that their assistance was urgently required. Godfrey and Robert raised the siege at Jabala and quickly brought their troops to Arqa, only to find that the reports about the gathering army had been false. Feeling betrayed, Albert states, they moved their forces two miles away from Arqa. They refused to assist Raymond's forces and personally disavowed his friendship. Albert claims that Raymond of Toulouse sent Godfrey the gift of a fine horse in the hope of a reconciliation. The chronicler states that since Godfrey was 'a man of great forbearance and love', and because he knew that many others would emulate how he responded to Raymond, he accepted the gift and restored their friendship.[276] This is a significant claim, for it indicates that Godfrey was beginning to act with the wider attitudes of the other crusaders in mind. Raymond of Aguilers casts the circumstances of Godfrey and Robert of Flanders' arrival at Arqa in a markedly different light. According to this chronicler – who was present in Raymond of Toulouse's force during the siege – it was the southern French themselves who had been given misinformation. This chronicler asserts that the reports of the gathering army had been fabricated by the crusaders' enemies with the aim of undermining their assault upon Arqa.[277] Whatever the origin of those reports, the recriminations of the episode signify how deeply divided Raymond's forces were from those of Godfrey and Robert of Flanders at this time.

A number of significant developments occurred while the crusaders were camped at Arqa between February and May 1099. In early April Peter Bartholomew – the man whose visions had led to the discovery of the Holy Lance at Antioch – reported that he had received a new vision. He stated that Christ, St Peter, and St Andrew had come to him to inform him about the presence in the armies of a number of sinners who deserved to be executed. This caused great uproar among the crusaders. Many challenged Peter's claims, and some even began to doubt the authenticity of the relic. A leading voice among these doubters was Arnulf of Choques, a chaplain of Robert of Normandy. Peter was charged to prove his claims by undergoing an ordeal, and on Good Friday he walked through a wall of fire holding the Holy Lance. The reports of the outcome of the trial differ, but it is clear that Peter died soon after, and that many among the crusaders thereafter ceased to believe in the authenticity of the relic.[278] The discovery of the Holy Lance at Antioch had bolstered Raymond of Toulouse's status, and the widespread repudiation of the relic at Arqa served badly to damage it. There was an attempt by the southern French contingent to use another visionary named Stephen of Valence to foster a new cult around the memory of Adhémar, but few seem to have taken it seriously.[279]

About a week after Peter Bartholomew's ordeal, Byzantine messengers arrived at the crusaders' camp, protesting Bohemond's retention of Antioch, which they asserted was in contravention of the oaths taken at Constantinople. The envoys reported that Alexios would reward the crusaders with large sums of gold and silver if they agreed to wait for him at Arqa until the feast of St John (24 June), so that they could unite and travel together to Jerusalem. Only Raymond of Toulouse among the leaders was willing to comply with this request. The other chief participants, along with the majority of the rank and file, had lost faith in Alexios because he had failed to help them at Antioch. Many believed that the emperor was trying to delay their progress so that they would be defeated, so that no future crusaders would seek to traverse the Byzantine Empire to reach the Holy Land.[280] Once again, Raymond of Toulouse acted in a manner that was at odds with the popular sentiment.

It was also at Arqa that the crusaders received ambassadors from Fatimid Egypt. No doubt at Alexios' suggestion, the crusaders had sought to exploit divisions in the Islamic world of the Near East by making an agreement with Egypt against the Turkish powers of Syria. During the siege of Antioch, emissaries from Egypt had visited the crusaders, who had then sent some representatives of their own to Cairo.[281] At Arqa, around a year later, the crusaders' representatives returned from Egypt to re-join the expedition, bringing with them Fatimid ambassadors. Crucially, in August 1098 the Fatimids had captured Jerusalem from the Turks. The Fatimid representatives at Arqa proposed a deal whereby the crusaders would be permitted to visit the Holy City in groups of 200 or 300 at a time. By now, though, the crusaders had become fixated on restoring Jerusalem to Latin possession, and so there was no chance they would accept this. They were now firmly set on capturing the Holy City by force.[282]

During the latter stages of the crusaders' time at Arqa there were further disruptions to the fragile peace which existed between the leaders. Godfrey and the other leaders reportedly became jealous of the tribute that local

Muslim princes were sending to Raymond of Toulouse. Albert claims that in an attempt at gaining a share of those spoils, they sent messages to those rulers claiming that they, not Raymond, led the army.[283] This incident provides a clear indication that the cracks in the leadership of the crusade were never far from the surface.

Jerusalem, May–July 1099

While Godfrey was at Arqa, Albert of Aachen asserts, the rest of the crusaders insistently urged him to leave and press on to Jerusalem. At the same time, the chronicler states, Raymond of Toulouse resisted these calls to depart, because he strongly desired to capture Arqa for himself.[284] Raymond's continued insistence on the authenticity of the now widely repudiated Holy Lance, and his unpopular wish to wait at Arqa for Alexios, caused his reputation to go into freefall. The chroniclers' accounts of the departure from Arqa strongly suggest that Godfrey had discerned the extent of the popular yearning to go to Jerusalem, and that Raymond was unable or unwilling to respond to it. He sensed in this situation an opportunity, and he acted to exploit it. Albert states that one day Godfrey, Robert of Flanders, and their followers suddenly burned their camp and departed Arqa. Destroying their camp served to demonstrate clearly that they had no intention of returning. According to Albert, Raymond's own army began to follow Godfrey at this point, forcing Raymond himself to follow in Godfrey's footsteps, even though he did not wish to.[285]

The departure from Arqa signals the point at which Godfrey became the dominant figure on the First Crusade. He may have acted out of a personal ambition to reach the Holy City; Albert explicitly attributes to him and his companions a 'constant desire to go to Jerusalem'.[286] But he may also have concluded that the resumption of the march was the best option available to him at that point. Despite his efforts in the Afrin valley, he had failed to establish a meaningful lordship of his own. Moreover, he did not wish to spend any more time and effort helping Raymond of Toulouse to capture Arqa and thereby extend his lordship around Rugia. Raymond of Aguilers explicitly states that Godfrey acted with the popular will in mind, noting that at this time 'the duke of Lotharingia was greatly anxious for the journey [to Jerusalem], and incited the people to it'.[287] Raymond of Toulouse, in contrast, 'broke into tears and began to despise himself and others, but God ignored his feeling in deference to the people's will'.[288]

The critical factor behind the crusaders' departure from Arqa was popular insistence on going to Jerusalem, and Godfrey astutely positioned himself at the head of it. As a result, his status among the rest of the crusaders began to surpass that of Raymond of Toulouse. At Arqa, Tancred perceived this shift in the balance of power, and he left Raymond's retinue to join that of Godfrey. Albert states that there had been a disagreement between Raymond and Tancred over pay, with the latter demanding more from the former. He noted that after Godfrey arrived at Arqa, Tancred 'stayed with the duke, bound faithfully to him in all military obedience'.[289] Raymond of Aguilers notes that Tancred wished to join Godfrey and so 'wickedly deserted' Raymond.[290]

On 13 May the crusaders departed Arqa, intent on reaching Jerusalem. As they travelled south over the following weeks, they kept to the coastal route, passing the port towns of Tripoli, Jubail, Beirut, Sidon, Tyre, Acre, Haifa, and Caesarea without major incident or meaningful opposition. On about 30 May, the crusaders left the coast at Arsuf and travelled inland towards Ramla, which lay on the road to Jerusalem (see Map 4.5). The inhabitants of nearby Jaffa destroyed the city before fleeing.[291] Between about 3 and 6 June they camped at Ramla, and installed as bishop of nearby Lydda a Norman prelate named Robert of Rouen.[292] The appointment of a Norman rather than a member of the clergy from southern France underscores Raymond's diminished status during the final stage of the journey to the Holy City.[293] The crusaders then moved on to Quebiba, and it was there that they received a request for assistance from native Christians in Bethlehem. The leaders despatched a force of knights under Tancred and Baldwin of Bourcq to take hold of it. After they captured the town, Tancred had his banner flown above the church of the Nativity there, an act which incurred the ire of some of the other crusaders.[294] Albert states that the Christians of Bethlehem specifically sought out Godfrey in the crusader camp, and that it was he who instructed the force of knights to head there.[295]

The armies of the First Crusade reached the Holy City on 7 June.[296] Raymond of Toulouse stationed his forces to the west of the city, outside the Tower of David, Jerusalem's citadel, before relocating to a spot near the Zion Gate at the south. Meanwhile, Godfrey and the rest of the northern French leaders arrayed their forces along the north-west stretch of the wall (see Map 4.6). Among them was Robert of Normandy, who had evidently brought his association with Raymond to an end. They were joined by Tancred, who had made the short journey to the Holy City from Bethlehem. Both the leaders who had entered Raymond's service at Marra were now aligned with Godfrey. The division of the crusaders into two forces outside the walls of Jerusalem was probably not a pre-ordained military strategy, but more likely a result of the rifts between the leaders at this point.[297]

The crusaders made their first assault on 13 June, but were repelled by the Fatimid garrison. They broke off their efforts and gathered in a council on 15 June to deliberate how to proceed. They resolved to build siege engines, and set about collecting wood to enable them to do so. The arrival of six Genoese ships at Jaffa on 17 June proved crucial; although a Fatimid fleet reached Jaffa the following day, trapping all but one of the Genoese ships there, the sailors quickly scuttled their boats and carried timber and other vital materials to Jerusalem, providing the two crusader armies with the means to build siege engines. During the next few weeks, the crusaders constructed a number of different machines. Both forces constructed their

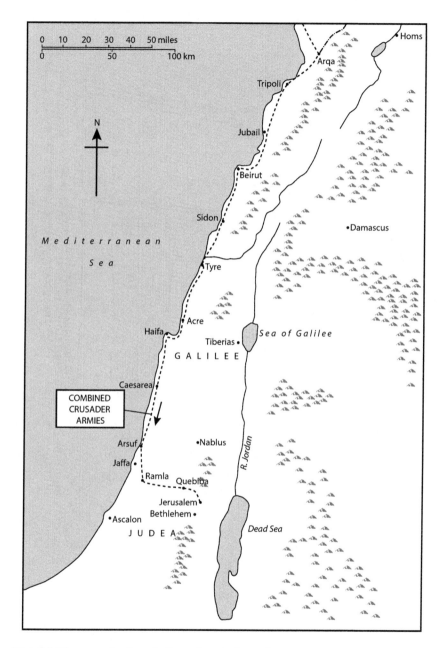

Map 4.5 The crusaders' route from Arqa to Jerusalem

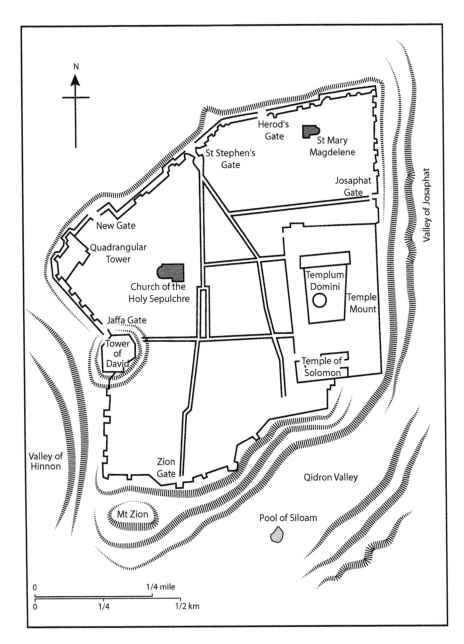

Map 4.6 Jerusalem

own siege towers.[298] Raymond of Toulouse appointed William Embracio –
who had arrived with the fleet at Jaffa on 17 June – to direct the construction of his siege tower, while Godfrey, Robert of Flanders, and Robert of
Normandy had Gaston of Béarn oversee the building of theirs.[299] Gaston,
a prominent nobleman from Spain, had been a member of Raymond of
Toulouse's contingent before he left it to join Godfrey and the northern
French.[300]

Raymond of Aguilers reports that around this time the crusaders broke
off from the siege to gather for a conference, in which they discussed disagreements between the leaders and Tancred's conduct in Bethlehem.[301]
The chronicler states that the discussions then turned to the question of
how the Latins would govern Jerusalem after its capture. He writes that the
assembly 'posed the question of the election of one of the princes as a king
[*regem*], to guard the city . . . if God grants it to us'.[302] The chronicler asserts
that the assembled clergy argued vehemently against the very notion of
appointing a king in the Holy City:

> What was the response of the bishops and the clergy to this? They stated
> that a king ought not to be elected in the place where the Lord has suf-
> fered and was crowned. Suppose that the elected man said in his heart,
> 'I sit upon the throne of David and I hold his kingdom [*regnum*]', his
> faith and virtue might degenerate like David's. The Lord might over-
> throw him and be angry with the place and the people. Moreover, the
> prophet cries out, 'when the Holy of Holies shall have come, unction
> will cease', because it was made clear to all people that he had come.
> But let there be some advocate [*advocatus*] to protect the city, and to
> divide the rents and tributes of the region to the guardians of the city.
> Because of these and other reasons, the election was delayed until eight
> days after the capture of Jerusalem.[303]

The chronicler asserts that the clergy invoked a passage from the book of
Daniel (9:24–7) to make their case.[304] The significance of this passage will
be explored in the following chapter. For present purposes, it is apposite to
note only that these discussions over the rule of Jerusalem were left unresolved at this point.

On 8 July, the crusaders prepared themselves for the next round of military activity by carrying instituting a fast, and making a procession around
the Holy City – as Joshua had before capturing Jericho – before climbing
the Mount of Olives, the place where Christ had ascended to heaven after
His resurrection.[305] On 13 July, they launched their new assault. Raymond
of Aguilers asserts that this new phase of activity came after Godfrey's men
surreptitiously shifted their siege equipment from its former position at
the north-west of the city to a new spot near the north-east corner. The
chronicler states that on the next day the Fatimid garrison – along with the
crusaders who had not been informed about the plan – were dumbfounded

when they realised what had happened. The crusaders, he stated, discerned the hand of God at work.[306] At this time, the crusaders deployed three mangonels near a point on the northern wall near St Stephen's gate, in order to launch stones against the city wall. The Fatimid garrison reportedly placed sacks of straw and chaff against the walls with the intention of cushioning the impact of stones hurled by the crusaders' mangonels. This prompted Godfrey to use his crossbow to launch burning arrows at the sacks, setting them alight, and thereby exposing the walls. The crusaders then moved a ram up against the outer wall, and succeeded in smashing a hole. Though the ram became lodged, they burned it, leaving behind a hole in the wall.[307]

At dawn on 15 July, Godfrey and the rest of the forces arrayed at the north of the city started to roll their siege tower up to the wall at a point near the north-east corner of the city. It was evidently a well-constructed device. It was three storeys high, and its exterior was covered with panels wrapped with animal hides, which provided protection against incendiary attacks from the besieged garrison. Atop it was placed a gold cross containing a statue of Christ.[308] Albert of Aachen provides a detailed account of what took place as the tower was rolled into position against the wall. On the lowest storey were the crusaders whose role was to push the tower forward. In the middle storey were two brothers named Lithold and Engilbert of Tournai and a number of other warriors.[309] Stationed on the top storey was Godfrey, with his brother Eustace alongside him. Together, the two brothers led another contingent of soldiers.[310] The Fatimid garrison deployed its mangonels to hurl rocks against the tower – aiming at the golden cross atop it – and though it was hit repeatedly, it remained upright and functional.[311] Godfrey was in the thick of the action as the tower was rolled forward. At one point a soldier standing at his side was killed instantly when he was struck on the head by a stone hurled from the city. During this phase in the fighting, Godfrey used his crossbow to pick off the Fatimid soldiers who were operating the mangonels, and personally repaired the tower by tying down the hide-covered panels when they came loose.[312] The Fatimids hurled fire-spitting pots against the tower, but they failed to set it alight. They also attempted to burn the tower using Greek fire, but the crusaders had placed inside it wineskins containing vinegar, which they used to extinguish the flames. While the crusaders were repelling these incendiary attacks, Godfrey, Eustace, and their companions on the top storey of the tower hurled missiles at the Fatimids who were standing on the city walls. At this point, Lithold and Engilbert of Tournai sensed an opportunity, and so lowered some beams of wood from the tower's middle storey onto the city wall, and then dashed across them. Godfrey and Eustace quickly descended from top of the tower to the middle storey and followed them over onto the wall. At this point crusaders outside the tower raised scaling ladders against the wall.[313] The crusaders had infiltrated the Holy City, and Godfrey was the first of the leaders to enter.

Godfrey clearly distinguished himself during this critical phase in the siege. While Albert describes Godfrey's exertions atop the tower in great detail, the sources of the *Gesta Francorum* tradition praise his efforts in more general terms. Like Albert, several noted that Eustace was in the thick of the action alongside his brother. In the *Gesta Francorum* it is stated that during the assault on Jerusalem 'our knights [fought] bravely on the siege-tower, led by Duke Godfrey and Count Eustace his brother'.[314] Tudebode repeated this statement verbatim, and the author of the 'Bartolf' text closely replicated it.[315] The author of the *Gesta Francorum* claimed that the very first crusader to enter the city was Lithold of Tournai.[316] Tudebode repeated this assertion, adding to it the statement that after Lithold was 'closely followed by our knights of Christ along with Count Eustace and Duke Godfrey'.[317] Raymond of Aguilers asserts that Godfrey was the very man who extended the platform across which the crusaders went from the tower to the city walls.[318] Clearly, Godfrey and his brother stood out among the crusaders by taking such a prominent role in the fighting during this phase in the siege.

Soon after the crusaders under Godfrey infiltrated Jerusalem from the north, Raymond of Toulouse's men managed to enter from the south. As they overran the streets of the Holy City, they seized precious goods and animals, and brutally killed many of its inhabitants. Much blood was reportedly spilled in the Temple Mount, the rectangular complex at the southeast corner which enclosed the Templum Domini (the Dome of the Rock) and the Temple of Solomon (the al-Aqsa mosque).[319] Raymond of Aguilers used apocalyptic imagery drawn from the book of Revelation to describe these events, stating that 'in the Temple of Solomon and the portico [the crusaders] rode in blood to the knees and bridles of their horses'.[320] Tancred plundered many spoils from the Templum Domini, and, according to Albert, 'faithfully shared them with Duke Godfrey, whose knight he was'.[321] Amidst the mayhem and bloodshed, Raymond of Toulouse shrewdly negotiated control of the Tower of David from the city's Fatimid commander.[322]

Raymond of Aguilers – who was present when the crusaders captured Jerusalem – states that Godfrey (accompanied by Tancred) was one of the first to enter the city, and affirms that on that day the two spilled an incredible amount of blood as they helped capture the city.[323] Albert asserted that the crusaders had used excessive cruelty in their attacks on Jerusalem's inhabitants, before claiming that while 'the common crowd' were attacking Jerusalem's citizens near the Temple of Solomon, and the other princes were greedily eyeing the city's possessions and buildings, Godfrey acted in an entirely different manner. He states that:

> Duke Godfrey soon abstained from all slaughter, and, keeping only three of his men with him, Baldric [the seneschal], Adelolf and Stabelo [the chamberlain], he took off his hauberk and linen clothes, went out of the walls with bare feet and made a humble procession around the outside of the city; then, entering through that gate which looks out on the Mount of Olives, he presented himself at the Sepulchre of Lord Jesus Christ, son of the living God, keeping up steadfastly tears, prayers

and divine praises, and giving thanks to God because he had earnt the sight of that which had always been his greatest desire.[324]

Since Albert implies that Godfrey participated in the attacks before he chose to cease taking part in them, his account is not necessarily incompatible with that provided by Raymond of Aguilers. Significantly, Albert does not ascribe to Godfrey this 'pious desire' (*pio . . . desiderio*) of worshiping at the Holy Sepulchre in order to absolve him for the responsibility for the sack of Jerusalem and the violence meted out to its citizens. On a number of occasions throughout his account of the First Crusade, Albert had enthusiastically recounted how Godfrey had fought and killed Muslims. The aim of this passage was instead to draw a distinction between Godfrey and the rest of the crusaders. Whereas the other chroniclers state that many of the crusaders began to give prayer, Albert states that it was only Godfrey who did so. When it came to recounting the climactic moment of the First Crusade, then, Albert sought to cast Godfrey as the most devout participant.

On 15 July, as the crusaders tightened their grip on Jerusalem, many crusaders began to turn from acts of violence to acts of devotion, heading to the city's holy places to worship and give thanks to God for their victory. The author of the *Gesta Francorum* states that after the crusaders ceased pillaging and shedding blood, they 'all came rejoicing and weeping from excess of gladness to worship at the Sepulchre of our Saviour Jesus'.[325] Similarly, Raymond of Aguilers noted that as the city fell,

> it was rewarding to see the worship of the pilgrims at the Holy Sepulchre, the clapping of hands, the rejoicing and singing of a new song to the Lord. Their souls offered to the victorious and triumphant God prayers of praise which they could not explain in words.[326]

Fulcher of Chartres states that the crusaders went

> to the Lord's Sepulchre and His most glorious Temple, singing a new canticle to the Lord in a resounding voice of exultation, and making offerings and most humble supplications, joyously visited the holy places as they had long desired to do.[327]

The crusaders instantly regarded the capture of the Holy City as one of the most significant events in history. Fulcher asserted that what had happened on 15 July 1099 would 'resound and continue memorable in the tongues of all nations until the end of time', while Raymond of Aguilers asserted that the day of Jerusalem's capture was:

> A new day, new gladness, new and everlasting happiness, and the fulfilment of our toil and love brought forth new words and songs for all. This day, which I affirm will be celebrated in the centuries to come,

changed our grief and struggles into gladness and rejoicing . . . This day, [15 July], shall be commemorated to the praise and glory of the name of God, who in response to the prayers of His Church returned in faith and blessing to His children Jerusalem as well as its land which he had pledged to the Fathers.[328]

In this passage, the chronicler asserted that God had aided the crusaders on that day, and that their actions would resonate for the rest of time.

Notes

1   'Godefridus dux regni Lotharingie uir nobilissimus'. AA, pp. 60–1.
2   For a detailed study of Godfrey's march to Constantinople, see: John W. Nesbitt, 'The Rate of March of Crusading Armies in Europe', *Traditio*, 9 (1983), 167–81, esp. pp. 171–2, 181.
3   'medio mensis Augusti'. AA, pp. 60–3.
4   For the text in its original Hebrew, see: *Hebräische Berichte über die Judenverfolgungen während der Kreuzzüge*, ed. Adolf Neubauer and Moritz Stern (Berlin, 1892), pp. 1–35. For a translation, see: *The Chronicle of Solomon bar Simson*, in *The Jews and the Crusaders: The Hebrew Chronicles of the First and Second Crusades*, tr. Shlomo Eidelberg (Madison, 1977), pp. 21–72 (here pp. 24–5). For a critical discussion of the text, see: Chazan, *God, Humanity and History*, pp. 52–99.
5   While no imperial source records that Henry intervened on behalf of Jewish communities at this time, for the most part he did seek to protect Jews during his reign, for he regarded them as ready sources of cash. See: Robinson, *Henry IV*, pp. 301–2.
6   *The Chronicle of Solomon bar Simson*, tr. Eidelberg, p. 25.
7   AA, pp. 50–1.
8   Murray, *Crusader Kingdom*, p. 43.
9   Rudolf Hiestand, 'Juden und Christen in der Kreuzzugspropaganda und bei den Kreuzzugspredigern', in Alfred Haverkamp (ed.), *Juden und Christen zur Zeit der Kreuzzüge* (Sigmaringen, 1999), pp. 153–208, at pp. 177–8.
10 Chazan, *God, Humanity and History*, pp. 76–7.
11 Murray, *Crusader Kingdom*, p. 45.
12 Murray, *Crusader Kingdom*, p. 43; Idem, 'Money and Logistics', pp. 240–1.
13 France, *Victory*, pp. 101–2.
14 AA, pp. 62–3. *CPC*, no. 70, dates Godfrey's stay at Tulln from 9 to 30 September.
15 Though Nesbitt, 'The Rate of March', p. 172, questions Albert's dating for this phase of the march.
16 See above, p. 93. In 1096 Urban II wrote to Coloman, praising him highly, and asking him to take up the struggle against Clement III. See: *PL*, vol. 151, cols 480–2; JL 5662. On the kingdom of Hungary in this period, see: Nora Berend, 'Hungary in the Eleventh and Twelfth Centuries', *NCMH*, vol. 4, part 2, pp. 304–16.
17 AA, pp. 62–3.
18 AA, pp. 62–3.
19 AA, pp. 64–7.
20 AA, pp. 68–9.
21 AA, pp. 70–1.
22 'Hanc itaque imperatoris beniuolentiam dux intelligens, in omnibus se imperatoris parere pollicetur mandatis'. AA, pp. 70–3.

23 Andressohn, *Godfrey*, p. 55.
24 'in omni opulentia et iocunditate recreati sunt'. AA, pp. 72–3. *CPC*, no. 97, dates the stay at Niš to 7–12 November. Frankopan, *The First Crusade*, p. 115, argues that the abundance of supplies at Niš indicates how efficiently Alexios had prepared for the arrival of the crusaders.
25 AA, pp. 72–3. *CPC*, no. 100, suggests that the army was at Sofiya between 16 and 20 November.
26 *CPC*, no. 102, puts the stay at Philippopolis to 26 November to 3 December. On Hugh of Vermandois and his role in the First Crusade, see: Marcus Bull, 'The Capetian Monarchy and the Early Crusade Movement: Hugh of Vermandois and Louis VII', *Nottingham Medieval Studies*, 40 (1996), 25–46; James Naus, *Constructing Kingship: The Capetian Monarchs of France and the Early Crusades* (Manchester, 2016), pp. 42–5, 47–8.
27 AA, pp. 72–3.
28 AA, pp. 72–5. Albert describes the Westerners in Alexios' service as 'Franci'.
29 AA, pp. 76–7; *CPC*, no. 107. Nesbitt calculates that Godfrey's force had travelled from Tulln to Constantinople in 89 days (marching on 59 days and resting on the others), which equates to an average march of about 15.5 miles per day: Nesbitt, 'The rate of march', pp. 172–3.
30 'magno exercitu'. *GF*, p. 6.
31 On Alexios' dealings with the crusaders at Constantinople, see: Jonathan Shepard, 'Cross Purposes: Alexius Comnenus and the First Crusade', in *FCOI*, pp. 107–29; Frankopan, *The First Crusade*, pp. 118–36; Jonathan Harris, *Byzantium and the Crusades*, 2nd edn (London, 2014), pp. 59–69.
32 See above, p. 93.
33 Anna, p. 277.
34 On Alexios' preparations, see: Frankopan, *The First Crusade*, pp. 113–14.
35 Anna, p. 285, refers to Alexios' attempts to monitor communications between the crusaders.
36 Harris, *Byzantium*, p. 60, describes Alexios' tactics as 'tried and tested'.
37 See, for example: *GF*, p. 6.
38 On developments at Constantinople, see: *GF*, pp. 5–7; RA, pp. 42–3, tr. pp. 24; PT, pp. 38–48, tr. pp. 22–30; FC, pp. 176–80, tr. pp. 79–80; Anna, pp. 277–96. For comment, see: Frankopan, *The First Crusade*, pp. 118–37.
39 'quidam aduene de terra Francorum'. AA, pp. 74–5.
40 AA, pp. 74–7.
41 AA, pp. 76–7; *CPC*, no. 109.
42 Harris, *Byzantium*, p. 63.
43 AA, pp. 76–9.
44 AA, pp. 78–81.
45 AA, pp. 82–3; *GF*, p. 6; *CPC*, nos. 110–1.
46 AA, pp. 82–3.
47 Anna, p. 288.
48 France, *Victory*, pp. 106–7.
49 AA, pp. 82–5.
50 Anna, p. 285.
51 France, *Victory*, pp. 103–4, 114; Flori, *Bohémond*, pp. 87–9.
52 'dux . . . respondit se non causa questus aut pro destructione Christianorum a terra et cognatione sua exisse, sed in Christi nomine uiam Ierusalem institisse, et hanc uelle perficere et adimplere consilio imperatoris, si eius gratiam et bonam uoluntatem recuperare et obseruare possit'. AA, pp. 82–3.
53 *CPC*, no. 113.
54 'in splendore et ornatu preciosarum uestium tam ex ostro quam aurifrigio, et ex niueo opera harmelino, et ex mardrino grisioque et uario quibus Gallorum principes precipue utuntur'. AA, pp. 84–5.

55 'Audiui de te quoniam miles et princes potentissimus tua sis in terra, et uir prudentissimus ac perfecte fidei. Quapropter te in filium adoptiuum suscipio, et uniuersa que possideo in tua potestate constituo, ut per te imperium meum et terra a facie presentis et affuture multitudinis liberari et saluari possit'. AA, pp. 84–7.

56 'non solum se ei in filium, sicut mos est terre, sed etiam in uassalum iunctis manibus reddidit, cum uniuersis primis qui tunc aderant, et postea subsecuti sunt'. AA, pp. 86–7. The author of the 'Bartolf' text speaks of Alexios and the crusaders concluding a 'pact' (*pactio*). Bartolf, pp. 494–5.

57 'Sic uero imperatore et duce perfecte fidei et amicicie uinculo insolubili innodatis'. AA, pp. 86–7.

58 'Boemundus homo imperatoris factus est'. AA, pp. 88–9.

59 Anna, p. 289.

60 AA, pp. 86–7. The chronicler states that the coins from Alexios swiftly found their way back into Byzantine coffers when the crusaders used them to buy supplies.

61 'pax et honor imperatori et omnibus suis deinceps exhiberetur'. AA, pp. 86–9.

62 AA, pp. 88–9.

63 Shepard, 'Cross Purposes', p. 109.

64 On the discussions between Bohemond and Alexios, see, among others: Jonathan Shepard, 'When Greek Meets Greek: Alexius Comnenus and Bohemond in 1097–8', *Byzantine and Modern Greek Studies*, 12 (1988), 185–277; John H. Pryor and Michael J. Jeffreys, 'Alexios, Bohemond, and Byzantium's Euphrates Frontier: A Tale of Two Cretans', *Crusades*, 11 (2012), 31–86.

65 'plurimis blandiciis'. AA, pp. 88–9.

66 Anna, pp. 294–5. Pryor and Jeffreys, 'Alexios, Bohemond, and Byzantium's Euphrates Frontier', argue that it was Alexios who raised the prospect of Bohemond assuming that office, in the hope that the Norman would carve out a territory near the Euphrates which would act as a buffer against the Turks.

67 AA, pp. 90–1.

68 AA, pp. 92–3.

69 GF, p. 13; RA, p. 42, tr. p. 24. For comment, see: France, *Victory*, p. 115; John H. Hill and Laurita L. Hill, 'The Convention of Alexius Comnenus and Raymond of Saint Gilles', *American Historical Review*, 58 (1953), 322–7.

70 GF, p. 13; AA, pp. 90–1.

71 'callide fraudulenterque' . . . 'Propterea igitur, quia multa coacti erant necessitate'. GF, pp. 11–12.

72 For comments on the importance of Byzantine aid to the success of the First Crusade, see: France, *Victory*, pp. 368–9.

73 DK, pp. 138–40 (no. 4), tr. in LE, pp. 15–17 (no. 1).

74 DK, pp. 136–7; France, *Victory*, pp. 97–8.

75 France, *Victory*, pp. 23–4, 231–2.

76 'communi consilio et pari conductu moderabantur'. AA, pp. 180–1.

77 AA, pp. 114–15, 136–7.

78 On the dynamic between the leadership and the rank and file, see: Christopher Tyerman, '"Principes et Populus": Civil Society and the First Crusade', in Simon Barton and Peter Linehan (eds), *Cross, Crescent and Conversion: Studies on Medieval Spain and Christendom in Memory of Richard Fletcher* (Leiden, 2008), pp. 127–51.

79 On the siege of Nicaea, see: France, *Victory*, pp. 160–5.

80 GF, p. 14.

81 GF, p. 14; RA, p. 43, tr. p. 25; AA, pp. 94–5.

82 AA, pp. 96–7.

83 Tanner, 'In His Brothers' Shadow', p. 85.

84 *GF*, pp. 13–4; AA, pp. 94–103. France, *Victory*, pp. 160–2, suggests that this piecemeal approach to the investment of Nicaea indicates that at this stage the crusade lacked a clear military command.

85 AA, pp. 96–101.

86 AA, pp. 104–7.

87 RA, pp. 43–4, tr. pp. 25–6.

88 'Dux Godefridus, Boemundus, non equo tardantes, laxis frenis per medios hostes aduolant, hoc lanceis perforantes, hos ab equis deicientes, socios sepe hortantes ad trucidandos hostes uirili ammonitione consolantur'. AA, pp. 108–9. See also: *CPC*, no. 152.

89 France, *Victory*, p. 161.

90 AA, pp. 112–13.

91 'Dux Godefridus . . . arrepto arcu baleari, et stans post scuta duorum sociorum eundem Turcum trans uitalia cordis perculit'. AA, pp. 118–9.

92 AA, pp. 120–5.

93 Bartolf, p. 495; Anna, pp. 304–5.

94 RA, p. 45, tr. p. 27.

95 AA, pp. 128–9.

96 'nobis vero tunc deerant dux Godefridus et comes Raimundus atque Hugo Magnus, qui per duos dies, nescio qua de causa, se a nobis subtraxerant cum gente magna nostorum tramite bifurco'. FC, p. 194, tr. p. 85.

97 *GF*, p. 18; PT, p. 51, tr. p. 34. France, *Victory*, pp. 169–70, suggests that the lack of overall leadership may have been the cause of this division amongst the crusaders.

98 For a detailed assessment of this battle, see: France, *Victory*, pp. 174–85.

99 RA, p. 45, tr. p. 27.

100 'Tamquam si ad conuiuium omnium deliciarum uocarentur'. AA, pp. 132–3.

101 'Iam dies clarissima illuxerat, sol radiis fulgebat lucidissimus, cuius splendor in clipeos aureos et uestes ferreas refulsit, signa et uexilla gemmis et ostro florida, erecta et hastis infixa coruscabant. Caballi celeres calcaribus urgebantur, nullus socium aut fratrum expectabat, sed quisque quo uelocius poterat ad auxilium et uindictam Christianorum uiam insistebant'. AA, pp. 132–3.

102 AA, pp. 134–7.

103 *GF*, pp. 18–20; PT, p. 53, tr. p. 35.

104 France, *Victory*, p. 183, n. 106.

105 AA, pp. 138–41; *GF*, p. 23; PT, p. 57, tr. p. 38; FC, pp. 199–203, tr. pp. 87–8.

106 'Dux uero sicuti solitus erat et promptus ad omnia aduersa Christianis confratribus subuenire, educto raptim gladio, equo fortiter calcaribus ammonito, misello homini aduolat . . . Vrsus itaque, uiso equo eiusque sessore se celeri cursu premente, ferocitati sue fidens et rapacitati suorum unguium, non segnius facie ad faciem duci occurrens, fauces et iugulet aperit, totum se ad resistendum immo as inuadendum erigit, ungues suos acutissimos exerit ut laniet, caput et brachia ab ictu gladii diligenter cauens subtrahit . . . Dux uero astutum et pessimum animal considerans in feritate audaci resistere, motus animo vehementer indignatur, et uerso mucronis acumine, temerario et ceco impetu propinquat belue ut iecur eius perforet, sed infelici casu ictum gladii effugiens, belua subito curuos ungues tunice ducis infixit, ac complexum brachiis equo deuolutum, terre applicans, dentibus iugulare properabat. Dux itaque angustiatus, reminiscens suorum multorum insignium factorum, et de omni periculo se adhuc nobiliter ereptum nunc uero uili morte a cruenta bestia se suffocari dolens, recuperatis uiribus in momento resurgit in pedibus, gladiumque in hoc repentino lapsu ab equo et cum insana fera luctamine propriis cruribus implicitum celeriter in eiusdem fere iugulum rapiens et capulo retinens, suras et neruos proprii cruris graui incisione truncauit'. AA, pp. 142–5. For the date, see: *CPC*, nos. 175–6.

107 Piers D. Mitchell, *Medicine in the Crusades: Warfare, Wounds and the Medieval Surgeon* (Cambridge, 2004), pp. 149–50.
108 AA, pp. 144–5. For a study of the story, see: Natasha R. Hodgson, 'Lions, Tigers and Bears: Encounters With Wild Animals and Bestial Imagery in the Context of Crusading to the Latin East', *Viator*, 44 (2013), 65–93, at pp. 83–93.
109 AA, pp. 144–5.
110 Hodgson, 'Lions, Tigers and Bears', p. 84.
111 AA, pp. 584–5. On Wicher, see: Murray, *Crusader Kingdom*, pp. 235–6.
112 AA, pp. 228–9. See above, p. 138.
113 Sweetenham, 'What Really Happened to Eurvin De Créel's Donkey?'.
114 Hodgson, 'Lions, Tigers and Bears', pp. 84, 91.
115 *The Song of Roland*, tr. Gerard J. Brault, 2 vols (University Park, PA, 1978), vol. 1, pp. 163–5 (commentary), vol. 2, pp. 46–7 (text). See also: Frederick Whitehead, 'Charlemagne's Second Dream', *Olifant*, 3 (1976), 189–95.
116 'totumque exercitum impia fama conturbare'. AA, pp. 144–5.
117 'fortis athleta et uir consiliorum, caput peregrinorum'. AA, pp. 144–5. As Edgington notes in her edition of Albert, the description of Godfrey as a 'man of wisdom' (*uir consoliorum*) evokes Ecclesiasticus 32:22 and 1 Maccabees 2:65.
118 France, *Victory*, pp. 186–93. On interactions between Latins and Christians of the Near East during the First Crusade, see: Christopher MacEvitt, *The Crusades and the Christian World of the East: Rough Tolerance* (Philadelphia, 2008), pp. 50–73.
119 On the expedition into Cilicia, see: AA, pp. 145–67, GF, pp. 24–5, PT, pp. 58–9, tr. pp. 39–40; FC, pp. 203–9, tr. p. 89. For comment, see: France, *Victory*, pp. 193–5; MacEvitt, *Rough Tolerance*, pp. 55–8.
120 Murray, 'The Army of Godfrey of Bouillon', pp. 323–4.
121 'Boemundum et hunc Tancradum quos sic ueneramini ac formidatis, nequaquam maiores et potentiores magistros credatis Christiani exercitus, nec fratri meo Godefrido duci et principi milicie totius Gallie, nullique sui generis istos esse comparandos. Princeps enim idem frater meus Godefridus est dux regni magni et primi imperatoris Romanorum Augusti hereditario iure suorum antecessorum nobilium, ab omni honoratur exercitu, et cuius uoci et consiliis ad omnia magni paruique obtemperare non desistunt, cum caput et domnus ab omnibus electus et constitutus sit'. AA, pp. 152–3.
122 'communi consilio et pari conductu moderabantur'. AA, pp. 180–1.
123 'Godefridi ducis nunc primum nomen scintillabat'. AA, pp. 150–1. Andressohn, *Godfrey*, pp. 71–2, following Albert, suggests that Bohemond's territorial ambitions had already angered the other leaders, who would have looked to Godfrey as the spokesman for their discontent. However, this is merely supposition, for nowhere else is it suggested that Bohemond had provoked the ire of the other leaders by this point.
124 *GF*, pp. 24–5.
125 FC, pp. 203–9, tr. p. 89.
126 France, *Victory*, p. 194, notes that events at Tarsus 'smack of the "my brother is bigger than yours" syndrome'.
127 AA, pp. 154–61.
128 'cuiusdam Armenici militis'. AA, pp. 160–7.
129 *CPC*, nos. 193–4.
130 AA, pp. 182–3; Murray, *Crusader Kingdom*, p. 203.
131 FC, p. 206, tr. p. 89; *CPC*, no. 195.
132 FC, pp. 209–15, tr. pp. 89–92; AA, pp. 168–81. On the county of Edessa, see: Monique Amouroux-Mourad, *Le comte d'Edesse, 1098–1150* (Paris, 1988).
133 On the crusaders' arrival at Antioch and the initial dispersal of their forces, see: AA, pp. 198–203; GF, p. 28; PT, pp. 63–4, tr. pp. 43–4; RA, pp. 47–8, tr. pp. 30–1. For analysis, see: France, *Victory*, pp. 222–7. For the later name of the gate invested by Godfrey, see WT, p. 252.

134 'Inter hec assidui Martis ludibria, et creberrimas incursiones, mora aliquanti temporis transacta'. AA, pp. 216–17.

135 AA, pp. 204–7; RA, p. 49, tr. p. 32; FC, pp. 218–19, tr. pp. 93; France, *Victory*, pp. 229–30.

136 *GF*, p. 30; PT, p. 65, tr. p. 45.

137 AA, pp. 208–11.

138 AA, pp. 210–13.

139 France, *Victory*, pp. 236–41.

140 *GF*, pp. 32–3; PT, pp. 66–7, tr. pp. 46–7; RA, pp. 50–1, tr. pp. 32–3.

141 RA, p. 53, tr. p. 35.

142 RA, p. 50. The Hills rendered this phrase (at p. 33) simply as Godfrey 'was ill', a translation which does not account for the adverb *maxime*.

143 'gravi ac diuturno morbo'. RA, p. 62, tr. p. 45.

144 AA, pp. 220–1; *GF*, p. 33; PT, p. 68, tr. p. 47.

145 AA, pp. 220–3; Murray, *Crusader Kingdom*, pp. 217, 221.

146 *GF*, pp. 33–4; PT, pp. 68–9, tr. pp. 48–9; *CPC*, no. 229.

147 RA, p. 55, tr. p. 37.

148 'dux Godefridus iam a uulneris sui infirmitate conualuit' . . . 'Deo annuente actum est'. AA, pp. 228–31.

149 RA, p. 55, tr. p. 37.

150 'Godefridus dux, in officio belli semper indeficiens' . . . 'Dei uiui, et Domini Iesu Christi sumus cultores, cuius nomini militamus. Hii in uirtute sua; nos uero in nomine Dei uiuentis adunati sumus. In cuius gratia confidentes, impios et incredulos impetere non dubitemus; quia siue uiuimus siue morimur Domini sumus'. AA, pp. 232–5.

151 France, *Victory*, pp. 245–6.

152 PT, p. 71, tr. p. 51.

153 *GF*, pp. 35–8; PT, pp. 70–3, tr. pp. 50–2; RA, pp. 56–8, tr. pp. 38–40; France, *Victory*, pp. 250–1; *CPC*, no. 233.

154 'estuans desiderio conserendi prelia'. AA, pp. 236–7; France, *Victory*, p. 248.

155 'Dux uero inperterritus et uindictam adtritorum fidelium sitiens, prorsus hinc abire aut aliqua formidine locum hunc se deserere contradixit, sed cum iuramento se asseruit aut hodie montem quo firmandum erat presidium conscendere, aut in eodem cum suis uitam amittere'. AA, pp. 240–1.

156 On Godfrey's reputed exploit in the Bridge Gate battle, see: Simon John, '"Claruit Ibi Multum Dux Lotharingiae": The development of the epic tradition of Godfrey of Bouillon and the Bisected Turk', in Simon T. Parsons and Linda M. Paterson (eds), *Literature of the Crusades* (Woodbridge, 2018), pp. 7–24.

157 'Claruit ibi multum dux Lotharingię. Hinc namque hostes at pontem prevenit, atque assenso gradu venientes per medium dividebant'. RA, p. 61. John, '"Claruit Ibi Multum Dux Lotharingiae"', pp. 9–10, argues that a better reading of this passage renders the last word as *dividebat*, i.e., in the singular rather than in the plural, as the Hills have it in their edition. To this, it should be added that the Hills' translation of this passage (p. 43) is unsatisfactory.

158 'Dux uero Godefridus, cuius manus bello doctissima erat, plurima capita licet galea tecta ibidem amputasse refertur, ex ore illorum qui presentes oculis perspexerunt. Dum sic plurimo belli labore desudaret et mediis hostibus plurimam stragem exerceret, Turcum, mirabile dictu, sibi arcu inportunum acutissimo ense duas diuisit in partes, lorica indutum. Cuius corporis medietas a pectore sursum sabulo cecidit, altera adhuc cruribus equum complexa in medium pontem ante urbis menia refertur ubi lapsa remansit'. AA, pp. 244–5.

159 John, 'Historical truth and the miraculous past', p. 280.

160 'Qui gladio suo quo Turcum trans loricas et uestes super pontem Antiochie medium secuit, non modicam regi opem hic contulisset', AA, pp. 584–5.
161 See above, p. 132.
162 Though note that the account of the battle in *GF*, pp. 39–41, does not include any reference to Godfrey. One of the four manuscripts of Peter Tudebode's *Historia* contains a unique passage describing Godfrey's exploit in the Bridge Gate battle: 'Tunc dux Godefredus Christi miles potentissimus irruens in eos evaginato ense, percussit quendam gentilem ferocissimum tam viriliter ut in duas partes ipsum divideret a vertice videlicet usque in sellam equi. Actumque est ex Dei providentia ut quamvis in duo discissus minime ex toto de equo dilaberetur. Post hunc aggressus alium ex oblico secuit eum per medium. Ex hinc maximus timor et horror omnes inimicos Christianitatis perculet, non solum qui presentes aderant sed omnes qui hoc utcumque audire potuerunt. Deinde dux per omnia memorandus illos in fugam versos persequens, nunc hos nunc illos ut leo fortissimus invadens detruncabat et in annem precipitabat'. PT, p. 75, n. *t.* The absence of this passage from the other three manuscripts, however, suggests that it was not included in Tudebode's original account.
163 On this, see: John, ' "Claruit Ibi Multum Dux Lotharingiae" ', pp. 23–4.
164 'ipse habebat plus milites in sua familia quam alii, et plus poterat dare'. PT, p. 78, tr. pp. 56–7 (adapted)
165 RA, p. 62, tr. pp. 44–5.
166 'adeo lenita est ut ab omnibus pater et conservator exercitus appellaretur. Ab eo itaque tempore crevit comitis nomen'. RA, p. 63, tr. p. 45 (adapted).
167 *GF*, pp. 43–4; PT pp. 81–2, tr. pp. 59–60; RA p. 63, tr. p. 46; France, *Victory*, pp. 254–5.
168 See above, p. 135.
169 'plurima talenta auri et argenti'. AA, pp. 262–3.
170 'tentorium miri operis et decoris Godefrido duci misit, ut gratiam et amiciciam illius inueniret'. AA, pp. 262–3.
171 AA, pp. 262–3. The incident suggests that alongside their efforts to increase their stranglehold on Antioch, the crusaders had become embroiled in the rivalries of the local Armenian lords. See: France, *Victory*, p. 256. MacEvitt, *Rough Tolerance*, p. 71, notes that Baldwin and Nicusus had earlier acted against Pakrad, and it may have been this that led him to target the gift bound for Godfrey.
172 Riley-Smith, *First Crusaders*, pp. 110–11.
173 AA, pp. 262–3.
174 *DK*, pp. 153–5 (no. 12), tr. in *LE*, pp. 25–6 (no. 6).
175 'sine ulla dubitatione uita gloriantur aeterna'. *DK*, p. 154, tr. *LE*, p. 26.
176 'Boemundus filius Rotberti, atque Raimundus, comes S. Aegidii, simulque Godefridus dux'. *DK*, p. 153, tr. in *LE*, p. 25. The letter also lists Hugh of Vermandois after Godfrey.
177 France, *Victory*, p. 255.
178 AA, pp. 264–7; Bartolf, pp. 500–1; FC, pp. 242–3, tr. p. 101.
179 *GF*, pp. 44–6; PT, p. 84, tr. p. 62.
180 AA, pp. 268–73.
181 On Bohemond and Firuz, see: *GF*, pp. 44; PT, pp. 82–3, tr. p. 61; AA, pp. 270–3; Anna, pp. 306–7.
182 *GF*, p. 63; PT, pp. 104–5, tr. p. 81; RA, p. 77, tr. p. 59; FC, p. 228, tr. p. 97; AA, pp. 266–9. On Stephen and his reputation, see: Brundage, 'An Errant Crusader'.
183 For what follows, see: France, *Victory*, pp. 262–7.
184 'Eia! fidelissimi milites Christi, non pro terrena remuneratione hoc periculum incurritus, sed illius meritum expectantes, qui post mortem presentem eterne uite premia suis conferre nouit'. AA, pp. 276–7.

185 RA, pp. 64–5, p. 47; AA, pp. 280–1.
186 AA, pp. 280–1; France, *Victory*, pp. 263–4.
187 France, *Victory*, pp. 299, 301.
188 RA, pp. 66–7, tr. p. 49; AA, pp. 296–9.
189 AA, pp. 292–3. France, *Victory*, pp. 272–4, dates Godfrey's unsuccessful sortie to the first few days after Kerbogha's arrival.
190 *GF*, pp. 56–7; PT, p. 97, tr. p. 73; AA, pp. 304–5; RA, p. 74, tr. p. 57; FC, pp. 246–7, tr. p. 102.
191 *GF*, pp. 58–9; PT, p. 100, tr. p. 76; RA, p. 74, tr. p. 56.
192 AA, pp. 312–15.
193 *GF*, pp. 62–3; PT, p. 104, pp. 79–80; RA, pp. 76–7, tr. p. 59; FC, p. 247, tr. p. 103; AA, pp. 299–301.
194 'cameli uilissimi'. AA, pp. 300–1.
195 AA, pp. 322–5. On Hartmann and Henry, see: Murray, *Crusader Kingdom*, pp. 208–9.
196 In general, see: John France, 'Two Types of Vision on the First Crusade: Stephen of Valence and Peter Bartholomew', *Crusades*, 5 (2006), 1–20.
197 Stephen of Valence's vision probably spurred Adhémar's efforts to encourage the leaders to swear an oath not to flee Antioch: France, *Victory*, p. 278.
198 *CPC*, nos. 284 and 288. On the relic, see: Thomas Asbridge, 'The Holy Lance of Antioch: Power, Devotion and Memory on the First Crusade', *Reading Medieval Studies*, 33 (2007), 3–36; Colin Morris, 'Policy and Visions: The Case of the Holy Land Found at Antioch', in John Gillingham and J. C. Holt (eds), *War and Government in the Middle Ages: Essays in Honour of J. O. Prestwich* (Woodbridge, 1984), pp. 33–45.
199 *DK*, pp. 157–65 (no. 16), tr. in *LE*, pp. 30–3 (no. 8).
200 *GF*, pp. 66–7; PT, pp. 108–9, tr. p. 84. RA, p. 79, tr. pp. 60–1; Bartolf, pp. 502–3; FC, pp. 247–9, tr. p. 103.
201 AA, pp. 316–20.
202 AA, pp. 320–1.
203 On the battle, see: France, *Victory*, pp. 279–96.
204 AA, pp. 332–3.
205 AA, pp. 334–5.
206 *GF*, pp. 70–1; RA, p. 83, tr. p. 65.
207 *DK*, pp. 156–60 (no. 15), at p. 160, tr. in *LE*, pp. 26–30 (no. 7), at p. 29. France, *Victory*, p. 285, describes this as a 'slip of memory' on Anselm's part.
208 *GF*, pp. 68–71; PT, pp. 110–14, tr. pp. 86–9; RA, pp. 79–83, tr. pp. 61–4; FC, pp. 251–8, tr. pp. 104–7.
209 'equitabant iuxta aquam, ubi uirtus illorum erat. Isti primitus signo crucis muniti, unanimiter inuaserunt illos'. *GF*, pp. 69–70.
210 'dux Lothariensis cum pluribus comitibus Lotharingis et legione gladiatoria'. Bartolf, p. 503.
211 'in nomine Iesu filii Dei uiui triumphantem'. AA, pp. 328–9.
212 AA, pp. 328–31.
213 AA, pp. 326–7.
214 France, *Victory*, pp. 292, 295–6.
215 On this phase of the crusade, see: John France, 'Moving to the Goal, June 1098–July 1099', in *JG*, pp. 133–49.
216 *GF*, p. 72. FC, pp. 265–6, tr. p. 112, asserts that the crusaders delayed for four months to rest.
217 PT, p. 114, tr. p. 90.
218 'Quippe nostri ocio, et diuiciis remissi, de itinere propter quod uenerant, usque in Kalendas nouembris contra Dei preceptum distulerunt'. RA, p. 84, tr. p. 65.

219 *GF*, pp. 70–1, 76; AA, pp. 340–1. Bartolf, p. 506, asserts that Bohemond was granted Antioch with common assent, saying nothing of Raymond's opposition.

220 Albert of Aachen, who was often critical of Raymond of Toulouse, states that the count had designs of his own upon the city, accusing him of insatiable acquisitiveness. AA, pp. 340–1. Asbridge, *First Crusade*, pp. 244–5, suggests that Raymond's apparent loyalty to Alexios was in fact a smokescreen for his own ambitions on Antioch.

221 RA, p. 83, tr. p. 65.

222 *DK*, pp. 155–6 (no. 13); France, 'Moving to the Goal', p. 138.

223 AA, pp. 340–1.

224 RA, p. 83, tr. p. 65.

225 *GF*, p. 72. This claim certainly chimes with the postponement of the crusade until 1 November, a delay which would have afforded Alexios ample time to come to Antioch: France, 'Moving to the Goal', p. 137.

226 AA, pp. 340–3.

227 Anna, pp. 312–13, seeks to exonerate Alexios of the charge of abandoning the crusaders, stating that he was afraid that if he went to their aid he might leave Constantinople defenceless.

228 'Denique deuisi sunt seniores, et unusquisque profectus est in terram suam, donec esset prope terminus eundi'. *GF*, pp. 72–3. AA, pp. 368–9, also mentions the dispersal of the leaders from Antioch to the nearby regions. France, 'Moving to the Goal', p. 142, suggests that the leaders sought to cement their positions in northern Syria in the knowledge that the dispute over Antioch would eventually erupt.

229 AA, pp. 354–5; RA, p. 84, tr. p. 66; *CPC*, nos. 323–4.

230 Though RA, p. 84, tr. p. 66, suggests that the leaders dispersed from Antioch after Adhémar's death, France, 'Moving to the Goal', p. 140, is certain that they did so before it.

231 AA, pp. 342–5. On Albert's claim regarding the siege of Rome, see above, pp. 71–2.

232 Asbridge, *First Crusade*, pp. 251–8.

233 *DK*, pp. 161–5 (no.16), tr. in *LE*, pp. 30–3 (no. 8); RRR, no. 6. On the letter, see: Luis García-Guijarro, 'Some Considerations on the Crusaders' Letter to Urban II (September 1098)', in *JG*, pp. 151–71. France, 'Moving to the Goal', p. 141, suggests that the leaders sent this letter after they heard Alexios had turned back at Philomelion in June 1098 rather than continue to Antioch.

234 *DK*, p. 161, tr. in *LE*, p. 30.

235 AA, pp. 354–5, and 370–1 (the latter passage refers to Godfrey meeting Baldwin at a halfway point between Antioch and Edessa). On Baldwin's grants to Godfrey during the siege of Antioch, see above, pp. 141–2.

236 'Godefridum ducem Christiani exercitus qui Antiochiam, Corbahan fugato, potenter obtinet, amicum datis dextris tibi facere non tardabis, et sic universam Christianorum opem et comtitatum in hac instanti necessitate scias te adepturum'. AA, pp. 346–7.

237 'uir et princeps es potens uiribus'. AA, pp. 346–7.

238 AA, pp. 348–53. RA, pp. 88–9, tr. p. 70, which gives a far briefer account, notes that Raymond of Toulouse accompanied Godfrey to Azaz.

239 For other agreements between Muslims and the crusaders between 1097 and 1099, see: Morton, *Encountering Islam*, pp. 166–8. Omar's son died in Godfrey's custody in spring 1099, apparently through ill health rather than treachery. When the crusaders finally moved away from Antioch around that time, Omar was left exposed. He was captured by Ridwan's forces and executed: AA, pp. 378–9; Asbridge, *First Crusade*, pp. 253–4.

240 See above, p. 142.
241 'ducem uidentes uirum pacificum et amatorem iusticie'. AA, pp. 354–7.
242 AA, pp. 356–7.
243 'uirtute militum'. AA, pp. 356–7.
244 'hoc unum pretereundum non videtur de duce Lotharingie, qui cum Antio-
    cham eo tempore cum duodecim militibus veniret, .c.^{tum} l.^{ta} Turcos obviam
    habuit. Tunc adsumptis armis, et cohortatus milites suos viriliter hostes aggres-
    sus est. Turci autem ut viderunt quia Franci mortem magis pugnando, quam
    fugam cum salute eligerent, quedam pars Turcorum descendit ut altera pars
    securius pugnaret, cum scirent socios suos a bello dimisis equis suis non disces-
    suros. Sic itaque bellum inceptum cum diu graviterque duraret, confortati
    adinvicem milites ducis, qui et numerum .xii. apostolorum continerent, et
    dominum suum quasi vicarium Dei haberent imperterriti agmina Turcorum
    invadunt. Contulit ibi Deus tantam victoriam duci'. RA, pp. 92–3, tr. p. 74. For
    the date, see: *CPC*, no. 320.
245 AA, pp. 370–3.
246 *GF*, pp. 75–6; RA, p. 93, tr. pp. 74–5.
247 *GF*, pp. 75–6; PT, p. 118, tr. pp. 94–5. Asbridge, *First Crusade*, p. 260, asserts that
    on this issue Godfrey and the other leaders acted with 'feeble ineptitude'.
248 PT, p. 118, tr. pp. 94–5.
249 'Etenim dux et comes Flandrensis leviter de civitate Antiochie habebant. Prop-
    terea licet ut de Boimundo vellent quod haberet eam, tamen non audebant ei
    eam laudare, metuentes incurrere periurii infamiam'. RA, p. 93, tr. p. 75.
250 RA, pp. 93–4, tr. p. 75.
251 *GF*, p. 76; PT, pp. 118–19, tr. pp. 95–6; RA, p. 94, tr. pp. 75–6; Tyerman, ' "Princ-
    ipes et Populus" ', pp. 131–2.
252 RA, pp. 91–2, tr. p. 73.
253 AA, pp. 368–9.
254 *GF*, p. 77; PT, p. 121, tr. p. 98; RA, p. 94, tr. pp. 75–6.
255 'dux aberat'. RA, p. 99, tr. p. 79.
256 AA, pp. 370–1.
257 AA, pp. 376–7.
258 RA, pp. 98–9, tr. p. 79.
259 'ductor et dominus exercitus eisdem fieret'. RA, p. 99, tr. pp. 79–80.
260 *GF*, pp. 80–1.
261 Asbridge, *First Crusade*, p. 273.
262 RA, p. 100, tr. p. 80. Nicholson, *Tancred*, pp. 76–7, suggests that Tancred joined
    Raymond's entourage as Bohemond's spy. France, 'Moving to the Goal',
    pp. 144–5, discusses the extent and possible origin of Raymond's funds. Later
    in his account, Raymond of Aguilers noted that Tancred's fee amounted to
    5,000 *solidi* and two fine Arabian horses: RA, p. 112, tr. p. 92.
263 RA, p. 104, tr. p. 85; FC, p. 268, tr. p. 113; France, *Victory*, p. 315.
264 *GF*, p. 81; PT, 125, tr. p. 102.
265 *GF*, p. 80; PT, pp. 124–5, tr. p. 102; RA, p. 101, tr. p. 81; FC, p. 266–7, tr.
    pp. 112–13; AA, pp. 374–5.
266 RA, p. 100, tr. p. 81.
267 'comes . . . discalciatus incedebat, invocantes Dei misericordiam et sanctorum
    presidia'. RA, p. 102, tr. p. 83. Cf. *GF*. p. 81; PT, p. 126, tr. p. 104.
268 As above, n. 263.
269 On Bohemond's seizure of Raymond's towers at Antioch, see: RA, p. 125, tr.
    p. 105. Andressohn, *Godfrey*, p. 90, describes Godfrey at this point as 'singularly
    passive'.
270 RA, p. 102, tr. p. 83.

271 RA, p. 103, tr. p. 84.
272 France, *Victory*, p. 317.
273 On the siege of Arqa, see: France, *Victory*, pp. 319–24.
274 'facta est dissensio magna in populo'. AA, pp. 372–3. Edgington in her edition notes the similarities with John 7:43 and Acts 15:39, 23:10.
275 AA, pp. 380–1. Bohemond soon set about carving out a state based upon the city of Antioch. See: Thomas Asbridge, *The Creation of the Principality of Antioch, 1098–1130* (Woodbridge, 2000). GF, p. 84, and PT, p. 130, tr. p. 107, have Bohemond turning back to Antioch at Laodicea rather than Jabala.
276 'uirum magne patientie et amoris'. AA, pp. 380–5.
277 RA, pp. 110–11, tr. p. 90. This agrees with the account given in *GF*, p. 84.
278 On Peter's trial, see: RA, pp. 112–24, tr. pp. 93–103; AA, pp. 378–9; Bartolf, p. 507; FC, pp. 236–41, tr. pp. 100–1.
279 RA, pp. 127–8, tr. pp. 106–8.
280 RA, pp. 125–6, tr. pp. 105–6.
281 *GF*, pp. 37, 42; RA, p. 58, tr. p. 40; AA, pp. 238–9. On the crusaders' understanding of the conflict between the Turks and the Fatimids, see Morton, *Encountering Islam*, pp. 141–50.
282 RA, pp. 109–10, tr. pp. 89–90; *CPC*, nos. 371–84.
283 AA, pp. 387–8; Andressohn, *Godfrey*, p. 93.
284 AA, pp. 386–7.
285 AA, pp. 386–7. The burning of the camp is also noted in RA, 130, tr. p. 110.
286 'ob desiderium semper eundi in Ierusalem'. AA, pp. 386–7.
287 'dux Lotharingię maxime volebat hoc iter, et plebem ad hoc commonefaciebat'. RA, p. 131, tr. p. 110 (altered).
288 'Conturbabatur itaque comes usque ad lacrimas, et usque ad sui atque suorum odium. Neque tamen ob hoc voluntatem suę plebis Deus imminuebat'. RA, pp. 130–1, tr. p. 110 (altered). On this point there is a clear contrast with the claim in GF, p. 85, that the leaders took counsel and jointly agreed to resume the march.
289 'cum duce remanens fideliter illi in omni subiectione militari astrictus'. AA, pp. 384–5
290 'male discessit a comite'. RA, p. 112, tr. p. 92. For comment, see: France, *Victory*, pp. 321–2.
291 RA, p. 141, tr. p. 119; Bartolf, p. 508; France, *Victory*, p. 329.
292 *GF*, p. 87, PT, pp. 133–4, tr. p. 111; RA, p. 136, tr. p. 115; FC, pp. 275–8, tr. p. 115; AA, pp. 396–9.
293 This is the suggestion of Asbridge, *First Crusade*, p. 297.
294 Bartolf, pp. 508–9; FC, pp. 278–81, tr. pp. 115–16; RA, p. 143, tr. p. 121.
295 AA, pp. 398–401.
296 On the siege of Jerusalem, see: France, *Victory*, pp. 330–66.
297 Bartolf, p. 513, explicitly notes that Godfrey took up position at the corner of the city overlooking the valley of Josaphat. See: France, *Victory*, pp. 330–3.
298 *GF*, pp. 89–90; AA, pp. 406–9; France, *Victory*, pp. 346–7.
299 RA, p. 145, tr. p. 123.
300 Randall Rogers, *Latin Siege Warfare in the Twelfth Century* (Oxford, 1997), pp. 51, 237–8.
301 Murray, *Crusader Kingdom*, p. 63, suggests that the debate was provoked by Tancred's activities in Bethlehem.
302 'Quesitum est, etiam ut aliquis de principibus in regem eligeretur, qui civitatem custodiret. Ne communis facta si nobis eam traderet Deus, a nullo custodita communiter, destrucretur'. RA, p. 143, tr. p. 121 (altered).
303 'Quibus ab episcopis et a clero responsum est? Non debere ibi eligere regem ubi Dominus passus et coronatus est. Quod si in corde suo diceret, sedeo super

solium David et regnum eius obtineo, deneger a fide et virtute David. Fortas-
sis disperdet eum Dominus et loco et genti irasceretur. Propterea clamabat
propheta: Cum venerit sanctus sanctorum, cessabit unctio, qui advenisse cunctis gentibus manifestum erat. Sed esset aliquis advocatus qui civitatem custodiret, et custodibus civitatis tributa regionis divideret, et redditus. Atque his et
aliis multis de causis dilatata est electio, et impedita, donec ad octavum diem
post captam Iherusalem'. RA, p. 143, tr. p. 121 (altered).

304 This is considered in closer detail in the following chapter. See below, pp. 178–9.
305 *GF*, p. 90; AA, pp. 412–15. Raymond of Aguilers reports that this was instigated
by the visions of a crusader named Peter Desiderius, who claimed to have been
visited by the spirit of Adhémar, who had advised it: RA, p. 143–5, tr. pp. 121–3.
On the parallel with Joshua, see: France, *Victory*, p. 347.
306 RA, p. 147, tr. p. 124–5. France, *Victory*, pp. 348–9, dates the relocation of the
tower to the night of 9–10 July.
307 AA, pp. 414–19.
308 AA, pp. 408–9, 416–19, 422–5. Albert dates the construction of Godfrey's tower
to the period between 2 and 7 July. On the tower, see: Rogers, *Latin Siege Warfare*, pp. 54–6.
309 On these men, see: Murray, *Crusader Kingdom*, pp. 192, 216.
310 AA, pp. 416–19.
311 AA, pp. 422–5. RA, p. 125, tr. p. 125, also refers to the garrison using stone-
hurling machines.
312 AA, pp. 422–5.
313 AA, pp. 426–9.
314 'nostri milites fortiter pugnabant in castello, uidelicet dux Godefridus, et
comes Eustachius frater eius'. *GF*, 90.
315 PT, pp. 139–40, tr. p. 118; Bartolf, pp. 514–15.
316 *GF*, p. 90.
317 'Continuo autem quod noster miles Christi ascendit supra murum quem secuti
sunt comes Eustachius et dux Godefredus'. PT, p. 140, tr. p. 118.
318 RA, p. 150, tr. p. 127. Raymond describes the platform as a bridge.
319 *GF*, pp. 91–2; PT, pp. 141–2, tr. pp. 119–20; FC, pp. 299–303, tr. pp. 121–2; AA,
pp. 428–43. On the crusaders' treatment of Jerusalem's inhabitants, see: Kedar,
'The Jerusalem Massacre of July 1099'.
320 'in templo et porticu Salominis equitabatur in sanguine ad genua, et usque ad
frenos equorum'. RA, p. 150, tr. pp. 127–8, drawing from Revelation 14:20.
321 'duci Godefrido cuius erat miles fideliter diuisit'. AA, pp. 432–3.
322 *GF*, p. 91, RA, p. 151, tr. p. 128.
323 'Inter primos vero ingressus est Tancredus et dux Lotharingię qui quantum
sanguinis ea die fuderit vix credibile est'. RA, p. 150, tr. p. 127.
324 'dux Godefridus ab omni mox strage se abstinens, tribus tantum suorum
secum retentis, Baldrico, Adelolfo, et Stabelone, exutus lorica et linea ueste,
nudatis pedibus muros egressus in circuitu urbis in humilitate processit, ac
per eam portam que respicit ad montem Oliuarum introiens, ad sepulchrum
Domini Iesu Christi filii Dei uiui presentatus est, in lacrimis, orationibus et
diuinis laudibus persistens, et Deo gratias agens quia uidere meruit quod illi
semper fuit in summo desiderio'. AA, pp. 436–7. On Baldric and Stabelo, see:
Murray, *Crusader Kingdom*, pp. 184, 229. Adelolf is not otherwise known.
325 'Venerunt autem omnes nostri gaudentes et prae nimio gaudio plorantes ad
nostri Saluatoris Iesu sepulchrum adorandum'. *GF*, p. 92. Cf. PT, p. 141, tr. p.
119.
326 'Capta autem urbe opere precium erat videre devotionem peregrinorum ante
sepulchrum Domini. Quomodo plaudebant exultantes et cantantes canticum

novum Domino. Etenim mens eorum Deo victori et triumphanti vota laudum offerebat, quę explicare verbis non poterat'. RA, p. 151, tr. p. 128.

327 'tunc autem ad Sepulcrum Domini et Templum eius gloriosum euntes, clerici simul et laici, exsultationis voce altisona canticum novum Domino decantando, loca sacrosancta tamdiu desiderata, cum oblationibus faciendis supplicationibusque humillimis, laetabundi omnes visitaverunt'. FC, pp. 304–5, tr. p. 123. This 'most glorious Temple' must have been the Templum Domini.

328 'in finem saeculi memoriale linguis tribuum universarum personabit et permanebit'. FC, p. 306, tr. p. 123; 'Nova dies, novum gaudium, nova et perpetua leticia laboris atque devotionis consummatio, nova verba nova cantica, ab universis exigebat. Hęc inquam dies celebris in omni seculo venturo, omnes dolores atque labores nostros gaudium et exultationem fecit . . . Hęc celebrabitur dies, idus Iulii, ad laudem et gloriam nominis Dei, qui dedit precibus ęcclesię suę urbem et patriam quam iuravit patribus et reddidit in fide et benedictione filiis'. RA, p. 151, tr. p. 128. The events of 15 July 1099 were subsequently memorialised in a feast observed by the Latin inhabitants of twelfth-century Jerusalem. See: Simon John, 'The "Feast of the Liberation of Jerusalem": remembering and reconstructing the First Crusade in the Holy City, 1099–1187', *JMH*, 41 (2015), 409–31.

5   In Jerusalem, 1099–1100

Godfrey's appointment as ruler of Jerusalem, July 1099

Against overwhelming odds, the First Crusaders had captured Jerusalem.[1] Their next task was to decide how they would govern it. As noted in the previous chapter, they had begun to consider this issue while they were besieging the city. Raymond of Aguilers relates that in early July, when the crusaders were still camped outside the city, they had discussed how the Holy City ought to be ruled. Members of the clergy had strongly cautioned against the appointment of a king, asserting instead that an 'advocate' should be appointed to rule over the new state. Those prelates reportedly then invoked a passage from the book of Daniel (9:24–7).[2] The siege had progressed quickly, however, and the issue was unresolved when the crusaders captured the city on 15 July. A week later, on 22 July, they appointed Godfrey as the ruler of Latin Jerusalem.[3] The following pages examine the circumstances in which he was selected, and the nature of the title that he assumed. Historians have devoted a great deal of attention to these topics.[4] It will be suggested here that Godfrey was selected to hold the office because in the aftermath of the capture of Jerusalem he was the best regarded of the leaders who planned to remain in the Holy Land, and that while he did not take the title of king as a result of the deliberations among the crusaders, he nevertheless assumed the highest authority in the incipient polity based on the Holy City.

According to Raymond of Aguilers, the Latins present in Jerusalem after its capture 'turned to the election of a king to run the government, collect the taxes of the region, to serve as a counsellor to the people, and protect the countryside from further devastation'.[5] He suggests, then, that the Latins resumed the discussion where they had left it in early July, and began to deliberate the appointment of a king. The same author states that members of the clergy intervened once again to voice their concerns to the secular leaders. He attributes to them the following words:

> We applaud your election, but only if you do it rightly and properly. Since eternal matters are more important than temporal matters, a

spiritual leader should first be elected, and after that a king, to take care of secular matters. If you do not do this, we will not recognise whomever you choose.[6]

This claim suggests that after the capture of the city the clergy no longer opposed the very idea of appointing a king, but that they instead wanted the spiritual rulership of Jerusalem to be decided first. This intervention reportedly angered the princes, who then hastened to appoint a secular ruler.[7]

The Latins sought to select a candidate to hold the office. Raymond of Aguilers reported that Raymond of Toulouse 'was encouraged to accept the *regnum*. He confessed that he shuddered at the name of kings in that city, but stated that he would consent if another man accepted it'.[8] While Raymond may have been offered the rule of Jerusalem first, it is possible that the chronicler was attempting to preserve his lord's reputation with this claim. Raymond of Toulouse's purported refusal of the offer seems rather out of keeping with his concerted efforts to build his own lordship around Rugia after the capture of Antioch.[9] A few passages later, the chronicler indicated that Raymond's own followers made up damaging stories about their lord to block his election as king, which may be closer to the truth.[10] Albert of Aachen, writing independently, also claims that Raymond of Toulouse was first offered the office. He states that 'the faithful and the leaders of the Christians took counsel and decided to give Count Raymond lordship of the city [*dominum urbis*] and guardianship of the Lord's Sepulchre'.[11] This chronicler then asserted that Raymond 'refused, and so did all the rest of the chiefs who were chosen for this office'.[12] Albert provided no explanation for why Raymond or the others turned down the office. He then stated that 'Duke Godfrey, although reluctant [*inuitus*], was at last put forward to hold the principate of the city [*urbis principatum*]'.[13] Throughout his account, Albert was critical of Raymond of Toulouse, and it is unlikely that this claim was designed to safeguard the count's reputation. Albert's treatment of these events likely has more to do with his overall authorial intentions regarding Godfrey. His description of the appointment suggests that the Latins regarded the office as a burden, and that Godfrey merited particular praise for accepting it even though he was unwilling.[14]

Whether or not Raymond of Toulouse was first offered the rulership of Jerusalem, it would no doubt have been evident to all present in July 1099 – including Raymond – that Godfrey had become the most popular of the leading crusaders by this time. Raymond of Aguilers even acknowledged that in the aftermath of the capture of Jerusalem, 'the counts of Flanders and Normandy [favoured] Godfrey as well as almost all from [Raymond's own] land'.[15] As the preceding chapter demonstrated, Godfrey had secured much admiration in the latter stages of the First Crusade.[16] In July 1099, then, a number of factors stood in his favour. He commanded a loyal retinue, had fought well in a number of military encounters, and had been the first of the leaders to enter Jerusalem. Moreover, he had been able to rely on support from his brother Baldwin in Edessa, while the other leaders had sometimes suffered when resources were scarce. Perhaps most significantly, by casting himself as the spearhead of the clamour at Arqa to resume the march to Jerusalem, Godfrey enabled the rank and file to see him as sympathetic to their wishes and expectations. In addition, he had not attracted serious criticism for devoting time and energy to establish his own lordship after the capture of Antioch. It is important to note, however, that Godfrey's standing among the leaders was not entirely of his own making. Until the latter phases of the First Crusade, he had been relatively passive for long periods, and he had not contributed as overtly or as consistently as other of the leaders to its ongoing success. Bohemond's decision to remain at Antioch served to rule him out of contention to lead the crusade at its culmination at the Holy City. Raymond of Toulouse had been chiefly responsible for his falling reputation in the latter phases of the expedition.[17] Moreover, Robert of Flanders and Robert of Normandy had evidently both signalled that they intended to return to the West. By avoiding controversy, staying with the main forces of the crusade, and aligning himself with the popular fervour to reach the Holy City, Godfrey emerged as the only real choice to hold the rulership of Jerusalem.

The contemporary sources are highly equivocal on the nature of the title that Godfrey assumed upon his appointment, and as a result, the topic has proved highly contentious. A well-known letter sent from the Holy Land to the pope and the Christian faithful in the West in September 1099 refers to Godfrey as 'Duke Godfrey, now by the grace of God advocate [*aduocatus*] of the church of the Holy Sepulchre'.[18] This letter forms the kernel of an influential tradition which has it that in July 1099 Godfrey assumed the title 'advocate of the Holy Sepulchre'.[19] The term *aduocatus* denotes the practice of secular advocacy of a religious house, and some modern scholars have interpreted its ascription to Godfrey as a sign that he had committed to provide lay service to the church of the Holy Sepulchre.[20] Certainly, Godfrey would have been familiar with the practice, having fulfilled the role for several ecclesiastical houses in the West; for example, like his uncle and grandfather before him, he had been advocate of St Hubert in Lotharingia.[21] As Hagenmeyer demonstrated over a century ago, however, this tradition rests upon shaky foundations, for Godfrey had no input to the letter of September 1099.[22] It was written at Laodicea when neither Godfrey nor any of his associates were present. Moreover, its author was a member of Raymond of Toulouse's contingent, possibly the chronicler Raymond of Aguilers, who, as noted above, used the term *advocatus* in his narrative of the First Crusade when recounting the crusaders' discussions about the rule of Jerusalem in early July.[23] Given that the document was written in the name of Daibert of Pisa – who, as the following pages will show, may have possessed a vision for the rulership of Jerusalem that clashed with Godfrey's – the document cannot be accepted as reflecting Godfrey's own conception of his title.

On balance, the available evidence weighs against the idea that Godfrey assumed the title of king. Significantly, prominent figures in the early history of the Latin East did not regard Godfrey as king. A charter issued by Tancred in about March 1101 states that he had received Tiberias 'from Duke Godfrey, the most serene prince of the entire East'.[24] Even more significantly, in a charter of 1104, Godfrey's successor, Baldwin, described himself as 'the first king of Jerusalem' (*rex Hierosolymitanas primus*).[25] If Godfrey had been king of Jerusalem, these documents would surely have ascribed that title to him.

While one or two of the chroniclers described Godfrey as a king, or associated the rule of Jerusalem with royal authority, most carefully evaded clarifying his precise title. They either continued to describe him as duke, attributed to him another non-royal style, or simply outlined the duties of the office to which he had been appointed. The author of the *Gesta Francorum* asserted that the Latins gathered to select a man 'to reign [*regnare*] over the others and to rule the city', a claim which invokes a sense of royal authority.[26] This author then stated that Godfrey 'was elected prince of the city [*principem civitatis*] so that he might fight against the pagans and protect the Christians'.[27] Recasting this passage, Tudebode asserted that the Latins 'held a council, in which Duke Godfrey was elected prince of the city, so that he might battle the pagans and guard the Christians'.[28] Curiously, a few passages later, Tudebode referred to 'Duke Godfrey, who had now been elected king in Jerusalem'.[29] Only a few lines later, though, Tudebode once again referred to Godfrey as 'duke'.[30] As noted above, Raymond of Aguilers states that the Latins had discussed appointing a king, causing the clergy to express disapproval and Raymond of Toulouse to quail. Immediately after this, the chronicler noted that the Latins 'together elected Godfrey and brought him to the sepulchre of the Lord'.[31] A few passages later, this author noted that 'it was agreed that the duke of Lotharingia ought to hold the city [of Jerusalem]'.[32] Raymond of Aguilers continued to describe Godfrey as duke after his appointment.[33]

The author of the 'Bartolf' text asserts that the clergy and the people rested after the capture of the Holy City, and then, 'with the consent of all the community, they appointed Duke Godfrey king and prince of the city of Jerusalem and all its regions'.[34] This author described him as 'King Godfrey' a few passages later, and also noted that Godfrey had ruled over a 'kingdom'.[35] Elsewhere, he wrote that Godfrey had been 'raised to the kingship'.[36] In describing Godfrey's death, however, this author self-contradictorily noted that 'while [Godfrey] lived, he was neither duke nor king, but stood out as servant and protector of the country'.[37] Fulcher commenced his chapter covering Godfrey's appointment with a short poem in which he noted that the 'Franks' (*Franci*) captured Jerusalem, and soon made Godfrey 'prince of the country' (*patriae . . . principe*).[38] He then noted that 'all the people of the Lord's army in the Holy City elected [Godfrey] prince of the kingdom [*regni principem*] to protect and rule it'.[39] Two chapter titles in this section of

Fulcher's account refer to the 'creation of a king' and to 'King Godfrey'.[40] It seems probable, however, that these chapter titles were added after Fulcher wrote the first version of his account of the crusade.

Albert of Aachen discussed Godfrey's appointment at length. He states that Godfrey was chosen 'to hold the principate of the city'.[41] He also noted that Godfrey was 'promoted on the advice of all the Christians and with their goodwill', and then referred to the process as an 'election and promotion'.[42] Albert conveyed a sense of Godfrey's duties as ruler, stating that he was appointed 'prince of the Christians to protect the city and its inhabitants'.[43] The chronicler also referred to the Latins' decision to 'raise up Godfrey, magnificent prince of Christians, to protect the defences in the city after the victory'.[44] Albert also used an array of vague and non-committal styles in respect of the title held by Godfrey, but persisted in calling him duke.[45] While this chronicler did not describe Godfrey as king, he did think that Godfrey had ruled over a kingdom, relating at one point that he was 'prince and ruler of his brothers on the throne of the kingdom of Jerusalem'.[46] He also noted that Godfrey had been 'raised up on the throne of the Jerusalem'.[47] This author also described the polity over which Godfrey ruled as a *regnum*, or 'kingdom'.[48]

A number of figures who wrote in the West also referred to Godfrey's position in Jerusalem. In November or December 1099, Archbishop Manasses of Rheims wrote a letter to Bishop Lambert of Arras, in which he claimed that he had received 'most humble entreaties from Duke Godfrey, whom the army of Christ raised by divine ordination into a king [*in regem sublimauit*]'.[49] Manasses then went on to exhort Lambert to ensure that the inhabitants of his diocese prayed and fasted so that 'the King of kings and Lord of lords would crown the king of the Christians [*Christianorum regi*] with victory over the enemy'.[50] While Manasses implied in this missive that he had received a letter from Godfrey, this is not reliable evidence for how Godfrey or any of his fellow Latins in Jerusalem during his tenure conceived of his authority. Pope Paschal II, Urban II's successor, referred to the outcome of the First Crusade in three letters which date to the eighteen months between the capture of Jerusalem and the appointment of Godfrey's successor, his brother Baldwin, on Christmas Day 1100.[51] Not once in these letters did Paschal refer to the new state in the Holy Land as a kingdom or its ruler as a king. Only in the third of these, sent to the consuls of Pisa in about August 1100, did Paschal mention Godfrey. In that letter, the pope referred to 'Godfrey and the other Christian princes still in Syria and the parts across the sea'.[52] The pope, then, evidently regarded Godfrey as one of a number of 'Christian princes' who held authority in the Holy Land. In one of the very last passages of the *Cantatorium*, written around 1106, it is related that 'Duke Godfrey' had gone to Jerusalem a decade earlier, but said nothing of his achievements on the expedition or his appointment as Jerusalem's ruler.[53] Frutolf of Michelsberg's 1106 continuator had seen a copy of the letter written at Laodicea in September 1099, and it was on the basis of that document's contents that he referred to 'Duke Godfrey the defender of the church in Jerusalem'.[54]

If Godfrey did not take the title of king, then, what title *did* he take? Modern historians have offered a number of suggestions. Riley-Smith concluded that where *dux* ('duke') did not suffice, Godfrey was described as *princeps*.[55] France suggests that Godfrey could have had many titles, including *defensor* ('defender'), *advocatus* ('advocate'), and *custos* ('guardian'), since all essentially denote the same function.[56] Murray has asserted that Godfrey may have assumed a style which reflected his twofold responsibilities of governing the kingdom and protecting the Christians and churches of the Holy Land. He thus contended that Godfrey's title might have incorporated the term *princeps* as well as a term such as *advocatus* (or its cognate *defensor*), and that the two would not have been mutually exclusive. Murray's hypothesis is of particular interest, for he suggests that in adopting a dual title, Godfrey followed a practice with which he would have been familiar in the West, namely that used by the emperor, who was often styled in a manner that denoted his role of protector of the Western Church.[57] Murray's hypothesis underlines the utility of interpreting Godfrey's involvement in the First Crusade in the light of his experiences in Lotharingia. The key point is that these suggestions are not incompatible with one another. It is possible that Godfrey's title was never formally fixed, leaving scope for contemporary writers to ascribe to him styles which reflected their own conceptions of the new political order in Latin Jerusalem.

The next issue to consider is *why* Godfrey took a title other than that of king. A range of explanations – not necessarily mutually exclusive – must be explored. Most modern historians have generally taken it for granted that the Latins regarded the new state based on Jerusalem as a kingdom from the very moment that they captured the Holy City on 15 July 1099.[58] Yet, there is no source dating to the period between Godfrey's appointment as ruler in July 1099 and his brother Baldwin's inauguration as king of Jerusalem on Christmas Day 1100 which records that the Latin inhabitants of the incipient state regarded it as a kingdom. It is possible that the 'kingdom' of Jerusalem entered existence with Baldwin's inauguration, only for the authors who wrote after that event retrospectively to rationalise the new polity's early history by backdating its foundation to 15 July 1099. If the precise status of the new polity did remain unfixed until Baldwin was inaugurated a year and a half after Godfrey's appointment, then there may have been less impetus to appoint a king in July 1099 than modern historians have sometimes supposed.[59]

Modern historians have also suggested that Godfrey may not have taken the title of king in deference to the arguments advanced by clergy who were present in Jerusalem at the time of his appointment.[60] As noted above, Raymond of Aguilers asserts that in early July members of the clergy voiced theological qualms over the prospect of appointing a king, and then after the capture of Jerusalem asserted that a spiritual leader ought to be appointed before a secular counterpart.[61] Historians have sometimes interpreted Raymond of Aguilers' testimony as evidence that those prelates intended for Jerusalem's spiritual leader to be the chief authority in the new state.[62] It was demonstrated earlier in this book that Godfrey had interacted with assertive prelates during his career in the West – Bishops Henry and Otbert of Liège, and Abbots Thierry I and II of St Hubert, to name but a few – and that he may have been aware of his predecessors' links to the reform papacy. As such, the possibility should not be ruled out that in July 1099 Godfrey was susceptible to the clergy's views on how spiritual and secular authority should interact in Jerusalem.

Modern scholars have sometimes made the connected suggestion that Godfrey assumed the rulership of Jerusalem but refused the title of king because he did not wish to be crowned in the city where Christ had worn a crown of thorns.[63] Yet, this suggestion seems to conflate Godfrey's appointment in July 1099 with Baldwin's inauguration as king on Christmas Day 1100. The theological concern centred upon the precedent of Christ's crown of thorns appears to have been expressed not by Godfrey but by Baldwin. Albert of Aachen states that Baldwin was inaugurated king in Bethlehem rather than the Holy City because

> he was unwilling and did not presume to be exalted and wear a diadem of gold or with precious stones, and to be made king in Jerusalem, where Lord Jesus, King of kings and Lord of lords, was brought low and subject even to death for the redemption of the world, and was crowned with terrible and sharp thorns.[64]

Fulcher of Chartres wrote in his account of Baldwin's inauguration that he had been anointed and crowned, before noting that 'this had not been done for his brother and predecessor because Godfrey had not wished it, and there were others who did not approve of it'.[65] However, Fulcher did not specify the concerns voiced in July 1099 over the prospect of Godfrey assuming the kingship. While it is possible that Godfrey or others present in Jerusalem in July 1099 articulated the Christic precedent that reportedly shaped Baldwin's considerations a year and a half later, no contemporary source is explicit that this was the case.

Apocalyptic expectations among the Latins may also have led Godfrey to avoid taking the title of king of Jerusalem.[66] Over the course of the First Crusade, its participants had reached a state of profound religious fervour. They punctuated their military activities with periodic fasts, almsgiving, and ritual processions, with the aim of securing divine favour and intercession. Their fervour only intensified as they neared Jerusalem, the site of many of the most important events in Christian history.[67] Their procession around Jerusalem in the manner of Joshua constitutes one notable manifestation of this trend.[68] In such a climate, it is eminently possible that ideas about the Endtimes were prevalent at the expedition's culmination. By the time of the First Crusade, there was in Christendom a long-established and influential eschatological tradition which centred upon a figure known as the 'Last World Emperor'. Propounded in the work of figures such as Pseudo-Methodius (*c.*700) and the tenth-century monk Adso, this tradition stated that the onset of the Endtimes would be preceded by the appearance of an emperor who would defeat Islam and capture Jerusalem, where he would be crowned. A number of modern scholars including Ferrier, Flori, and Rubenstein have emphasised the importance of millenarian ideas to the discussions which surrounded Godfrey's appointment in July 1099.[69]

The contemporary sources do convey the sense that the crusaders might have framed their own actions in the light of apocalyptic motifs. As noted above, Raymond of Aguilers drew from apocalyptic imagery in his description of the capture of Jerusalem, and in his account of the discussion in early July over the idea of appointing a king in Jerusalem.[70] Even more significant evidence in this regard is contained in the above-mentioned letter sent in September 1099 in the name of Daibert from Laodicea to the pope and the faithful in the West. This letter – which, as already indicated, may have been written by Raymond of Aguilers – highlights two aspects of the siege of Jerusalem: the barefoot procession around the Holy City, and the fact that as the crusaders overran the city, they rode up to their ankles in the blood of their enemies near the Temple of Solomon.[71] In a close study of the letter, Althoff suggested that its contents demonstrate that the crusaders interpreted their actions in Jerusalem in the light of Psalm 79's theme of purifying the Temple.[72] When Paschal II wrote in April 1100 to the Latins who were still in the Holy Land, he invoked similar motifs, asserting that 'we acknowledge that what the Lord promised to his people through the prophet has been fulfilled by you', and asserting that the crusaders' hands had been 'consecrated by the blood of your enemies'.[73] Frutolf of Michelsberg's continuator stated that by setting up the Church in Jerusalem, the Latins transformed 'mystical prophecies' into 'visible events', and then invoked two passages from the book of Isaiah (60:1 and 66:10).[74]

It is possible that apocalyptic ideas informed Godfrey's actions. He would likely have been familiar with such ideas, at least, given his links to Peter the Hermit and his followers, who seem to have been partially responsible for circulating them.[75] Whatever the nature of Godfrey's own beliefs, though, what is perhaps most important is that others *could interpret* his actions in the light of millenarian thinking.[76] Raymond of Aguilers had noted that Godfrey had spilled vast amounts of blood during the capture of Jerusalem, which could be seen in alignment with Psalm 79's theme of purification.[77] Similarly, Albert's claim that Godfrey ceased attacking the inhabitants of Jerusalem in order to make a barefoot procession around the city also had prophetic overtones.[78] Most critically, Godfrey's assumption of a title other than that of king could be attributed to concerns founded in the Last World Emperor tradition, namely, that the appointment of a king in Jerusalem would bring about the onset of the Endtimes. If some of the Latins present in Jerusalem in July 1099 had been stimulated by apocalyptic ideas, then, they might well have seen in Godfrey a leader who deported himself in a manner that was in tune with their beliefs.

While a number of previous studies have attributed Godfrey's assumption of a title other than that of king to his acquiescence to the arguments of others, it is possible to draw a rather different picture of his approach to this issue based on the wider appraisal of his career offered in this book. It was suggested in the preceding chapter that from the point that the crusaders departed in Arqa in May 1099, Godfrey had begun to conduct himself in a manner that responded to the wishes of the wider crusading masses. As such, the possibility should not be ruled out that at the time of his appointment he was cognisant of the potential advantages of exhibiting deference to the arguments put forward by others. Crucially, if he did assent to the vision of rulership articulated by members of the clergy, and showed sympathy for those who were concerned about the apocalyptic implications of the royal title, he did so at no cost to his own authority. He would surely have learned during his time in Lotharingia – and above all during his relatively constrained career as duke – that a prestigious title counted for very little if it was not associated with meaningful practical authority. Given the parlous military state of the Latin outposts in the Holy Land in July 1099, and the ambition of those who remained to keep hold of Jerusalem, Godfrey would have been in no doubt that the secular power would be dominant in the new polity. The crucial point, then, is this: although Godfrey was not king of Jerusalem, after his appointment in July 1099 he did hold the highest authority in the Holy City. As Albert of Aachen lucidly put it, Godfrey was 'duke and after God the highest ruler in Jerusalem'.[79]

Several of the chroniclers sought to explain why Godfrey was the chosen candidate to rule Jerusalem. Fulcher of Chartres wrote that Godfrey had been selected to hold the office 'because of the nobility of his character, military skill, patient conduct, no less than for his elegance of manners, to protect and govern it'.[80] Fulcher also states that Godfrey ruled 'with the consent of all' and with a 'firm hand'.[81] A number of writers suggested that God had played a part in Godfrey's appointment. As noted above, in late 1099 Manasses of Rheims wrote to Lambert of Arras, reporting that Godfrey had been appointed by 'divine ordination' (*diuina ordinatione*).[82] The author of the *Gesta Francorum* stated that when it came to selecting a ruler, the leaders ordered the rest to 'give alms and pray that God would choose for himself whomsoever he wished'.[83] Tudebode replicated this passage closely.[84] This version of the process of selecting a leader cast Godfrey as God's chosen candidate.

Albert of Aachen placed considerable emphasis on the role of providence in Godfrey's appointment. Indeed, this chronicler wrote outright that Godfrey's 'election and promotion . . . is believed not to have been the result of human will at all, but done entirely by God's arrangement and favour'.[85] He later stated that Godfrey's appointment had occurred 'in accordance

with God's command . . . and with the goodwill of the Christian people'.[86]
Albert reported in his account a series of three visions which he claimed signified that Godfrey had been divinely chosen. He inserted the first of these
visions in his account immediately after recounting how Godfrey removed
himself from the attacks on Jerusalem's inhabitants on 15 July to make a
barefoot procession around the city, before worshipping at the Holy Sepulchre, accompanied only by three members of his household, namely Baldric, Adelolf, and Stabelo.[87] Albert stated that the prayers Godfrey gave at
Christ's tomb on 15 July proved the veracity of a vision Stabelo had received
some time before the First Crusade. In that vision, Stabelo reportedly saw
a golden ladder rising from the earth to heaven, which Godfrey was climbing. With him on the ladder was his steward Rothard, carrying a lamp. After
Rothard's lamp went out and he reached a broken rung in the ladder, he
turned back and descended toward the earth. At this point, Stabelo took
the lamp and reignited it, before climbing the ladder with Godfrey all the
way to heaven. There, they found a table 'made ready for them [which was]
covered with all kinds of heaped up sweetness of delicious things'.[88] Upon
arriving in heaven, 'the duke reclined at this table with the chosen ones and
those worthy of it, and he shared in all the sweetness which was there'.[89]
Albert asserted that there was only one possible interpretation of this vision:

> What is signified by this ladder leading to the palace of heaven, unless
> the journey which the duke undertook with the entire purpose of his
> mind to the city of Jerusalem, which is the gate of the heavenly home-
> land? For the ladder was of purest gold, because one must come to this
> journey and the gate of heaven with pure heart and perfect free will.[90]

Albert then noted that this vision reflected the fact that while Rothard
had deserted the First Crusade – and Godfrey – during the siege of Antioch, Stabelo had remained steadfast and accompanied him all the way to
the Holy City, thereby proving his worthiness to pray alongside Godfrey
at the Holy Sepulchre, 'which is the table and the desire of all sweetness
of the saints'.[91]

Albert included the second and third instalments of his trilogy of visions
a few passages later in his account, just after the point at which he had
recorded Godfrey's appointment as ruler of Jerusalem. One of these had
apparently been experienced by Hecelo, 'a certain good and truthful
knight' from a place called Kenzvillare (possibly modern Kinzweiler, near
Aachen). According to the chronicler, ten years before the First Crusade,
Hecelo was on a hunt in a wood, and became tired and so was overcome
by sleep. As soon as he began to slumber, he received the following vision:

> [At] once he was transported in spirit to Mount Sinai, where Moses the
> Lord's servant, after he had fasted for forty days, was worthy to see the
> splendour of God's glory and receive the law from the hand of the Most

High. Then upon the peak of this mountain, he could see [Godfrey] being raised up with awe and gentleness in an easy ascent, and two men hurrying to meet him in white clothes and the insignia of bishops. As they came up to him there they offered him their blessing in these words: 'May you be filled with the blessings of the living God who conferred blessing and favour on His servant and faithful follower Moses and may you find favour in His eyes. May you be appointed duke and commander of His Christian people in all faith and truth.' After this was said the knight woke up and the vision disappeared.[92]

Albert stated outright that Hecelo's vision was proof that 'Godfrey was chosen by God and appointed leader and prince and commander of the Christian army, and before all the officers he was more blessed in deed, victory, and counsel, more perfect in faith and truth'.[93] As he had with the first, Albert affirmed that the second vision upheld only one possible interpretation: 'What else is to be perceived in this vision, except that in the spirit and gentleness of Moses there may arise a spiritual leader of Israel, preordained by God and appointed prince of the people?'[94] The aim of this passage, as Rubenstein has put it, was to cast Godfrey as 'a new Moses to the Christian people'.[95] By presenting Godfrey in this light, Albert inferred that, like the Israelites, the participants in the First Crusade had reached their Promised Land.

Albert attributed the third and final vision he included in his account to 'a certain Catholic brother and canon of St Mary's in Aachen, called Giselbert', and asserted that the witness had received it seven months *after* Godfrey's departure on the First Crusade.[96] Albert may have been a canon at St Mary's, and it is thus possible that he knew this witness personally. Giselbert's vision, according to Albert, presaged that Godfrey 'would be chief of all and prince in Jerusalem, preordained and appointed by God'.[97] In the vision, Giselbert reportedly witnessed a scene in which:

[Godfrey] powerfully took a seat in the sun, and a countless number of birds of all the kinds under heaven flocked around him. A part of them began little by little to diminish by flying away, but the greater part remained fixed and motionless to right and left. After this the sun was for the most part obscured by the rays of its brightness, and the duke's seat was utterly blotted out for a short period, and almost all the multitude of birds which had remained flew away.[98]

After this, according to Albert, Godfrey

took a seat in the sun, as he was promoted to the throne of the kingdom of Jerusalem, which exceeds all the towns in the world in name and holiness, just as the sun exceeds all the stars in the sky with its brilliance.[99]

Albert then wrote that the celestial birds

> were gathered around the seated duke, like those from all Christian lands, great and small, noble and lesser people, who were joined with him and subject to him. The birds flew away, just as a very great number of pilgrims returned to the land of their birth with the duke's consent and permission. But very many birds remained fixed and motionless, as many were attached to him by dutiful love, and having delighted in his intimate and comforting speech they vowed to stay longer with him.[100]

The chronicler employed avian imagery in this passage to articulate the difference between those who returned to the West after the capture of Jerusalem, and those who remained alongside Godfrey in the Holy Land. The image of Godfrey surrounded by birds of many different kinds, representing those who came from 'all Christian lands', was no doubt intended to symbolise the unity – and new shared identity – of the peoples who remained under Godfrey's rule in Jerusalem after his appointment.

The vision Albert attributed to the canon Giselbert bears a striking resemblance to a well-known passage included by Dudo of St Quentin in his account of the early history of Normandy, which he wrote around 1015. In that passage, Dudo related how another divinely selected ruler, Rollo, had united many disparate peoples under his authority as part of his efforts in founding Normandy. According to Dudo, on one occasion Rollo fell asleep and experienced a dream in which he was transported to a mountain. While he was there,

> he saw about the base of it many thousands of birds of different kinds and various colours, but with red left wings, extending in such numbers and so far and so wide that he could not catch sight of where they ended, however hard he looked. And they went one after the other in harmonious incoming flights and sought the spring on the mountain, and washed themselves, swimming together as they do when rain is coming; and when they had all been anointed by this miraculous dipping, they all ate together in a suitable place, without being separated into genera or species, and without any disagreement or dispute, as if they were friends sharing food. And they carried off twigs and worked rapidly to build nests; and furthermore, they willingly yielded to his command, in the vision.[101]

Another figure in Dudo's account then interpreted the vision for Rollo, stating that the image signified that 'the birds of different sorts will obey you: men of different kingdoms will kneel down to serve you'.[102] There is considerable similarity between Albert and Dudo's accounts of these visions. It is possible that Albert knew Dudo's work, as a number of copies of it had circulated by the time Albert wrote.[103] Equally, it may be that the two writers independently drew from a long-standing tradition of using birds to prophesise the establishment of authority.[104]

Albert's trilogy of visions foretelling Godfrey's appointment as ruler of Jerusalem strike a notably different tone to that which characterises the remainder of his account of the First Crusade. As Morris noted, throughout the rest of Albert's account, he 'appears as a conservative in his theology of the crusade', that is, he does not consistently emphasise the role of God in the expedition.[105] In these passages, however, Albert forcefully asserted that Godfrey had been providentially selected to rule Latin Jerusalem. While it is unclear whether these visions were actually reported at the time of Godfrey's appointment, rather than originating closer to the time at which Albert wrote his account, they at the very least yield insights into how Godfrey's appointment was perceived in the first years of the twelfth century.[106]

Ruling Jerusalem

Immediately after Godfrey's appointment, he demanded the Tower of David from Raymond of Toulouse. (As noted above, Raymond had secured possession of Jerusalem's citadel as the crusaders overran the city on 15 July.) Godfrey's motive for the demand is clear enough; he needed control of the citadel if his position in the Holy City was to be viable. Raymond of Aguilers highlighted the military importance of the Tower of David, asserting that it was the 'key of the whole kingdom of Judea'.[107] According to this chronicler, Godfrey claimed the Tower of David from Raymond of Toulouse, who refused to relinquish it because he planned to stay in the region of Jerusalem until Easter. Godfrey reportedly responded to this by asserting that he regarded the citadel as the most important part of the city, and the last place he would forsake. As a result of this mutual obstinacy, a serious rift developed between the two men. The rest of the Latins put pressure on Raymond, and he eventually agreed to surrender the citadel to Peter of Narbonne, bishop of Albara, to await a judgement on the matter. Almost as soon as Peter took hold of the citadel, however, he surrendered it to Godfrey. When Peter was reproached for not awaiting the outcome of the judgement, he asserted that he had been coerced by individuals who had brought 'many weapons' (*plurima arma*) to his quarters near the church of the Holy Sepulchre. Raymond of Aguilers claimed that Peter spoke of violence committed against him, and that he secretly blamed Raymond of Toulouse's men for what had happened.[108] The loss of the citadel compelled the angry Raymond to withdraw from Jerusalem, and he travelled out to the river Jordan. Raymond of Aguilers spoke of the sense of 'grief and injustice' that the count felt at the loss of the Tower of David.[109] Albert of Aachen depicted the episode in a similar light. According to this chronicler, as soon as Godfrey was installed as Jerusalem's ruler, he asked Raymond of Toulouse for control of the Tower of David; Albert stated that although Godfrey acted with the support and goodwill of all the rest of the Latins, Raymond refused to turn possession of the citadel over. He then wrote that Raymond was eventually forced 'by threats from the duke himself and the Christians' to relinquish it.[110] According to Albert, then, Godfrey personally threatened Raymond with the aim of gaining control of the citadel. The rift between Godfrey and Raymond would have a significant bearing on the Latins' early efforts to carve out their new state in the Holy Land.

With Jerusalem's secular government decided, the Latins turned to the matter of its spiritual rulership. On 1 August, just over a week after Godfrey's appointment, they selected Arnulf of Chocques to become patriarch of Jerusalem.[111] As noted above, Arnulf had vocally challenged the authenticity of the Holy Lance while the crusaders were at Arqa.[112] The new patriarch evidently sent letters to the West to announce his appointment.[113] Several of the chroniclers described Arnulf as a sound choice. The author of the *Gesta Francorum* described him as 'a most experienced and distinguished man', while Albert called him a 'cleric of wonderful wisdom and eloquence'.[114] Raymond of Aguilers, in contrast, raised a number of objections regarding Arnulf's suitability for the office. He asserted that Arnulf was of low birth and a philanderer, that he had not previously held a bishopric, and that after he assumed the office, he unjustly took benefices which belonged to other members of the clergy in Jerusalem. The chronicler's hostility to the new patriarch was no doubt connected to his earlier criticism of the Holy Lance, which had been associated so closely with the southern French contingent.[115] During the First Crusade Arnulf had generally been associated with the forces led by Godfrey and the two Roberts, and this must have played a role in his appointment.[116]

A few days later, reports circulated among the Latins that a piece of the True Cross was hidden somewhere in Jerusalem. On 5 August, they uncovered a relic which they immediately revered as a fragment of the cross upon which Christ had been crucified.[117] Though Raymond of Aguilers asserted that Arnulf had instigated the discovery, the chronicler's hostility to the newly installed patriarch did not cause him to question the relic's authenticity. This chronicler explicitly stated that the Latins regarded the discovery of the True Cross as a sign of divine approbation for their efforts on the First Crusade. According to him, when the Latins unearthed the relic, they rendered thanks to God for granting them Jerusalem and the fragment, a symbol of Christ's crucifixion.[118] Albert of Aachen stated that when the relic was discovered, the Latins made a ritual procession to the place in Jerusalem where it had been unearthed, before carrying it to the church of the Holy Sepulchre while giving prayer and singing hymns.[119] A few passages later, Albert placed in Godfrey's mouth a speech in which he outlined the relic's significance:

[Assuredly] we have been redeemed by the wood of the Holy Cross from the hand of death and hell, and by angelic power from harm, and we have been cleansed in the blood of Lord Jesus, son of the living God, from all the filth of former error, and we have confidence in eternal life.[120]

With this, Albert singled Godfrey out among the rest of the Latins as a figure who understood the spiritual potency of the relic.

Several days after the discovery of the True Cross, Godfrey and the other Latins in Jerusalem received word that the Fatimids were preparing an invasion force with the aim of retaking the Holy City.[121] According to the *Gesta Francorum* and Tudebode, a few days after his election, Godfrey had instructed his brother Eustace and Tancred to go to Nablus and receive the surrender of its citizens. This claim is of interest in its own right, for it illuminates the fact that in the period immediately after Godfrey was appointed ruler of Jerusalem, his brother Eustace was acting as his agent. Upon discovering the buildup of the Fatimid force, Godfrey sent a messenger to Eustace and Tancred, asking them to hurry to him because he had heard that the Fatimid army was gathering at Ascalon. Eustace and Tancred reportedly encountered Fatimid troops at Ramla, before despatching their own message to Godfrey in Jerusalem, informing him of what they had discovered.[122]

On 9 August the forces under Godfrey left Jerusalem and headed toward Ascalon pre-emptively to strike the Fatimids. The sources record that Raymond of Toulouse was initially reluctant to contribute his forces to Godfrey's initiative. The author of the *Gesta Francorum* related that Raymond of Toulouse and Robert of Normandy wished to ensure that the Fatimids really were gathering an army before they acted.[123] This seems like an attempt to conceal divisions, as other chroniclers stated outright that Raymond demurred on departing toward Ascalon because he still harboured resentment toward Godfrey. Raymond of Aguilers wrote that Raymond of Toulouse was nursing a sense of injustice at the loss of the Tower of David.[124] Albert provided the most detailed account of Raymond's reluctance to participate. He related that Godfrey left some troops in Jerusalem (with some placed in the Tower of David) before departing towards the plains around Ascalon, accompanied by his brother Eustace and Tancred – who had evidently linked up with him by this point – as well as Robert of Flanders. Upon discovering that the reports were accurate and that a Fatimid army was gathering, they sent messengers back to Jerusalem to exhort Raymond and Robert of Normandy to join them. They also asked Peter the Hermit and Arnulf to bring the relic of the True Cross to them so that they could take it with them into battle.[125] According to Albert, Raymond was 'still feeling the goad of envy against Duke Godfrey because he had lost the Tower of David', and so refused the request to come to Ascalon. It was only after he was 'pushed and incited to action by threats from the duke and all the princes' and received counsel from his own advisers that he agreed to bring his troops into the fray.[126] He joined up with the contingents led by Godfrey on 10 August, and the next day, their combined forces advanced further towards Ascalon.

A number of sources relate that as the Latins neared Ascalon on 11 August, they encountered large herds of cattle and other beasts. When the leaders learned that these herds had been left by the Fatimids as a distraction – the aim was to trick the Latins into plundering and thereby lose their focus on battle – they had it proclaimed that anyone who broke formation to seize the animals would be punished. The next day, the Latins found the Fatimid army camped just to the north of Ascalon itself. The Latins arrayed their forced into three lines, with Raymond of Toulouse to the right next to the sea, Robert of Flanders, Robert of Normandy, and Tancred in the middle, and Godfrey to the left. The *Gesta Francorum* and Tudebode note that Eustace was among the leaders who directed the final preparations.[127] In the battle that followed, the Latins prevailed, with their cavalry charge reportedly proving decisive.

The *Gesta Francorum* and the sources derived from it describe the battle of Ascalon rather cursorily. Albert of Aachen, though, provided a far fuller account, in which he once again prioritised Godfrey's role. This chronicler wrote that after the prefect of Ramla – a recent convert to Christianity – questioned Godfrey why so many of the Latins were openly rejoicing as they marched to battle, Godfrey, 'full of Christ's faith and instructed in spiritual response, responded to the man's enquiry by discoursing widely about these things'.[128] According to Albert, Godfrey proceeded to deliver a speech in which he articulated the spirituality and beliefs of his fellow Latins:

> Know that these people, whom you see and hear singing in exultation as they hurry toward their enemies and join battle in the name of the Lord Jesus Christ their God, are certain today of the crown of the kingdom of heaven, and know that they will pass on to a better life, in which they shall begin to live more happily for the first time, if they are found worthy to die in this battle for his name and favour.[129]

Godfrey reportedly stated, then, that the Latins rejoiced at this point because they believed that, whatever their fate in the battle, they had already guaranteed themselves a place in heaven. According to Albert, Godfrey then discussed the protective capabilities of the sign of the cross, before speaking about the particular qualities of the True Cross.[130] The chronicler also has Godfrey play a central role in the battle itself, stating that when the Fatimids began at one point to retreat, he initiated a cavalry charge which forced them to flee their camp. While this reportedly put victory within the Latins' grasp, some were reportedly distracted from the battle by the opportunity to plunder the abandoned camp. This prompted Godfrey quickly to unleash another cavalry charge against the enemy lines, in order to ward off any potential fightback. According to Albert, with this second charge Godfrey 'visited severe destruction on the enemy and then spurred on all those with him', before pursuing the fleeing Fatimid warriors up to the gates of Ascalon.[131]

The *Gesta Francorum* and the accounts derived from it state that after the Latins prevailed in the battle of Ascalon, they returned in triumph to Jerusalem.[132] While Albert of Aachen agrees that the Latins returned to the Holy City after the battle, he stated that a few days later – he is not precise on the timing – Godfrey led a combined force of 2,000 infantry and cavalry back to Ascalon and began to besiege it. The chronicler reports that the inhabitants of the city were soon contemplating surrender to Godfrey, only for Raymond of Toulouse to intervene. Raymond was reportedly 'envious of all Duke Godfrey's glory on account of the Tower of David which he had lost', and so secretly sent a legation into the city to encourage its inhabitants to resist him.[133] Those messengers reportedly affirmed that many of Godfrey's companions would return to the West, leaving him with only a small force. Encouraged by this report, the people of Ascalon refused to surrender their city to Godfrey. After the other leading figures among the Latins departed Ascalon, Godfrey was forced to raise the siege and move his forces away from the city.[134] He led his troops north toward the port of Arsuf, where Raymond of Toulouse had commenced a new siege. However, when Raymond discovered that Godfrey was approaching his location, he was mindful of 'the trick he had played on [Godfrey] through envy', and so broke the siege off and moved his force away.[135]

After Raymond departed Arsuf, he linked up with Robert of Flanders and Robert of Normandy, and moved to a region which lay between Haifa and Caesarea. Godfrey made his own brief attack on Arsuf, but could not break its inhabitants' resistance. Before departing the city, Raymond had reportedly exhorted its citizens not to fear Godfrey, just as he had done at Ascalon. Albert stated that when Godfrey discovered that the people of Arsuf 'were ready for war and ready to resist him because of Raymond's persuasion and testimony, he turned aside from the city with sorrowful heart'.[136] After leaving Arsuf, he sought revenge against Raymond:

> [Godfrey] told his comrades to seek out Raymond immediately in the camp and return on his head all the injustice he had enacted against him. At once, after telling his comrades, he put on his hauberk and raised the banners; while he had arranged to go into the count's camp in an angry mood, Raymond had likewise had the foresight to arm for defence and decided to attack him.[137]

According to Albert, it was only the intervention of Robert of Flanders and the other leaders that prevented a full-scale conflict between Godfrey and Raymond. He claimed that the other princes 'came between them, reproved the men severely, and at length with much endeavour they soothed both sides and brought them back into agreement'.[138]

While Godfrey and Raymond were reconciled, though, the damage caused by their dispute was considerable, for both Ascalon and Arsuf remained in enemy hands.[139] On balance, the greater responsibility for the dispute and its repercussions lies with Godfrey, as he had been charged with the defence of Jerusalem. He had acquired the Tower of David in a manner that angered and disaffected Raymond. The capture of Arsuf or Ascalon (or both) would have bolstered the new state. The position of the Latins was precarious at this time, and this episode must have made it clear to them that they had to avoid internecine conflict if they were to maintain hold of the Holy City and the other places they had captured by that point.[140]

In the aftermath of the capture of Jerusalem, the Latins who remained in its vicinity essentially possessed only a few outposts, which were isolated from each other and surrounded by Muslim-held territory on all sides. Although Bohemond held Antioch and Baldwin was in possession of Edessa, both were too far away to the north to provide military assistance. In the south, the Latins held Jaffa – the closest port to Jerusalem, though the Fatimids had destroyed it before fleeing – and, inland, Ramla and the adjacent Lydda, Bethlehem, and the Holy City itself (see Map 5.1). Godfrey's territory thus amounted to a thin corridor of land which extended about thirty miles from Jaffa on the coast to Jerusalem (encompassing Ramla and Lydda) and then about five miles south from the Holy City to Bethlehem.[141]

With Jerusalem captured, many of the Latins felt that they had fulfilled the obligations to which they had committed upon joining the First Crusade. As a result, a significant number began to depart the Holy Land to return to their homelands. The most prominent figures to leave at this time were Robert of Flanders and Robert of Normandy. They travelled north to Laodicea, and in September set sail from there for the West.[142] The sources relate that the departure of so many of the Latins at this time left the newly-established states short of numbers.[143] Albert of Aachen put one group who left at 20,000. While this is surely an exaggerated figure, it is one which emphasises the perceived scale of the exodus.[144] The above-mentioned vision that Albert attributed to the canon Giselbert – of flocks of birds representing different peoples from the West flying away from the figure of Godfrey – highlighted the effect of the widescale departures to the Latins' early efforts to settle the Holy Land.[145] One letter sent from Jerusalem to Germany in April 1100 stated that Jerusalem was 'under attack on all sides from pagans and infidels, more than all other places because of its considerable sanctity'.[146] In describing this early settlement period, Fulcher of Chartres emphasised the uncertain plight of those who remained in the Holy City. This chronicler wondered why it was that the Latins' 'little kingdom' (*regnulum*) managed to survive at this time, before concluding it must have done so because its inhabitants had secured God's favour.[147]

The departure of many veterans of the First Crusade in the months following the battle of Ascalon created difficulties for those who remained. Godfrey seems only to have had a limited military force at his disposal during his tenure in Jerusalem. In the weeks after Easter 1100, for example, he conducted a campaign in which he led a contingent consisting of only 200 knights and 1,000 infantry. Though he no doubt left other warriors

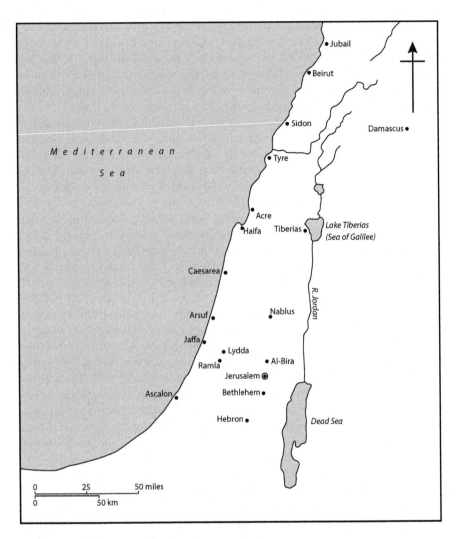

Map 5.1 The early Latin settlements in the Holy Land

to garrison Jerusalem and other fortified places at that time, even taking those probable additional troops into account, he still commanded far smaller numbers than had fought during the major military encounters of the First Crusade.[148] Godfrey evidently attempted to alleviate this shortage of manpower by encouraging more Latins to come to the Holy Land. As noted above, when Manasses of Rheims wrote to Lambert of Arras in late 1099, he implied that he had received a letter from Godfrey in Jerusalem. Perhaps acting on a request from Godfrey, Manasses instructed Lambert to encourage individuals who had taken the vow to go on crusade but not departed to fulfil their obligations and travel to the Holy Land.[149] Moreover, Albert of Aachen states that Godfrey told those who departed for the West at this time

> that they should be mindful, and should impress on their Christian brothers that they should not hesitate to come to the Lord's Sepulchre, but should flock daily to assist him and the other comrades who were staying in exile to oppose the many barbarous peoples.[150]

Since Albert largely based his account on information provided by crusaders who had returned to the West, he would likely have been well-placed to describe the valedictory injunctions placed upon them just before they departed the Holy Land.

Over the course of the First Crusade, political associations among its participants had shifted considerably. Many participants had swapped their allegiances from one leader to another. As a result, the composition and identity of Godfrey's circle of associates in Jerusalem was markedly different to that which had departed Lotharingia in 1096.[151] Murray has carried out a close prosopographical analysis of the named figures who were part of Godfrey's circle after the end of the First Crusade, and concluded that only about half of those who were associated with him during his tenure in Jerusalem were of Lotharingian origin.[152] The Lotharingians attested alongside him in the Holy City include Baldric, his seneschal, Stabelo, his chamberlain, and Warner of Grez. Other Lotharingians who had set out with him had died during the crusade, entered the service of another lord, or returned to the West.[153] To compensate for these losses, Godfrey took into his household individuals from places other than Lotharingia. These included figures from other duchies of the kingdom of Germany (such as Wicher the Swabian) and a number of Normans (such as Robert of Apulia). A few ecclesiastical figures are also attested alongside Godfrey in the Holy City, chief among them Arnulf of Chocques, patriarch of Jerusalem, and Robert of Rouen, bishop of Lydda.[154]

The Latins' approach to settling the Holy Land was dictated by the repercussions of the First Crusade. Since the Byzantines had ceased aiding the Latins in light of Bohemond's refusal to relinquish Antioch, future crusaders from the West would be unable to take the land route to Jerusalem through imperial territory. This increased the Latins' reliance on the port cities of the Holy Land. The strategic value of those ports was immense, for they not only facilitated the arrival of new recruits and supplies, but they also functioned as centres of trade and commerce. The Latins who remained in the Holy Land realised quickly that if they were to survive, let alone prosper, it was essential for them to deal aggressively with the nearby Muslim powers. In this regard, they were able to exploit the fearsome reputation that the First Crusaders had acquired during the course of the expedition. The

Latins' renown as formidable warriors compelled a number of Muslim lords to make peace or render tribute rather than face them in battle. Albert of Aachen recorded that the Muslim inhabitants of Acre, Tyre, Sidon, Tripoli, and Beirut all refrained from attacking the new inhabitants of Jerusalem because they 'were terrified and trembling' after hearing how the Latins had defeated the Fatimid forces at Ascalon.[155]

One of Godfrey's first substantial acts was to conclude a treaty with the citizens of Arsuf. According to Albert, the people of that city instigated the agreement with the Latins after they discovered that Godfrey had decided to stay in Jerusalem and had reconciled with Raymond of Toulouse. Under the terms of the agreement, the two sides agreed to a peace, Arsuf committed to pay tribute to Godfrey, and the two sides exchanged hostages. Godfrey sent to Arsuf a number of hostages, including Gerard of Avesnes, whom Albert described as Godfrey's 'faithful knight'.[156] After a few weeks, however, certain unspecified 'envious men' (*inuidorum*) reportedly advised the citizens of Arsuf to cease paying tribute to Godfrey. The departure of many First Crusaders in August and September left Godfrey with too few warriors to enforce the terms of the agreement, and this bolstered Arsuf's resistance. Although the hostages sent from Arsuf managed to escape Godfrey's custody and return to their city, its people refused to return Godfrey's own hostages to him.

Albert states that Godfrey was angered by the dispute with Arsuf, and so began a new siege on the city. He started the operation on 15 October.[157] The chronicler reports that over the course of a few weeks Godfrey's men built siege engines, one of which was a three-storey siege tower which seems to have resembled those used by the crusaders a few months earlier at the siege of Jerusalem. During the siege, the inhabitants of Arsuf raised over the city wall a large ship's mast, to the end of which they had tied Gerard of Avesnes, Godfrey's hostage. Gerard reportedly begged Godfrey to show mercy on the people Arsuf so that his life would be spared. Godfrey refused, but reportedly consoled Gerard about his fate by asserting to him that 'if you die in this present life, you will live with Christ in heaven'.[158] The Latins then attacked the city, and Gerard seemed to have been killed after being struck by arrows and other projectiles. The citizens of Arsuf succeeded in destroying the Latins' siege tower, killing many of the fifty warriors who had been stationed within it. At this point, according to Albert, Godfrey realised that the siege was not progressing well, and this prompted him to make a long speech in which he reproached his fellow Latins and encouraged them to renew their efforts. This was followed by another speech by Patriarch Arnulf.[159] After this, the Latins constructed another siege tower, only for the defenders to destroy it as they had the first. In mid-December, Godfrey decided to abandon the siege. The Latins had been unable to make progress with their siege engines, and the cold and snow of winter had set in further to hamper their efforts. Albert of Aachen devoted a lengthy passage in his account to describing the two-month siege of Arsuf. He recounted the brutal fighting that characterised the siege, and described in visceral detail the deaths and serious injuries sustained on both sides. His treatment of the siege makes it clear that the Latins made a very serious effort to capture the city.

Before Godfrey departed for Jerusalem, he appointed a force of 100 knights and 200 infantry at nearby Ramla and instructed them to harass the citizens of Arsuf. However, those troops were unable to inflict many casualties among the citizens, and so they resorted to destroying their crops and vineyards. After some time, the troops stationed at Ramla abandoned even those efforts, and followed Godfrey back to Jerusalem.[160] Barber has suggested that Godfrey and his companions in Jerusalem survived during the winter of 1099–1100 through foraging expeditions, and by carrying out raids intended to compel nearby rulers to render tribute.[161]

Godfrey spent Advent at the Holy City. On 21 December, he was joined at Jerusalem by Baldwin and Bohemond, who had come there to visit the Holy Sepulchre. They were accompanied by Daibert, archbishop of Pisa, one of the more inscrutable figures in the early history of the Latin East.[162] In the West, Daibert had been a close associate of Urban II. Urban had appointed Daibert bishop of Pisa in 1088, and then raised him to the status of archbishop in 1092. In Autumn 1098, the pope sent Daibert at the head of a large fleet of Pisan ships to the Holy Land to reinforce the First Crusade, which at that time was mired at Antioch. Adhémar, Urban's original legate on the expedition, had died at Antioch in 1097, and it may be that the pope invested Daibert with legatine powers. If he had, though, those powers would have expired with Urban's death in July 1099. In September 1099 Daibert and his fleet arrived at Laodicea, held at that time by Bohemond.[163] There, he met Robert of Flanders, Robert of Normandy, and Raymond of Toulouse, who had travelled up from Jerusalem. Daibert's meeting with those three veterans of the First Crusade occasioned the composition of the well-known letter in which Godfrey is described as 'advocate'.[164]

Albert of Aachen was highly critical of Daibert, writing that he impiously ingratiated himself to Bohemond and Baldwin, and that when the three arrived at Jerusalem around 21 December, the archbishop sought to do the same to Godfrey, in order to obtain the office of patriarch. Daibert's efforts in this regard were successful. At Christmas, Godfrey presided over a council in Jerusalem. As a result of that gathering, Arnulf of Choques was removed from the office of patriarch and Daibert was appointed to it in his place.[165] Albert wrote that Daibert

> had assiduously sought Bohemond and Baldwin as his patrons [and then] began to make himself so pleasing and delightful to [Godfrey] that he was rewarded with promotion to the position of patriarch, but rather by means of a contribution of money than by choice of the new Church.[166]

That Albert should so explicitly accuse Daibert of buying the office of patriarch underlines exactly how badly the chronicler regarded him.

Daibert quickly asserted his authority as patriarch in Jerusalem. Fulcher of Chartres, who was present at the Holy City in late 1099 as part of Baldwin's retinue, wrote that 'in Jerusalem Duke Godfrey and Lord Bohemond received their land from Patriarch Daibert for the love of God'.[167] Fulcher appears to be stating in this passage that Godfrey and Baldwin took part in a ceremony in which Daibert formally confirmed them in their lands. It is possible that a ritual of this kind was intended symbolically to subserviate the two secular figures to the spiritual authority. Daibert's apparent aim here might have correlated with the arguments advanced by members of the clergy at Godfrey's appointment. As Murray has noted, there are a number of possible explanations for Daibert's conduct after he reached Jerusalem. Some historians have suggested that his adherence to the policies of the reform papacy led Daibert to see in Jerusalem the opportunity to establish the ultimate Church state.[168] Other scholars have suggested that Daibert acted out of personal ambition. The likeliest explanation, as Murray points out, is that at Christmas 1099, Daibert, Godfrey, Bohemond, and Baldwin concocted an agreement which would work to their mutual benefit.[169] Daibert's confirmation would have been of real benefit to Bohemond. His hold on Antioch was opposed by the Byzantines, meaning he was in need of legitimacy, and since his lands lay far to the north of Jerusalem, Bohemond would surely have known that any agreement with Daibert would not entail close dealings with him. At first sight, such an agreement would have been far less beneficial to Godfrey, who faced no challenges to his position in Jerusalem, where he would have to rule in close proximity to Daibert.[170] For Godfrey, though, practical considerations were crucial; he needed the assistance of the Pisan fleet which Daibert commanded to bolster his efforts to capture port cities near Jerusalem. The 'Bartolf' text is quite explicit on this point, stating that the fleet was pivotal to the discussions.[171] On 5 January (the day before the feast of the Epiphany), Godfrey, Baldwin, Bohemond, and Daibert met at the river Jordan, the place where John had baptised Christ, and they bathed in the river together. After this, Godfrey and Daibert returned to Jerusalem, and Bohemond and Baldwin departed north to return to Antioch and Edessa respectively.[172]

In mid-February 1100, Godfrey resumed his efforts against Arsuf.[173] Albert of Aachen states that a certain inhabitant of the city informed Godfrey that its citizens were happily going about the business of cultivating their crops, without fearing attacks from the Latins at all. Godfrey and the traitor agreed that on an appointed day, the former would send a force of forty mounted warriors to ambush the people of Arsuf. The chronicler reports that the Latins massacred the city's inhabitants, inflicting many casualties and taking many women and boys as prisoners. As a result of this, the inhabitants of Arsuf requested assistance from Egypt. The Fatimids duly despatched a force of 100 Arab cavalry and 200 Ethiopian footmen. News of the arrival of the Fatimid force at Arsuf prompted a small force of ten knights to travel with their squires from Jerusalem to Arsuf, unbeknownst to Godfrey. The knights succeeded in killing several of the Arab horsemen, and they carried their heads back to Jerusalem. This success prompted Godfrey to despatch a larger force of 140 knights under the command of Warner of Grez and Robert of Apulia to set ambushes against the remainder of the Fatimid warriors. A skirmish ensued, in which the Latins again prevailed. Godfrey's men captured more horses and soldiers and took them back to Jerusalem. 'Duke Godfrey', Albert states, 'rejoiced not a little at the success of his men'.[174] Albert claims that the defeat of the Fatimid force prompted the people of Arsuf to realise that they could no longer resist the Latins, and so they 'made peace [and] presented the keys of the gates and towers to the duke and became liable to pay tribute to him besides'.[175] As Edgington notes in her edition of Albert's account, this is something of an over-exaggeration on the chronicler's part, for the Latins did not actually take possession of Arsuf at this point. Rather, this passage should be read as an indication of the fact that the Latins had finally compelled its citizens to render tribute reliably.[176]

Albert of Aachen states that in the aftermath of the campaign against Arsuf, Godfrey turned his attention back to Ascalon and the Fatimids. He wrote that Godfrey wanted 'yet further to oppress and subdue the town of Ascalon and to overthrow and vanquish the rest of the towns of the Egyptian kingdom'.[177] With this in mind, Godfrey decided to rebuild and fortify the port of Jaffa.[178] Albert states that as soon as the port was once again operational, it became a centre of trade, a place for the Latins already in the Holy Land to go for recreation, and an arrival point for visitors from the West. When the inhabitants of the nearby Muslim towns of Ascalon, Caesarea and Acre realised how much the rebuilding of Jaffa had bolstered the Latins' position, they sent a combined delegation to Jerusalem to make an offer of peace to Godfrey, promising to send him ten fine horses, three mules, and a monthly sum of 5,000 bezants in tribute. Godfrey accepted the offer, and in the period that followed, friendly relations were established between him and those Muslim lords. Ascalon sent to Godfrey gifts of foodstuffs, wine, and oil, while Caesarea and Acre sent payments of gold and silver. Albert explained this development by noting that 'fear of the most Christian duke was instilled in all the lands and regions of the gentiles'.[179] This chronicler claims that other Muslim princes from Arabia likewise sought to make peace with Godfrey, but only if he permitted trade between Christians and Muslims in Jerusalem and Jaffa. Godfrey assented to this, though he reportedly prohibited the Latins from engaging in maritime trade, fearing it might lead to the Muslim-held port cities growing so rich that they would terminate their agreements with him.[180] As a result of these arrangements, relations between Godfrey and the lord of Ascalon became so warm that one day the latter sent back to Jerusalem Gerard of Avesnes, whom the Latins had assumed had been killed during the siege of Arsuf in late 1099.[181]

The sources yield tantalising glimpses into Godfrey's efforts to establish the institutions of the new state over which he ruled. Since he spent significant portions of his tenure on campaign away from Jerusalem, he probably would not have had much opportunity to work towards establishing the infrastructure of government. More likely, he adopted a pragmatic and contingent approach to ruling in the Holy City. One aspect of his tenure for which there is good evidence is his policy toward enfeoffment. As Murray has argued, since Godfrey had so few towns and cities in his possession, he seems to have been reluctant to grant land away by bestowing lordships on his followers. As an alternative, in several instances he assigned the tribute rendered by certain Muslim-held areas to his associates.[182] As noted above, after Godfrey and his fellow Latins defeated a Fatimid army in early 1100, Arsuf began to pay tribute. According to Albert of Aachen, Godfrey granted this tribute to Robert of Apulia, 'in return for a cash settlement'.[183] Godfrey did nevertheless make a number of conventional land grants. After the lord of Ascalon returned Gerard of Avenses to Jerusalem in 1100, Godfrey bestowed upon his repatriated knight fiefs worth 100 marks of land, including the castle of Hebron (which the Latins called St Abraham). Albert states that Godfrey made these grants to Gerard to compensate him for the suffering he had endured while acting as a hostage at Arsuf.[184] While Godfrey lay ill in bed in the summer of 1100, he granted the port of Haifa – which the Latins had yet to capture at that point – to Geldemar Carpenel, a prominent member of his household.[185] Most significantly, in the months following the capture of Jerusalem, Godfrey helped Tancred to carve out a lordship around the sea of Galilee by granting him the castle of Tiberias. Albert states that Godfrey had rebuilt that fortress during Advent 1099, and then granted it to Tancred, in recognition of the military service that he had provided.[186] As previously noted, Tancred stated in a charter issued in about March 1101 that he had received his land from Godfrey. That document relates that Tancred had been constituted lord of Tiberias, and all of Galilee.[187] While the contemporary sources provide information on only these few grants, Godfrey apparently made a number of others whose details have not been preserved. This is evident from the fact that when Baldwin reached Jerusalem in late 1100 to succeed his brother, he enquired among the Latins there about the fiefs that had been granted there from the revenues of Muslim-held towns.[188]

The sources also indicate that Godfrey played a role in the development of ecclesiastical institutions in the new Latin state.[189] Immediately after he was appointed ruler of Jerusalem in July 1099, he installed twenty canons to observe the Divine Office in the church of the Holy Sepulchre. Godfrey and other prominent figures also ordered the manufacture of bells which were then used to sound the canonical hours.[190] At some point during his tenure, Godfrey also granted the revenues of twenty-one villages in the region of al-Bira (which lay ten miles north of Jerusalem) and all but two of the ovens in the Holy City to the canons of the church of the Holy Sepulchre.[191] Godfrey was also likely responsible for installing canons in the Templum Domini.[192] There are indications that he made donations to other houses. He is documented as having granted a village called Hessilia and two ovens in Jerusalem to the Hospital of St John in Jerusalem.[193] Beyond Jerusalem, Godfrey is reputed to have ordered the foundation of a hospice (*hospitium*) in Jaffa.[194] Godfrey was also involved in the organisation of the Latin Church in Jerusalem. The 'Bartolf' text records that at Christmas 1099, Godfrey presided over a gathering of the clergy and the people in the Temple of Solomon, in order to discuss 'the state of the kingdom and the church of Jerusalem'.[195] Frutolf of Michelsberg's 1106 continuator made a similar claim, noting that Godfrey presided over a large council in Jerusalem at Christmas 1099, the purpose of which, according to this author, was to invest a number of bishops:

> Under Duke Godfrey . . . a vast meeting [*conventus ingens*] took place in Jerusalem of all those in the East who were Christian, but especially of the pilgrims who had settled in Antioch, Syria, Edessa or Palestine, so that on the feast of Christmas . . . many bishops were consecrated for the surrounding areas.[196]

The author implies in this passage that the native Christians of the Holy Land participated in the Christmas gathering. Whether or not this was the case, the author clearly regarded Godfrey as a ruler who worked to build links between the Latin and Eastern Christians.

Godfrey's death and the succession of Baldwin I

Shortly after Easter 1100, Tancred came from his castle at Tiberias to Jerusalem to complain to Godfrey that a local Muslim ruler near his lands had ceased to pay him tribute.[197] Albert states that the Latins called the Muslim ruler in question the Fat Peasant, on account of his corpulence and unrefined character. Godfrey was annoyed by the report, and he accompanied Tancred back to his lands with a force of warriors. The two spent a week plundering the Fat Peasant's lands, killing some and capturing others. Albert states that this prompted the Fat Peasant to seek military assistance from Damascus. In response, the ruler of Damascus sent a band of 500 Turks to battle Godfrey and Tancred's forces. After Tancred's rearguard force became detached from Godfrey's vanguard, they skirmished against the Damascene warriors. Albert states that when the Turks discovered that Godfrey was nearby, though, they swiftly returned to Damascus.[198] With this campaign concluded, Godfrey travelled back to Jerusalem and Tancred returned to Tiberias. The chronicler noted that in the aftermath of this campaign, Tancred concluded peace terms with a number of nearby local rulers. Apparently emboldened by this, Tancred sent six messengers to Damascus, stating to its ruler that he should surrender and convert to

Christianity, for he could not buy peace from Tancred by tribute. The ruler of Damascus, gravely angered by this message, killed five of the six messengers and only spared the last because he converted to Islam. When Godfrey discovered what had happened to Tancred's men, he led a force to the lands around Damascus and ravaged them for a fortnight. Albert states that Godfrey's campaign compelled the Fat Peasant to cease seeking aid from Damascus, and come to terms with Godfrey and Tancred instead.

After Godfrey ended his campaign in Damascene territory, he departed, planning to visit the ports of Acre, Caesarea, and Haifa en route south along the coastal road back to Jerusalem. Albert reports that while Godfrey was at Caesarea (about 10 June), he was offered a meal by its Muslim lord. Though Godfrey politely declined the offer, he accepted some citrus fruit. Very shortly after, he began to feel ill. With his symptoms worsening, he travelled on to Jaffa, and there he encountered a newly arrived fleet of ships from Venice.[199] The chronicler states that at Jaffa, Godfrey was carried into a hospice which he had recently had built, and he then lay in that place gripped by illness, while some of his companions supported his feet and head, and others tearfully looked on. After the rest of the Latins in the region learned that Godfrey had become ill, many reportedly came to see him at Jaffa. Among those who visited him as he lay on his sickbed were the leaders of the Venetian fleet. However, Godfrey felt too unwell to speak with them, and he sent them back to their ships, promising that if he felt better the next day, he would grant them an audience. His illness grew worse during the night, though, and the next day (*c.*12 June) he asked his men to carry him back to Jerusalem. The Venetians dealt instead with Warner of Grez and Tancred, and those two men then went to confer with Godfrey over the military uses to which the Venetian fleet could be put. Through this process, the decision was reached that the Venetians should attack the port of Haifa, and that Warner and Tancred would lead the Latins in place of Godfrey. Bolstered by the Venetian aid, the Latins prepared siege engines and began their attack on Haifa, but broke it off after a rumour reached them that Godfrey had died. Though the rumours proved false, Godfrey's illness had worsened, though he was able to reassure his fellow Latins and the Venetians that he expected to recover, spurring them to resume the siege on Haifa. Tancred and Warner, joined now by Daibert, left for Jaffa to travel back to Haifa. However, Warner fell ill at Jaffa, and was carried back to Jerusalem, arriving there on 14 July.

On 18 July, Godfrey died as a result of the illness from which he had been suffering for the previous five weeks. The 'Bartolf' text simply states that Godfrey died in the second year after the capture of Jerusalem.[200] According to Albert, Godfrey 'made confession of his sins in true remorse of heart and with tears, took communion of the Lord's body and blood and, thus secured and protected by a spiritual shield, he was taken from this light'.[201] The chronicler claimed that after 'the distinguished duke and noble champion of Christ' died, there followed five days of 'very great lamentation and bitter weeping by all the Christians there – Gauls, Italians, Syrians, Armenians, Greeks – and by very many gentiles: Saracens, Arabs, and Turks'.[202] Frutolf's continuator asserted that the entire Church lamented Godfrey's passing, and that death had snatched him away too soon. This author stated Godfrey 'had so united both the natives and his fellow pilgrims by his gentleness that it was hard to tell whether the Franks lamented more than the Greeks or Syrians'.[203] Fulcher of Chartres noted that Godfrey died, before offering Jerusalem's first Latin ruler the following elegy:

> At the beginning of the year after the city was captured, upon you, Duke Godfrey, as a crown of merit, the Lord Bestowed this rule. But not for long did you exercise it when by Nature's decree you perished. When the rising sun entered the Sign of the glowing Leo you rejoicing ascended to Heaven borne by Michael the Archangel.[204]

Five days after his death, Godfrey's body was placed in a tomb at Golgotha, in front of Mount Calvary, near the entrance of the church of the Holy Sepulchre.[205]

Though Godfrey had made the anticipatory grant of Haifa to Geldemar Carpenel, his illness presented Tancred and Daibert with the opportunity to advance their positions. After the Latins captured Haifa, Tancred quickly expelled Geldemar and his followers and, with Daibert's support, claimed the city for himself.[206] Albert states that after this, Tancred and Daibert heard of Godfrey's death, and resolved to take hold of Jerusalem, just as they had Haifa. They reportedly sent a messenger to Antioch, requesting Bohemond to come and take control of Jerusalem. That messenger, though, was intercepted by Raymond of Toulouse in Laodicea, thereby exposing the plan.[207] Crucially, members of Godfrey's household took charge of the situation in Jerusalem after his death. A group including Arnulf of Choques, Wicher the Swabian, and Geldemar Carpenel sent a delegation led by Robert of Rouen, bishop of Lydda, to Edessa, to inform Baldwin of Godfrey's death and enjoin him to come to the Holy City to succeed his brother. The group also placed guards in the Tower of David.[208] Murray has suggested that these figures acted in this way out of the belief that Godfrey had formally nominated Baldwin as his heir.[209] While Albert states that Baldwin 'dissolved into very great weeping and lamentation' at the news of Godfrey's death, Fulcher states that 'he grieved somewhat [at the death of his brother] but he rejoiced more' at the opportunity it had presented him.[210] Baldwin promised the delegation from Jerusalem that he would come to the Holy City after he had set his affairs in Edessa in order. To that end, he summoned his kinsman, Baldwin of Bourcq, to succeed him as count of Edessa. He took a number of followers, including the chronicler Fulcher of Chartres, and departed for Jerusalem. Baldwin and his retinue had a fraught journey south from Edessa, battling several Muslim contingents en route.[211]

On the way to the Holy City, Baldwin and his men stopped at Haifa in order to confer with Tancred. After Baldwin discovered Tancred and Daibert's plan to seize Jerusalem, he sent several of his companions ahead to Jerusalem to safeguard the Tower of David and thereby secure his succession. Baldwin himself reached the Holy City around 9 November.[212] After enquiring about the grants made by Godfrey, Baldwin asked the Latins who were present there about Godfrey's equipment and money, only to be told that it had all been given away in alms and to settle debts.[213] Albert states that at this point, Baldwin 'was confirmed on oath by all, and was raised powerfully onto the throne of Jerusalem, where he remained gloriously'.[214] This should be read as an indication that the people of Jerusalem accepted Baldwin as their ruler, although he would have to wait to be formally appointed. Crucially, if there was any meaningful opposition to the prospect of appointing a king of Jerusalem at this time, Baldwin was able to overcome it. It is likely that, in the interval between Godfrey's appointment in July 1099 and Baldwin's arrival in Jerusalem in November 1100, apprehensions about the idea of appointing a monarch – perhaps including concerns about thereby inviting the Endtimes – had dissipated.

The 'Bartolf' text and Fulcher both state that Baldwin was in dispute with Daibert at this time.[215] Perhaps Baldwin had sought to punish Daibert for his intrigue with Tancred, or Daibert had voiced opposition to the idea of Baldwin assuming the royal title. Either way, Baldwin was not to be denied by Daibert. Godfrey's successor convinced – or, more likely, compelled – the patriarch to inaugurate him king of Jerusalem. He was evidently soon confident in his succession, for only six days after arriving in the Holy City, he went out on campaign to the Dead Sea. He was away from Jerusalem for six weeks, returning only on 21 December. Four days later, on Christmas Day, in the church of the Nativity in Bethlehem, Daibert inaugurated Baldwin king of Jerusalem.[216] It is at this point in his account that Albert stated that Baldwin opted to be crowned in Bethlehem rather than in the Holy City, because he did not wish to wear a crown of gold where Christ had worn one of thorns.[217] While Baldwin did not wish to be crowned king in Jerusalem, however, he had no qualms with fulfilling the office in the Holy City. The day after his inauguration, he returned to the Holy City as its king. He held court in the Temple of Solomon, and remained in Jerusalem for fifteen days to dispense law and justice amongst the Christians.[218] At Christmas 1100, then, Baldwin established the institution of Latin kingship in the Holy City, creating a royal dynasty in the polity founded by the First Crusaders in 1099.[219]

Notes

1 As many of the First Crusaders felt that they had fulfilled their obligations by reaching the Holy City – the goal of their expedition – the present chapter will generally refer to those who remained in the Holy Land after July 1099 as 'Latins'.

2 RA, p. 143. See above, p. 161.

3 *GF*, p. 92; PT, p. 142, tr. p. 120; Bartolf, p. 516; Fulcher, pp. 306–8, tr. pp. 124–5. Though no contemporary source states explicitly where the Latins met on 22 July, they most likely did so in the church of the Holy Sepulchre. Godfrey's appointment on that day probably came at the end of discussions which had been carried out over the preceding days. AA, pp. 444–5, suggests that the discussions about the rulership of Jerusalem recommenced on 17 July, and Murray, *Crusader Kingdom*, p. 66, and *CPC*, no. 408, both accept that the discussions began on that day.

4 See, among others: Jay Rubenstein, 'Godfrey of Bouillon vs. Raymond of Saint-Gilles: How Carolingian Kingship Trumped Millenarianism at the End of the First Crusade', Matthew Gabriele and Jace Stuckey (eds), *The Legend of Charlemagne in the Middle Ages: Power, Faith, and Crusade* (Basingstoke, 2008), pp. 59–75; Luc Ferrier, 'La couronne refusée de Godefroy de Bouillon: eschatologie et humiliation de la majesté aux premiers temps du royaume latin de Jérusalem', in *Le Concile de Clermont de 1095 et l'appel à la croisade. Actes du colloque universitaire international de Clermont-Ferrand (23–25 juin 1995)* (Rome, 1997), pp. 245–65; Alan V. Murray, 'The Title of Godfrey of Bouillon as Ruler of Jerusalem', *Collegium Medievale*, 3 (1990), 163–78; Murray, *Crusader Kingdom*, pp. 63–7; John France, 'The Election and Title of Godfrey de Bouillon', *Canadian Journal of History*, 18 (1983), 321–30; Jonathan Riley-Smith, 'The Title of Godfrey of Bouillon', *Bulletin of the Institute for Historical Research*, 52 (1979), 83–6. For a narrative study of Godfrey's tenure, see: Malcolm Barber, *The Crusader States in the Twelfth Century* (New Haven, 2012), pp. 18–25, 50–62.

5 'ut aliquis eligeretur in regem, qui omnium curam gerens, et tributa regionis colligeret, et ad quem plebs terrę reverteretur et provideret ne ulterius terra desolaretur'. RA, p. 152, tr. p. 129 (adapted).

6 'Laudamus electionem vestram, verum si recte et ordine faciatis. Sicut sunt ęterna priora temporalibus sic vicarium spiritalem prius eligite post hęc, regem qui rebus agendis seculariter presit. Alioquin, invalidum esse censemus, quicquid eligitis'. RA, p. 152, tr. p. 129 (adapted).

7 RA, p. 152, tr. p. 129. The chronicler states that the princes rejected this 'advice and protest' (*amonicione et contradictione*).

8 'ortabantur comitem Sancti Eigidii ut acciperet regnum. At ille nomen regium se perorrescere fatebatur in illa civitate, sed prebere se aliis consensum si id acciperent'. RA, p. 152, tr. p. 129 (adapted).

9 France, 'The election and title of Godfrey de Bouillon', p. 321, is certain that Raymond of Toulouse was the first to be offered the office. The Hills accepted the suggestion that Raymond probably was the first to be offered Jerusalem. They state that this happened because he was the most senior of the crusaders, but aver that he refused the position on the basis that he was a pilgrim: Hills, *Raymond IV*, pp. 132–4. Rubenstein, *Armies of Heaven*, p. 298, suggests that Raymond refused the office in an attempt to demonstrate humility.

10 'verum multa de eo turpia conposuerunt ne in regem eligeretur'. RA, p. 153, tr. p. 130.

11 'fideles et primores Christianorum, inito consilio, dominium urbis et custodiam dominici sepulchri comiti Reimundo dare decreuerunt'. AA, pp. 444–7.

12 'Quo renitente, et ceteris uniuersis capitaneis ad id officium electis'. AA, pp. 446–7.

13 'Godefridus dux tandem licet inuitus ad tenendum urbis principatum promouetur'. AA, pp. 446–7.

14 By stating that Godfrey was reluctant to assume the office, Albert may have had in mind the topos of the *rex renitens* or 'unwilling king'. In the Middle Ages

those men who held a reluctance to assume the office of king were regarded as suitable because of their unwillingness. See: Björn Weiler, 'The Rex Renitens and the Medieval Ideal of Kingship, ca.900–ca.1250', *Viator*, 31 (2000), 1–42. This study invokes Godfrey as a prime example of a king who was held to be an unwilling recipient of his office.

15 'Flandrensis et Normannię comites favebant duci, et omnes etiam pene de terra comitis Raimundi'. RA, p. 153, tr. p. 130.

16 See above, pp. 157–8.

17 See above, pp. 157–8.

18 'Godefridus dux, gratia Dei ecclesiae S. Sepulcri nunc aduocatus'. *DK*, pp. 167–74 (no. 18), at p. 168. See also: RRR, no. 16. For a translation of the letter, see: *LE*, pp. 33–7 (no. 9), though note that on p. 34, the term 'aduocatus' is rendered as 'defender'.

19 A range of modern writers have ascribed to Godfrey this title. See, for example: Asbridge, *First Crusade*, p. 321, and the works cited in Murray, 'The Title of Godfrey of Bouillon', p. 163, n. 1.

20 France, 'The Election and Title of Godfrey de Bouillon', p. 327; Riley-Smith, 'The Title of Godfrey of Bouillon', p. 84; Murray, *Crusader Kingdom*, pp. 74–6.

21 See above, pp. 7, 63, 68, 73, 75–6, 77–80, 81, 98.

22 Heinrich Hagenmeyer, 'Der Brief der Kreuzfahrer an den Pabst im Jahre 1099 nach der Schlacht bei Askalon', *Forschungen zur Deutschen Geschichte*, 13 (1873), 400–12. Hagenmeyer's argument is summarised in Riley-Smith, 'The Title of Godfrey of Bouillon', pp. 83–5. Important studies of the letter and its manuscript tradition have recently been carried out by Thomas W. Smith. See his 'The First Crusade Letter Written at Laodicea in 1099: Two Previously Unpublished Versions From Munich, Bayerische Staatsbibliothek Clm 23390 and 28195', *Crusades*, 15 (2016), 1–25, and the same scholar's 'Scribal Crusading: Three New Manuscript Witnesses to the Regional Reception and Transmission of First Crusade Letters', *Traditio*, 72 (2017) (forthcoming).

23 See above, pp. 161, 199.

24 'a duce Godefrido, totius Orientis serenissimo principe'. *DULKJ*, vol. 1, pp. 124–5 (no. 20); *Cartulaire general de l'Ordre des Hospitaliers de Saint-Jean de Jérusalem, 1100–1300*, ed. Joseph Delaville de Roulx, 4 vols (Paris, 1894–1906), vol. 2, pp. 897–8 (no. 1); RRR, no. 56.

25 *DULKJ*, vol. 1, pp. 131–2 (no. 27); RRR, no. 56.

26 'uellet regnare super alios et regere ciuitatem'. *GF*, p. 92.

27 'elegerunt ducem Godefridum principem civitatis, qui debellaret paganos et custodiret Christianos'. *GF*, pp. 92–3 (translation adapted).

28 PT, p. 142, tr. p. 120 (adapted).

29 'Dux quoque Godefredus, qui iam ad regem electus erat in Iherusalem'. PT, p. 145, tr. p. 123 (adapted).

30 'dux Godefredus'. PT, p. 146, tr. p. 124.

31 'pariter elegerunt ducem, et obtulerunt eum ad sepulchrum Domini'. RA, p. 152, tr. pp. 129–30 (adapted).

32 'duce Lotharingie ordinatum esset quod civitatem retinere deberet'. RA, p. 154, tr. p. 132 (adapted).

33 RA, pp. 152–9, tr. pp. 132–5, which contains five references to Godfrey as 'duke' in relation to events after his appointment on 22 July.

34 'primates et populi requie modica refecti sunt, omnes communi assensu Godefridum ducem in regem ac principem civitatis Iherusalem et totius regionis extulerunt'. Bartolf, p. 516.

35 'rege Godefrido' . . . 'regnum'. Bartolf, pp. 519, 520.

36 'dux Godefridus . . . sublimatus in regem'. Bartolf, p. 518.

37 'dum viveret, non dux vel rex, sed servus et protector patriae exstitit'. Bartolf, p. 520.

38 'Iherusalem Franci capiunt virtute potentia, | Quippe Godefrido patriae mox principe facto'. FC, p. 307, tr. p. 124 (adapted).

39 'Quem . . . in urbe sancta regni principem omnis populus dominici exercitus ad illud conservandum atque regendum elegit'. FC, pp. 307–8, tr. p. 124 (adapted).

40 'De rege . . . in urbe procreatis' . . . 'regis Godefridi'. FC, pp. 306, 349, tr. pp. 124, 136.

41 'ad tenendum urbis principatum promouetur'. AA, pp. 446–7.

42 'Promotus igitur consilio et beniolentia omnium Christianorum' . . . 'electio et promotio'. AA, pp. 446–7.

43 'princeps Christianorum . . . at protegendam urbem et eius habitatores'. AA, pp. 452–3.

44 'et in ea post uictoriam ad tuenda menia Godefridum magnificum Christianorum principem exaltaret'. AA, pp. 480–1. This passage features in Albert's account as speech attributed to Daibert of Pisa.

45 AA: 'leader and prince and commander of the Christian army' ('ductorem et principem et preceptorem Christiani exercitus') (pp. 446–7); 'duke and commander of His Christian people' ('Dux et preceptor populi sui Christiani') (pp. 446–7); 'ruler of the city and commander of the people' ('urbis rectorem ac populi preceptorem prefecerunt') (pp. 448–9); 'chief of all and prince in Jerusalem' ('caput omnium et princeps . . . in Ierusalem') (pp. 448–9); 'the highest prince of Jerusalem' ('summus princeps Ierusalem') (pp. 466–7); 'distinguished duke and noble champion of Christ' ('egregio duce et nobilissimo Christi athleta') (pp. 514–15); 'the duke and after God the highest ruler in Jerusalem' ('Godefridus dux et summus post Deum dominator Ierusalem') (pp. 462–3). For an example of Albert's continued use of the title 'duke', see: pp. 506–7, where the chronicler refers to Godfrey as the 'most Christian duke' ('duci Christianissimo').

46 'principem et rectorem suorum confratrum in solio regni Ierusalem'. AA, pp. 450–1.

47 'in throno Ierusalem exaltatus'. AA, pp. 452–3.

48 At one point there is a reference to the 'kingdom of Duke Godfrey' ('regno Godefridi ducis'). AA, pp. 522–3 (translation adapted).

49 'per preces humillimas Godefridi ducis, quem exercitus Christi diuina ordinatione in regem sublimauit'. DK, pp. 175–6 (no. 20).

50 'ut Rex regum et Dominus dominantium contra hostes Christianorum regi impendat uictoriam'. DK, p. 176.

51 For Paschal's letters, see: DK, pp. 174–5 (no. 19, dated December 1099); DK, pp. 178–9 (no. 22, dated 28 April 1100); DK, pp. 179–81 (no. 23, dated August 1100).

52 'Godefrido aliisque principibus Christianis adhuc in Syria et transmarinis partibus'. DK, pp. 180–1.

53 *Cantatorium*, pp. 253–4.

54 'Gotefrido duce Hierosolimitanam ęcclesiam defensante'. Frutolf 1106, p. 158, tr. p. 159.

55 Riley-Smith, 'The Title of Godfrey of Bouillon', p. 86.

56 France, 'The Election and Title of Godfrey de Bouillon', p. 328.

57 Murray, 'The Title of Godfrey of Bouillon', pp. 169–71; Murray, *Crusader Kingdom*, pp. 74–7.

58 Murray, *Crusader Kingdom*, pp. 65–6; Idem, *Crusader Kingdom*, pp. 5; Riley-Smith, 'The Title of Godfrey of Bouillon', p. 83; France, 'The Election and Title of Godfrey de Bouillon', p. 326.

59 On the early political status of Latin Jerusalem, see: Simon John, 'The Papacy and the Establishment of the Kingdoms of Jerusalem, Sicily and Portugal: Twelfth-Century Papal Political Thought on Incipient Kingship', *Journal of Ecclesiastical History*, 68 (2017), 223–59, esp. pp. 230–5.

60 France, 'The Election and Title of Godfrey de Bouillon', p. 328, asserts that 'it was the status of Jerusalem as the property of the church which dictated the form of Godfrey's election'. For a wider study, see: John G. Rowe, 'Paschal II and the Relation Between the Spiritual and Temporal Powers in the Kingdom of Jerusalem', *Speculum*, 32 (1957), 470–501.

61 See above, pp. 178–9.

62 France, 'The Election and Title of Godfrey de Bouillon', pp. 323–9.

63 See, for example: Bernard Hamilton, *The Latin Church in the Crusader States: The Secular Church* (London, 1980), p. 12; Rubenstein, *Armies of Heaven*, p. 299.

64 'Noluit enim nec presumpsit in Ierusalem diademate auro uel gemmis precioso exaltari, adornari et in regem promoueri, ubi Dominus Iesus rex regum et dominus dominantium humiliatus et obediens usque ad mortem pro mundi redemptione spinis horridis et acutis coronatus est'. AA, pp. 550–1.

65 'et quod fratri suo praedecessori non fecerant, quoniam noluit et tunc laudatum a quibusdam non fuit'. FC, 385, tr. p. 148.

66 A number of recent works have examined medieval ideas about the apocalypse. See, among others: Brett Whalen, *Dominion of God: Christendom and Apocalypse in the Middle Ages* (Cambridge, MA, 2009); James T. Palmer, *The Apocalypse in the Early Middle Ages* (Cambridge, 2014).

67 For an influential treatment of the religious ideas of the crusaders during the expedition, see: Riley-Smith, *First Crusade*, pp. 91–119.

68 See above, p. 161.

69 Ferrier, 'La couronne refusée'; Jean Flori, *La croix, la tiare et l'épée. La croisade confisquée* (Paris, 2010), pp. 205–20; Rubenstein, *Armies of Heaven*, esp. pp. 293–303; Rubenstein, 'Godfrey of Bouillon'. Riley-Smith, *First Crusaders*, p. 26, briefly highlights eleventh-century anxieties about the Endtimes in his study of the response to the First Crusade appeal.

70 See above, pp. 161, 163, 178–9.

71 *DK*, p. 171, tr. *LE*, p. 35.

72 Gerd Althoff, *"Selig sind, die Verfolgung ausüben"*. *Päpste und Gewalt im Hochmittelalter* (Darmstadt, 2013), pp. 130–1, 137–9.

73 'Quod per prophetam populo suo Dominus pollicetur, impletum uobis agnoscimus' . . . 'manus uestras, quas hostium suorum sanguine consecrauit'. *DK*, p. 178. On the letter's imagery, see: Althoff, *"Selig sind . . ."*, p. 139.

74 'versis in hystorias visibiles eatenus mysticis prophetiis'. Frutolf 1106, p. 160, tr. p. 159.

75 Flori, *La croix*, pp. 217–19.

76 Cf. Rubenstein, *Armies of Heaven*, pp. 293–301, where it is strongly implied that Godfrey actively manipulated prophetic ideas to his advantage.

77 RA, p. 150, tr. p. 127.

78 AA, pp. 436–7. Rubenstein, *Armies of Heaven*, pp. 291–4, accepts Albert's account of Godfrey's procession, and describes the act as a 'brilliant first step' in manipulating prophecy.

79 'Godefridus dux et summus post Deum dominator Ierusalem'. AA. pp. 462–3. See also: Rubenstein, *Armies of Heaven*, p. 299 ('Despite the . . . ambiguous title, Godfrey's office seemed no less splendid or royal'); Murray, 'The Title of Godfrey of Bouillon', p. 167 ('while he may not have been king in name, a man chosen by God to be his regent in Jerusalem was clearly in a strong constitutional position').

80 'Quem ob nobilitatis excellentiam et militiae probitatem atque patientiae modestiam, necnon et morum elegantiam in urbe sancta regni principem omnis populus dominici exercitus ad illud conservandum atque regendum elegit'. FC, pp. 307–8, tr. p. 128.

81 'Dux . . . Godefridus . . . principatum Iherosolymitanum rexit: quem consensu omnium susceperat obtinendum'. FC, pp. 321–2, tr. p. 128.

82 *DK*, p. 176.
83 'faceret elemosinas cum orationibus, quatinus sibi Deus eligeret quem vellet'. *GF*, p. 92.
84 PT, p. 142, tr. p. 120.
85 'Huius uero ducis electio et promotio nequaquam humana uoluntate fuisse credatur, sed totum Dei ordinatione et gratia factum'. AA, pp. 446–7.
86 'ex Dei ordinatine et populi Christiani beniuolentia'. AA, pp. 450–1.
87 See above, pp. 163–4.
88 'Vbi mensa illis parata et omni deliciarum dulcedine cumulata reperta est'. AA, pp. 436–7, invoking Psalm 22(23): 5. The steward Rothard is attested in no other source.
89 'Ad hanc denique dux cum electis et ea dignis recumbens, de omni que aderat dulcedine partitus est'. AA, pp. 436–9.
90 'Quid per hanc scalam ad celi palacium ducentem, nisi uia quam dux tota mensis intentione apprehendit ad urbem Ierusalem que porta celestis est patrie significatur? Ex auro enim purissimo erat scala, quia ad hanc uiam et portam celi puro corde et perfecta uoluntate ueniendum est'. AA, pp. 438–9.
91 'sepulchrum Domini, quod mensa est et desiderium totius dulcedinis sanctorum'. AA, pp. 438–9.
92 'cuiusdam boni et ueridici militis' . . . 'statim in spiritu ad montem Syna translatus, ubi Moyses famulus Domini ieiunio quadraginta dierum expleto claritatem glorie Dei meruit uidere, et legem de manu altissimis accipere. Super huius denique montis cacumen uidebat predictum ducem cum timore et mansuetudine facili ascensu attolli, et duos ei in uestibus albis et pontificali ornatu obuiam festinare. Qui ilico ut ad eum peruentum est in hiis uerbis hanc sibi porrexere benedictionem et gratiam benedictionem. "Qui seruo et fideli suo Moysi contulit benedictionem et gratiam benedictionibus Dei uiuentis replearis, et gratiam in oculis eius inuenias. Dux ac preceptor populi sui Christiani in omni fide et ueritate constitueris." Hoc dicto miles fit expergefactus, et subtracta est uisio'. AA, pp. 446–7.
93 'hunc [Godfrey] a Deo electum et constitutum ductorem et principem et preceptorem Christiani exercitus, et pre omnibus primatibus, actu, uictoria, consiliis beatiorem, fide et ueritate integriorem'. AA, pp. 446–7.
94 'Quid in hac uisione aliud considerandum nisi quia in spiritu et lenitate Moysi surgeret dux spiritualis Israhel, a Deo preordinatus et princeps populi constitutus?' AA, pp. 448–9.
95 Rubenstein, *Armies of Heaven*, p. 300.
96 'cuidam catholico fratri et canonico Sancte Marie Aquis, Giselberto nomine'. AA, pp. 448–9.
97 'caput omnium et princeps futurus esset in Ierusalem, a Deo prescitus et constitutus'. AA, pp. 448–9.
98 'dux in sole potenter accepiset sedem, et ex omni genere auium que sub celo sunt in circuitu illius infinite copie confluxissent. Quarum pars paulatim auolando minui cepit, amplior uero pars fixa et inmobilis a dextris et sinistris remanebat. Post hec sol a radiis sue claritatis maxima ex parte obscuratus est, sedesque ducis breui interuallo prorsus deleta, ex tota fere auium multitudo que remanserat auolauit'. AA, pp. 448–9.
99 'In sole sedem dux accepit, cum in in solio regni Ierusalem promouetur, que omnes mundi superat ciuitates nomine et sanctitate, sicut sol sua claritate uniuersas celi stellas'. AA, pp. 450–1.
100 'Congregate sunt aues celi circa sedentem, cum de universis regnis Christianorum magni et parui, nobiles et ignobiles, illi associati et subditi facti sunt. Auolauerunt aves, cum plurima peregrinorum multitudo ad terram cognationis sue reuersa est ex illius consensu et licentia. Sed plurime aues fixe et inmobiles permanserunt, cum multi pio amore illius innodati, et familiari eius

allocutione delectati, cum illo ultra remanere deuouerunt'. AA, pp. 450–1 (translation adapted).

101 'denique illius montis cacumine adhuc superstes, circa basim illius hinc inde et altrinsecus, multa millia avium diversorum generum, varii coloris, sinistras alas quin etiam rubicundas habentium, quarum diffusae longe laleque multiludinis inexhaustam extremitatem perspicaci et angustalo obtutu nonpoterat comprehendere; caeterum congruenti incessu atque volatu eas sibi alternis vicibus invicem cedentes, fontem montis petere, easque se convenienti natatione sicuti solent tempore futurae pluviae abluere, omnibusque mira infusione dellbutis, congrua eas statione sine discretione generum et specierum, sine ullo contentionis jurgio, mutuo vicissim pastu quasi amicabililer comedere; easque deportatis ramusculis festinanti labore nidificare: quin etiam suae visionis imperio voluntarie succumbere'. Dudo of St Quentin, *De moribus et actis primorum Normanniae ducum*, ed. Jules Lair (Caen, 1865), pp. 146–7, tr. in Dudo of St Quentin, *History of the Normans*, tr. Eric Christiansen (Woodbridge, 1998), pp. 29–30.

102 'Tibi aves diversarum specierum obtemperabunt; tibi homines diversorum regnorum serviendo accubitati obedient'. Dudo, *De moribus*, p. 147, tr. p. 30.

103 The most recent study of Dudo's account lists fifteen known manuscripts, all but four of which were produced in the eleventh or twelfth century. See: Benjamin Pohl, *Dudo of St Quentin's Historia Normannorum: Tradition, Innovation and Memory* (Woodbridge, 2015), pp. 34–108.

104 Other instances of avian imagery employed for this purpose include Genesis 40:17 and Virgil's *Aeneid* (book 1, 393–401, and book 12, 247–56). See: Dudo, *History*, tr. Christiansen, p. 188, n. 135.

105 Morris, 'The Aims and Spirituality of the First Crusade', pp. 110–11.

106 Cf. Rubenstein, *Armies of Heaven*, p. 299, who is more confident that the visions were recounted at the time of Godfrey's appointment.

107 'arcem David . . . tocius regni iudaici capud'. RA, p. 154, tr. p. 132.

108 RA, pp. 152–3, tr. pp. 130–1.

109 'dolore et iniuria'. RA, p. 154, tr. p. 132.

110 'donec minis ipsius ducis et Christianorum restituere coactus est'. AA, pp. 446–7.

111 On Arnulf, see: Raymonde Foreville, 'Un chef de la première croisade: Arnoul Malecouronne', *Bulletin historique et philologique du Comité des travaux historiques* (1954–1955), 382–5; Murray, *Crusader Kingdom*, pp. 182–3; Hamilton, *Latin Church*, pp. 12–14. Hamilton notes that the previous incumbent of the office, the orthodox Patriarch Symeon II, died in Cyprus around the time the crusaders captured Jerusalem. Whether or not the crusaders knew this, they would no doubt have sought to appoint a Latin patriarch whatever the circumstances.

112 See above, p. 156.

113 Manasses of Rheims asserted in his letter of November or December 1099 that he had received a missive from Arnulf, the newly-installed patriarch: *DK*, p. 176.

114 'sapentissimum et honorabilem uirum'. *GF*, p. 93 (cf. PT, p. 142, tr. p. 120); 'clericum mire prudentie et facundie'. AA, pp. 452–3. Bartolf, p. 516, records Arnulf's appointment rather matter-of-factly, while FC, p. 308, tr. p. 124, refers to the appointment of a patriarch, but does not specify that it was Arnulf who was appointed.

115 RA, pp. 153–4, tr. p. 131.

116 France, 'The election and title of Godfrey de Bouillon', p. 328, suggests that Arnulf may have been selected for the very purpose of smoothing over some of the disagreements that had coloured Godfrey's earlier appointment.

117 The chroniclers provided varied and sometimes conflicting reports of the dis-
    covery of the True Cross. See: RA, 154, tr. 131–2; Bartolf, p. 516; FC, 309–10,
    tr. 125; AA, pp. 450–3. On the relic, see: Deborah Gerish, 'The True Cross
    and the Kings of Jerusalem', *Haskins Society Journal*, 8 (1996), 137–55; Alan V.
    Murray, ' "Mighty Against the Enemies of Christ": The Relic of the True Cross
    in the Armies of the Kingdom of Jerusalem', in John France and William G.
    Zajac (eds), *The Crusades and Their Sources: Essays Presented to Bernard Hamilton*
    (Aldershot, 1998), pp. 217–38. For wider medieval traditions concerning the
    True Cross, see: Barbara Baert, *A Heritage of Holy Wood: The Legend of the True
    Cross in Text and Image*, tr. Lee Preedy (Leiden, 2004).
118 RA, 154, tr. 131–2.
119 AA, pp. 450–3.
120 'In hoc utique ligno sancte crucis redempti sumus de manu mortis et inferi,
    et potestate angeli nequam, et in sanguine Domini nostri Iesu filii Dei uiui ab
    omni inquinamento ueteris erroris emundati, fiduciam habemus eterne uite'.
    AA, pp. 460–1.
121 For what follows here on the buildup to and course of the battle of Ascalon, see
    France, *Victory*, pp. 357–66. France suggests that the Latins probably expected
    an attack from Egypt in retaliation for their capture of the Holy City. For the
    chroniclers' accounts, see: GF, pp. 94–7; PT, pp. 145–9, tr. pp. 123–7; RA,
    pp. 157–9, tr. p. 135; Bartolf, pp. 517–18; FC, pp. 312–18, tr. pp. 126–8; AA,
    pp. 456–71.
122 *GF*, p. 93; PT, p. 143, tr. p. 121.
123 *GF*, pp. 93–4; PT, p. 144, tr. p. 122.
124 RA, pp. 154–5, tr. p. 132. The chronicler states that Raymond had been plan-
    ning to depart Jerusalem, only to postpone his departure when he heard of the
    gathering of the Fatimid forces.
125 AA, pp. 454–7.
126 'Reimundus adhuc stimulo inuidie seuiens aduersus ducem Godefridum eo
    quod turrim David amiserit' . . . 'denuo a duce et cunctis principibus minis
    pulsatus et ammonitus, tandem ex consilio suorum'. AA, pp. 456–7.
127 *GF*, p. 95; PT, p. 145, tr. p. 123–4.
128 'Ad hec dux, fide Christi plenus, et spirituali responsione instructus, sciscitanti
    uiro super hiis sapienter exposuit'. AA, pp. 460–1.
129 'Populus hic quem uides et audis in uoce exultationis aduersum inimicos prop-
    erare, et prelium in nomine Domini Iesu Christi Dei sui committere, scito quia
    certus est hodie de corona regni celorum, et quia ad meliorem transibit uitam,
    in qua primum felicius uiuere incipiet, si pro eius nomine et gratia in hoc
    prelio mori meruerit'. AA, pp. 460–1.
130 See above, pp. 191–2.
131 'grave hostium reddidit exterminium, ac tunc uniuersos a preda reuocatos
    secum acuit'. AA, pp. 466–7.
132 *GF*, pp. 96–7; PT, p. 148–9, tr. p. 126–7; Bartolf, p. 518; FC, p. 318, tr. p. 128.
133 'inuidus omnis glorie ducis Godefridi propter turrim David quam amiserat'.
    AA, pp. 470–1. The very last entry in the account of Raymond of Aguilers refers
    to Raymond of Toulouse's decision to send a converted Turk named Bohe-
    mond to the ruler of Ascalon in order to discuss peace terms. RA, pp. 157–8,
    tr. p. 135. It may be that this chronicler referred in this passage to the same
    incident as Albert, but presented it in a different light. Ibn al-Qalānisī, it is
    worth noting, wrote that the leaders of the Latins quarrelled at Ascalon: *The
    Damascus Chronicle of the Crusades: Extracted and Translated From the chronicle of Ibn
    al-Qalānisī*, ed. and tr. H. A. R. Gibb (London, 1932), p. 49.
134 AA, pp. 470–1.

135 'conscius doli quem aduersus eum per inuidiam fecerat'. AA, pp. 472–3. *CPC*, nos. 425–6, date the incident at Ascalon to mid-August.

136 'Sed Reimundi suasione et attestatione hos . . . rebelles ac resistentes inueniens, tristi animo ab urbe diuertit'. AA, pp. 472–3.

137 'Sociosque ammonuit quatenus Reimundum in castris subito impeterent, et omne nefas quod aduersum se egerat in caput illius redderent. Qui statim, sociis ammonitis, lorica indutus, uexillis erectis, dum in castra comitis animo irato tendere disposuisset, Reimundus partier ex prouidentia armatus ad resistendum illi occurrere decreuisset'. AA, pp. 472–3.

138 'interuenerunt, uiros grauiter arguerunt, quos tandem utrimque multo conatu placatos in concordiam reduxerunt'. AA, pp. 472–3.

139 Baldwin I captured Arsuf in 1102. Ascalon, however, remained uncaptured until 1153. In the intervening time, in Prawer's oft-cited words, the city remained 'a thorn in the flesh' of the Latins in Jerusalem: Joshua Prawer, *The Latin Kingdom of Jerusalem: European Colonialism in the Middle Ages* (London, 1973), p. 21.

140 Barber, *Crusader States*, pp. 51–2.

141 Barber, *Crusader States*, pp. 18, 54; Murray, *Crusader Kingdom*, p. 78.

142 Their departure is recorded in *DK*, p. 173, tr. *LE*, p. 36, AA, pp. 484–5, and Bartolf, p. 518.

143 Though note that Raymond of Aguilers states that the Fatimids prepared to attack the Latins immediately after they captured Jerusalem because of the small size of their army, and because both men and horses were in a poor state after the end of the First Crusade. RA, p. 158, tr. p. 135.

144 AA, pp. 484–5.

145 See above, pp. 188–9.

146 'Hierusalem in maiore propter excellentiam sanctitatis maximae omnium locorum undique a paganis gentibus et incredulis esse oppressam'. *DK*, pp. 176–7 (no. 21), tr. in *LE*, pp. 37–8 (no. 10). For a study of the letter and a new critical edition, see Smith, 'Scribal Crusading'. The author of the letter was Daibert of Pisa, who in April 1100 was patriarch of Jerusalem. On Daibert, see above, pp. 199–200. Admittedly, the description of Jerusalem's parlous condition at this time may be a result of the fact that the aim of the letter was to persuade inhabitants of Germany to take the cross and come to the Holy Land.

147 FC, pp. 388–90, tr. pp. 149–50. In this passage, Fulcher stated that in 1101 there only 300 knights and 300 infantry in Jerusalem and the nearby towns. Cf. Barber, *Crusader States*, p. 53, where it is argued that the repercussions of the widescale departures after the battle of Ascalon were not as damaging to the Latins' plight as the sources suggest. He argues that there developed in the twelfth century a degree of aristocratic cohesion, but this holds more relevance to a generation or so later than the initial settlement phase.

148 AA, pp. 506–7. Albert notes that during this particular campaign, Tancred added to Godfrey's force a contingent of 100 knights.

149 *DK*, pp. 173–4. Requests for new recruits and assistance were a central theme of the communication from the Latins in the Holy Land to the West in the twelfth century. See: Jonathan Phillips, *Defenders of the Holy Land: Relations Between the Latin East and the West, 1119–1187* (Oxford, 1996).

150 'ut sui memores existant, confratres Christianos commoneant, quatenus ad sepulchrum Domini uenire non dubitent, sed sibi ceterisque consociis in exilio remanentibus auxilio de die in diem adversus tot barbaras nationes concurrant'. AA, pp. 474–5.

151 In describing events in Jerusalem, Albert of Aachen refers several times to the 'household of Duke Godfrey' or similar. See, for example, the reference to the 'domo ducis Godefridi'. AA, pp. 538–9.

152 For what follows, see: Murray, *Crusader Kingdom*, pp. 77–81, Murray, 'The Army of Godfrey of Bouillon', pp. 327–9; Jonathan Riley-Smith, 'The Motives of the Earliest Crusaders and the Settlement of Latin Palestine, 1095–1100', *EHR*, 98 (1983), 721–36, at pp. 724–7.

153 Count Cono of Montaigu is one Lotharingian who returned to the West after the First Crusade: his presence there is recorded in *Cantatorium*, pp. 253–4. On Cono, see: Murray, *Crusader Kingdom*, pp. 189–91.

154 Bartolf, p. 518, states that some clerics as well as laymen stayed in Jerusalem with Godfrey, but does not name them.

155 AA, pp. 474–5.

156 'deuotum sibi militem'. AA, pp. 474–5. On Gerard, see: Murray, *Crusader Kingdom*, p. 199.

157 AA, pp. 486–91. For the dates of the siege, see: *CPC*, no. 431.

158 'Si enim presenti uita moriaris, uiuere habes cum Christo in celestibus'. AA, pp. 488–9.

159 AA, pp. 492–3.

160 AA, pp. 494–5.

161 Barber, *Crusader States*, p. 52.

162 Much has been written on Daibert and his dealings with Godfrey. See, among others: Hamilton, *Latin Church*, pp. 14–15; Murray, *Crusader Kingdom*, pp. 81–93; Michael Matzke, *Daibert von Pisa. Zwischen Pisa, Papst und erstem Kreuzzug* (Sigmaringen, 1998); Patricia Skinner, 'From Pisa to the Patriarchate: Chapters in the Life of (Arch)bishop Daibert', in Patricia Skinner (ed.), *Challenging the Boundaries of Medieval History: The Legacy of Timothy Reuter* (Turnhout, 2009), pp. 155–72; Jay Rubenstein, 'Holy Fire and Sacral Kingship in Post-Conquest Jerusalem', *JMH*, 43 (2017) (forthcoming). The last of these chiefly investigates relations between Daibert and Godfrey's brother, Baldwin.

163 Raymond of Toulouse had taken Laodicea, before handing it over the Byzantines after the capture of Antioch. Bohemond had then wrested it away and incorporated it into his burgeoning state based around Antioch. See: AA, pp. 479–85.

164 See above, pp. 180, 182–3, 185.

165 Bartolf, pp. 518–19; FC, pp. 333–4, tr. p. 132; AA, pp. 496–7; *CPC*, no. 439. A charter of Baldwin I issued in late 1102 or early 1103 refers to Arnulf as archdeacon of Jerusalem, which suggests that he was granted a significant consolation after being removed from the office of patriarch: *CCSSJ*, pp. 72–4 (no. 19); *DULKJ*, vol. 1, pp. 128–30 (no. 24); RRR, no. 69.

166 'episcopus Pisanus, multum fautoribus Boemundo et Baldwino sibi adquisitis, duci gratus et dilectus adeo fieri cepit, quousque ad patriarchatus dignitatem prouehi meruit, sed potius collectione pecunie quam electione noue ecclesie'. AA, pp. 496–7.

167 'in Hierusalem quoque dux Godefridus et dominus Boamundus acceperunt terram suam a patriarcha Daiberto propter amorem Dei'. FC, pp. 741–2, tr. p. 269. It is important to note, however, that this claim is not included in the 'Bartolf' account, and Fulcher included it in his narrative not in chronological sequence, but as part of an event which took place many years later. For these reasons, caution must be exercised when interpreting this passage.

168 In this regard, it is not without interest that Daibert made no mention of Godfrey in connection to the rulership of Jerusalem in the account of the Holy City's plight that the patriarch included in his letter to Germany in April 1100: DK, pp. 176–7, tr. LE, pp. 37–8

169 Murray, *Crusader Kingdom*, pp. 83–5.

170 France, 'The Election and Title of Godfrey de Bouillon', pp. 323–4.

171 'Ideoque necessarium et valde opportunum reipublicæ suæ duxerunt, si talem virum haberent cujus industria et sollertia civitates super mare sitas navigio caperent'. Bartolf, p. 519.

172 AA, pp. 496–9.

173 On what follows, see: AA, pp. 498–503.

174 'Dux denique Godefridus de prospero euentu suorum non ad modicum letatus est'. AA, pp. 502–3.

175 'pacem composuit, claues portarum et turrium duci contulit, facta ei ultra tributaria'. AA, pp. 502–3.

176 AA, p. 503, n. 13.

177 'dux, uolens amplius adhuc urgere et subiugare, ciuitatem Ascalona et ceteras ciuitates de regno Babylonie opprimere ac debellare'. AA, pp. 502–3.

178 The Fatimids had abandoned the port as the First Crusaders neared Jerusalem in the summer of 1099. See above, p. 158.

179 'Incubuit enim timor Christianissimi ducis in uniuersas terras et regiones gentilium'. AA, pp. 504–5.

180 AA, pp. 504–5.

181 AA, pp. 506–7.

182 Murray, *Crusader Kingdom*, pp. 80–1.

183 'tributa Roberto . . . pro conuentione solidorum a duce concessa sunt'. AA, pp. 502–3.

184 AA, pp. 506–7.

185 AA, pp. 616–17. On anticipatory grants of this nature, see: Robert Bartlett, *The Making of Europe: Conquest, Colonisation and Cultural Change, 950–1350* (London, 1993), pp. 90–2.

186 AA, pp. 506–7, 508–9.

187 'Tyberiade cum tota Galilea eiusque pertinentiis accepta', in *DULKJ*, vol. 1, pp. 124–5; *Cartulaire general de l'Ordre des Hospitaliers*, vol. 2, pp. 897–8 (no. 1); RRR, no. 56. When Tancred captured the port of Haifa in August 1100 – ignoring Godfrey's prospective grant to Geldemar Carpenel – he established the basis of a Latin state that had the potential to break away from Jerusalem. However, Tancred left Galilee behind in mid-1101 to travel north to assume the regency of Antioch after Bohemond was taken captive. On Tancred's activities in Galilee, see: Murray, *Crusader Kingdom*, pp. 95–6; Barber, *Crusader States*, p. 20. On his time in Antioch, see: Asbridge, *Principality of Antioch*, pp. 52–3.

188 AA, pp. 540–1.

189 The key work on the foundation and development of ecclesiastical institutions in the Latin East remains Hamilton, *Latin Church*, esp. pp. 52–85, on Jerusalem.

190 AA, pp. 454–5 (who specifies that it was twenty); Bartolf, p. 516; FC, p. 310, tr. p. 124; RRR, no. 12.

191 This was confirmed in an act of Baldwin I issued in 1114: *CCSSJ*, pp. 86–8 (no. 26); *DULKJ*, vol. 1, pp. 183–5 (no. 56); RRR, no. 147. See also: Barber, *Crusader States*, p. 17.

192 FC, p. 310, tr. p. 124, notes that canons were installed soon after Godfrey was appointed, but does not specifically attribute the installation to him. AA, pp. 528–9, asserts that one of those in Jerusalem at the time of Godfrey's death was 'Arnulf the dignatory of the Lord's temple' ('Arnolfo prelato templi Domini'), which also suggests a religious community existed there in Godfrey's tenure; *DULKJ*, vol. 1, p. 98 (no. 2); RRR, no. 13; Denys Pringle, *The Churches of the Crusader Kingdom of Jerusalem*, 4 vols (Cambridge, 1993–2010), vol. 3, p. 401.

193 He seems to have done so in August 1099: *DULKJ*, pp. 98–9 (no. 3); RRR, no. 14. Though the Hospital had no military function in Godfrey's day, in about

1113 it was refounded as the headquarters of the Knights Hospitaller. See: Anthony Luttrell, 'The Earliest Hospitallers', in Benjamin Z. Kedar, Jonathan Riley-Smith and Rudolf Hiestand (eds), *Montjoie: Studies in Crusade History in Honour of Hans Eberhard Mayer* (Aldershot, 1997), pp. 37–54.

194 AA, pp. 512–13; *DULKJ*, vol. 1, pp. 104–5 (no. 8); RRR, no. 30.

195 'de statu regni et Ecclesiæ Iherosolymitanæ'. Bartolf, p. 519. It was as a result of this gathering that Daibert was appointed patriarch. See above, pp. 199–200. For a brief discussion of the Christmas gathering, see: Hamilton, *Latin Church*, p. 16.

196 'Sub Gotefrido duce . . . conventus ingens factus est in Hierusalem, ab omnibus qui sunt in oriente Christicolis, maximeque qui vel Antiochię vel in Syria, Rohas vel Palestina resederant peregrinis, in tantum, ut in ipsis nativitatis dominicę festis quam plures regionibus adiacentibus consecrarentur episcopi'. Frutolf 1106, pp. 158–60, tr. p. 159.

197 AA, pp. 506–11; *CPC*, no. 459.

198 AA, pp. 508–9.

199 On the Venetian involvement in the early phases of Latin settlement in the Holy Land, see: Elena Bellomo, 'The First Crusade and the Latin East as Seen From Venice: The Account of the Translatio sancti Nicolai', *Early Medieval Europe*, 17 (2009), 420–43.

200 Bartolf, p. 520.

201 'Qui confessione delictorum suorum in uera cordis compunctione et lacrimis peracta, dominici uero corporis et sanguinis communione percepta, sic spirituali scuto munitus et protecus, ab hac luce subtractus est'. AA, pp. 514–15. The nature of the illness which claimed Godfrey's life is unclear; Frutolf of Michelsberg's 1106 continuator states that Godfrey was only one of a number of victims of a pestilence that inflicted many casualties among the Latins in the summer of 1100. Frutolf 1106, p. 160, tr. pp. 159–60.

202 'Mortuo igitur tam egregio duce et nobilissimo Christi athleta . . . maxima lamenta et nimius ploratus omnibus illic Christianis, Gallis, Italicis, Syris, Armenicis et Grecis, gentilibus plerisque Sarracenis, Arabitis, Turcis, fuere per quinque dies'. AA, pp. 514–7. For the date see: *CPC*, no. 482.

203 'tanta se mansuetudine coniunxerat tam indigenis quam comperegrinis, ut vix adverteretur, Francisne plus plangeretur quam Syris vel Grecis'. Frutolf 1106, p. 160, tr. p. 160.

204 'Ad caput hoc anni post captum contigit urbem, | Ad meriti cumulum Dominus tibi, dux Godefride, | Contigit hoc regnum. sed tempore non diuturno | Tu perfunctus eo, natura dante, ruisti. | Orto sole semel sub fervescente Leone, | Aethera scandisti laetans, Michaele levante'. FC, pp. 350–1, tr. p. 136.

205 AA, pp. 516–17; Frutolf 1106, p. 160, tr. p. 160 (which states that the tomb was made of Parian stone). On Godfrey's tomb, see: Pringle, *Churches*, vol. 3, pp. 64–5; Jaroslav Folda, *The Art of the Crusaders in the Holy Land, 1098–1187* (Cambridge, 1995), pp. 37–40. A number of visitors to Jerusalem in the centuries after 1100 reported seeing Godfrey's resting place. Vicenzo Fava visited the Holy Land in the seventeenth century and included a drawing of Godfrey's tomb in his account. See: Vicenzo Fava, *Relatione del Viaggio di Gierusalemme*, British Library, MS. Add. 33566, fol. 90r. The tomb was destroyed along with several of his successors' in a fire in 1808.

206 AA, pp. 520–3.

207 AA pp. 522–5.

208 AA, pp. 538–9, speaks of Tancred travelling to Jerusalem in the hope of corrupting the guards placed in the Tower of David. Bartolf, p. 520, also describes the sending of the message from Jerusalem to Baldwin in Edessa, though does not name any of the protagonists. On the succession of Baldwin, see: Alan V.

Murray, 'Daimbert of Pisa, the *Domus Godefridi* and the Accession of Baldwin I of Jerusalem', in *FCTJ*, pp. 81–102; Idem, *Crusader Kingdom*, pp. 94–7.

209 Murray, 'Daimbert of Pisa', p. 89.

210 'in nimios ploratus et lamenta cor Baldwini defluxit'. AA, pp. 528–9; 'dolens aliquantulum de fratris morte, sed plus gaudens de hereditate'. FC, p. 353, tr. 2.1.

211 Bartolf, pp. 520–1; FC, pp. 352–70, tr. pp. 137–43; AA, pp. 528–41.

212 AA, pp. 540–1.

213 AA, pp. 540–1.

214 'unde ab omnibus iureiurando firmatus, in throno Ierusalem potenter exaltatus gloriose resedit'. AA, pp. 540–1.

215 Bartolf, p. 523; FC, pp. 368–9, tr. p. 143.

216 Bartolf, p. 523; FC, 385, tr. 148; AA, 550–1. The location, setting and form of Baldwin's inauguration were all intended to convey liturgical messages aimed at bolstering his new royal authority. See: Simon John, 'Liturgical Culture and Royal Inauguration in the Latin Kingdom of Jerusalem, 1099–1187', *JMH*, 43 (2017) (forthcoming).

217 See above, p. 184.

218 AA, pp. 550–1.

219 Though note that it was some time before the papacy accepted the status of Jerusalem as a kingdom. See: John, 'The papacy', pp. 232–5.

6 Conclusion

This book has examined the ancestry and career of Godfrey of Bouillon. It has considered his involvement in the First Crusade, but has also investigated his experiences in the West and the careers of his forebears. By exploring the ways in which Godfrey's formative experiences and dynastic influences may have shaped his worldview and outlook, the book has aimed to shed new light on his activities on the expedition which brought him to wider historical attention.

The opening chapter examined the history of the house of Ardennes-Bouillon, Godfrey's maternal forebears, focussing on the eleventh century. It suggested that its most prominent members were active in Lotharingia and further afield in the Western Empire. Most significantly, the family had meaningful connections to the reform papacy between the 1050s and 1070s. Godfrey the Bearded emerged as the principal secular supporter of the papacy in Italy in the mid-eleventh century. His brother Frederick (Godfrey of Bouillon's great-uncle) held the office in 1057–1058 as Stephen IX. Godfrey the Hunchback enjoyed amicable relations with Gregory VII in the years after his election as pope in 1073. Moreover, the house of Ardennes-Bouillon had close ties to the bishop of Liège and the monks of St Hubert. The chapter also surveyed the history of the comital house of Boulogne (his paternal lineage) and identified channels of communication to which the family belonged in the latter part of the eleventh century. The chapter also discussed Godfrey's paternal ancestry, detailing the participation of his father, Eustace II of Boulogne, in the Norman Conquest of England, and the epistolary activities of his mother, Ida of Boulogne.

The second chapter focussed on Godfrey's career in the West. It speculated on the possible course of his life before he emerged in contemporary sources when, in 1076, at the age of about sixteen, he succeeded his uncle Godfrey the Hunchback to the lands and holdings of the house of Ardennes-Bouillon. It was posited that Godfrey may have been associated with his uncle before this time. The chapter then charted Godfrey's career in Lotharingia. He supported the institution of the Peace of God by his kinsman Bishop Henry of Liège in about 1082, and interacted with reform-minded prelates, including the abbots of St Hubert and St Laurent. He was appointed to the office of duke of Lower Lotharingia in 1087. While other modern studies have suggested that Godfrey was a close partisan of Henry IV during his time in Lotharingia, this book has taken a different view, arguing that the contemporary evidence which ties Godfrey to Henry is problematic, and that sources written in proximity to Henry make no mention of a strong political connection to Godfrey. Moreover, at times Godfrey was at odds with Henry's surrogates in Lotharingia, among whom were Count Albert III of Namur and Bishop Otbert of Liège.

The third chapter discussed Godfrey's response to the appeal for the First Crusade, and explored the ways in which his response may have been shaped by his formative experiences and by dynastic precedents. Significant in this respect were the activities of his father in support of William the Conqueror in 1066, the connections of members of the house of Ardennes-Bouillon to the reform papacy, the long-standing tendency of the monks of St Hubert to instruct members of the family on sin and penitence, and Godfrey's involvement in the institution of the Peace of God in Liège by his kinsman Bishop Henry. Moreover, Godfrey belonged to a number of communication networks which encompassed prominent secular and ecclesiastical figures, and which permeated the notional frontier between Lotharingia (and the kingdom of Germany) and the kingdom of France, thereby connecting Godfrey to elites in northern France, Normandy, and England. It is clear that Godfrey responded to Urban II's appeal for the expedition, and was not stimulated to join the crusade by the preaching activities of Peter the Hermit. It was also suggested that Godfrey's decision to join the First Crusade may have been at least in part a result of the fact that his time as duke between 1087 and 1095 had been – in comparison to his predecessors' careers – relatively inauspicious and constrained. Indeed, 'Godfrey of Bouillon' may have become so-known because, in contrast to his predecessors, who had wielded considerable influence in Lotharingia and beyond, he was primarily associated with his family's chief holding near the Middle Meuse.

The fourth chapter charted Godfrey's exploits on the First Crusade, investigating his role in each of the military set pieces of the expedition and in the machinations between its most prominent participants. It identified the different ways in which the various sources present his character and activities, and suggested that while Godfrey consistently garnered praise for his exploits in combat, and thereby earned himself a reputation as an accomplished warrior, in respect of the overall direction of the First Crusade, he was consistently outshone by Bohemond (an exceptional general and wily strategist) and Raymond of Toulouse (who had the deepest pockets and possessed the greatest prestige among the leaders). It was only in the last months of the First Crusade in 1099 that Godfrey rose to prominence among the leaders, and, even then, his ascendance was only partially a result of his own conduct. Godfrey maintained mutually supportive relations with his brothers during the course of the First Crusade. Godfrey and Baldwin marched from Lotharingia and joined up with Eustace – who had travelled with the other forces from northern France – at Constantinople. Thereafter, the three brothers worked to support each other's interests during the expedition. Baldwin enjoyed success pursuing his own ambitions after he departed the main forces, and this culminated in his acquisition of Edessa in 1098. Thereafter, Baldwin supported his brothers in their efforts during the siege of Antioch. As Godfrey neared death in the summer of 1100, he nominated his younger brother to succeed him in Jerusalem. Similarly, Eustace seems to have explored his own interests at points during the expedition: for example, in late 1098, he persisted in Raymond of Toulouse's attack on Marra, after Godfrey had departed the city. For the most part, though, Eustace remained closely associated with Godfrey. He fought with his younger brother atop the siege tower at Jerusalem. After Godfrey was appointed ruler of Jerusalem, Eustace worked as his agent by accepting the surrender of Nablus in his name.

The fifth chapter examined the circumstances in which Godfrey was chosen as the first ruler of Latin Jerusalem in July 1099, suggesting that he did not take the title of king upon assuming the office. The chapter then explored various explanations for why he did not take a royal title, highlighting the possibility that he simply adopted a pragmatic approach out of deference to the interests of others. The chapter then considered the course of his year-long tenure in the Holy City and evidence which sheds light on his role in the establishment of new institutions in Latin Jerusalem, before examining his death and the succession of his brother Baldwin, who was inaugurated king of Jerusalem in Bethlehem on Christmas Day 1100.

The book has considered a range of sources which cast Godfrey in different lights. The texts which detail the careers of Godfrey's ancestors and his experiences in the West were written in the age of the 'Investiture Conflict', and so focus chiefly on the struggles of the German crown against the Saxon rebels and the reform papacy. The accounts written in the kingdom of Germany – such as the *Annals of Niederaltaich* and the work of Lampert of Hersfeld, Berthold of Reichenau, Bernold of St Blasien, and Frutolf of Michelberg – refer to the activities of the members of the house of Ardennes-Bouillon only when they were relevant to the wider dimensions of the 'Investiture Conflict'. An important exception in this regard is Frutolf's 1106 continuator, who provided important insights into the response to the First Crusade in Germany and Godfrey's actions on the expedition. Of the authors who worked in Lotharingia, Sigebert of Gembloux referred to Godfrey only very infrequently. While the author of the *Cantatorium* did provide much more information on Godfrey's career in the West, he did so only when it helped to detail how St Hubert acquired its lands and property in the eleventh and early twelfth centuries. This author included in his account very little about the First Crusade, and said nothing about Godfrey's exploits on the expedition.

The study of Godfrey's exploits on the First Crusade and in Jerusalem relied above all on the Latin chronicles of the expedition. While these texts provide much detail on this phase of his life, they must be approached critically. The *Gesta Francorum* and the accounts based on it focus chiefly on Bohemond, and generally accord Godfrey a less prominent role. The *Gesta Francorum* itself is dominated by the 'most valiant champion of Christ' Bohemond, and its narrative accentuates events at Antioch in order to maximise Bohemond's importance to the crusade.[1] After Bohemond left the crusade in the aftermath of the capture of Antioch, the narrative of the *Gesta Francorum* recounted the course of the rest of the expedition without bringing Godfrey or any other of the leaders to the fore. Peter Tudebode made a few alterations to the *Gesta Francorum*, several of which shed further light on Godfrey's activities at certain points during the crusade. While Raymond of Aguilers drew from the *Gesta Francorum*, his substantially original account provides a southern French perspective which counterbalances the *Gesta*'s focus on Bohemond. Raymond of Aguilers' proximity to Raymond of Toulouse meant that he was privy to the interactions between the leaders of the expedition. While this chronicler devoted much of his attention to the ongoing conflict between Raymond and Bohemond, he nonetheless provided valuable information on matters relating to Godfrey. The 'Bartolf' text likely conveys a sense of what Fulcher of Chartres included in his recension. In both the 'Bartolf' text and Fulcher's extant version, Godfrey is devoted no more attention than any of the other leaders of the First Crusade.

In contrast to the sources of the *Gesta Francorum* tradition, Godfrey is indisputably the chief protagonist of Albert of Aachen's account of the First Crusade. Albert consistently casts Godfrey as the dominant figure on the crusade, the individual who had the greatest role in the shaping of the expedition's course. He is depicted fighting with superlative skill in practically every military encounter, and as a pious Christian who was devoted to the aims of the expedition. Albert also used Godfrey at several points as a mouthpiece for articulating the theological significance of the crusade. Crucially, whereas the narratives of the *Gesta Francorum* and the accounts which were based on it often hinged on providential intervention – Raymond of Aguilers' treatment of the discovery of the Holy Lance represents a prime example of this – Albert for the most part adopted an approach toward causation which prized the role of human agency on the crusade. Yet, in the sections of his account in which Albert did accord influence to divine intervention, Godfrey acts as the cornerstone. This approach toward articulating the cosmic significance of the crusade is most obvious in his description of the trilogy of visions which he claimed presaged that Godfrey had been selected by God to become the ruler of Jerusalem. As a result, while the sources of the *Gesta Francorum* tradition characterised the entire crusading army as God's elect, in Albert's account of the crusade Godfrey stands alone as the human conduit through which divine will had been enacted. Morris has argued that Albert's portrayal of Godfrey was intended to convey the sense that the First Crusade as a whole had benefitted from divine support.[2] However, since Albert consistently singled Godfrey out from the rest of the crusaders, the sense that emerges from his account is not that God had benevolently overseen the progress of the crusade as a whole, but that He had intervened through His sponsorship of Godfrey.

It is striking that the Lotharingian and imperial evidence focussed on Godfrey's ancestry and career in the West barely mentioned his activities after his departure on the First Crusade, while the sources devoted to the crusade related hardly anything about his exploits before he set out on the expedition. In contemporary perception, then, there was something of a disjuncture between Godfrey's career in the West and his time on the crusade. The explanation for this must lie in the fact that the repercussions of the 'Investiture Conflict' continued to reverberate in the Empire in the late eleventh century and the first years of the twelfth. As a result, many of the chroniclers who wrote from an imperial perspective were not disposed to extol the achievements of the papally-instigated First Crusade. Moreover, even the authors in the kingdom of Germany who were aligned with the papacy – such as the author of the *Cantatorium* – were often concerned above all to detail the repercussions of the 'Investiture Conflict' in their own locality. It was no doubt for this reason that Albert of Aachen overlooked Urban II's role in the origin of the First Crusade, and focussed instead on the activities of Peter the Hermit. For the expedition itself, Godfrey, the holder of one of the principal secular offices of the kingdom of Germany, constituted a politically acceptable protagonist. As a result of this disinterest in – or perhaps ignorance of – Godfrey's background and origin, the contemporary authors of the First Crusade made nothing of the associations of the house or Ardennes-Bouillon with the reform papacy. Where the authors of the crusade did accord more attention to Godfrey than the other leaders of the expedition, they chiefly did so in relation to his appointment as ruler of Jerusalem in July 1099. In the eyes of contemporary authors, this event, more than any other, differentiated Godfrey from the rest of the leading crusaders.

Among the contemporary portrayals of Godfrey, a number of recurrent patterns emerge. He repeatedly garnered praise for his skill as a warrior. Lampert of Hersfeld wrote that at the point of Godfrey the Hunchback's death in 1076, Godfrey was 'an energetic young man, very eager for military action'.[3] This is an assessment of Godfrey that appears to have held true for the rest of his life. Even taking into account Albert of Aachen's predilection for lauding Godfrey, it is clear that he fought well during the military encounters of the First Crusade. Comparing the accounts of the various battles and skirmishes of the crusade demonstrates that on a number of occasions, Albert provided detailed accounts of Godfrey's exploits in a given encounter, which the *Gesta Francorum* or one of its derivatives corroborated by noting simply that he had fought well, without giving more precise details. The most revealing example of this trend emerges in the various reports of the battle fought in early March 1098 near the Bridge Gate at Antioch. Raymond of Aguilers remarked that in that encounter Godfrey distinguished himself by forcing an enemy contingent to split into two, while Albert provided a detailed report of how in that battle Godfrey, with a single blow, sliced an armoured Muslim warrior clean in two.[4] Albert's hyperbole, then, is compatible with the respect accorded to Godfrey's exploits in the sources of the *Gesta Francorum* tradition.

Albert of Aachen sought to cast Godfrey as a profoundly pious man who was beyond reproach in spiritual matters. However, a closer study of Godfrey's conduct hints at a more complex picture. A feature of his behaviour was an apparent tendency to act out of self-interest rather than in support of ecclesiastical figures or out of pure spiritual concerns. The author of the *Cantatorium* subtly reproached Godfrey for being slow to come to the assistance of the deposed abbots of St Hubert and St Laurent in the early 1090s, and implied that Godfrey had even attempted to benefit – at St Hubert's expense – from the problems which Bishop Otbert had created in the diocese of Liège in that era. Moreover, Godfrey's efforts on the crusade sometimes seemed to have been intended to bolster his own position rather than benefit the expedition as a whole. After the First Crusaders captured Antioch, for example, Godfrey was content to devote his energy to attempting to establish a fief in the region between Antioch and Edessa. Several months elapsed before he sought to act as the spearhead of the popular clamour to go to Jerusalem. In many respects, he does not seem to have behaved all that differently to Raymond of Toulouse, but, fortunately for him, he managed to avoid earning the obloquy that was heaped upon Raymond for his apparent fixation on carving out a lordship. Whether or not Godfrey abstained from the slaughter carried out by the crusaders on 15 July in Jerusalem, he shared in the spoils which Tancred appropriated from the Templum Domini as the crusaders overran the city. While it has sometimes been suggested that in July 1099 Godfrey acquiesced to clerical concerns by avoiding a royal title, equally, he may also have acted out of expedience in doing so.

Godfrey's interactions with the range of figures whom he encountered during the course of the First Crusade are revealing of his predilections. He was not beyond adopting an aggressive approach in his dealings with the other leaders of the crusade. He threatened violence against Bohemond in the first part of 1098 in order to gain a pavilion which had originally been gifted to him, and did so again to Raymond of Toulouse in July 1099 to wrest control of the Tower of David. Godfrey appears to have been instructed in the art of realpolitik. Throughout the First Crusade, he enjoyed amicable relations with Robert of Flanders, despite the fact that Robert's father had been a longtime adversary of Godfrey the Hunchback, and had even been implicated in the fatal attack upon Godfrey's uncle in 1076. Moreover, it is crucial to point out that Godfrey's interactions with other potentates were not automatically conditioned by their religious beliefs. During the expedition, Godfrey pursued an alliance with Omar, the lord of Azaz, and as ruler of Jerusalem, he reputedly enjoyed amicable relations with the Muslim rulers of nearby cities, permitting trade between Christians and Muslims in Jerusalem and Jaffa. Divested of the anti-Muslim rhetoric which characterised Urban II's preaching as well as the chronicles of the First Crusade, Godfrey's deportment on the crusade is suggestive of a man who was comfortable dealing with potentates who had vastly different backgrounds, beliefs, and worldviews. His formative experiences in the cultural and political melting pot of Lotharingia might well have prepared him in this regard.

In many ways, Godfrey's time in Lotharingia set the parameters for his career on the First Crusade. His decision to respond positively to the appeal for the expedition, his dealings with other prominent figures, and the circumstances in which his brother succeeded him in 1100 were all contingent, to greater and lesser extents, on the course of his life before he departed on the expedition. Unlike our medieval forebears, then, modern historians cannot overlook the experiences of Godfrey, duke of Lower Lotharingia, if they are fully to understand the career of Godfrey, First Crusader and ruler of Latin Jerusalem.

Notes

1 'fortissimus Christi athleta', in *GF*, p. 29; Wolf, 'Crusade and Narrative', pp. 211–16.
2 '[In] a certain sense . . . Godfrey [stands] in this chronicle as [a representative] of God's purpose in the place which, in the French tradition, had been occupied by Pope Urban and the whole crusading host'. Morris, 'The Aims and Spirituality', p. 112.
3 See above, p. 57.
4 See above, pp. 139–41.

Epilogue
Godfrey's reputation in the twelfth and thirteenth centuries

The First Crusade was a defining moment in history. The names of its most prominent participants quickly became emblazoned onto the collective consciousness of Latin Christendom. Some of those who took part in the expedition came to be revered in their own lifetimes. Veterans who returned to Europe in the years after 1099 were celebrated for their exploits. Robert of Normandy was welcomed home as a conquering hero, while Robert of Flanders gained the sobriquet 'Robert the Jerusalemite'.[1] Bohemond very deliberately harnessed his reputation as a leading figure in the crusade when he toured France in 1106–1107 to recruit men for his expedition against the Byzantine Empire, regaling audiences with stories of his exploits in the Holy Land.[2] As Godfrey remained in the Holy Land after the end of the First Crusade and died only a year later, it was left to others to shape his reputation.

The success of the First Crusade created shockwaves which permeated throughout the Latin Christian world. Contemporaries expressed a sense of appreciative wonder at the capture of Jerusalem, and instantly regarded that event as a pivotal moment in Christian history.[3] In the early twelfth century, there was an explosion of historiographical interest in the expedition, and further monumental accounts of the crusade were composed in the period down to the end of the thirteenth century. In ecclesiastical houses throughout the West, scribes patiently copied manuscripts of these texts, the circulation of which in turn further helped to spread information about the crusade.[4] As Bull and Kempf have put it, the First Crusade 'lived on in and through the transmission of its textual articulations' and 'remained an active site of memory through the sustained demand for copies of narratives of it'.[5] As a result, reports and stories concerning the events of 1096–1099 were transmitted widely throughout Latin Christendom. Crucially, even as the capture of Jerusalem was still fresh in the mind, writers began to use the First Crusade as a benchmark for assessing subsequent crusading activity. In 1101–1102, a new wave of crusaders set out from areas including northern Italy, Burgundy, and Germany, before travelling through Europe and Asia Minor, where they were defeated by the Turks. The failure of the expeditions of 1101–1102 served to add lustre to the memory of the First Crusade and its participants.[6] Purkis has suggested that very soon after its conclusion, the expedition which culminated in 1099 was 'allocated a numerical "first-ness"', that is, it came to be regarded as the first in a sequence of military campaigns conducted under the banner of the cross.[7] The memory of the First Crusade permeated Latin Christendom in other ways; for example, in the twelfth and thirteenth centuries, noble families extolled the achievements of ancestors who had taken part in the expedition.[8] It was these two linked processes – the writing of crusade history, and the exaltation of the memory of the First Crusade – that set the framework for how Godfrey was remembered in the two centuries after his death.[9] The following pages will sketch in broad terms how his reputation evolved in that time, in anticipation of a more comprehensive study of the process.

During the first half of the twelfth century, the success of the First Crusade was widely celebrated throughout Latin Christendom, in texts including prose histories, poems, and liturgy, as well as in sculpture, paintings, and other visual depictions.[10] One author who wrote in this era declaimed that the expedition was a 'noble and marvellous theme for exposition', while another noted that its history 'deserves to be publicised through a faithful account as much to those living now as for future generations, so that through it the Christian's hope in God may be strengthened and more praise inspired in their minds'.[11] As previously noted, an array of historical accounts of the crusade were composed in the early twelfth century. Between about 1105 and 1110, Robert the Monk, Baldric of Bourgueil, and Guibert of Nogent each used the *Gesta Francorum* as the basis for their own chronicles of the crusade.[12] They all concluded that the *Gesta Francorum* was insufficiently sophisticated to commemorate the crusade fittingly, and they sought in their own accounts to place the expedition within a more elaborate theological framework.[13] Robert's account achieved an astonishing level of popularity; around 100 manuscripts of it were produced between the twelfth and seventeenth centuries, prompting Bull and Kempf, the text's most recent editors, to deem it 'a medieval "bestseller"'.[14] Gilo of Paris probably wrote his *Historia vie Hierosolimitane* – an account of the crusade in Latin verse – within a few years of Bohemond's visit to France in 1106–1107.[15] His work survives in five copies, one of which contains substantial additions by an author known as the Charleville Poet. Other authors of this era included treatments of the First Crusade in wider historiographical projects. Between 1112 and 1118 Ralph of Caen wrote the *Gesta Tancredi*, a biography of Tancred, in which he treated the First Crusade at length.[16] Orderic Vitalis wrote his *Historia Ecclesiastica* at the monastery of St Evroul on the southern frontier of Normandy between about 1122 and his death in 1142.[17] Orderic devoted book IX (*c*.1135) of his *Historia* to the First Crusade. William of Malmesbury finished the first version of his *Gesta Regum Anglorum* in about 1125. He included an account of the First Crusade in book IV.[18]

In the texts which formed part of this early–twelfth-century wave of writing on the First Crusade, Godfrey is cast in a particular light. While the *Gesta*

Francorum and its earliest derivatives exhibited a cautious respect for Godfrey, the authors who contributed to the new wave of historiography on the crusade were much more fulsome in their praise of him, especially his skill as a warrior. Baldric described Godfrey as a 'very shrewd and fierce warrior' and a 'most fierce knight'.[19] Guibert asserted that Godfrey was 'worthy of the title duke, a model warrior'.[20] Ralph believed that Godfrey stood comparison with one of the most renowned warriors from history, noting that he 'gave up nothing to Hector in fervor, in strength, in will or in spirit. He excelled in arms and was happy'.[21] William related that although Godfrey brought 'great companies to battle in his train; and though his knights were tough and experienced, none was found either readier than he to join battle or more effective when it was joined'.[22] Gilo referred to Godfrey at one point in his account as *dux Bullicus* ('the duke of Bouillon'). Intriguingly, this phrase is rendered in two of the surviving manuscripts of his account as *dux bellicus*: 'the duke of war'.[23] These writers extolled Godfrey's martial ability by recounting stories about his exploits in battle. Guibert, the Charleville Poet, and William all discussed the story of his fight with a wild bear.[24] Authors including Guibert, Robert, Orderic, Gilo, and Ralph of Caen also included in their account the story of Godfrey cutting an armoured Muslim warrior in two in a battle fought during the siege of Antioch.[25]

A number of the authors who worked in this era also sought to cast Godfrey as a sincere and devout Christian. Gilo of Paris related that in the aftermath of the capture of Antioch, Godfrey's motives for encouraging the crusaders to resume the march to Jerusalem were pure and unselfish.[26] Guibert asserted that 'no one was wiser in his faith in God' than Godfrey.[27] Robert the Monk described Godfrey as a 'shining light of Christendom'.[28] Significantly, Guibert and Robert even suggested that God had intervened in the First Crusade to assist Godfrey at certain moments. According to Guibert, Baldwin of Bourcq asserted that Godfrey and his men believed that they enjoyed support from God.[29] Robert stated that during one clash at the siege of Antioch 'God looked after his soldier' by ensuring that Godfrey escaped unscathed.[30] Robert also related that as Godfrey fought atop his tower with sword and bow during the siege of Jerusalem, 'the Lord guided his hand in the battle and his fingers in the combat'.[31] Most of the writers of this era asserted that Godfrey had taken the title of king of Jerusalem; Robert, Baldric, Guibert, Orderic, and William all state that Godfrey assumed a royal title.[32] Guibert, William, and Orderic all attributed the theological concern with wearing a crown of thorns in the Holy City to Godfrey rather than his brother and successor, Baldwin.[33]

Most significantly, several of the authors of this era directly linked the martial and spiritual sides of Godfrey's character. Robert drew a direct connection between Godfrey's pious demeanour and his prowess as a warrior:

Godfrey was handsome, of lordly bearing, eloquent, of distinguished character, and so lenient with his soldiers as to give the impression of being a monk rather than a soldier. However, when he realised that the enemy was at hand and battle imminent, his courage became abundantly evident and like a roaring lion he feared the attack of no man. What breastplate or shield could withstand the thrust of his sword?[34]

Ralph believed that the military and spiritual were effectively fused in Godfrey because he had inherited the distinct qualities of his warlike father and his pious mother:

> The nobility of [Godfrey] was marked by many virtues, both secular and divine. These included, charity to the poor, mercy to wrongdoers, humility, clemency, sobriety, justice and chastity. In fact, the duke demonstrated more of the qualities of a monk than he did of a soldier. However, he was not less experienced in secular virtues. He knew how to wage war, to arrange a line of battle and to find glory in arms. As a youth, he was the first or among the first in learning to kill the enemy. He grew more skilled as a young man and did not give up his practise as a mature man. Thus as the son of a fighting count and a most religious countess, even when he had been observed by a rival he deserved to hear: 'in the eagerness for war look to the father, in his cultivation of God behold the mother.'[35]

This author also described Godfrey more succinctly – yet no less significantly – as 'a man totally devoted to war and to God'.[36]

The presentations of Godfrey as a pious warrior were consonant with the wider spirit of celebration that characterised Latin Christian attitudes towards the crusades in the first half of the twelfth century. This was an era in which the crusaders' feat of capturing Jerusalem continued to be widely extolled, and in which the Latin states founded in the Holy Land were experiencing notable successes.[37] The depictions of Godfrey which took shape in this era may also be seen as echoing wider contemporary discussions on spirituality which were instigated by the crusades, and above all, by the establishment of the Military Orders. In his *De Laude Novae Militiae* (1128–1131), Bernard of Clairvaux deliberated whether the Knights Templar ought to be classed as monks or as warriors. To him, the Templars

> in some wonderful, unique way [seemed] to be meeker than lambs and fiercer than lions, so that I am almost in doubt whether they ought to be called knights or monks. Unless, of course I were to call them by both names, which would be more exact, as they are known to have the gentleness of a monk and the bravery of a knight.[38]

The parallel between Bernard's description of the Templars and the image of Godfrey fashioned by writers in this era is striking. Bernard's aim in writing the *De Laude* was to depict the Templars as perfect spiritual warriors who were ideally suited to protect the Latin East. Similar considerations may well have conditioned how writers of the first half of the twelfth century depicted Godfrey, the first ruler of Latin Jerusalem.

The atmosphere of optimism and celebration which was stimulated in Latin Christendom by the success of the First Crusade was severely jolted by the loss of Edessa to Muslim forces on Christmas Eve 1144. In the years that followed, the West organised a new large-scale crusade, an expedition which became known as the Second Crusade. The memory of 1099 seems to have been strong in the minds of figures involved in the new expedition. Pope Eugenius III (1145–1153) stated in *Quantum Praedecessores* – the bull that he issued to promote the call for the new crusade – that he had 'learned from what men of old have said and we have found written in their histories' about the First Crusade.[39] He challenged those who took part in the Second Crusade to seek to emulate the achievements of those who had helped capture Jerusalem.[40] Significantly, however, Eugenius conjured up the memory of the First Crusade as a whole, rather than pinpointing any of its leading participants. A similar interpretation may be seen in the Anglo-Norman nobleman Brian FitzCount's 1143 letter to Henry of Blois, bishop of Winchester. In that missive, Brian affirmed that he had reflected upon the history of the First Crusade, and that his cogitations had galvanised his conviction to support the Empress Matilda in her struggle to claim the English throne from King Stephen. In the letter, he listed the expedition's chief participants as Stephen of Blois (King Stephen's father), Robert of Normandy, Raymond of Toulouse, Bohemond, Robert of Flanders, Eustace of Boulogne, and Godfrey.[41] While Brian did note that Godfrey was appointed ruler of Jerusalem, he did not substantially differentiate Godfrey from the other leading participants of the crusade. On balance, then, in the mid-twelfth century, the most prominent figures in the First Crusade were generally accorded equal status in recollections of expedition.

The fall of Edessa and the failure of the Second Crusade prompted a significant readjustment in wider attitudes toward crusade history and in perceptions of the Latin East. Afterwards, it became clear to Latin Christian observers that the security of the states founded by the First Crusaders was in grave danger. Between 1144 and 1187, the Latin East was increasingly reliant on assistance from the West for its survival.[42] At the same time, the Muslim powers of Syria and Egypt became increasingly united in opposition to the Latins in the Holy Land, principally as a result of the efforts of Nur ad-Din and Saladin. At the battle of Hattin on 4 July 1187, Saladin's army defeated the combined military forces of the Latin East, and, in the months that followed, captured Jerusalem and much of the Latin-held territory in the Holy Land.[43] In the years between the Second Crusade and Hattin, the Latins who inhabited the Holy Land were aware that their plight was growing increasingly parlous, just as the nearby Muslim powers were becoming united against them. In the early 1180s one observer who wrote in Jerusalem mournfully noted that

> the enemy has become stronger than ourselves, and we who used to
> triumph over our foes and customarily bore away the glorious palm

of victory, now, deprived of divine favour, retire from the field in igno-
minious defeat after nearly every conflict.[44]

The era of celebration inaugurated by the success of the First Crusade was
over. Latin Christian authors who wrote in the second half of the twelfth
century continued to extol the memory of 1099. But many also sought to
employ its memory to encourage efforts aimed at preserving the Latin East.
This recalibration in attitudes toward the Latin East and crusading history
underpinned how Godfrey was portrayed in this era.

While the second half of the twelfth century witnessed the composition
of fewer full-length accounts of the First Crusade than in the years down to
about 1144, one of the most significant treatments of the expedition dates
to this period. Working between about 1170 and 1184, William of Tyre wrote
a monumental *Historia* of the First Crusade and Latin East.[45] William held
important offices in the kingdom of Jerusalem, serving as chancellor from
1174 and archbishop of Tyre from 1175. He was closely associated with the
monarchy of Latin Jerusalem. He apparently began writing at the behest
of King Amalric, and he acted as tutor to Amalric's young son, the future
Baldwin IV. William's authorial aims evolved over the course of his career.
Most significantly, while he was in the West attending the Third Lateran
Council in 1179, he gained insights into how he could tailor the *Historia* to
a Western audience. Thereafter, he seems to have written with the aim of
encouraging people in the West to support the Latin East.[46] He also sought
to demonstrate that the ruling dynasty of Latin Jerusalem had a glorious
and rich history.[47] William drew from a wide range of evidence, including
the *Gesta Francorum* (or a related text), the chronicles of Raymond of Aguilers, Fulcher of Chartres, Baldric of Bourgueil, and the first six books of
Albert of Aachen's *Historia*. He also had access to the documents kept in
Jerusalem's chancery, and used spoken traditions on the First Crusade that
had been passed down through successive generations in the Latin East.

In William's eyes, the leading participants in the First Crusade were the
founding fathers of the kingdom of Jerusalem. Since Godfrey was the first
Latin ruler of the Holy City, he occupied an especially prominent place in
William's account. This author accumulated a wide range of stories and traditions regarding Godfrey. He explicitly noted at one point in his account
that in his day numerous tales about Godfrey circulated by word of mouth,
stating 'that many splendid deeds, well worthy of admiration, were done by
[Godfrey], works which even today are still told as familiar stories'.[48] Unlike
earlier chroniclers of the First Crusade, William collected a significant level
of information about Godfrey's life in the West. William knew that Godfrey had been a son of the comital house of Boulogne, which he correctly
identified as part of the kingdom of France.[49] William also included in his
account stories about Godfrey's youth, recounting a tradition which had it
that when he was very young, his mother Ida had received a vision which
foretold the future achievements of her progeny.[50] William noted that

Godfrey succeeded his uncle as duke of Lower Lotharingia, neatly sidestepping the fact that over a decade passed between Godfrey's the Hunchback's death and Godfrey's appointment as duke.[51] William devoted particular effort to extolling Godfrey's illustrious character and abilities as a warrior. He included in his *Historia* an account of Godfrey's fight with a bear.[52] He also related the tradition that Godfrey had bisected a Muslim warrior at Antioch, citing the story as enduring proof of his skill as a warrior.[53] William also asserted that Godfrey was 'a pious man, whose heart was filled with pious care for all that pertained to the honour of the house of God'.[54] Elsewhere, this author described Godfrey as 'a man of humble and gentle nature, who stood in fear of the rebuke of the Lord'.[55]

Since William aimed to emphasise the legitimacy of the ruling dynasty of Jerusalem, he sought to cast its founder in a positive light. He provided a unique account of the circumstances in which Godfrey was selected as the ruler of Jerusalem in July 1099. According to this chronicler, after the crusaders captured the Holy City, the retinues of each of the leading candidates were interviewed to ascertain which man was best suited to rule the city.[56] William affirmed that when Godfrey's men were interviewed, they complained that he often spent too long in church, staying behind to ask questions after religious services had concluded. According to the chronicler, the electors regarded this as a favourable quality, and promptly selected him to hold the office.[57] William omitted Albert of Aachen's suggestion that Godfrey accepted the appointment unwillingly, and stated that the clergy who argued at the time of Godfrey's election that the authority of Jerusalem's spiritual leader should hold the highest authority had acted out of self-interest.[58]

At several points in his *Historia*, William revealed that he was aware Godfrey had not held the title king of Jerusalem. In his prologue, which he wrote around 1183–1184, William noted that Christian kings had ruled in Jerusalem for 84 years, 'if Lord Godfrey who ruled there as duke be included'.[59] Elsewhere, he referred to Godfrey as 'the first Latin ruler of the kingdom of Jerusalem'.[60] William also noted that some of his contemporaries, 'not appreciating Godfrey's services, hesitate to place his name in the catalogue of kings'.[61] On the other hand, since William sought to assert the legitimacy of the ruling dynasty, he explicitly ascribed to Godfrey the royal title at certain points in his account. Indeed, in one passage, he asserted that Godfrey had been 'not merely a king, but the best of kings, a light and mirror to others'.[62] William included in his *Historia* the tradition that Godfrey had refused to wear a crown of gold, citing the story as proof of his inimitable temperament. Yet, William also sought to convey the sense that Godfrey's refusal to wear a crown in no way undermined his authority in Jerusalem (and, by extension, that of his successors).[63] In William's eyes, then, Godfrey was a heroic figure, a model for the chronicler's contemporaries to emulate.

In was in this period that there was a significant transformation in how the First Crusade was remembered. In the late twelfth century, in northern

France (most likely Picardy), three songs recounting the crusade which existed prior to that point in spoken form – the *Chanson d'Antioche*, the *Chanson des Chétifs* and the *Chanson de Jérusalem* – were reworked and amalgamated into a unified trilogy of *chansons de geste* known to modern scholars as the 'cycle rudimentaire'. The *Antioche* covers the First Crusade from its origins to the aftermath of the battle of Antioch.[64] The narrative of the *Jérusalem* commences with the crusaders' arrival at the Holy City, and describes how they captured it, before relating an embellished version of the battle of Ascalon.[65] *Les Chétifs* purports to describe events that took place after the events recounted in the *Chanson d'Antioche* and before those narrated in the *Jérusalem*, though its content seems to have been almost entirely confected.[66] Taken as a whole, the 'cycle rudimentaire' provides an embellished account of the history of the First Crusade from its origins to its conclusion. It is important to note that these songs' content was not primarily governed by the aim of providing a historically accurate account of the First Crusade, but by the conventions of the *chansons de geste*. Most significantly, these *chansons* may have been intended to serve as recruitment material for new crusading expeditions.

The *chansons* of the 'cycle rudimentaire' depict Godfrey as an epic hero in the mould of figures like Charlemagne and Roland. The *Antioche* and the *Jérusalem* repeatedly extol his noble character and military prowess. In the *Antioche*, most references to Godfrey are accompanied with an adjective or short description intended to cast him in a positive light. Hence, he is described with phrases including – but by no means limited to – 'brave and shrewd', 'noble-looking', and 'lion-hearted'.[67] The tradition of Godfrey hacking an enemy warrior in two is a recurrent thread in this song. The first allusion to the feat appears during the description of fighting that took place during the siege of Nicaea, at which point it is stated that Godfrey 'fell upon the Turks with furious determination; anyone he struck ended up sliced in half'.[68] At Antioch, he is ascribed with accomplishing the feat several times. It is recounted in one passage that Godfrey 'sliced a Turk in half right down to his lungs so that one half hung down on each side of the saddle'.[69] It is related that shortly after this, Godfrey's lance broke, prompting him to draw his sword: 'He struck a Saracen on top of his helmet, slicing downwards so far into his vital organs that the two halves hung right down to ground level'.[70] The passage culminates in the most fearsome iteration of the feat: 'The duke slashed straight through the spine so that one half of the Turk fell to the ground whilst the other half stayed in the golden saddle, the body gripping on tight though the soul had gone, with the leg as stiff as if it had been fixed in position'.[71] Later still, Godfrey is depicted cutting a mounted foe from the head to pelvis, with only the horse's saddle preventing his blade from slicing even further.[72] The tradition also reoccurs in the *Chanson de Jérusalem*. At one point in this song, Godfrey is described as cleaving an unfortunate warrior almost in two.[73] Later, it is related that after the crusaders had captured Jerusalem, Godfrey entered single combat with a Muslim warrior. Godfrey permitted his foe to strike two unopposed blows at the outset. Godfrey is described as cleaving both his foe and his foe's horse apart with a single blow of his sword, before sending the dismembered body to the sultan of Persia as a warning.[74] Towards the end of the song, Godfrey is once more described as enacting a similar kind of feat in the battle that followed the capture of Jerusalem.[75] Within a few generations of the First Crusade, then, this tradition had evidently become a cornerstone of Godfrey's reputation.

The songs also cast Godfrey as a man of profound piety. He is used in a number of passages in the *Antioche* to articulate the spiritual importance of the First Crusade. In one passage, Godfrey makes a heartfelt speech to encourage his fellow crusaders to maintain their efforts in the siege of Antioch. In that speech, Godfrey outlines the purpose of the First Crusade, and hubristically vows to take the fight against Islam on to Mecca itself.[76] The *Chanson de Jérusalem* repeatedly describes Godfrey as a devoted Christian, referring to him as 'much favoured by God' and 'Duke Godfrey, who placed a profound trust in God'.[77] He is customarily referred to throughout the song after his appointment as 'King Godfrey'.[78] The songs of the 'cycle rudimentaire' also feature the tradition that Godfrey refused a crown of gold upon his appointment as ruler of Jerusalem. At one point in the *Antioche* it is related that Godfrey 'did not wear a crown of beaten gold or other metal. Instead he had a circlet made for him from the garden of Saint Abraham'.[79] In the *Jérusalem*, Godfrey articulates the reason for this refusal: 'my lords . . . it is unthinkable that a crown of pure gold should ever be placed on my head. Jesus after all had a crown of thorns when He suffered for us; so my crown shall not be of gold, or silver, or brass'.[80] Godfrey is then said to have proceeded to the garden of St Abraham, where he picked some thorns which were fashioned into a crown.

In the second half of the twelfth century, images of Godfrey shifted in accordance with the atmosphere of concern created by the loss of Edessa and the failure of the Second Crusade. Godfrey was depicted in the songs of the 'cycle rudimentaire' and by William of Tyre as a heroic figure who had repeatedly exhibited his prowess by enacting remarkable martial feats. These portrayals of Godfrey may well have been intended to help generate much-needed support for the Latin East by encouraging would-be crusaders to seek to follow in Godfrey's footsteps and emulate his exploits.

Just as sources written around the time of the Second Crusade shed light on how Godfrey was remembered in the middle of the twelfth century, evidence dating to the time of battle of Hattin (4 July 1187) and the Third Crusade can be used to gauge the nature of his reputation in the years around 1200. The loss of Jerusalem in the aftermath of the defeat of the forces of the Latin East at Hattin fostered a renewed interest in the figures who had helped capture the city in 1099. The author of one of the

Old French continuations of William of Tyre's chronicle asserted that when Saladin captured Jerusalem in 1187, 'he found in the city two aged men; one was called Robert of Coudre who had been with Godfrey of Bouillon at the conquest'.[81] This claim is of considerable interest. Since an individual who participated in the First Crusade and who remained alive in 1187 would have had to have been about one hundred years old, it is unlikely to have been true. Yet, even if Robert of Coudre himself or William of Tyre's continuator invented this claim, it provides clear evidence that the capture of Jerusalem 1099 and its loss to Saladin's forces in 1187 were linked in contemporary perception. It is also of note that this author associated the capture of Jerusalem with Godfrey alone and not any other of the leading figures of the First Crusade.

In contrast, other chroniclers who wrote about the Third Crusade maintained an interest in the First Crusade as a whole. In the last years of the twelfth century, an author named Ambroise wrote an Old French verse account of Richard I of England's experiences on the Third Crusade. This author recorded that when Richard decided not to make an assault upon Jerusalem in the summer of 1192, many among his army were disappointed, and some were even critical of the king. Duke Hugh III of Burgundy reportedly sponsored the production of a bawdy song mocking Richard, only for the king to respond by ordering the composition of a poetic rebuttal. In commenting on this episode, Ambroise drew a comparison between men like Hugh and the participants in the First Crusade:

> [Never] will a good song be sung about such uncontrolled men, nor will God look upon their deeds as on those who went on a different pilgrimage, when Antioch was besieged and taken by force by our men. The story is still told of those for whom God gave the victory, of Bohemond and Tancred, who were distinguished pilgrims, and of Godfrey of Bouillon and high princes of high renown and of the others who died in the service of God, so that He gave back to them according to their desires and plans. He raised their deeds to great heights and they and all their family are exalted and still honoured.[82]

The early-thirteenth-century author of the *Itinerarium Peregrinorum et Gesta Regis Ricardi* – another text focussed on Richard's exploits on the Third Crusade – mournfully stated that before Saladin captured the Holy City in 1187:

> our people had held this most sacred city for around eighty-nine years. The victorious Christian force recovered it together with Antioch after the Gentile had held it for forty years . . . For in the year of Our Lord 1099 Bohemond, Raymond, Tancred, Duke Godfrey, Count Robert of Normandy and the other Franks had captured it and expelled the Saracens.[83]

Elsewhere in his account, this author followed Ambroise in asserting that the participants of the Third Crusade

> were not like the pilgrims who were once on the expedition to Antioch, which our people powerfully captured in a famous victory which is still related in the deeds of Bohemond and Tancred and Godfrey [of] Bouillon and the other most outstanding chiefs, who triumphed in so many glorious victories, whose feats even now are like food in the mouth of the narrator. Because they performed their service freely and wholeheartedly for God, God 'rewarded their labours' [Wisdom of Solomon, 10:17], and exalted their magnificent feats so that they would be remembered forever and all their descendants would also be praised with ample reverence.[84]

Ambroise and the author of the *Itinerarium* asserted that the participants in the Third Crusade were inferior to the men who had helped capture Jerusalem in 1099, further exemplifying how the memory of the First Crusade was used as a benchmark for assessing later crusading activity. A late twelfth-century scribe who copied Baldric of Bourgueil's account of the First Crusade included in his manuscript an original poem in which he praised all the 'great men' [*magnates*] of the First Crusade, listing Adhémar of Le Puy, Peter the Hermit, Godfrey, Baldwin, Stephen of Blois, Robert of Normandy, Hugh of Vermandois, Eustace, Bohemond and Raymond of Toulouse. As the scribe put it, '[many] excellent lords took part in this expedition, but the aforesaid were the greatest and all of the others followed these men'.[85] Around the end of the twelfth century and the beginning of the thirteenth, then, Godfrey for the most part continued to be remembered as one of a number of First Crusade heroes.

The loss of the Holy City in 1187 stunned Latin Christendom. Just as the capture of Jerusalem in 1099 inaugurated an era of celebration in the Latin Christian world, reports of its capture by Saladin sowed devastation in the West. It also ignited a new phase in the history of the crusades, for it stimulated a number of new large-scale expeditions which were aimed at recovering the Holy City. The century after 1187 witnessed the organisation and prosecution of a series of major crusades, including the Third (1187–1193), Fourth (1202–1204), Fifth (1217–1221), Sixth (1228–1229), Seventh (1248–1254), Eighth (1270) and Ninth (1271–1272).[86] Although the forces of the Sixth Crusade under Emperor Frederick II managed to restore Jerusalem to Christian rule in 1229, it was permanently lost in 1244. In 1291 Muslim forces finally overran the last vestiges of Latin territory in the Holy Land. Between 1187 and 1291, Latin Christians often expressed the aim of recovering Jerusalem and rebuilding the Latin East. These were ambitions which were widespread throughout the West: at the Fourth Lateran Council in 1215, for example, it was declared that the *negotium Terrae Sanctae* – 'the business of the Holy Land' – was the concern of all Christendom.[87] This atmosphere, which combined devastation at the loss of Jerusalem with desperation for its recovery, conditioned another shift in perceptions of Godfrey. In the thirteenth century, then, he was often held up more explicitly than before as a paradigm of behaviour.

In the first quarter of the thirteenth century, an unknown author translated William of Tyre's *Historia* into Old French.[88] The French rendition, targeted at aristocratic audiences in northern France, was extremely popular in the Middle Ages; over fifty manuscripts produced before 1500 survive today. The translator adjusted William's portrayal of Godfrey to suit the proclivities of his target audience. For instance, at one point in his *Historia*, William of Tyre had referred to the 'illustrious and magnificent lord Godfrey'.[89] The translator rendered this phrase simply as 'the *preudhome* Godfrey', a term which denoted that, as well as possessing prodigious military talent, Godfrey was a man of upstanding character and morals.[90] The thirteenth century also witnessed the composition of two new groups of *chansons de geste* which served to extend the narrative established in the 'cycle rudimentaire'. One group, consisting of the *Naissance du Chevalier au Cygne*, the *Chevalier au Cygne*, and *Les Enfances Godefroi*, extended the narrative established in the 'cycle rudimentaire' back in time to cover the history of Godfrey's family in the generations leading up to the First Crusade.[91] These songs cast Godfrey as the descendant of a mysterious warrior known as the Swan Knight, and recount an embroidered version of his early exploits.[92] Their overall effect was to cast Godfrey as the scion of a noble Christian dynasty, and the presignified champion of the First Crusade whose ultimate achievement was the capture of Jerusalem. A second group of new *chansons*, known as the *Jérusalem* continuations, provide a rendition of Godfrey's tenure as ruler of the Holy City, and of the doings of his successors down to the eve of Saladin's conquests.[93] Taken together, these texts form a coherent cycle of *chansons de geste*. Godfrey acts as the cycle's main character, a status he shared with the champions of other cycles of epic songs such as Charlemagne, Roland, and Guillaume d'Orange.

It was also in this period that traditions which cast Godfrey as a founding lawgiver in the kingdom of Jerusalem took shape. In his *Livre de Forme de Plait*, a legal treatise on the procedures and laws of the high court of Cyprus written in the 1250s, Philip of Novara asserted that the laws of the kingdom of Jerusalem had from its earliest days been written down on decorated parchments, signed by the king, and kept in a box at the Holy Sepulchre. Philip noted that the practise of using these 'Letters of the Sepulchre' had been maintained in the kingdom for many years, but did not specify when it was instituted.[94] Between about 1262 and 1264 John of Ibelin used the *Livre de Forme de Plait* and other sources to write his *Livre des Assises*, a treatise on the legal procedures of the Latin East. In one recension of the *Livre des Assises* the prologue was altered to include the history of the 'Letters of the Sepulchre', and in this version, the establishment of the practice was attributed to Godfrey.[95] In John's original prologue to his

Livre des Assises, he wrote that Godfrey had played a key role in the foundation of the legal system of the kingdom of Jerusalem, stating that Godfrey had instituted a division between Jerusalem's High Court (where matters concerning fiefs and vassals were heard) and the Burgess Court (where people of lesser rank could plead their cases). John also states that Godfrey assented to a request made by the *suriens* (the native Christians of the Holy Land) to allow them to hold their own tribunals as a way of regulating their own issues.[96]

Most significantly, between 1187 and 1291, a range of authors invoked the memory of Godfrey to stimulate enthusiasm for new crusades or to comment on contemporary crusading activity. The writer known as the Minstrel of Rheims compared information he gained about Godfrey's preparations for the First Crusade in 1095–1096 with the steps taken by King Louis IX between 1244 and 1248 to prepare for the Seventh Crusade. The Minstrel asserts that Louis had erred by granting his knights a period of grace to set their financial affairs in order, rather than setting out as soon as possible:

> One thing [Louis] did from which no good came: he agreed to a respite of three years which the knights requested of the legate, to postpone paying the debts they owed to the citizens, except for what the legate took for their faith. With this settled, they left to go overseas. [Godfrey of Bouillon], however, did not do this, but sold his duchy forever, and went overseas entirely at his own expense, without caring what the others were doing. This is what he did, and Scripture says that God never wants to be served by theft of any kind.[97]

The author contrasts Louis with Godfrey, who, he claims, had taken his own money and possessions with him on his crusade, to make the case that it was necessary to finance a crusading expedition with money which was not ill-gotten. Another tradition (albeit an ahistorical one) concerning Godfrey's preparations for the First Crusade circulated in Champagne in the 1260s, before the cathedral chapter of Rheims included it in a 1264 document which recorded a protest against crusade taxation. In the preceding years, a series of taxes had been levied in the region to raise funds for a number of crusades, including Count Thibault IV of Champagne's expedition of 1239–41 and the Seventh Crusade. According to the tradition, as it was recorded in 1264, Godfrey had been so determined to fulfil his crusade vow that he extorted excessive taxes from his subjects in order to raise the necessary funds, only to lose it all during his expedition to the Holy Land. The Champagne tradition then had it that during Godfrey's journey home, Godfrey stopped off in Rome to visit his brother – who held the office of pope – who advised him to sell his lands so that he could restore his subjects' money to them, and thereafter to only use money which was rightfully his to fund an expedition to the Holy Land. Godfrey is reputed to have heeded his brother's counsel, embarked on the First Crusade with the money he had legitimately accumulated, and ultimately gained victory in the Holy Land.[98]

Stephen of Bourbon used another tradition centred upon Godfrey as the narrative basis for an *exemplum* which he included in his *Tracatus de Materiis Praedicabilibus*, a handbook for preaching. The *exemplum*, titled 'self-control of the flesh aids bravery', recounted that:

> When Godfrey of Bouillon, who was the first of the Franks to reign in Jerusalem, captured Antioch and Jerusalem and the land of Syria by force, after he had killed and expelled the obscene Saracens, who marvelled at his bravery, which no Saracen was able to resist, nor sustain a blow from his hand. At the time when there was peace, some Turks sent him presents in admiration, visiting him and questioning how his hands were so strong. Godfrey publicly cut the head off a horse with his sword. When the Turks said that the strength and goodness was in the sword, he accepted another sword which they handed over to him and did the same to another horse. And then, when they wondered why he was so strong, when he was not bigger than other men, they said that it was because his hands never touched the flesh of prostitutes and certainly not filthy luxuries.[99]

Stephen harnessed the memory of Godfrey in this moral story to argue that an individual's bravery relied not upon their strength and ability but on the nature of their character.

A number of thirteenth-century authors discussed contemporary crusading activity by invoking Godfrey's career on the First Crusade. A few years after the conclusion of the Fourth Crusade Gunther of Pairis wrote an account of that expedition. At the outset of it, Gunther described a recruitment sermon preached by Martin, the abbot of Pairis, to a crowd gathered at the church of the Blessed Virgin Mary at Basel in 1201. Gunther relates that Martin commenced his orations with a lament for the loss of Jerusalem, before asserting that all of Christendom should strive towards its recovery. Martin acknowledged that those who took part in a new expedition would face grave dangers, but stated that they could draw courage from the precedent set down by the participants in the First Crusade. He reportedly then delivered an *exemplum* in which he recounted the events which had culminated in the capture of Jerusalem in 1099:

> I want you to remember the accomplishments of our predecessors. At the time when that famous expedition led by the noble Duke Godfrey and other French and German princes was made, that infidel people, then as now, had occupied that land, having killed or captured all Christians. They had held in secure and fearless domination for forty years the holy city of Jerusalem, Tyre, Sidon, Antioch itself, and other fortified cities, in fact all territory right up to Constantinople. Yet, by

God's will, all of these places were recovered by that army in the briefest span of time, as in a flash. Also, the very capital of the kingdom, Jerusalem, was restored to our people.[100]

After Martin invoked the memory of the most resounding success story from crusading history, he outlined the spiritual rewards which were on offer to those who took the cross. He closed his sermon by asserting that he too would take part in the new expedition. Gunther states that the sermon moved the gathered audience to floods of tears. Crucially, Martin attempted to cultivate enthusiasm for the Fourth Crusade not by reciting the deeds of figures from classical or biblical history, but by speaking of the accomplishments of Godfrey and the other participants in the First Crusade, whom he encouraged listeners to regard as models of behaviour. By stating that Jerusalem had been in the hands of the 'infidel people' for forty years at the time it had been captured by the forces of the First Crusade, Martin subtly implied that the task which faced the Fourth Crusade was less onerous.

In his Old French prose history of the Fourth Crusade, written in about 1207, Geoffrey of Villehardouin claimed that when the crusaders met in the newly captured Constantinople on 9 May 1204 to deliberate which of Margrave Boniface I of Montferrat and Count Baldwin IX of Flanders should be ruler of the new Latin Empire, Godfrey was at the forefront of their minds. According to Villehardouin, as the discussions at Constantinople became increasingly fraught, it was suggested that the crusaders should be mindful of the circumstances in which Godfrey had been appointed ruler of Jerusalem in July 1099. The chronicler states that some of those who were present argued that

> if we elect one of these two eminent men, the other will be so jealous that he will leave with all his men, and the land might be lost as a result. The land of Jerusalem was nearly lost in a similar situation, when Godfrey of Bouillon was chosen as ruler in the wake of its conquest. [Raymond of Toulouse] was so jealous that he persuaded some of the other barons and as many other people as he could to leave the army; a good number of them did as he wished and so few remained in Jerusalem that they would have lost that land had God not come to their aid. We must be mindful of this, and take care that the same thing doesn't happen to us.[101]

In the end, the crusaders decided to appoint Baldwin of Flanders. Since Villehardouin was a leading participant in the Fourth Crusade, he would have taken part in these discussions, and so would have been well-placed to know the arguments that were put forward. His account of Baldwin's selection as Latin Emperor of Constantinople suggests not only that the events surrounding Godfrey's appointment as ruler of Jerusalem in 1099 were known to participants of the Fourth Crusade, but that this knowledge helped to shape how those participants acted.

The *Ordinatio de Predicatione Sancti Crucis,* a preaching guide probably written in England around the time of the Fifth Crusade, features an *exemplum* which recounts the experiences of two crusaders from Flanders who were brothers named Godfrey and Eustace. It relates that:

> Eustace and Godfrey, Flemish knights and brothers, went together to the Holy Land. Godfrey received a serious wound and, before he was healed the Christians entered battle with the Saracens. Godfrey, laid low by this grave injury, was not able to take part in the battle, and for that reason he requested that his brother Eustace refrain from fighting for fifteen days. Then, after that time, Godfrey, his health restored by the grace of God, would enter battle with his companions. However, Eustace answered that he was a true knight of Christ, and that he desired *to depart and to be with Christ* [Philippians, 1:23]: He did not want to avoid battle, indeed, he wanted to attack the enemies of Christianity . . . He entered battle and became a martyr of God.[102]

The purpose of this *exemplum* appears to have been to highlight the risks of setting out on crusade prematurely. While the named individuals are not explicitly identified as Count Eustace III of Boulogne and Godfrey of Bouillon, and the narrative of the *exemplum* has no parallel with any known event from their lives, on balance these individuals were probably named Eustace and Godfrey in order to invoke the precedent of the First Crusade. Between 1266 and 1268, Humbert of Romans wrote his *De predicatione crucis contra Saracenos,* a handbook for crusade preaching. He devoted one chapter to praising the military accomplishments of famous Christian warriors, beginning with the deeds of Old Testament figures including Judas Maccabeus and Job, before proceeding to discuss the achievements of Charlemagne. Humbert then offered a précis of the First Crusade:

> [In] the year 1095, on account of the *comotionem* of Peter the Hermit and the preaching of Urban II at the council of Clermont and other preachers mandated by him, Godfrey of Bouillon and other noble men along with clergy and innumerable people took the cross. They travelled through Greece, and sustaining many toils and deaths and exertions, they captured Antioch and Jerusalem. Remaining in those regions, they captured other places in succession. And so the Holy Land was removed from the hands of the Saracens and handed over to Christians.[103]

Among the leading participants, Humbert named only Peter the Hermit and Godfrey. After this summary of the First Crusade, Humbert briefly mentioned the exploits of the leaders of the Third Crusade: Frederick

Barbarossa, Philip Augustus, and Richard I. Humbert evidently believed that invoking Godfrey and these other prominent crusaders would help preachers to stimulate participation in future expeditions.

The manner in which Godfrey was invoked in these thirteenth-century texts suggests that he had become an iconic figure of both the First Crusade and crusading history more generally. Significantly, there are signs that in this era, the memory of Godfrey actively influenced – or was used with the intention of influencing – how individuals thought and acted. On 11 November 1247, Count Robert I of Artois (d.1250) had a charter drawn up as part of his preparations for his brother Louis IX's crusade. In this document, Robert states that he had donated relics to the abbey of Lens after being inspired by the 'the most Christian king of Jerusalem Godfrey of Bouillon, duke of Brabant, lord of Lens in Artois and count of Boulogne on the sea'.[104] While the tradition of Godfrey's donation to Lens actually belonged to the *Jérusalem* continuations, Robert nevertheless evidently had it in mind as he prepared for his own crusading expedition. Similarly, in 1261, Bishop Florence of Acre wrote to King Henry III of England, in order to request military assistance for the Latin East. Although Henry had already taken the cross twice by this time, he had not actually embarked for the East. Bishop Florence implied that if Henry made good on his vow and brought an army to the Holy Land, he would be regarded as the most famous crusader 'since the time of Godfrey'.[105] While Henry III never personally fulfilled his crusade vow, that Florence attempted to persuade him to come to the Latin East by invoking Godfrey is revealing of the presumed utility of his reputation in this era.

As well as emerging as a hero of the cycle of *chansons de geste* which focussed specifically on the crusades, Godfrey made guest appearances in other vernacular poetry. He features in several late-thirteenth-century *chansons de geste* which are not part of the Crusade Cycle. At the outset of *Doon de Maience*, a *chanson* belonging to the cycle concerned with feudal revolt, reference is made to the Swan Knight and his ancestor Godfrey, the conqueror of Jerusalem.[106] Godfrey also appears in *Gaufrey*, another song of the cycle of revolt.[107] He is mentioned four times in the *Enfances Renier*, a *chanson* from the cycle of Guillaume d'Orange.[108] Moreover, one manuscript containing the crusade *chansons* also features several romances of Alexander, suggesting that Godfrey's exploits had come to be seen in alignment with the deeds of established poetical heroes from the more distant past.[109] Near the end of the twelfth century, an unknown (possibly Norman) author composed an Old French poem on the First Crusade based largely on the account of Baldric of Bourgueil.[110] Godfrey features prominently throughout this text.[111]

Godfrey was also invoked in this era in a number of verse texts which were not directly concerned with the First Crusade. He is mentioned in the late-thirteenth-century *Le Pas Saladin*, a short Old French poem on the exploits of Richard I and Philip Augustus on the Third Crusade. At one point this text invokes Guy of Lusignan and King Amalric of Jerusalem, and then 'Godfrey of Bouillon, who conquered Jerusalem, and who sent so many pagans to their death'.[112] Godfrey is one of many figures mentioned in John of Howden's *Rossignos* (1272). At one point the poet named figures including Judas Maccabeus, Hector, Julius Caesar, Charlemagne, and Roland, before listing the famous First Crusaders Robert of Normandy, Bohemond, Tancred, and 'Godfrey of the holy journey, who was a noble king in Syria'.[113] John then mentioned a series of figures from history and legend, including Gawain, Lancelot, Perceval, Robert Guiscard, Richard I, Louis IX, Henry III, Raymond of Provence, Alexander, Arthur, and Edward I of England. One of the most significant of Godfrey's posthumous appearances is that in Rutebeuf's *La Complainte d'Outremer*, a 173-line Old French poem written in 1266. In this poem Rutebeuf related how the Latin East had fallen into ruin, before setting out how it could be restored. At one point, Rutebeuf invoked Godfrey's name in a manner which serves not only to evince how far his reputation had developed by this time, but also as a reminder of the fact that his reputation continued to be shaped by crusading history: 'Alas! Antioch, Holy Land, what a poor state you are in when you have no more Godfreys!'[114]

By the end of the thirteenth century, then, Godfrey had been transformed into a hero of crusading history. Writers held him up as an example for contemporary crusaders to follow. His memory was used to add stimulus to new crusading enterprises, and his name was invoked in order to provide a point of comparison with contemporary crusading activity. Crucially, whereas earlier authors had produced fully rounded treatments of Godfrey's life, character, and exploits on the First Crusade, in the thirteenth century, Godfrey was often conjured up with little or no introduction. By the end of the thirteenth century, then, Godfrey had become iconic of crusading history. It is as a crusading icon that he appears in Dante's *Divine Comedy*, one of the most celebrated pieces of world literature. Dante wrote his *Divine Comedy* between about 1308 and 1321. In it, he recounted an imagined journey through the three realms of the Christian afterlife, during which he met the spirits of famous historical figures. While traversing *Paradiso's* fifth sphere (the heaven of Mars), the residence of warriors of the faith, Dante described meeting a series of men famed for their military exploits, including Joshua, Judas Maccabeus, Charlemagne, Roland, Guillaume d'Orange, and Renoart (the latter four of whom were widely celebrated in knightly literature during the Middle Ages). Then, Dante wrote, he encountered none other than Godfrey of Bouillon.[115] The popularity of Dante's masterpiece has helped to ensure that Godfrey has continued to be remembered in the centuries since its composition.

Godfrey's reputation did not cease to evolve at the turn of the fourteenth century. The last vestiges of Latin-held territory in the Holy Land fell in 1291, and in the years that followed, a number of authors wrote treatises setting out plans for the recovery of Jerusalem and the reconstruction of the Latin East.[116] Significantly, Godfrey is mentioned in a number of these recovery treatises. In his *De recuperatione Terre Sancte* (1305–1307) the Norman lawyer Pierre Dubois provided a comprehensive plan for the organisation of a new crusade to the Holy Land. Dubois suggested that the new army should be divided into four parts, three of which should go to the Holy Land by sea, with the fourth following the land route taken by Charlemagne, Barbarossa, and Godfrey.[117] In 1306 Fulk of Villaret, Grand Master of the Knights Hospitaller, wrote a Latin recovery treatise in which he included a brief history of the First Crusade, noting that its 'leader was Godfrey of Bouillon, who acquired Jerusalem'.[118] In 1307–8 Fulk also assisted in the composition of another recovery treatise in which Godfrey was mentioned.[119] The anonymous 'Memoria Terre Sancte', written between 1289 and 1308, contains an exemplary story concerning Godfrey's preparations for the First Crusade.[120] The Venetian Marino Sanudo Torsello mentioned Godfrey in various contexts throughout his *Liber Secretorum Fidelium Crucis*. At one point Sanudo discussed various attempts which had been made throughout history by Christians to conquer Egypt, and listed Godfrey as one of those who had tried.[121] Sanudo also included in his treatise a history of the First Crusade and an assessment of Godfrey's character, both of which he drew from the *Historia* of William of Tyre.[122] In one chapter of his recovery treatise of 1332, Roger of Stangrave provided an *exemplum* which focussed on 'the good duke Godfrey of Boulogne'.[123] The *Directorium ad passagium faciendum* (1332) implored its dedicatee, Philip VI of France, to lead an army to Constantinople, following the route taken by Peter the Hermit and Godfrey of Bouillon.[124]

But while the events of 1291 conditioned many recollections of Godfrey at the turn of the fourteenth century, the same era also heralded the moment at which his reputation assumed a monumentally significant new dimension. In about 1312, the Lotharingian poet Jacques de Longuyon composed the *Voeux du paon*, a poem of over 8,000 lines, which he interpolated into his romance on the life of Alexander.[125] At one point in this text, it is recounted that a character named Porrus fought with such ferocity that he had surpassed the feats of nine of the most formidable warriors from history. The poet then related the careers of each of these nine men. Hector, Julius Caesar, and Alexander featured as a trio of 'pagan' heroes. Then came three biblical figures: Joshua, David, and Judas Maccabeus. The final three consisted of a triad of Christian heroes: King Arthur, Charlemagne, and Godfrey of Bouillon.[126] These nine figures from history were carefully selected to epitomise the ideals of chivalry. The roster had a powerful symmetry which neatly reflected the medieval division of history into three ages. Arthur and Charlemagne were by this time the chief protagonists of the 'matters' of Britain and France, and they were incorporated into the roster to bring chivalry into the context of Christian history. By this time, Godfrey too had attained iconic status. His memory was therefore conscripted into the list in order to symbolise the contemporary relevance of the crusades to the aspirations of chivalry. This roster of nine historical warriors became known as the *Neuf Preux*: the Nine Worthies. The cult of the Nine Worthies evolved into one of the most influential cultural motifs of the Later Middle Ages, one which was celebrated and commemorated in a wide range of literature, art, and music in the centuries that followed. It was as a member of this illustrious pantheon that Godfrey was chiefly remembered in the Later Middle Ages.[127] Godfrey's posthumous apotheosis as a member of the Nine Worthies, and the evolution of his reputation across the centuries down to the present day, is, however, a story that will have to be told in another book.

Notes

1 On Robert of Normandy's career after his return to the West, see: Aird, *Robert Curthose*, pp. 191–244.
2 Flori, *Bohémond*, pp. 253–72; Paul, 'A Warlord's Wisdom', pp. 556–60.
3 See above, pp. 164–5. For assessments of how thinkers in Latin Christendom made sense of the First Crusade, see John, 'Historical Truth and the Miraculous Past', and William J. Purkis, 'Rewriting the History Books: The First Crusade and the Past', in *WEC*, pp. 140–54.
4 For an insightful analysis of one such manuscript, see: Jay Rubenstein, 'Putting History to Use: Three Crusade Chronicles in Context', *Viator*, 35 (2004), 131–68. The manuscript in question is Bibliothèque nationale de France, MS Latin 14378. It was apparently presented to King Louis VII of France in 1137, and it contains copies of the accounts of Fulcher of Chartres and Raymond of Aguilers.
5 Marcus Bull, and Damien Kempf, 'Introduction', in *WEC*, pp. 1–8, at p. 5.
6 Albert of Aachen and Fulcher of Chartres both suggested that the crusaders of 1101–2 had been sinful, and so had suffered divine punishment as a result. AA, pp. 610–11; FC, pp. 428, 433, tr. pp. 165–6.
7 Purkis, 'Rewriting the History Books', p. 143.
8 In general, see: Nicholas L. Paul, *To Follow in Their Footsteps: The Crusades and Family Memory in the High Middle Ages* (Ithaca, 2012).
9 To this it should be added that wider medieval processes of memorialisation and recollection of the past also had a determining influence on how Godfrey was remembered. Modern literature in this area is far too vast to do justice to here, but profitable starting points may be found in the essays collected in Gerd Althoff, Johannes Fried, and Patrick J. Geary (eds), *Medieval Concepts of the Past: Ritual, Memory and Historiography* (Cambridge, 2002), and in Elisabeth van Houts, *Memory and Gender in Medieval Europe, 900–1200* (Basingstoke, 1999). On the memorialisation of crusading history, see the essays in Megan Cassidy-Welch (ed.), *Remembering the Crusades and Crusading* (Abingdon, 2017).
10 For a fuller study of how the First Crusade was remembered in the first half of the twelfth century, see: Jonathan Phillips, *The Second Crusade: Extending the Frontiers of Christendom* (New Haven, 2007), pp. 17–36.
11 'insigne thema referendi mira prestruitur dictatorum studio'. OV, vol. 5, pp. 4–5; 'et ideo litterali compaginatione commendari debet notitie tam praesentium quam futurorum, ut per hoc et spes in Deum Christiana magis solidetur, et laus eius in eorum mentibus vivacior incitetur'. RM, p. 4, tr. p. 77.
12 RM; BB; GN.
13 Riley-Smith, *First Crusade*, pp. 135–52.
14 RM.
15 Gilo.

16 RC.

17 OV.

18 WM.

19 'Dux . . . sicut erat huiusce rei sagacissimus et bellator acerrimus' . . . 'erat miles accerimus'. BB, pp. 17–18, 32.

20 'Ducis . . . nomine dignus, specimen militiae'. GN, p. 155, tr. p. 66.

21 '[Dux Godefridus] cuius non feruor, non uires, non animosus | spiritus Hectoreis cessit, sed prefuit armis, | letus adest'. RC, p. 31, tr. p. 53.

22 'magnas in bellum trahens cateruas, et quanuis durum et exercitatum militem haberet, nullus tamen eo uel prior in congressu uel promptior in effectu habebatur'. WM, vol. 1, pp. 658–9.

23 Gilo, p. 120, n. *m.*

24 GN, pp. 285–6, tr. p. 133–4; Gilo, pp. 94–5; WM, vol. 1, pp. 658–9. William described the beast as a lion.

25 GN, pp. 284–5, tr. p. 133; RM, pp. 44–5, tr. p. 133; OV, vol. 5, pp. 84–5; Gilo, pp. 120–3; RC, p. 53, tr. p. 79.

26 Gilo, pp. 226–9.

27 '[Godfrey] quo post dei fidem nemo sagacior'. GN, p. 295, tr. p. 138.

28 'tantam militie Christiane . . . lucem'. RM, p. 45, tr. p. 133.

29 'At nos, sumpto de expertis dei adminiculis iugibus ausu superque ipsum spiritu innitentes'. GN, p. 338, tr. p. 159.

30 'Deus militem suum custodivit'. RM, p. 45, tr. p. 133.

31 'Godefridus . . . Cuius *manus ad prelium et digitos ad bellum* Dominus dirigeba, quoniam, iactis sagittis inimicorum pectora et utraque latera transforabat'. RM, p. 98, tr. p. 199, invoking Psalm 143:1.

32 RM, p. 101, tr. p. 202; BB, p. 113; GN, p. 284, tr. p. 132; OV, vol. 5, pp. 174–5; WM, vol. 1, pp. 650–1.

33 GN, pp. 317–8, tr. p, 149; WM, vol. 1, pp. 660–1; OV, vol. 5, pp. 340–1.

34 'Hic vultu elegans, statura procerus, dulcis eloquio, moribus egregius, et in tantum militibus lenis ut magis in se monachum quam militem figuraret. Hic tamen, cum hostem sentiebat adesse et imminere prelium, tunc audaci mente concipiebat animum, et quasi leo frendens, ad nullius pavebat occursum. Et quae lorica vel clipeus sustinere poterat impetum mucronis illius?' RM, p. 9, tr. p. 84.

35 'Iunioris huius nobilitas multis polluit uirtutibus cumulata, cum secularibus, tum diuinis; largitate erga pauperes, erga delinquentes misericordia; porro humilitate, mansuetidine, sobrietate, iustitia, castitate insignis, potius monachorum lux quam militum dux emicabat. Nec minus tamen ea, quae seculi sunt, nouerat tractare: preliari, ordinare acies, armis gloriam propagare; primus aut in primus ferire hostem adolescens didicit, iuuenis assueuit, senex non destitit. Adeo belligeri comitis ac comitissae religiossimae filius, ut etiam ab emulo conspectus, audire mereretur: "Ad belli studium, ecce pater; circa Dei cultum, ecce mater."' RC, p. 18, tr. pp. 36–7.

36 'Dux Godefridus, homo totus bellique Deique'. RC, p. 31, tr. p. 53.

37 The prosperity of the Latin states should not be overstated, however. The Latins in the Holy Land faced considerable strategic problems. They also suffered a number of significant defeats, such as that endured at the battle of the Field of Blood in 1119, on which see: Thomas Asbridge, 'The Significance and Causes of the Battle of the Field of Blood', *JMH*, 24 (1997), 301–16.

38 'Ita denique miro quodam ac singulari modo cernuntur et agnis mitiores, et leonibus ferociores, ut pene dubitem quid potius censeam appellandos, monachos videlicet, an milites: nisi quod utrumque forsan congruentius nominarim, quibus neutrum deesse cognoscitur, nec monachi mansuetudo, nec militis

fortitudo'. *Sancti Bernardi Opera*, ed. Jean Leclercq, et al., 9 vols in 10 (Rome, 1957–77), vol. 3, p. 221, tr. in *The Templars: Selected Sources*, tr. Malcolm Barber and Keith Bate (Manchester, 2002), p. 224.

39 'antiquorum relatione didicimus et in gestis eorum scriptum repperimus'. Rolf Große, 'Überlegungen zum Kreuzzugsaufruf Eugens III. von 1145/46: Mit einer Neuedition von JL 8876', *Francia*, 18 (1991), pp. 85–92, at p. 90, tr. in *The Crusades: Idea and Reality, 1095–1274*, tr. Louise Riley-Smith and Jonathan Riley-Smith (London, 1981), pp. 57–9, at p. 57. For a close study of the bull's contents, see: Phillips, *The Second Crusade*, pp. 37–60.

40 'Maximum namque nobilitatis et probitatis indicium fore cognoscitur, si ea, que patrum strenuitas acquisiuit, a bonis filiis strenue defendantur. Verumtamen si, quod absit, secus contigerit, patrum fortitudo in filiis imminuta esse probatur'. Große, 'Überlegungen', p. 91, tr. p. 58.

41 H. W. C. Davis, 'Henry of Blois and Brian FitzCount', *EHR*, 25 (1910), 297–303, at pp. 301–3.

42 Phillips, *Defenders*, pp. 100–281.

43 Carole Hillenbrand, ' "Abominable Acts": The Career of Zengi', in Jonathan Phillips and Martin Hoch (eds), *The Second Crusade: Scope and Consequences* (Manchester, 2001), pp. 111–32; Malcolm C. Lyons and D. E. P. Jackson, *Saladin: The Politics of the Holy War* (Cambridge, 1982).

44 'Iam enim ad ea tempora, quibus nec nostra vicia nec eorum remedia pati possumus, perventum est: unde, nostris id merentibus peccatis, facti sunt hostes in capite, et qui de inimicis triumphantes palmam frequentius solebamus referre cum gloria, nunc in omni pene conflictu, divinia destituti gratia'. WT, p. 1061, tr. vol. 2, p. 506.

45 WT; Peter Edbury and John G. Rowe, *William of Tyre: Historian of the Latin East* (Cambridge, 1988).

46 Edbury and Rowe, *William of Tyre*, pp. 13–29.

47 Edbury and Rowe, *William of Tyre*, pp. 61–84.

48 'Fuerunt et alia multa eiusdem incliti viri magnifica et admiratione digna opera, que usque in presens in ore hominum pro celebri vertuntur historia'. WT, p. 430, tr. vol. 1, p. 391.

49 WT, pp. 425–6, tr. vol. 1, p. 386.

50 WT, p. 427, tr. vol. 1, pp. 387–8.

51 WT, p. 426, tr. vol. 1, p. 386.

52 WT, p. 219, tr. vol. 1, p. 176.

53 WT, pp. 278–9, tr. vol. 1, pp. 233–4.

54 'vir religiosus erat, in his que ad decorum domus dei habebant respectum'. WT, p. 431, tr. vol. 1, p. 391.

55 'vir humilis erat et mansuetus ac tremens sermones domini'. WT, p. 441, tr. vol. 1, p. 404.

56 WT, pp. 422–3, tr. vol. 1, pp. 381–3.

57 WT, p. 423, tr. vol. 1, p. 382.

58 WT, p. 421, tr. vol. 1, p. 379.

59 'domino duce Godefrido, qui primus regnum obtinuit'. WT, p. 100, tr. vol. 1, p. 57.

60 'primo ex Latinis regni Ierosolimorum moderatore insigni'. WT, p. 453, tr. vol. 1, p. 415.

61 'Unde quidam in catalogo regum, non distinguentes merita, eum dubitant connumerare'. WT, p. 431, tr. vol. 1, p. 392.

62 'non solum rex, sed regum optimus, lumen et speculum videtur aliorum'. WT, p. 431, tr. vol. 1, pp. 392–3.

63 WT, pp. 431–2, tr. vol. 1, pp. 392–3.

64 *ChAnt.*

65 *OFCC*, vol. 6, tr. in *ChJér*, pp. 173–353.

66 *OFCC*, vol. 5, tr. in *ChJér*, pp. 67–172.

67 'Godefrois . . . li praus et li saçans', 'le duc de Buillon a la ciere hardie', 'Gode-frois qui cuer a de lion'. *ChAnt*, vol. 1, pp. 64, 225, 442, tr. pp. 130, 204, 311.

68 'Lors se feri es Turs par molt fier maltalant, | Qui il ataint a coup tot le vait por-fendant'. *ChAnt*, vol. 1, p. 97, tr. p. 146.

69 'Tot en fendi un Turc desci que el pomon | Que le moitiés en pent d'ambes pars l'arçon'. *ChAnt*, vol. 1, pp. 200–1, tr. p. 192.

70 'Et fiert un Sarrazin parmi la teste armee. | Tout li fendi le cors desci qu'en la coree, | Que les moitiés en pendent tot contreval la pree'. *ChAnt*, vol. 1, p. 201, tr. p. 192.

71 'Tot le coupa li dus tres parmi l'eskinee, | L'une moitiés del Turc caï emmi le pree, | Et li autre est remese en la sele doree, | Li cars del Turc s'estraint, car l'arme en est alee, | Si fu roide la jambe com s'ele fust plantee'. *ChAnt*, vol. 1, p. 202, tr. p. 193.

72 *ChAnt*, vol. 1, pp. 318–9, tr. p. 254.

73 *OFCC*, vol. 6, p. 189, tr. in *ChJér*, pp. 300–1.

74 *OFCC*, vol. 6, p. 199, tr. in *ChJér*, pp. 308–9.

75 *OFCC*, vol. 6, p. 248, tr. in *ChJér*, p. 346.

76 *ChAnt*, vol. 1, pp. 191–2, tr. pp. 187–8.

77 '[Godfrey] que Dex par ama tant' . . . 'li dus Godefrois, qui en Diu molt se fie'. *OFCC*, vol. 6, pp. 41, 45, tr. in *ChJér*, pp. 179, 182.

78 See, e.g., the reference to 'Li rois Godefrois': *OFCC*, vol. 6, p. 154, tr. in *ChJér*, p. 274.

79 'Ainc n'i porta corone d'or fin ne de metaus, | De l'ort Saint Abraham li fu fait uns cerchaus, | Si li mist ens el cief li boins rois des ribaus, | car premiers i entra par desous les muraus'. *ChAnt*, vol. 1, p. 167, tr. p. 176.

80 'Segnor, bien le saciés, ja nel nos penseron | Que ja en mon cief ait corone d'or en son: | Car Jhesus l'ot d'espines quant sofri passion: | Ja la moie n'ert d'or, d'argent, ne de laiton'. *OFCC*, vol. 6, pp. 152–3, tr. in *ChJér*, p. 272.

81 'qu'il trova en la citè .ij. anciens homes. L'un avoit non Robert de Coudre, qui avoit esté avec Godefroi de Buillon a la conqueste'. *La Continuation de Guillaume de Tyr (1184–1197)*, ed. Margaret Ruth Morgan (Paris, 1982), p. 52, tr. in *The Conquest of Jerusalem and the Third Crusade: Sources in Translation*, tr. Peter Edbury (Aldershot, 1998), p. 45.

82 'N'iert ja bone chançon chantee, | N'ovraine feite que Deu veie, | Si com il fist a l'autre veie, | Quant Antioche fud assise | E nostre gent par force enz mise – | Dont l'en raconte encore l'estorie, | De cels qui Deus dona victorie, | De Buiamont e de Tancré – | C'erent pelerein esmeré – | E de Godefrei de Buil-lon, | E de hauz princes de grant non, | E des autres qui lors i furent | Qui Deus servirent e mururent | Tant qu'il lor rendi lor servise | A lur gré e a lur devise, | E lor ovraines suzhauça | Par tantes feiz e eshauça, | E il e totes lor lignees; | Si en sunt encore eshaucees'. Ambroise, *Estoire de la Guerre Sainte*, ed. and tr. Mari-anne Ailes and Malcolm Barber, 2 vols (Woodbridge, 2003), vol. 1, p. 172, vol. 2, p. 174.

83 'Hanc autem sacratissimam civitatem circiter octoginta novem annos gens nostra tenuerat, ex quo ipsam pariter cum Antiochia victoriosa Christianorum recuperavit potentia, cum eam prius gentiles per annos quadraginta possedis-sent. Anno enim Domini M°XC°IX° Boimundus, Raimundus, Tancredus, dux Godefridus, Robertus comes Normanniae, et alii Franci eam ceperant, expulsis

Saracenis'. *Itinerarium Peregrinorum et Gesta Regis Ricardi*, in *Chronicles and Memorials of the Reign of Richard I*, ed. William Stubbs, 2 vols (London, 1864), vol. 1, pp. 1–450, at p. 22, tr. in *The Chronicle of the Third Crusade: The Itinerarium Peregrinorum and the Gesta Regis Ricardi*, tr. Helen J. Nicholson (Aldershot, 1997), p. 39.

84 'Non enim hi fuerant quales olim vere peregrini in Antiochena expeditione, quam gens nostra potenter obtinuit, unde quoque et adhuc recitatur in gestis super tam famosa Victoria Boimundi et Tancredi, necnon et Godefridi de Builun, et aliorum procerum praestantissimorum, qui tot praeclaris triumpharunt victoriis, quorum opera jam nunc fiunt tanquam cibus ab ore narrantium, qui quia corde non ficto gratuitum Deo praestabant obsequium, reddidit eis Deus mercedem laborum suorum, et exaltavit magnifica opera sua immortali memoria, ut etiam ipsorum tota posteritas ampliori praedicetur veneratione'. *Itinerarium*, p. 396, tr. p. 346.

85 'Multi alii proceres probi in hac expeditione extiterunt. | Sed isti predicti maiores et sub his omnes alii fuerunt'. Nicholas L. Paul, 'Crusade, Memory and Regional Politics in Twelfth-Century Amboise', *JMH*, 31 (2005), 127–41, at pp. 140–1.

86 The post-1187 era also witnessed a shift in how the First Crusade was remembered. After this point, some observers devoted more attention to the Third Crusade than to the First. See: Purkis, 'Rewriting the History Books', pp. 151–4.

87 Björn Weiler, 'The *Negotium Terrae Sanctae* in the Political Discourse of Latin Christendom, 1215–1311', *International History Review*, 25 (2003), 1–36.

88 *Guillaume de Tyr et ses continuateurs: Text français du XIIIᵉ siècle, revu et annote*, ed. Paulin Paris, 2 vols (Paris, 1879–1880); Philip Handyside, *The Old French William of Tyre* (Leiden, 2015).

89 'vir magnificus et illustris dominus Godefridus Lotaringie dux'. WT, p. 161, tr. vol. 1, p. 116.

90 'Cil preudome Godefroiz'. *Guillaume de Tyr*, vol. 1, p. 56.

91 *OFCC*, vols 1, 2 and 3.

92 In general, see: Simon John, 'Godfrey of Bouillon and the Swan Knight', in Simon John and Nicholas Morton (eds), *Crusading and Warfare in the Middle Ages: Realities and Representations. Essays in Honour of John France* (Farnham, 2014), pp. 129–42, and Trotter, 'L'ascendance mythique de Godefroy de Bouillon'.

93 *OFCC*, vols 7.i, 7.ii, and 8.

94 Philip of Novara, *Le Livre de Forme de Plait*, ed. and tr. Peter Edbury (Nicosia, 2009), pp. 118–21 and 259–61; Peter Edbury, 'Law and custom in the Latin East: *les letres dou sepulcre*', *Mediterranean Historical Review*, 10 (1995), 71–9.

95 John of Ibelin, *Le Livre des Assises*, ed. Peter Edbury (Leiden, 2003), pp. 628–9.

96 Ibelin, *Livre*, pp. 51–7.

97 'Mais une chose fist li rois dont il ne vint nus biens; car il s'acorda au respit de trios ans que li chevalier quisent au legat pour avoir respit des detes qu'il devoient aus bourjois, sauf ce que li legaz ne pourprenoit pas leur foiz. Et sour ce il s'en alerent outre meir; et ainsi ne fist mie Godefrois de Bouillon, qui vendi sa duchée à touz jourz, et ala outre meir proprement au sien, et n'enporta rien de l'autrui. Si esploita, et l'Escriture dit que Dieus ne se veut mie servir de rapine ne de toute'. *Récits d'un ménestrel de Reims au XIIIᵉ siècle*, ed. Natalis de Wailly (Paris, 1876), p. 190, tr. in *A Thirteenth-Century Minstrel's Chronicle*, tr. Robert Levine (Lampeter, 1990), p. 88.

98 *Archives législatives de la ville de Reims*, ed. Pierre Varin, 2 vols in 4 (Paris, 1840–1852), vol. 1.1, pp. 453–4. For comment, see: E. A. R. Brown, 'Taxation and Morality in the Thirteenth and Fourteenth Centuries: Conscience and Political Power and the Kings of France', *French Historical Review*, 8 (1973), 1–28, at pp. 13–15.

99 'Juvat fortitudinem carnis continencia' . . . 'Cum Godefridus de Bullione, qui primus de Francis regnavit in Jerusalem, cepissit armis Antochiam et Jerusalem et terram Syrie, concisis et expulsis Saracenis obscenis, cum mirarentur ejus fortitudinem, cui nullus Saracenus posset resistere, nec ictum manus ejus sustinere, tempore treuge, [aliqui] Turcorum admirati miserunt ei munera, visitantes eum et querentes unde tanta ejus manibus esset fortitudo. Qui coram eis ense suo scidit ictu equi caput. Et [cum] dicerunt quod erat virtute et bonitate ensis sue, accepto ense ab eis sibi traditio, idem fecit de alio equo. Et tunc cum quererent [unde] hoc virtus ei [venerat], cum ipse non esset major aliis hominibus, ait quod manus sue nunquam carnes tractaverant meretricis nec luxuria fuerant inquinate'. *Anecdotes historiques. Légendes et apologues tirés du recueil inédit d'Étienne de Bourbon*, ed. A. Lecoy de la Marche (Paris, 1877), p. 442. For comment, see: James B. MacGregor, 'The First Crusade in Late Medieval *Exempla*', *The Historian*, 68 (2006), 29–48, at pp. 34–5.

100 'Ac ne vos illud terreat quod hoc tempore gentilis rabies super nostros adeo invaluit, rerum praecedentium vos cupio reminisci. Eo tempore quo celebris ista expeditio sub nobili duce Gotefrido, caeterisque Francorum ac Theutonicorum principibus facta est, infidelis ille populus, ita ut nunc, Christianis omnibus occisis vel captis, terram illam occupaverat, sanctamque civitatem Jerusalem, et Tyrum, ac Sidonem, ipsamque Antiochiam, et alias urbes munitas, imo totam terram usque Constantinopolim secure et absque ullo metu annis quadraginta possederant. Quae tamen omnia, volente Domino, per eumdem exercitum brevissimo tempore, velut in transcursu recepta sunt. Nicaea, Iconium, Antiochia, Tripolis, et aliae civitates expugnatae sunt. Ipsa etiam sedes regni Jerusalem populo nostro restituta'. Gunther of Pairis, *Historia Captae a Latinis Constantinopoleos, PL*, vol. 212, cols 221–56, at cols 227–8, tr. in Gunther of Pairis, *Hystoria Constantinopolitana*, tr. Alfred J. Andrea (Philadelphia, 1997), p. 70.

101 'Seigneur, sé l'on eslist l'un de ces deus haus homes, li autres en aura si grant envie qui il enmenra toute sa gent, et ensi porrons-nous perdre la terre; car toute ensi dut estre cele de Jèrusalem perdue, quant il eslurent Godefroi de Bouillon, et la terre fu conquise; et li quens de Saint-Gile en ot si grant envie que il porchaça as autres barons, et à tous ceus qu'il pot qu'il se départissent de l'ost, et tant s'en alèrent de l'ost de gens, que cil remestrent si poi en la terre que sé nostre Sires proprement ne les eust soustenus, la terre fust toute reperdue. Et pour ce, devons-nous garder qu'il ne nos aviegne autresi'. Geoffrey of Villehardouin, *De La Conqueste de Constantinople*, ed. Paulin Paris (Paris, 1838), p. 84, tr. in *Joinville and Villehardouin: Chronicles of the Crusades*, tr. Caroline Smith (London, 2008), pp. 1–144, at p. 69.

102 'Eustachius & Gaufridus, milites Flandrenses & fratres, ad invicem venerunt in Terram Sanctam, & in amplicando Gaufridus grave vulnus recepit &, antequam ipse sanaretur, Christiani cum Sarracenis bellum inierunt, cum ipse Gaufridus, infirmirate vulneris gravatus, interesse non potuit & ideo rogavit fratrem suum Eustachium, quod ipse non intraret bellum, sed per XV dies exspectaret, donec per Dei graciam, sanitate recuperata, consortes bellum inirent. Respondit autem Eustachius tanquam verus miles Christi cupiensque *dissolvi & esse cum Christo* [Phillipians, 1:23]: Disserre nolo, quin invadam inimicos crucifixi, "kar grant avantage aueroie de venir à Deu xv. iurs plus tot ke vus," & ivit in bellum & martyr Dei factus est'. *Ordinatio de Predicatione Sancti Crucis*, in *Quinti Belli Sacri Scriptores Minores*, ed. Reinhold Röhricht (Geneva, 1879), pp. 2–26, at p. 20.

103 'Item circa annum Domini 1095 ad comotionem Petri heremite et predicationem sancti alias Urbani secundi in concilio claremonteum et aliorum

prelatorum de mandato eius cruce signati sunt Gotfridus de Boillon et alij viri nobiles et clerus et populus innumerabilis. qui transeuntes per Greciam et sustinentes labores innumerabiles et mortes et angustias. ceperunt Anthiochiam et Jerusalem. et commorantes in partibus illis alia loca successiue ceperunt. et extunc- terra sancta erepta de manibus saracenorum. in manus transit christianorum. Triumphis'. Humbert of Romans, *De predicatione crucis contra Saracenos*, ed. Peter Wagner (Nuremberg, *c*.1495), an *incunabulum* transcribed by Kurt V. Jensen and published online at www.jggj.dk/saracenos.htm. For this extract, see ch. XVI.

104 'Christianissimus Jerosolymorum Rex GODEFRIDUS DE BULLON, Dux Brabantiae, Dominus de Lens in Artesio, & Comes de Bolonia supra mare', in *ODEH*, vol. 1, pp. 204–5 (no. 88). On this, see: Peter R. Grillo, 'Note sur le Cycle de la Croisade du MS BN fr. 12569: les reliques de Lens', *Romania*, 94 (1973), 258–67.

105 'a tempore Godefridi', *Diplomatic Documents preserved in the Public Record Office, 1, 1101–1272*, ed. Pierre Chaplais (London, 1964), pp. 241–2 (no. 343).

106 'Le Chevalier o chisne fu pour li combatans, | Quant il sa fille prist, dont il ot. III. enfans. | Godefroi en sailli, qui puis fu roy puissans | Là en Jerusalem, outre les mescréans'. *Doon de Maience*, ed. Alexandre Pey (Paris, 1859), p. 242.

107 'Le Chevalier o chisne o li cinq compengnon, | Et une gentil dame qui fu de grant renon; | Du chu lignage fu Godefroi de Billon'. *Gaufrey*, ed. François Guessard and Polycarpe Chabaille (Paris, 1859), p. 4.

108 *Les Enfances Renier*, ed. Delphine Dalens-Marekovic (Paris, 2009), pp. 408, 713, 853–4, 874.

109 See: *OFCC*, vol. 1, pp. xxvii–xxviii.

110 'Un récit en vers Français de la Première Croisade fondé sur Boudri de Bourgueil', ed. Paul Meyer, *Romania*, 5 (1876), 1–63, 6 (1877), 489–94.

111 'Un récit en vers', ed. Mayer, p. 22.

112 'Godefroy de Bulon | Qui Jerusalem conquist, | Et tant paiens a la mort mist'. *Le Pas Saladin*, ed. Frank E. Lodeman (Baltimore, 1897), p. 10.

113 'Ne Godefrai de sainte vie | Ki fu reis nobles en Surie'. John of Howden, *Rossignos*, ed. Glynn Hesketh (London, 2006), pp. 141–2.

114 'Ha! Antioche, Terre sainte, | Con ci at delireuze plainte | Quant tu n'as mais nuns Godefrois!' Rutebeuf, *Oeuvres Complètes*, ed. Michel Zink (Paris, 1990), pp. 854–5.

115 Dante Alighieri, *The Divine Comedy*, tr. Charles S. Singleton, 3 vols in 6 (Princeton, 1971–5), vol. 3.1, pp. 200–1 (*Canto* XVIII of the *Paradiso*).

116 On these texts, see in general: Antony Leopold, *How to Recover the Holy Land: The Crusade Proposals of the Late Thirteenth and Early Fourteenth Centuries* (Aldershot, 2000); Jacques Paviot, *Projets de Croisade (v. 1290–1330)* (Paris, 2008).

117 Pierre Dubois, *De recuperatione Terre Sancte*, ed. Charles V. Langlois (Paris, 1891), p. 88, tr. in Pierre Dubois, *The Recovery of the Holy Land*, tr. Walther I. Brandt (New York, 1956), p. 156.

118 'Cujus passagii, in hoc quod factum armorum spectabat, fuit capitaneus Godofredus et Bulhon qui Jherusalem acquisivit'. Fulk of Villaret, *Informatio et instructio super faciendo generali passagio pro recuperatione Terre Sancte*, ed. Jospeh Petit, 'Mémoire de Foulques de Villaret sur la croisade', *Bibliothèque de l'école des chartes*, 60 (1899), 602–10, at p. 604.

119 Fulk of Villaret, et al., *Qualiter Terra Sancta possit per Christianos recuperari*, ed. Benjamin Z. Kedar and Sylvia Schein, 'Un projet de "passage particulier" proposé par l'ordre de l'Hôpital, 1306–1307', *Bibliothèque de l'école des chartes*, 137 (1979), 211–26, with edition of the tract at pp. 221–26, and the reference to Godfrey at p. 222.

120 'Memoria Terre Sancte', ed. Charles Kohler, 'Deux projets de croisade en Terre Sainte (XIIIᵉ–XIVᵉ siècle)', *Mélanges pour servir à l'histoire de l'Orient latin et des Croisades*, 2 vols, c.p. (Paris, 1906), pp. 545–67, at pp. 546–7.

121 Marino Sanudo Torsello, *Liber Secretorum Fidelium Crucis*, in *Gesta Dei per Francos*, ed. Jacques Bongars, 2 vols in 3 (Hannover, 1611), vol. 2, pp. 1–288, at pp. 39–47, tr. in Marino Sanudo Torsello, *The Book of the Secrets of the Faithful of the Cross*, tr. Peter Lock (Farnham, 2011), pp. 76–87.

122 Sanudo, *Liber Secretorum*, pp. 130–52, tr. pp. 210–42.

123 'De l'ensample del bon Duk Godfrey de Bolyonne'. Roger of Stangrave, *Li charboclois d'armes du conquest precious de la terre saint de promission*, ed. Jacques Paviot, *Projets de Croisade*, pp. 293–387, at p. 340.

124 *Directorium ad passagium faciendum*, *RHC Arm.*, vol. 2, pp. 367–517, at p. 419.

125 An edition of the *Voeux du paon* can be found interspersed throughout *The Buik of Alexander or the Buik of the most Noble and Valiant Alexander the Great*, ed. Graeme Ritchie, 4 vols (Edinburgh, 1919–27). On the poem and its influence, see: Catherine Gaullier-Bougassas, 'Les *Voeux du Paon*, une grande oeuvre à succès de le fin du Moyen Âge', in Catherine Gaullier-Bougassas (ed.), *Les Voeux du Paon de Jacques de Longuyon: originalité et rayonnement* (Paris, 2011), pp. 7–32.

126 *Buik of Alexander*, vol. 4, p. 406.

127 See, among others: Jacqueline Cerquiglini-Toulet, 'Fama et Les Preux: Nom et Renom à La Fin du Moyen Âge', *Médiévales*, 24 (1993), 35–44.

Bibliography

NB: For abbreviations, see above, pp. viii–xiii.

Manuscripts

London, British Library
    MS. Add. 33566 [Vicenzo Fava, *Relatione del Viaggio di Gierusalemme*].
    MS. Henry Yates Thompson 12.

Source collections

Monumenta Germaniae Historica.
    Constitutiones et acta publica imperatorum et regum.
    Diplomata Regum et Imperatorum Germaniae.
        Diplomata Heinrici III.
        Diplomata Heinrici IV.
    Epistolae: Die Briefe der deutschen Kaiserzeit.
    Epistulae selectae.
    Libelli de lite imperatorum et pontificum.
    Scriptores (In Folio).
    Scriptores rerum Germanicarum in usum scholarum separatim editi.
    Scriptores rerum Germanicarum, Nova series.
The Old French Crusade Cycle, ed. Emmanuel J. Mickel and Jan A. Nelson, 10 vols in 11 (Tucsaloosa, 1977–2003).
    La Naissance du Chevalier au Cygne, ed. Emmanuel J. Mickel and Jan A. Nelson.
    Le Chevalier au Cygne and La Fin d'Elias, ed. Jan A. Nelson.
    Les Enfances Godefroi and Le Retour de Cornumarant, ed. Emmanuel J. Mickel.
    La Chanson d'Antioche, ed. Jan A. Nelson.
    Les Chétifs, ed. Geoffrey M. Myers.
    La Chanson de Jérusalem, ed. Nigel R. Thorp.
    The Jérusalem Continuations, Part I: La Chrétienté Corbaran, ed. Peter R. Grillo.
    The Jérusalem Continuations, Part II: La Prise d'Acre, La Mort Godefroi, and La Chanson des Rois Baudoin, ed. Peter R. Grillo.
    The Jérusalem Continuations: The London-Turin Version, ed. Peter R. Grillo.
    La Geste du Chevalier au Cygne, ed. Edmond A. Emplaincourt.
    Godefroi de Buillon, ed. Jan B. Roberts.

Patrologia Latina, ed. Jacques-Paul Migne, 217 vols.
Recueil des Historiens des Croisades.
   Documents Arméniens, 2 vols.
   Historiens Occidentaux, 5 vols.
Recueil des Historiens des Gaules et de la France, ed. Martin Bouqet et al., 24 vols.
Regesta Pontificum Romanorum ab condita ecclesia ad annum post Christum natum MCX-CVII, ed. Philippe Jaffé, S. Loewenfeld et al., 2 vols, 2nd edn (Leipzig, 1885–8).
Revised Regesta Regni Hierosolymitani Database [http://crusades-regesta.com/].

Primary sources

Actes des comtes de Flandre, 1071–1128, ed. Fernand Vercauteren (Brussels, 1938).
Actes des Comtes de Namur de la première race (946–1196), ed. Félix Rousseau (Brussels, 1937).
Albert of Aachen, *Historia Ierosolimitana: History of the Journey to Jerusalem*, ed. and tr. Susan B. Edgington (Oxford, 2007).
Alighieri, Dante, *The Divine Comedy*, tr. Charles S. Singleton, 3 vols in 6 (Princeton, 1971–1975).
Ambroise, *Estoire de la Guerre Sainte*, ed. and tr. Marianne Ailes and Malcolm Barber, 2 vols (Woodbridge, 2003).
Anecdotes historiques. Légendes et apologues tirés du recueil inédit d'Étienne de Bourbon, ed. A. Lecoy de la Marche (Paris, 1877).
The Anglo-Saxon Chronicle, tr. Dorothy Whitelock and David C. Douglas (London, 1961).
Anna Komnene, *The Alexiad*, tr. E. R. A. Sewter, rev. Peter Frankopan (London, 2009).
Annales Altahenses Maiores, MGH SS, rer. Germ., vol. 4.
Annales Mosomagenses, MGH SS, vol. 3, pp. 160–6.
Annales S. Iacobi Leodiensis, MGH SS, vol. 16, pp. 635–45.
Annales Yburgenses, MGH SS, vol. 16, pp. 434–8.
Anselm of Liège, *Gesta Episcoporum Tungrensium, Trajectensium, et Leodiensium, MGH SS*, vol. 7, pp. 161–234.
Archives législatives de la ville de Reims, ed. Pierre Varin, 2 vols in 4 (Paris, 1840–1852).
Baldric of Bourgueil, *Historia Ierosolimitana*, ed. Steven Biddlecombe (Woodbridge, 2014).
'Bartolf of Nangis', *Gesta Francorum Iherusalem Expugnantium, RHC Occ.*, vol. 3, pp. 487–543.
Benzo of Alba, *Ad Heinricum IV, imperatorem libri VII, MGH SS rer. Germ.*, vol. 65.
Bertholds und Bernolds Chroniken, ed. I. S. Robinson (Darmstadt, 2002).
Bonizo of Sutri, *Liber ad amicum, MGH Libelli*, vol. 1, pp. 568–620, tr. in *The Papal Reform of the Eleventh Century: Lives of Pope Leo IX and Pope Gregory VII*, tr. I. S. Robinson (Manchester, 2004), pp. 158–261.
Die Briefe Heinrichs IV., Q H IV, pp. 5–20, 51–141, 469–83.
Brunonis Saxonicum Bellum, Q H IV, pp. 191–405.
The Buik of Alexander or the Buik of the Most Noble and Valiant Alexander the Great, ed. Graeme Ritchie, 4 vols (Edinburgh, 1919–1927).
Carmen de Bello Saxonico, Q H IV, pp. 143–89.

The Carmen de Hastingae Proelio of Guy Bishop of Amiens, ed. and tr. Frank Barlow (Oxford, 1999).

Cartulaire de l'abbaye de Gorze, ed. Armand d'Herbomez (Paris, 1898).

Cartulaire de l'abbaye de Saint-Trond, ed. Charles Piot, 2 vols (Brussels, 1870–1874).

Le Cartulaire du Chapitre du Saint-Sépulcre de Jérusalem, ed. Geneviève Bresc-Bautier (Paris, 1984).

Cartulaire de la Commune de Couvin, ed. Stanislas Bormans (Namur, 1875).

Le Cartulaire de Marcigny-sur-Loire, 1045–1144, ed. Jean Richard (Dijon, 1957).

Cartulaire general de l'Ordre des Hospitaliers de Saint-Jean de Jérusalem, 1100–1300, ed. Joseph Delaville de Roulx, 4 vols (Paris, 1894–1906).

La Chanson d'Antioche, ed. Suzanne Duparc-Quioc, 2 vols (Paris, 1977–1978), tr. in *The Chanson d'Antioche: An Old French Account of the First Crusade*, tr. Susan B. Edgington and Carol Sweetenham (Farnham, 2011).

The Chanson des Chétifs and Chanson de Jérusalem: Completing the Central Trilogy of the Old French Crusade Cycle, tr. Carol Sweetenham (Farnham, 2016).

Les Chartes du Clermontois, conservées au musée Condé, à Chantilly, ed. André Lesort (Paris, 1904).

Chartes de l'abbaye de Saint-Hubert en Ardenne, ed. Godefroid Kurth, 2 vols (Brussels, 1903).

Chronicon Wirziburgense, MGH SS, vol. 6, pp. 17–31.

La Chronique de Saint Hubert dite Cantatorium, ed. Karl Hanquet (Brussels, 1906).

Chroniques des comtes d'Anjou et des seigneurs d'Amboise, ed. Louis Halphen and René Poupardin (Paris, 1913).

Codice Diplomatico Polironiano (961–1125), ed. Rosella Rinaldi, Carla Villani and Paolo Golinelli (Bologna, 1993).

La Continuation de Guillaume de Tyr (1184–1197), ed. Margaret Ruth Morgan (Paris, 1982), tr. in *The Conquest of Jerusalem and the Third Crusade: Sources in Translation*, tr. Peter Edbury (Aldershot, 1998).

The Crusades: Idea and Reality, 1095–1274, tr. Louise Riley-Smith and Jonathan Riley-Smith (London, 1981).

The Damascus Chronicle of the Crusades: Extracted and Translated From the Chronicle of Ibn al-Qalānisī, ed. and tr. H. A. R. Gibb (London, 1932).

Damian, Peter, *Die Briefe des Petrus Damiani, MGH Epistolae: Briefe*, vol. 4.

Diplomata belgica ante annum millesimum centesimum scripta, ed. M. Gysseling and A. C. F. Koch (Brussels, 1950).

Diplomatic Documents Preserved in the Public Record Office, 1, 1101–1272, ed. Pierre Chaplais (London, 1964).

Directorium ad passagium faciendum, RHC Arm., vol. 2, pp. 367–517.

'Documents extraits du cartulaire du chapitre de Fosses', ed. J. Barbier, *Analectes pour servir à l'histoire ecclésiastique de la Belgique*, 4 (1867), 396–422.

'Documents relatifs à l'abbaye de Flône', ed. M. Evrard, *Analectes pour servir à l'histoire ecclésiastique de belgique*, 23 (1892), 273–504.

Doon de Maience, ed. Alexandre Pey (Paris, 1859).

Dudo of St Quentin, *De moribus et actis primorum Normanniae ducum*, ed. Jules Lair (Caen, 1865), tr. in Dudo of St Quentin, *History of the Normans*, tr. Eric Christiansen (Woodbridge, 1998).

Eleventh-Century Germany: The Swabian Chronicles, tr. I. S. Robinson (Manchester, 2008).

Les Enfances Renier, ed. Delphine Dalens-Marekovic (Paris, 2009).

Epistulae et Chartae ad Historiam Primi Belli Sacri Spectantes Quae Supersunt Aevo Aequales ac Genuinae: Die Kreuzzugsbriefe aus des Jahren 1088–1100, ed. Heinrich Hagenmeyer (Innsbruck, 1901).

Frutolfi et Ekkehardi Chronica necnon Anonymi Chronica Imperatorum, ed. Franz-Josef Schmale and Irene Schmale-Ott (Darmstadt, 1972), tr. in *Chronicles of the Investiture Contest: Frutolf of Michelsberg and His Continuators*, tr. T. J. H. McCarthy (Manchester, 2014).

Fulcher of Chartres, *Historia Hierosolymitana*, ed. Heinrich Hagenmeyer (Heidelberg, 1913), tr. in Fulcher of Chartres, *A History of the Expedition to Jerusalem, 1095–1127*, tr. Frances R. Ryan (Knoxville, 1969).

Fulk of Villaret, *Informatio et instructio super faciendo generali passagio pro recuperatione Terre Sancte*, ed. Jospeh Petit, 'Mémoire de Foulques de Villaret sur la croisade', *Bibliothèque de l'école des chartes*, 60 (1899), 602–10.

Fulk of Villaret, et al., *Qualiter Terra Sancta possit per Christianos recuperari*, ed. Benjamin Z. Kedar and Sylvia Schein, 'Un projet de "passage particulier" proposé par l'ordre de l'Hôpital, 1306–1307', *Bibliothèque de l'école des chartes*, 137 (1979), 211–26.

Gaufrey, ed. François Guessard and Polycarpe Chabaille (Paris, 1859).

Genealogia Comitum Buloniensium, MGH SS, vol. 9, pp. 299–301.

Geoffrey of Villehardouin, *De La Conqueste de Constantinople*, ed. Paulin Paris (Paris, 1838), tr. in *Joinville and Villehardouin: Chronicles of the Crusades*, tr. Caroline Smith (London, 2008), pp. 1–144.

Gesta Francorum et aliorum Iherosolimitanorum, ed. and tr. Rosalind Hill (Oxford, 1962).

The Gesta Guillelmi of William of Poitiers, ed. and tr. R. H. C. Davis and Marjorie Chibnall (Oxford, 1998).

The Gesta Normannorum Ducum of William of Jumièges, Orderic Vitalis and Robert of Torigni, ed. and tr. Elisabeth van Houts, 2 vols (Oxford, 1992–1995).

Giles of Orval, *Gesta episcoporum Leodiensium, MGH SS*, vol. 25, pp. 1–129.

Giles of Orval, *Gesta episcoporum Leodensium abbreviata, MGH SS*, vol. 25, pp. 129–35.

Gilo of Paris and a second anonymous author, *The Historia vie Hierosolimitane*, ed. and tr. C. W. Grocock and Elizabeth Siberry (Oxford, 1997).

Guibert of Nogent, *Dei Gesta per Francos*, ed. R. B. C. Huygens (Turnhout, 1996), tr. in Guibert of Nogent, *The Deeds of God Through the Franks*, tr. Robert Levine (Woodbridge, 1997).

Guillaume de Tyr et ses continuateurs: Text français du XIIIe siècle, revu et annote, ed. Paulin Paris, 2 vols (Paris, 1879–1880).

Gunther of Pairis, *Historia Captae a Latinis Constantinopoleos, PL*, vol. 212, cols 221–56, tr. in Gunther of Pairis, *Hystoria Constantinopolitana*, tr. Alfred J. Andrea (Philadelphia, 1997).

Hebräische Berichte über die Judenverfolgungen während der Kreuzzüge, ed. Adolf Neubauer and Moritz Stern (Berlin, 1892).

Herman of Reichenau, *Chronicle, MGH SS*, vol. 5, pp. 67–133, tr. in *Eleventh-Century Germany: The Swabian Chronicles*, tr. I. S. Robinson (Manchester, 2008), pp. 58–98.

Humbert of Romans, *De predicatione crucis contra Saracenos*, ed. Peter Wagner (Nuremberg, c.1495), transcribed by Kurt V. Jensen (www.jggj.dk/saracenos.htm).

Imperial Lives and Letters of the Eleventh Century, tr. Theodor M. Mommsen and Karl F. Morrison (New York, 1962).

Itinerarium Peregrinorum et Gesta Regis Ricardi, in *Chronicles and Memorials of the Reign of Richard I*, ed. William Stubbs, 2 vols (London, 1864), vol. 1, pp. 1–450, tr. in *The*

Chronicle of the Third Crusade: The Itinerarium Peregrinorum and the Gesta Regis Ricardi, tr. Helen J. Nicholson (Aldershot, 1997).

The Jews and the Crusaders: The Hebrew Chronicles of the First and Second Crusades, tr. Shlomo Eidelberg (Madison, 1977).

Lampert of Hersfeld, *Annales*, ed. Oswald Holder-Egger, rev. by Adolf Schmidt and Wolfgang D. Fritz (Darmstadt, 1962), tr. in *The Annals of Lampert of Hersfeld*, tr. I. S. Robinson (Manchester, 2015).

Landulf Senior, *Historia Mediolanensis*, *MGH SS*, vol. 8, pp. 32–100.

Letters From the East: Crusaders, Pilgrims and Settlers in the 12th–13th Centuries, tr. Malcolm Barber and Keith Bate (Farnham, 2010).

Leo Marsicanus, *Chronica monasterii Casinensis, MGH SS*, vol. 34.

John of Howden, *Rossignos*, ed. Glynn Hesketh (London, 2006).

John of Ibelin, *Le Livre des Assises*, ed. Peter Edbury (Leiden, 2003).

'Memoria Terre Sancte', ed. Charles Kohler, 'Deux projets de croisade en Terre Sainte (XIIIᵉ–XIVᵉ siècle)', *Mélanges pour servir à l'histoire de l'Orient latin et des Croisades*, 2 vols, c.p. (Paris, 1906), pp. 545–67.

Opera diplomatica et historica, ed. Aubert Miraeus and Jean-François Foppens, 4 vols (Brussels, 1723–1748).

Orderic Vitalis, *The Ecclesiastical History of Orderic Vitalis*, ed. and tr. Marjorie Chibnall, 6 vols (Oxford, 1969–1980).

Ordinatio de Predicatione Sancti Crucis, in *Quinti Belli Sacri Scriptores Minores*, ed. Reinhold Röhricht (Geneva, 1879), pp. 2–26.

'Papsturkunden in Florenz', ed. Wilhem Wiederhold, *Nachrichten von der Gesellschaft der Wissenschaften zu Göttingen. Philosophisch-historische Klasse*, 3 (1901), 306–25.

Papsturkunden in Spanien: I Katalonien, ed. Paul Kehr (Berlin, 1926).

Le Pas Saladin, ed. Frank E. Lodeman (Baltimore, 1897).

Philip of Novara, *Le Livre de Forme de Plait*, ed. and tr. Peter Edbury (Nicosia, 2009).

Pierre Dubois, *De recuperatione Terre Sancte*, ed. Charles V. Langlois (Paris, 1891), tr. in Pierre Dubois, *The Recovery of the Holy Land*, tr. Walther I. Brandt (New York, 1956).

[*Quantum Praedecessores*] Rolf Große, 'Überlegungen zum Kreuzzugsaufruf Eugens III. von 1145/46: Mit einer Neuedition von JL 8876', *Francia*, 18 (1991), pp. 85–92.

Quellen zur Geschichte Kaiser Heinrichs IV., ed. Franz-Josef Schmale and Irene Schmale-Ott (Darmstadt, 1968).

Ralph of Caen, *Tancredus*, ed. Edoardo D'Angelo (Turnhout, 2011), tr. in Ralph of Caen, *Gesta Tancredi*, tr. Bernard S. Bachrach and David S. Bachrach (Aldershot, 2005).

Raymond of Aguilers, *Liber*, ed. John H. Hill and Laurita L. Hill (Paris, 1969), tr. in Raymond of Aguilers, *Historia Francorum qui ceperunt Iherusalem*, tr. John H. Hill and Laurita L. Hill (Philadelphia, 1968).

'Un récit en vers Français de la Première Croisade fondé sur Boudri de Bourgueil', ed. Paul Meyer, *Romania*, 5 (1876), 1–63, 6 (1877), pp. 489–94.

Récits d'un ménestrel de Reims au XIIIᵉ siècle, ed. Natalis de Wailly (Paris, 1876), tr. in *A Thirteenth-Century Minstrel's Chronicle*, tr. Robert Levine (Lampeter, 1990).

Recueil des chartes de l'abbaye de Stavelot-Malmédy, ed. Joseph Halkin and Charles G. Roland, 2 vols (Brussels, 1909).

Das Register Gregors VII., ed. Erich Caspar, *MGH Ep. sel.*, 2 vols (Berlin, 1920–3), tr. in *The Register of Pope Gregory VII 1073–1085: An English Translation*, tr. H. E. J. Cowdrey (Oxford, 2002).

Robert the Monk, *Historia Iherosolimitana*, ed. Damien Kempf and Marcus Bull (Woodbridge, 2013), tr. in *Robert the Monk's History of the First Crusade: Historia Iherosolimitana*, tr. Carol Sweetenham (Aldershot, 2005).

Roger of Stangrave, *Li charboclois d'armes du conquest precious de la terre saint de promission*, ed. Jacques Paviot, *Projets de Croisade (v. 1290–1330)* (Paris, 2008), pp. 293–387.

Rutebeuf, *Oeuvres Complètes*, ed. Michel Zink (Paris, 1990).

Sancti Anselmi Cantuariensis Archiepiscopi, Opera Omnia, ed. F. S. Schmitt, 6 vols (Edinburgh, 1946–1963), with translations of the letters in *The Letters of Saint Anselm of Canterbury*, tr. Walter Frölich, 3 vols (Kalamazoo, 1990).

Sancti Bernardi Opera, ed. Jean Leclercq, et al., 9 vols in 10 (Rome, 1957–1977).

Sigebert of Gembloux, *Chronicon, MGH SS*, vol. 6, pp. 300–74.

The Song of Roland, tr. Gerard J. Brault, 2 vols (University Park, PA, 1978).

Storia de'Normanni di Amato di Montecassino volgarizzata in antico francese, ed. Vincenzo de Bartholomaeis (Rome, 1935), tr. in Amatus of Montecassino, *The History of the Normans*, tr. Prescott N. Dunbar, rev. by Graham A. Loud (Woodbridge, 2004).

Table chronologique des chartes et diplômes imprimés concernant l'histoire de la Belgique, ed. Alphonse Wauters, et al., 12 vols (Brussels, 1866–1919).

The Templars: Selected Sources, tr. Malcolm Barber and Keith Bate (Manchester, 2002).

Translatio S. Servatii, MGH SS, vol. 12, pp. 85–126.

Trumphus Sancti Remacli, MGH SS, vol. 11, pp. 433–61.

Tudebode, Peter, *Historia de Hierosolymitano itinere*, ed. John H. Hill and Laurita L. Hill (Paris, 1977), tr. in Peter Tudebode, *Historia de Hierosolymitano itinere*, tr. John H. Hill and Laurita L. Hill (Philadelphia, 1974).

Udalric of Zell, *Consuetudines Cluniacenses, PL*, vol. 149, cols 635–778.

Die Urkunden der lateinischen Könige von Jerusalem, ed. Hans E. Mayer, 4 vols, c.p. (Hannover, 2010).

Die Urkunden und Briefe der Markgräfin Mathilde von Tuszien, ed. Elke Goez and Werner Goez (Hannover, 1998).

Vita Heinrici II. Imperatoris, auctore Adalboldo, MGH SS, vol. 4, pp. 679–95.

Vita Heinrici IV. Imperatoris, Q H IV, pp. 407–67.

William of Apulia, *Gesta Robertii Wiscardi, MGH SS*, vol. 9, pp. 239–98.

William of Malmesbury, *Gesta Regum Anglorum*, ed. and tr. R. A. B. Mynors, completed by Rodney M. Thomson and Michael Winterbottom, 2 vols (Oxford, 1998–9).

William of Tyre, *Chronique*, ed. R. B. C. Huygens, 2 vols, c.p. (Turnhout, 1986), tr. in William of Tyre, *A History of Deeds Done Beyond the Sea*, tr. Ernest A. Babcock and August C. Krey, 2 vols (New York, 1943).

Secondary sources

Aird, William M., *Robert Curthose, Duke of Normandy* (Woodbridge, 2008).

Althoff, Gerd, *"Selig sind, die Verfolgung ausüben": Päpste und Gewalt im Hochmittelalter* (Darmstadt, 2013).

Althoff, Gerd, Johannes Fried and Patrick J. Geary (eds), *Medieval Concepts of the Past: Ritual, Memory and Historiography* (Cambridge, 2002).

Amouroux-Mourad, Monique, *Le comte d'Edesse, 1098–1150* (Paris, 1988).

Andressohn, John C., *The Ancestry and Life of Godfrey of Bouillon* (Bloomington, 1947).

Arnold, Benjamin, *Princes and Territories in Medieval Germany* (Cambridge, 1991).

Asbridge, Thomas, *The Creation of the Principality of Antioch, 1098–1130* (Woodbridge, 2000).

———, *The First Crusade: A New History* (London, 2004).

———, 'The Holy Lance of Antioch: Power, Devotion and Memory on the First Crusade', *Reading Medieval Studies*, 33 (2007), 3–36.

———, 'The Significance and Causes of the Battle of the Field of Blood', *JMH*, 24 (1997), 301–16.

Aubé, Pierre, *Godefroy de Bouillon* (Paris, 1985).

'L'avouerie en Lotharingie', *PSHISGL*, 98 (1984).

Bachrach, David S., and Bernard S. Bachrach, 'Bruno of Merseburg and His Historical Method, c.1085', *JMH*, 40 (2014), 381–98.

Baert, Barbara, *A Heritage of Holy Wood: The Legend of the True Cross in Text and Image*, tr. Lee Preedy (Leiden, 2004).

Barber, Malcolm, *The Crusader States in the Twelfth Century* (New Haven, 2012).

Barlow, Frank, *Edward the Confessor*, new edn (New Haven, 1997).

———, *William Rufus*, new edn (New Haven, 2000).

Barthélemy, Dominique, *The Serf, the Knight, and the Historian*, tr. Graham R. Edwards (Ithaca, 2009).

Bartlett, Robert, *The Making of Europe: Conquest, Colonisation and Cultural Change, 950–1350* (London, 1993).

Bates, David, *William the Conqueror* (New Haven, 2016).

———, *William the Conqueror*, new edn (Stroud, 2004).

Bates, David, Julia Crick and Sarah Hamilton (eds), *Writing Medieval Biography, 750–1250: Essays in Honour of Professor Frank Barlow* (Woodbridge, 2006).

Baudhuin, Jean, 'Les relations entre le comte de Namur Albert III et l'abbaye de Saint-Hubert', in Joseph Balon (ed.), *Études d'histoire et d'archéologie namuroises dédiées à Ferdinand Courtoy*, 2 vols (Namur, 1952), vol. 1, pp. 327–34.

Bauer, N., 'Der Fund von Spanko bei St. Petersburg', *Zeitschrift für Numismatik*, 36 (1926), 75–94.

Becker, Alfons, *Papst Urban II. (1088–1099)*, 3 vols (Stuttgart, 1964–2012).

———, 'Urban II. und die deutsche Kirche', in Josef Fleckenstein (ed.), *Investiturstreit und Reichsverfassung* (Sigmaringen, 1973), pp. 241–75.

Bedos-Rezak, Brigitte, 'Medieval Seals and the Study of Chivalric Society', in Howell Chickering and Thomas H. Seiler (eds), *The Study of Chivalry: Resources and Approaches* (Kalamazoo, 1988), pp. 313–72.

Bellomo, Elena, 'The First Crusade and the Latin East as Seen From Venice: The Account of the Translatio sancti Nicolai', *Early Medieval Europe*, 17 (2009), 420–43.

Bennett, Matthew, 'Military Masculinity in England and Northern France, c.1050–c.1225', in Dawn M. Hadley (ed.), *Masculinity in Medieval Europe* (London, 1999), pp. 71–88.

Berend, Nora, 'Hungary in the Eleventh and Twelfth Centuries', *NCMH*, vol. 4, part 2, pp. 304–16.

Blake, E. O., and Colin Morris, 'A Hermit Goes to War: Peter and the Origins of the First Crusade', *SCH*, 22 (1985), pp. 79–107.

Blumenthal, Uta-Renate, *The Investiture Controversy: Church and Monarchy From the Ninth to the Twelfth Century* (Philadelphia, 1988).

———, 'Papal Registers in the Twelfth Century', in Peter Linehan (ed.), *Proceedings of the Seventh International Congress of Medieval Canon Law (Cambridge, 23–27 July 1984)* (Vatican City, 1988), pp. 135–51.

Bonenfant-Feytmans, Anne-Marie, 'Le plus ancien acte de l'abbaye d'Andenne', in *Etudes d'histoire dédiées à la mémoire de Henri Pirenne: par ses anciens élèves* (Brussels, 1937), pp. 19–33.

Bony, Pierre, 'L'image du pouvoir seigneurial dans les sceaux: codification des signes de la puissance de la fin du XIe au début du XIIIe siècle dans les pays d'Oïl', in *Seigneurs et seigneuries au moyen âge: actes du 117e congrès national des Sociétes savantes, Clermont-Ferrand 1992* (Paris, 1995), pp. 489–523.

Boshof, Egon, 'Lothringen, Frankreich und das Reich in der Regierungszeit Heinrichs III.', *Rheinische Vierteljahrsblätter,* 42 (1978), 63–127.

Bradbury, Jim, *The Medieval Archer* (Woodbridge, 1985).

Breysig, Kurt, 'Gottfried von Bouillon vor dem Kreuzzüge', *Westdeutsche Zeitschrift für Geschichte und Kunst,* 17 (1898), 169–201.

Bridgeford, Andrew, 'Was Count Eustace II of Boulogne the patron of the Bayeux Tapestry?', *JMH,* 25 (1999), 155–85.

Brown, E. A. R., 'Taxation and Morality in the Thirteenth and Fourteenth Centuries: Conscience and Political Power and the Kings of France', *French Historical Review,* 8 (1973), 1–28.

Brown, Shirley A., 'The Bayeux Tapestry: Why Eustace, Odo and William?', *ANS,* 12 (1990), 7–28.

Brundage, James A., 'Adhemar of Puy: The Bishop and His Critics', *Speculum,* 34 (1958), 201–12.

———, 'An Errant Crusader: Stephen of Blois', *Traditio,* 16 (1960), 380–95.

Buckley, Penelope, *The Alexiad of Anna Komnene: Artistic Strategy in the Making of a Myth* (Cambridge, 2014).

Bull, Marcus, 'The Capetian Monarchy and the Early Crusade Movement: Hugh of Vermandois and Louis VII', *Nottingham Medieval Studies,* 40 (1996), 25–46.

———, *Knightly Piety and the Lay Response to the First Crusade: The Limousin and Gascony, c.970–c.1130* (Oxford, 1993).

———, 'The Relationship Between the *Gesta Francorum* and Peter Tudebode's *Historia de Hierosolymitano Itinere.* The Evidence of a Hitherto Unexamined Manuscript (St. Catharine's College, Cambridge, 3)', *Crusades,* 11 (2012), 1–17.

Bull, Marcus, and Damien Kempf, 'Introduction', in *WEC,* pp. 1–8.

Bur, Michel, 'La Frontière entre la Champagne et la Lorraine du milieu du Xe à la fin du XIIe siècle', *Francia,* 4 (1976), 237–54.

Bysted, Ane L., *The Crusade Indulgence: Spiritual Rewards and the Theology of the Crusades, c.1095–1216* (Leiden, 2015).

Calmet, Augustin, *Histoire de Lorraine,* 7 vols, new edn (Nancy, 1747–1757).

Cassidy-Welch, Megan (ed.), *Remembering the Crusades and Crusading* (Abingdon, 2017).

Cauchie, Alfred, *La Querelle des investitures dans les diocèses de Liège et de Cambrai,* 2 vols (Louvain, 1890–1891).

Cerquiglini-Toulet, Jacqueline, 'Fama et Les Preux: Nom et Renom à La Fin du Moyen Âge', *Médiévales,* 24 (1993), 35–44.

Chazan, Robert, *God, Humanity, and History: The Hebrew First Crusade Narratives* (Berkeley, 2000).

Clouet, Louis, *Histoire de Verdun et du pays Verdunois,* 3 vols (Verdun, 1867–1870).

Cobb, Paul M., *The Race for Paradise: An Islamic History of the Crusades* (Oxford, 2014).

Cohen, Jeremy, *Sanctifying the Name of God: Jewish Martyrs and Jewish Memories of the First Crusade* (Philadelphia, 2004).

Cole, Penny J., *The Preaching of the Crusades to the Holy Land, 1095–1270* (Cambridge, MA, 1991).

Constable, Giles, 'The Financing of the Crusades in the Twelfth Century', in Benjamin Z. Kedar, Hans E. Mayer, and R. C. Smail (eds), *Outremer: Studies in the History of the Crusading Kingdom of Jerusalem presented to Joshua Prawer* (Jerusalem, 1982), pp. 64–88.

———, 'The Historiography of the Crusades', in Angeliki E. Laiou and Roy P. Mottahedeh (eds), *The Crusades From the Perspective of Byzantium and the Muslim World* (Washington, 2001), pp. 1–22.

Cosgrove, Walker R., 'Crucesignatus: A Refinement or Merely One More Term Among Many?', in Thomas F. Madden, James L. Naus, and Vincent Ryan (eds), *The Crusades: Medieval Worlds in Conflict* (Farnham, 2010), pp. 95–107.

Cowdrey, H. E. J., *The Cluniacs and the Gregorian Reform* (Oxford, 1970).

———, 'The Peace and the Truce of God in the Eleventh Century', *Past and Present*, 46 (1970), 42–67.

———, *Pope Gregory VII, 1073–1085* (Oxford, 1998).

———, 'Pope Gregory VII's "crusading" plans of 1074', in Benjamin Z. Kedar, Hans E. Mayer and R. C. Smail (eds), *Outremer: Studies in the History of the Crusading Kingdom of Jerusalem presented to Joshua Prawer* (Jerusalem, 1982), pp. 27–40.

———, 'Urban II's Preaching of the First Crusade', *History*, 55 (1970), 177–88.

Crozet, René, 'Le voyage d'Urbain II et ses négociations avec le clergé de France (1095–1096)', *Revue Historique*, 179 (1937), 271–310.

Davis, H. W. C., 'Henry of Blois and Brian FitzCount', *EHR*, 25 (1910), 297–303.

de Gaffier, Baudouin, 'Sainte Ide de Boulogne et l'Espagne', *Analecta Bollandiana*, 86 (1968), 67–82.

de Ram, Pierre, 'Notice sur un sceau inédit de Godefroi de Bouillon', *Bulletin de l'académie royale des sciences, des lettres et des beaux-arts de Belgique*, 13 (1846), 355–60.

Despy, Georges, 'Les actes des ducs de Basse-Lotharingie du XIᵉ siècle', *PSHIGL*, 95 (1981), 65–132.

———, 'La carrière lotharingienne du pape Étienne IX', *RBPH*, 31 (1953), 955–72.

———, 'La date de l'accession de Godefroid de Bouillon au duché de Basse-Lotharingie', *RBPH*, 36 (1958), 1275–84.

———, 'La fonction ducale en Lotharingie, puis en Basse-Lotharingie de 900 à 1100', *Revue du Nord*, 48 (1966), 107–9.

———, 'Godefroid de Bouillon et l'abbaye de Saint-Hubert en 1095', *Saint-Hubert d'Ardenne: Cahiers d'histoire*, 1 (1977), 45–50.

———, 'Godefroid de Bouillon, myths et réalitiés', *Academie royale de belgique, bulletin de la classe des lettres et des sciences morales et politiques*, 71 (1985), 249–75.

———, 'Notes sur les actes de Godefroid le Barbu, comme marquis de Toscane (1054–1069)', in *Mélanges offerts par ses confrères étrangers à Charles Braibant* (Brussels, 1959), pp. 65–81.

Dickès, Jean-Pierre, *Sainte Ide de Boulogne: mère de Godefroy de Bouillon* (Paris, 2004).

Dieckmann, Friedrich, *Gottfried III der Bucklige, herzog von Niederlothringen und gemahl Mathildens von Canossa* (Erlangen, 1885).

Dorchy, Henri, 'Godefroid de Bouillon, duc de Basse-Lotharingie', *RBPH*, 26 (1948), 961–99.

Douglas, David C., *William the Conqueror: The Norman Impact on England*, new edn (New Haven, 1999).

Dumville, David, 'What is a Chronicle?', in Erik Kooper (ed.), *The Medieval Chronicle II* (Amsterdam, 2002), pp. 1–27.

Dupont, Christian, 'Les domains des ducs en Basse-Lotharingie au XIe siècle', *PSHIGL*, 95 (1981), 217–40.

Dupréel, Eugene, *Histoire Critique de Godefroid le Barbu, Duc de Lotharingie, Marquis de Toscane* (Brussels, 1904).

Edbury, Peter, 'Law and Custom in the Latin East: *les letres dou sepulcre*', *Mediterranean Historical Review*, 10 (1995), 71–9.

Edbury, Peter and John G. Rowe, *William of Tyre: Historian of the Latin East* (Cambridge, 1988).

Edgington, Susan B., 'Albert of Aachen Reappraised', in *FCTJ*, pp. 55–68.

———, 'The First Crusade: Reviewing the Evidence', in *FCOI*, pp. 55–77.

———, 'The *Gesta Francorum Iherusalem expugnantium* of "Bartolf of Nangis"', *Crusades*, 13 (2014), 21–35.

Erdmann, Carl, *The Origin of the Idea of the Crusade*, tr. Marshall W. Baldwin and Walter Goffart (Princeton, 1977).

Evergates, Theodore, *Henry the Liberal: Count of Champagne, 1127–1181* (Philadelphia, 2016).

Ferrier, Luc, 'La couronne refusée de Godefroy de Bouillon: eschatologie et humiliation de la majesté aux premiers temps du royaume latin de Jérusalem', in *Le Concile de Clermont de 1095 et l'appel à la croisade: Actes du colloque universitaire international de Clermont-Ferrand (23–25 juin 1995)* (Rome, 1997), pp. 245–65.

Flori, Jean, *Bohémond d'Antioche: chevalier d'aventure* (Paris, 2007).

———, *Chroniqueurs et propagandistes: introduction critique aux sources de la première croisade* (Geneva, 2010).

———, *La croix, la tiare et l'épée. La croisade confisquée* (Paris, 2010).

———, *La Guerre Sainte. La formation de l'ideé de croisade dans l'Occident chrétien* (Paris, 2001).

———, 'Ideology and Motivation in the First Crusade', in Helen J. Nicholson (ed.), *Palgrave Advances in the First Crusade* (Basingstoke, 2005), pp. 15–36.

———, 'Les origines de l'adoubement chevaleresque: étude des remises d'armes et du vocabulaire qui les exprime dans les sources historiques latines jusqu'au début du XIIIe siècle', *Traditio*, 35 (1979), 209–72.

———, 'De le paix de Dieu à la croisade? Un réexamen', *Crusades*, 2 (2003), 1–23.

———, *Pierre l'Ermite et la première croisade* (Paris, 1999).

Folda, Jaroslav, *The Art of the Crusaders in the Holy Land, 1098–1187* (Cambridge, 1995).

Foreville, Raymonde, 'Un chef de la première croisade: Arnoul Malecouronne', *Bulletin historique et philologique du Comité des travaux historiques* (1954–1955), 382–5.

France, John, 'Anna Comnena, the Alexiad and the First Crusade', *Reading Medieval Studies*, 10 (1983), 20–32.

———, 'The Election and Title of Godfrey de Bouillon', *Canadian Journal of History*, 18 (1983), 321–30.

———, 'Holy War and Holy Men: Erdmann and the Lives of the Saints', in *EC1*, pp. 193–208.

———, 'Moving to the Goal, June 1098–July 1099', in *JG*, pp. 133–49.

———, 'Patronage and the Appeal of the First Crusade', in *FCOI*, pp. 5–20.

———, 'Two Types of Vision on the First Crusade: Stephen of Valence and Peter Bartholomew', *Crusades*, 5 (2006), 1–20.

———, 'The Use of the Anonymous *Gesta Francorum* in the Early Twelfth-Century Sources for the First Crusade', in *FCTJ*, pp. 29–42.

——, *Victory in the East: A Military History of the First Crusade* (Cambridge, 1994).

Frankopan, Peter, *The First Crusade: The Call From the East* (London, 2012).

Freed, John B., *Frederick Barbarossa: The Prince and the Myth* (New Haven, 2016).

Gabriele, Matthew, *An Empire of Memory: The Legend of Charlemagne, the Franks, and Jerusalem Before the First Crusade* (Oxford, 2011).

Ganshof, François-Louis, 'Les origines de la Flandre impériale: contribution à l'histoire de l'ancien Brabant', *Annales de la Société royale d'archéologie de Bruxelles*, 46 (1942–1943), 99–173.

García-Guijarro, Luis, 'Some Considerations on the Crusaders' Letter to Urban II (September 1098)', in *JG*, pp. 151–71.

Gaullier-Bougassas, Catherine, 'Les *Voeux du Paon*, une grande oeuvre à succès de le fin du Moyen Âge', in Catherine Gaullier-Bougassas (ed.), *Les Voeux du Paon de Jacques de Longuyon: originalité et rayonnement* (Paris, 2011), pp. 7–32.

Genicot, Léopold, 'Princes territoriaux et sang Carolingien: La Geneaologia Comitum Buloniensium', in Léopold Genicot (ed.), *Études sur les Principautés Lotharingiennes* (Louvain, 1975), pp. 217–306.

Gerish, Deborah, 'The True Cross and the Kings of Jerusalem', *Haskins Society Journal*, 8 (1996), 137–55.

Gilchrist, John T., 'The Erdmann Thesis and the Canon Law, 1083–1141', in Peter Edbury (ed.), *Crusade and Settlement: Papers Read at the First Conference of the Society for the Study of the Crusades and the Latin East and Presented to R. C. Smail* (Cardiff, 1985), pp. 37–45.

Gillingham, John, *Richard I* (New Haven, 1999).

Glaesener, Henri, 'Godefroy de Bouillon et la bataille de l'Elster', *Revue des études historiques*, 105 (1938), 253–64.

——, 'Un mariage fertile en conséquences (Godefroid le Barbu et Béatrice de Toscane)', *Revue d'histoire ecclésiastique*, 42 (1947), 379–416.

Golinelli, Paolo, *Matilde e i Canossa* (Milan, 2004).

Green, Judith A., *The Aristocracy of Norman England* (Cambridge, 1997).

Grillo, Peter R., 'Note sur le Cycle de la Croisade du MS BN fr. 12569: les reliques de Lens', *Romania*, 94 (1973), 258–67.

Guyotjeannin, Olivier, Jacques Pycke and Benoît-Michel Tock, *Diplomatique Médiévale*, 3rd edn (Turnhout, 2006).

Hagenmeyer, Heinrich, 'Der Brief der Kreuzfahrer an den Pabst im Jahre 1099 nach der Schlacht bei Askalon', *Forschungen zur Deutschen Geschichte*, 13 (1873), 400–12.

——, *Chronologie de la Premiére Croisade, 1094–1100* (Paris, 1902).

Hamilton, Bernard, *The Latin Church in the Crusader States: The Secular Church* (London, 1980).

Handyside, Philip, *The Old French William of Tyre* (Leiden, 2015).

Hanquet, Karl, *Étude critique sur la chronique de St Hubert dite Cantatorium* (Brussels, 1900).

Harris, Jonathan, *Byzantium and the Crusades*, 2nd edn (London, 2014).

Hay, David, *The Military Leadership of Matilda of Canossa, 1046–1115* (Manchester, 2008).

Healy, Patrick, *The Chronicle of Hugh of Flavigny: Reform and the Investiture Contest in the Late-Eleventh Century* (Aldershot, 2006).

Herrmann, Hans-Walter, and Reinhard Schneider (eds), *Lotharingia: Eine europäische Kernlandschaft um das Jahr 1000* (Saarbrücken, 1995).

Hiestand, Rudolf, 'Il cronista medievale e il suo pubblico: alcune osservazioni in margine alla storiografia della crociate', *Annali della Facoltà di lettere e filosofia dell'Università di Napoli*, 27 (1984–1985), 207–27.

———, 'Juden und Christen in der Kreuzzugspropaganda und bei den Kreuzzugspredigern', in Alfred Haverkamp (ed.), *Juden und Christen zur Zeit der Kreuzzüge* (Sigmaringen, 1999), pp. 153–208.

Hill, John H., and Laurita L. Hill, 'The Convention of Alexius Comnenus and Raymond of Saint Gilles', *American Historical Review*, 58 (1953), 322–7.

———, *Raymond IV, Count of Toulouse* (Syracuse, 1962).

Hillenbrand, Carol and Carole Hillenbrand, '"Abominable Acts": The Career of Zengi', in Jonathan Phillips and Martin Hoch (eds), *The Second Crusade: Scope and Consequences* (Manchester, 2001), pp. 111–32.

———, *The Crusades: Islamic Perspectives* (Edinburgh, 1999).

Hodgson, Natasha R., 'Lions, Tigers and Bears: Encounters With Wild Animals and Bestial Imagery in the Context of Crusading to the Latin East', *Viator*, 44 (2013), 65–93.

Holt, J. C., *Magna Carta*, 3rd edn (Cambridge, 2015).

Huyghebaert, Nicholas, 'La mère de Godefroid de Bouillon: La comtesse Ide de Boulogne', *PSHIGL*, 95 (1981), 43–63.

John, Simon, '"Claruit Ibi Multum Dux Lotharingiae": The Development of the Epic Tradition of Godfrey of Bouillon and the Bisected Turk', in Simon T. Parsons and Linda M. Paterson (eds), *Literature of the Crusades* (Woodbridge, 2018), pp. 7–24.

———, 'The "Feast of the Liberation of Jerusalem": Remembering and Reconstructing the First Crusade in the Holy City, 1099–1187', *JMH*, 41 (2015), 409–31.

———, 'Godfrey of Bouillon and the Swan Knight', in Simon John and Nicholas Morton (eds), *Crusading and Warfare in the Middle Ages: Realities and Representations. Essays in Honour of John France* (Farnham, 2014), pp. 129–42.

———, 'Historical Truth and the Miraculous Past: The Use of Oral Evidence in Twelfth-Century Historical Writing on the First Crusade', *EHR*, 130 (2015), 263–301.

———, 'Liturgical Culture and Royal Inauguration in the Latin Kingdom of Jerusalem, 1099–1187', *JMH*, 43 (2017) (forthcoming).

———, 'The Papacy and the Establishment of the Kingdoms of Jerusalem, Sicily and Portugal: Twelfth-Century Papal Political Thought on Incipient Kingship', *Journal of Ecclesiastical History*, 68 (2017), 223–59.

Joranson, Einar, 'The Great German Pilgrimage of 1064–1065', in Louis J. Paetow (ed.), *The Crusades and Other Historical Essays: Presented to Dana C. Munro by His Former Students* (New York, 1928), pp. 3–43.

Joris, André, 'Observations sur la proclamation de la Trêve de Dieu à Liège à la fin du XIe siècle', in André Joris (ed.), *Villes-Affaires-Mentalités. Autour du pays mosan* (Brussels, 1993), pp. 313–44.

Keats-Rohan, K. S. B., *Domesday People: A Prosopography of Persons Occurring in English Documents: 1066–1166, Vol. I: Domesday Book* (Woodbridge, 1999).

Kedar, Benjamin Z., 'The Jerusalem Massacre of July 1099 in the Western Historiography of the Crusades', *Crusades*, 3 (2004), 15–75.

Knappen, M. M., 'Robert II of Flanders on the First Crusade', in L. J. Paetow (ed.), *The Crusades and Other Historical Essays* (New York, 1968), pp. 79–100.

Kupper, Jean-Louis, *Liège et l'Église impériale (XIe–XIIe siècle)* (Paris, 1981).

————, 'La maison d'Ardenne-Verdun et l'eglise de Liège: Remarques sur les origines d'une principauté episcopale', *PSHIGL*, 95 (1981), 201–15.

————, 'Otbert de Liège: les manipulations monétaires d'un évêque d'Empire à l'aube du XIIe siècle', *Le moyen âge*, 35 (1980), 353–85.

Laret-Kayser, Arlette, 'La function et les pouvoirs ducaux en Basse-Lotharingie au XIe siècle', *PSHIGL*, 95 (1981), 133–52.

Leopold, Antony, *How to Recover the Holy Land: The Crusade Proposals of the Late Thirteenth and Early Fourteenth Centuries* (Aldershot, 2000).

Lieberman, Max, 'A New Approach to the Knighting Ritual', *Speculum*, 90 (2015), 391–423.

Lobet, Marcel, *Godefroid de Bouillon: Essai de Biographie Antilégendaire* (Brussels, 1943).

Lösek, Fritz, ' "Et bellum inire sunt coacti": The Great Pilgrimage of 1065', in Michael J. Herren, C. J. McDonough, and Ross J. Arthur (eds), *Latin Culture in the Eleventh Century: Proceedings of the Third International Conference on Medieval Latin Studies* (Turnhout, 2002), pp. 61–72.

Loud, Graham A., *The Age of Robert Guiscard: Southern Italy and the Norman Conquest* (Harlow, 2000).

Luttrell, Anthony, 'The Earliest Hospitallers', in Benjamin Z. Kedar, Jonathan Riley-Smith and Rudolf Hiestand (eds), *Montjoie: Studies in Crusade History in Honour of Hans Eberhard Mayer* (Aldershot, 1997), pp. 37–54.

Lyons, Malcolm C., and D. E. P. Jackson, *Saladin: The Politics of the Holy War* (Cambridge, 1982).

MacEvitt, Christopher, *The Crusades and the Christian World of the East: Rough Tolerance* (Philadelphia, 2008).

MacGregor, James B., 'The First Crusade in Late Medieval *Exempla*', *The Historian*, 68 (2006), 29–48.

Maquet, Julien, *'Faire Justice' dans le diocèse de Liège au Moyen Âge (VIIIe–XIIe siècles): Essai de droit judiciaire reconstitute* (Geneva, 2008).

Markowski, Michael, 'Crucesignatus: Its Origins and Early Usage', *JMH*, 10 (1984), 157–65.

Martens, Mina, 'Une reproduction manuscrite inédite du sceau de Godefroid de Bouillon', *Annales de la société royale d'archéologie de bruxelles*, 46 (1942–1943), 7–27.

Matthys, André, 'Les châteaux de Mirwart et de Sugny, centres de pouvoirs aux Xᵉ et XIᵉ siècles', in Jean-Marie Duvosquel and Alain Dierkens (eds), *Villes et campagnes au moyen âge: mélanges Georges Duby* (Liège, 1991), pp. 465–502.

Matzke, Michael, *Daibert von Pisa. Zwischen Pisa, Papst und erstem Kreuzzug* (Sigmaringen, 1998).

Mayer, Hans E., 'Baudouin Iᵉʳ et Godefroy de Bouillon avant la Première Croisade', in Hans E. Mayer, *Mélanges sur l'histoire du Royaume Latin de Jérusalem* (Paris, 1984), pp. 10–48.

————, *Die Kanzlei der lateinischen Königen von Jerusalem*, 2 vols in 4 (Hannover, 1996).

Meijns, Brigitte, 'Obedience to the Bishop, Apostolic Protection and Appeal to Rome: The Changing Representation of Abbot Theodoric I of St-Hubert (1055–1086) Against the Backdrop of the Investiture Conflict in the Diocese of Liège', *RBPH*, 91 (2013), 1–28.

Meyer von Knonau, Gerold, *Jahrbücher des Deutschen Reiches unter Heinrich IV. und Heinrich V.*, 7 vols (Leipzig, 1890–1909).

Mitchell, Piers D., *Medicine in the Crusades: Warfare, Wounds and the Medieval Surgeon* (Cambridge, 2004).

Morin, Germain, 'Godefroy de Bouillon et Adalbéron, Abbé de Saint-Vincent de Laon: A propos du manuscrit Rh. CVIII de Zurich', *Revue Bénédictine*, 42 (1930), 273–5.

———, 'Lettre inédite a A[nselme de Cantorbéry] a G[odefroy de Bouillon] ?', *Revue Bénédictine*, 34 (1922), 135–46.

Morton, Nicholas, *Encountering Islam on the First Crusade* (Cambridge, 2016).

Morris, Colin, 'The Aims and Spirituality of the First Crusade as Seen Through the Eyes of Albert of Aachen', *Reading Medieval Studies*, 16 (1990), 99–117.

———, 'The *Gesta Francorum* as Narrative History', *Reading Medieval Studies*, 19 (1993), 55–71.

———, 'Policy and Visions: The Case of the Holy Land found at Antioch', in John Gillingham and J. C. Holt (eds), *War and Government in the Middle Ages: Essays in Honour of J. O. Prestwich* (Woodbridge, 1984), pp. 33–45.

Murray, Alan V., 'The Army of Godfrey of Bouillon, 1096–1099: Structure and Dynamics of a Contingent on the First Crusade', *RBPH*, 70 (1992), 301–29.

———, *The Crusader Kingdom of Jerusalem: A Dynastic History, 1099–1125* (Oxford, 2000).

———, 'Daimbert of Pisa, the *Domus Godefridi* and the Accession of Baldwin I of Jerusalem', in *FCTJ*, pp. 81–102.

———, ' "Mighty Against the Enemies of Christ": The Relic of the True Cross in the Armies of the Kingdom of Jerusalem', in John France and William G. Zajac (eds), *The Crusades and Their Sources: Essays Presented to Bernard Hamilton* (Aldershot, 1998), pp. 217–38.

———, 'Money and Logistics in the Forces of the First Crusade: Coinage, Bullion, Service, and Supply, 1096–99', in John H. Pryor (ed.), *Logistics of Warfare in the Age of the Crusades* (Aldershot, 2006), pp. 229–49.

———, 'The Title of Godfrey of Bouillon as Ruler of Jerusalem', *Collegium Medievale*, 3 (1990), 163–78.

Musset, Lucien, *The Bayeux Tapestry*, new edn, tr. Richard Rex (Woodbridge, 2005).

Naus, James, *Constructing Kingship: The Capetian Monarchs of France and the Early Crusades* (Manchester, 2016).

The New Cambridge Medieval History, 8 vols (Cambridge, 1995–2005).

Nesbitt, John W., 'The Rate of March of Crusading Armies in Europe', *Traditio*, 9 (1983), 167–81.

Nicholas, David, *Medieval Flanders* (London, 1992).

Nicholson, Robert L., *Tancred: A Study of His Career and Work in Relation to the First Crusade and the Establishment of the Latin East* (Chicago, 1940).

Nip, Renée, 'Godelieve of Gistel and Ida of Boulogne', in Anneke B. Mulder-Bakker (ed.), *Sanctity and Motherhood: Essays on Holy Mothers in the Middle Ages* (London, 1995), pp. 191–223.

Oksanen, Eljas, *Flanders and the Anglo-Norman World, 1066–1216* (Cambridge, 2012).

Ott, John S., *Bishops, Authority and Community in Northwestern Europe, c.1050–1150* (Cambridge, 2015).

———, ' "Reims and Rome are Equals": Archbishop Manasses I (c.1069–1080), Pope Gregory VII, and the Fortunes of Historical Exceptionalism', in Sigrid Danielson and Evan A. Gatti (eds), *Envisioning the Bishop: Images and the Episcopacy in the Middle Ages* (Turnhout, 2014), pp. 275–302.

Overmann, Alfred, *Gräfin Mathilde von Tuscien: Ihre Besitzungen* (Innsbruck, 1895).

Ozeray, Michel, *Histoire de la ville et du duché de Bouillon*, 2nd edn (Brussels, 1864).

Palmer, James T., *The Apocalypse in the Early Middle Ages* (Cambridge, 2014).

Parisse, Michel, 'Généalogie de la Maison d'Ardenne', *PSHIGL*, 95 (1981), 9–41.

———, 'Lotharingia', in *NCMH*, vol. 3, pp. 310–27.

———, *La Noblesse Lorraine, XIe – XIIIe siècles*, 2 vols (Paris, 1976).

Paul, Nicholas L., 'Crusade, Memory and Regional Politics in Twelfth-Century Amboise', *JMH*, 31 (2005), 127–41.

———, *To Follow in Their Footsteps: The Crusades and Family Memory in the High Middle Ages* (Ithaca, 2012).

———, 'A Warlord's Wisdom: Literacy and Propaganda at the Time of the First Crusade', *Speculum*, 85 (2010), 534–66.

Paviot, Jacques, *Projets de Croisade (v. 1290–1330)* (Paris, 2008).

Peirce, Ian, 'The Knight, His Arms and Armour in the Eleventh and Twelfth Centuries', in Christopher Harper-Bill and Ruth Harvey (eds), *The Ideals and Practice of Medieval Knighthood* (Woodbridge, 1986), pp. 152–64.

Perry, Guy, *John of Brienne: King of Jerusalem, Emperor of Constantinople, c.1175–1237* (Cambridge, 2013).

Peters, Wolfgang, 'Zur Gründung und frühen Geschichte des Benediktinerpriorates St. Peter in Bouillon', *Revue Bénédictine*, 109 (1999), 341–58.

Phillips, Jonathan, *Defenders of the Holy Land: Relations Between the Latin East and the West, 1119–1187* (Oxford, 1996).

———, *Holy Warriors: A Modern History of the Crusades* (London, 2009).

———, *The Second Crusade: Extending the Frontiers of Christendom* (New Haven, 2007).

Pohl, Benjamin, *Dudo of St Quentin's Historia Normannorum: Tradition, Innovation and Memory* (Woodbridge, 2015).

Powell, James M., 'Myth, Legend, Propaganda, History: The First Crusade, 1140–ca.1300', in Michel Balard (ed.), *Autour de la Première Croisade* (Paris, 1996), pp. 127–41.

Prawer, Joshua, *The Latin Kingdom of Jerusalem: European Colonialism in the Middle Ages* (London, 1973).

Prestwich, Michael, 'Medieval Biography', *Journal of Interdisciplinary History*, 40 (2010), 325–46.

Pringle, Denys, *The Churches of the Crusader Kingdom of Jerusalem*, 4 vols (Cambridge, 1993–2010).

Pryor, John H., and Michael J. Jeffreys, 'Alexios, Bohemond, and Byzantium's Euphrates Frontier: A Tale of Two Cretans', *Crusades*, 11 (2012), 31–86.

Purkis, William J., *Crusading Spirituality in the Holy Land and Iberia, c.1095–c.1187* (Woodbridge, 2008).

———, 'Rewriting the History Books: The First Crusade and the Past', in *WEC*, pp. 140–54.

Rapports de MM. De Ram, Gachard et de Reiffenberg faits à la séance de la classe des lettres du 5 février 1849 concernant la status de Godefried de Bouillon (s.l.,1849).

Richard, Jean, *The Crusades, c.1071–c.1291* (Cambridge, 1999).

Riley-Smith, Jonathan, 'Casualties and the Number of Knights on the First Crusade', *Crusades*, 1 (2002), 13–28.

———, *The Crusades: A History*, 3rd edn (London, 2014).

———, *The First Crusade and the Idea of Crusading* (London, 1986).

———, *The First Crusaders, 1095–1131* (Cambridge, 1997).

———, 'First Crusaders to the East and the Costs of Crusading, 1095–1130', in Michael Goodich, Sophia Menache and Sylvia Schein (eds), *Cross Cultural Convergences in the Crusader Period* (New York, 1995), pp. 237–57.

———, 'The Motives of the Earliest Crusaders and the Settlement of Latin Palestine, 1095–1100', *EHR*, 98 (1983), 721–36.

———, 'The Title of Godfrey of Bouillon', *Bulletin of the Institute for Historical Research*, 52 (1979), 83–6.

Reuter, Timothy, 'The "Imperial Church System" of the Ottonian and Salian Rulers: A Reconsideration', *Journal of Ecclesiastical History*, 33 (1982), 347–74.

Robert, Ulysee, *Un pape belge: histoire du Pape Étienne X* (Brussels, 1892).

Robinson, I. S., *Henry IV of Germany, 1056–1106* (Cambridge, 1999).

———, *The Papacy, 1073–1198: Continuity and Innovation* (Cambridge, 1990).

Rogers, Randall, *Latin Siege Warfare in the Twelfth Century* (Oxford, 1997).

Rowe, John G., 'Paschal II and the Relation Between the Spiritual and Temporal Powers in the Kingdom of Jerusalem', *Speculum*, 32 (1957), 470–501.

Rubenstein, Jay, *Armies of Heaven: The First Crusade and the Quest for the Apocalypse* (New York, 2011).

———, 'Godfrey of Bouillon vs. Raymond of Saint-Gilles: How Carolingian Kingship Trumped Millenarianism at the End of the First Crusade', in Matthew Gabriele and Jace Stuckey (eds), *The Legend of Charlemagne in the Middle Ages: Power, Faith, and Crusade* (Basingstoke, 2008), pp. 59–75.

———, 'Holy Fire and Sacral Kingship in Post-Conquest Jerusalem', *JMH*, 43 (2017) (forthcoming).

———, 'Putting History to Use: Three Crusade Chronicles in Context', *Viator*, 35 (2004), 131–68.

———, 'What Is the *Gesta Francorum* and Who Is Peter Tudebode?', *Revue Mabillon*, 16 (2005), 179–204.

Runciman, Steven, *A History of the Crusades*, 3 vols (Cambridge, 1951–1954).

Saur, Léon, 'Entre Bar, Namur et Liège: Bouillon, place stratégique', *PSHIGL* 95 (1981), 258–82.

Shepard, Jonathan, 'Cross Purposes: Alexius Comnenus and the First Crusade', in *FCOI*, pp. 107–29.

———, 'When Greek Meets Greek: Alexius Comnenus and Bohemond in 1097–8', *Byzantine and Modern Greek Studies*, 12 (1988), 185–277.

Skinner, Patricia, 'From Pisa to the Patriarchate: Chapters in the Life of (Arch)bishop Daibert', in Patricia Skinner (ed.), *Challenging the Boundaries of Medieval History: The Legacy of Timothy Reuter* (Turnhout, 2009), pp. 155–72.

Smith, Thomas W., 'The First Crusade Letter Written at Laodicea in 1099: Two Previously Unpublished Versions From Munich, Bayerische Staatsbibliothek Clm 23390 and 28195', *Crusades*, 15 (2016), 1–25.

———, 'Scribal Crusading: Three New Manuscript Witnesses to the Regional Reception and Transmission of First Crusade Letters', *Traditio*, 72 (2017) (forthcoming).

Somerville, Robert, 'The Council of Clermont (1095) and Latin Christian Society', *Archivum Historiae Pontificiae*, 12 (1974), 55–90.

———, *The Councils of Urban II: I Decreta Claromontensia* (Amsterdam, 1972).

———, *Pope Urban II's Council of Piacenza* (Oxford, 2011).

Stiegemann, Christoph and Matthias Wemhoff (eds), *Canossa 1077: Erschütterung der Welt. Geschichte, Kunst und Kultur am Aufgang der Romanik*, 2 vols (Munich, 2006).

Strack, Georg, 'Pope Urban II and Jerusalem: A Re-Examination of His Letters on the First Crusade', *The Journal of Religious History, Literature and Culture*, 2 (2016), 51–70.

———, 'The Sermon of Urban II in Clermont and the Tradition of Papal Oratory', *Medieval Sermon Studies*, 56 (2012), 30–45.

Sweetenham, Carol, 'What Really Happened to Eurvin De Créel's Donkey? Anecdotes in Sources for the First Crusade', in *WEC*, pp. 75–88.

Tanner, Heather J., 'The Expansion of the Power and Influence of the Counts of Boulogne Under Eustace II', *ANS*, 14 (1992), 251–77.

——, *Families, Friends and Allies: Boulogne and Politics in Northern France and England, c.879–1160* (Leiden, 2004).

——, 'In His Brothers' Shadow: The Crusading Career and Reputation of Eustace III of Boulogne', in Khalil I. Semaan (ed.), *The Crusades: Other Experiences, Alternate Perspectives* (Binghamton, 2003), pp. 83–99.

Theotokis, Georgios, *The Norman Campaigns in the Balkans, 1081–1108* (Woodbridge, 2014).

Tollebeek, Jo, 'An Era of Grandeur: The Middle Ages in Belgian National Historiography, 1830–1914', in R. J. W. Evans and Guy P. Marchal (eds), *The Uses of the Middle Ages in Modern European States: History, Nationhood and the Search for Origins* (Basingstoke, 2011), pp. 113–35.

Tourneur, Victor, 'Un denier de Godefroid de Bouillon frappé en 1096', *Revue belge de numismatique et de sigillographie*, 83 (1931), 27–30.

Trotter, David A., 'L'ascendance mythique de Godefroy de Bouillon et le Cycle de la Croisade', in Laurence Harf-Lancner (ed.), *Métamorphose et bestiaire fantastique au moyen âge* (Paris, 1985), pp. 107-35.

Tyerman, Christopher, *The Debate on the Crusades, 1099–2010* (Manchester, 2011).

——, *God's War: A New History of the Crusades* (London, 2006).

——, *The Invention of the Crusades* (Basingstoke, 1998).

——, ' "Principes et Populus": Civil Society and the First Crusade', in Simon Barton and Peter Linehan (eds), *Cross, Crescent and Conversion: Studies on Medieval Spain and Christendom in Memory of Richard Fletcher* (Leiden, 2008), pp. 127–51.

——, 'Were There Any Crusades in the Twelfth Century?', *EHR*, 110 (1995), 553–77.

van Bavel, Bas, *Manors and Markets: Economy and Society in the Low Countries* (Oxford, 2010).

van Houts, Elisabeth, *Local and Regional Chronicles* (Turnhout, 1995).

——, *Memory and Gender in Medieval Europe, 900–1200* (Basingstoke, 1999).

Vanderlinden, Herman, 'La date de la nomination de Godefroid de Bouillon comme duc de Lotharingie (1087)', *Bulletin de la commission royale d'histoire*, 90 (1926), 189–92.

——, 'Le tribunal de la Paix de Henri de Verdun et la formation de la principauté de Liège', in Herman Vanderlinden, François-Louis Ganshof and Gaston G. Dept (eds), *Mélanges d'histoire offerts à Henri Pirenne par ses anciens élèves et ses amis à l'occasion de sa quarantième année d'enseignement à l'Université de Gand, 1886–1926*, 2 vols, c.p. (Brussels, 1926), pp. 589–96.

Vanderputten, Steven, *Monastic Reform as Process: Realities and Representations in Medieval Flanders, 900–1100* (Ithaca, 2013).

Vanderputten, Steven, Tjamke Snijders and Jay Diehl (eds), *Medieval Liège at the Crossroads of Europe: Monastic Society and Culture, 1000–1300* (Brepols, 2016).

Vaughn, Sally N., 'Anselm in Italy, 1097–1100', *ANS*, 16 (1994), 245–70.

——, *St Anselm and the Handmaidens of God: A Study of Anselm's Correspondence With Women* (Turnhout, 2002).

Verlinden, Charles, *Robert Ier le Frison, comte de Flandre: Étude d'histoire politique* (Antwerp, 1935).

Waeger, Gerhart, *Gottfried von Bouillon in der Historiographie* (Zurich, 1969).

Weiler, Björn, 'The *Negotium Terrae Sanctae* in the Political Discourse of Latin Christendom, 1215–1311', *International History Review*, 25 (2003), 1–36.

——, 'The Rex Renitens and the Medieval Ideal of Kingship, ca.900–ca.1250', *Viator*, 31 (2000), 1–42.

Weinfurter, Stefan, *The Salian Century: Main Currents in an Age of Transition*, tr. Barbara M. Bowlus (Philadelphia, 1999).

Werner, Matthias, 'Der Herzog von Lothringen in salischer Zeit', in Stefan Weinfurter (ed.), *Die Salier und das Reich*, 3 vols (Sigmaringen, 1991), vol. 1, pp. 367–473.

West, Charles, 'Monks, Aristocrats and Justice: Twelfth-Century Monastic Advocacy in a European Perspective', *Speculum*, 92 (2017), 372–404.

——, *Reframing the Feudal Revolution: Political and Social Transformation Between Marne and Moselle, c.800–c.1100* (Cambridge, 2014).

Wetzstein, Thomas, 'Europäische Vernetzungen: Straßen, Logistik und Mobilität in der späten Salierzeit', in Bernd Schneidmüller and Stefan Weinfurter (eds), *Salisches Kaisertum und neues Europa: Die Zeit Heinrichs IV. und Heinrichs V.* (Darmstadt, 2007), pp. 341–70.

Whalen, Brett, *Dominion of God: Christendom and Apocalypse in the Middle Ages* (Cambridge, MA, 2009).

Whitehead, Frederick, 'Charlemagne's Second Dream', *Olifant*, 3 (1976), 189–95.

Wolf, Kenneth B., 'Crusade and Narrative: Bohemond and the *Gesta Francorum*', *JMH*, 17 (1991), 207–16.

Wolfzettel, Friedrich, 'Gottfried von Bouillon: Führer des ersten Kreuzzugs und König von Jerusalem', in Inge Milfull and Michael Neumann (eds), *Mythen Europas: Schlüsselfiguren der Imagination. Mittelalter* (Regensburg, 2004), pp. 126–42.

Yewdale, Ralph B., *Bohemond I, Prince of Antioch* (Princeton, 1924).

Index